AS OTHERS SAW US

Cork through European Eyes

Edited by
Joachim Fischer and Grace Neville

The Collins Press

Published in 2005 by
The Collins Press
West Link Park
Doughcloyne
Wilton
Cork

British Library Cataloguing in Publication Data

As others saw us : Cork through European eyes
    1. Cork (Ireland) - Description and travel 2. Cork (Ireland)
    - Literary collections 3. Cork (Ireland) - In literature
    I Fischer, Joachim II. Neville, Grace
    913.1'956'04

ISBN: 1903464854

Typesetting: The Collins Press

Font: AGaramond 11 point

Printed in Ireland by ColourBooks

Front cover image: 'Bard of the Lee' by John Fitzgerald, watercolour on paper, *c.* 1870 –
Elizabeth Fort and old St Finbarr's, from the parapet of the Southgate, as seen in 1796:
courtesy Crawford Municipal Art Gallery;

Back cover image: Elizabeth Fort and St Finbarr's Cathedral from the parapet of the
Southgate Bridge, as seen in 2005, by Sarah Farrelly

Cork 2005

European Capital of Culture

*Dedicated to all our European friends
in Cork and elsewhere*

Dr Joachim Fischer is Senior Lecturer in German and
Joint Director of the Centre for Irish-German Studies in
the University of Limerick.

Dr Grace Neville is Statutory Lecturer in French and
Chair of the Post-Graduate Programmes in
Women's Studies at University College Cork.

Both have been published widely in
their areas of specialisation.

CONTENTS

Acknowledgements

W E WOULD like to thank Cork 2005 and in particular, Tom McCarthy, without whose enthusiastic support and subsequent generous financial subvention this book would not have seen the light of day. We are also grateful to our editor Maria O'Donovan who took on the difficult task of setting the parallel text.

We would like to express our thanks to the translators who undertook, often under considerable time pressure, to work on the texts, many of which are challenging from both a linguistic and stylistic point of view. Credit is also due to the subeditors, Anne O'Connor (NUI Galway) for Italian, Irene Gilsenan-Nordin (University College Dalarna) for Swedish, Micheál Briody (University of Helsinki) for Finnish and Martín Veiga (NUI Cork) for Galician.

We would like to acknowledge the help and support we received from the following: Gabrielle and Martin Alioth, Julianstown, Co. Meath; Anders Alqvist, Galway; Michael Alstadt, Karlsruhe, Germany; Garrett Barden, Cork; John Barry, Cork; Peter Berninger, Brussels; Theo Bögels, Amsterdam; Michael Bøss, Arhus, Denmark; Anna Borzecka, Krakow; Damian Bracken, Cork; Katariina Briody, Helsinki; Jean Brihault, Rennes; Neil Buttimer, Cork; Rui Carvalho Homem, Porto; Houchang Chehabi, Boston and Vienna; Nora Clarke, Oslo; Tom and Verena Conley, Harvard; Marie Corneloup, Paris; Simon Coveney MEP, Brussels; David Cox, Cork; Pat Cronin, Cork; Brian Crowley MEP, Brussels; Aidan Doyle, Cork; Nuala Finnegan, Cork; Terry Folley, Cork; Adrian Gebruers, Cork; Marieke Krajenbrink, Limerick; Martin, Matthew and Ben Krasa, Cork; David Lilburn, Limerick; Aled Llion, Galway; Marisol Morales Ladrón, Alcala, Spain; Valentina McCarthy, Cork; François Moureau, Paris; Annika Musall, Gaisberg, Germany; Ken Nicholls, Cork; Catherine O'Brien, Galway; Conall Ó Caoimh, Dublin; Diarmuid Ó Giolláin, Cork; Gearóid Ó Néill, Limerick; Jennifer and Terence O'Reilly, Cork; Pádraig and Dagmar Ó Riain, Cork; Adrian Otoiu, Baia Mare, Romania; Ann Rigney, Utrecht; Diarmuid Scully, Cork; Keith Sidwell, Cork; Eoin Stephenson,

Limerick; Malachy Vallely, Louvain, Belgium; and many many others. We would like to acknowledge the help of the staff of the Boole Library, University College Cork – especially the staff in the Special Collections section, the Royal Irish Academy (Dublin), the National Library (Dublin), the British Library (London), the Bibliothèque Nationale (Paris), the Musée Albert Kahn (Paris), the Widener Library (Harvard), the Yale University Library, and the Arts Faculty (UCC). We are grateful to the Centre for Human Settlement and Historical Change (NUI Galway) which supported and financed Sebastian Stumpff's translation.

Lastly, we appreciate the permission to reprint extracts granted to us by Rowohlt Verlag, Reinbek; Kiepenheuer & Witsch Verlag, Cologne; Rosa Pock-Artmann, Vienna; Sabine Boebé, Erftstadt, Germany; Jean-Michel Picard, Dublin; the Gerold family, Berlin; *Le Monde* and *Libération* newspapers, Paris; Denoël, Paris; Gallimard publishers, Paris; CNRS publications, Paris; Cistercian Publications, Kalamazoo, USA; Hachette, Paris; and Four Courts Press, Dublin. While every effort has been made to obtain copyright permission, in some cases it was not possible to establish contact. Any queries should be addressed to the editors.

Editorial Note

The foreign language texts appear largely as they are in the printed original. This means that spelling will vary within one language depending on the period the texts were composed. This is particularly noticeable in texts in German. In a number of instances paragraphs have been reorganised to facilitate reading. Occasionally, punctuation has also been modified where the original impedes understanding by modern readers.

The different ways of marking direct speech have been standardised. In all texts including foreign language texts only single quotation marks (' ') are used for this purpose. Also the often highly idiosyncratic and inconsistent use of italics has been standardised: they mark foreign words (not proper names), book and periodical titles, and emphasis.

Misspellings and grammatical errors in English words and sentences in the foreign language originals have mostly been retained to emphasise the authenticity of the texts. Occasional misunderstandings and factual errors have been left stand for the same reason. The attentive reader will easily spot them and is welcome to an occasional feeling of superiority due to her or his own expert local knowledge.

With very few exceptions, we have refrained from annotating the texts by means of footnotes. While we have aimed at the highest editorial standards we did not find it appropriate to clutter this book with elaborate scholarly additions or corrections, although we felt sorely tempted every so often. The texts are meant to stand on their own and to speak for themselves. Where footnotes appear they are generally part of the original text.

In order to arrive at parallel texts the length of text on matching pages varies. This deviation from normal editorial practice was unavoidable.

About the Authors

(in chronological order)

BROTHER MARCUS was an Irish monk who wrote the *Vision of Tnugdal* in 1149 while in Ratisbon, Bavaria. It became a very popular text in medieval Europe and was translated into Middle High German and many other languages.

BERNARD DE CLAIRVAUX (1090-1153). Of noble birth, he became the founder of the Cistercian order in 1115. He was one of the most important figures in medieval mysticism and wrote the life of his friend St Malachy (1094-1148).

GEORG BRAUN (1542-1622) was a German theologian and geographer, and FRANS HOGENBERG (*c.* 1538-*c.* 1590) a Flemish engraver. Their magnificent six-volume atlas, *Civitates Orbis Terrarum*, was published in Cologne between 1575 and 1618. It contains maps with commentaries on about 530 major towns in Europe, Africa, Asia and even America.

FRANÇOIS DE LA BOULLAYE-LE-GOUZ (1623-1668), Catholic traveller from the Anjou region around the Loire, left extensive accounts of his travels in India, Persia, Greece and the Middle East. He visited Ireland in 1644.

JACQUES-NICOLAS BELLIN (1703-1772) was a cartographer and hydrographer with the French Ministry of the Marine. A specialist in the mapping of coastal areas, he was honoured in 1741 by being made France's first official *ingénieur-cartographe*. Mapping and describing territories were, of course, key activities for France's expanding empire at that time.

PHILIP (FILIPPE) MAZZEI (1730-1816) was an Italian physican, merchant and author, and an ardent supporter of the American Revolution. He studied medicine in Florence and practised in Turkey before moving in 1755 to London, where he became a wine merchant. In December 1778 he travelled to Virginia and took an active part in supporting the movement for independence. He became a friend and correspondent of Thomas Jefferson. A zealous republican, he published *Recherches historiques et politiques sur les États-Unis de l'Amérique septentrionale* (Paris, 1788).

JACQUES LOUIS (DE BOURGENET, CHEVALIER) DE LATOCNAYE, var. DE LA TOCNAYE, was a Breton aristocrat and émigré in 1791. He toured Ireland in 1795-96 and recorded his experieicnes in the book from which our extract is taken. It is a frequently quoted source for many aspects of Irish social history. The English translation, *Rambles through Ireland by a French Emigrant*, was fist published in Cork in 1798.

CHARLES BARON BAERT-DUHOLAND (1751-1825) was a member of parliament for the Pas-de-Calais region in northern France.

CORNELIUS DE JONG (VAN RODENBURG) (1762-1836) joined the Dutch Navy as a young cadet and rose to the rank of captain in 1786. In 1791 he was given command of the frigate *Scipio* on which he travelled to the Cape of Good Hope, Norway and Ireland. This journey is described in the book from which our extract is taken.

HERMANN VON PÜCKLER-MUSKAU (1785-1871) was one of the most popular German travel authors of the nineteenth century. His *Letters of a Deceased Person*, which decribe a Romantically-inspired journey through Britain and Ireland, was perhaps his best known work. Influenced by English gardens he became one of the most renowned landscape and garden designers of his time in Germany.

CHARLES COMTE DE MONTALEMBERT (1810-1870) was a leading public representative, author, lawyer and member of the Académie Française. For him, as for other contemporary writers such as Henri-Dominique Lacordaire (1802-1861) and Félicité de Lamennais (1787-1854), Ireland encapsulated the twin interests and ideals of Catholicism and liberalism. He said later that the two months he spent in Ireland in 1830 were among the happiest of his entire life.

ALEXIS DE TOCQUEVILLE (1808-1859) is one of Europe's foremost political scientists. A leading French writer, historian, politician and traveller, Alexis de Tocqueville, is author of a series of seminal works such as *De la Démocratie en Amérique* (1835-40).

PIERRE ETIENNE DENIS SAINT GERMAIN-LEDUC was author of a collection of interviews: *Les Campagnes de Mlle Thérèse Figueur, aujourd'hui Madame la veuve Sutter, ex-dragon au 15e et 9e régiments de 1793 à 1815* (Paris:

Dauvinet et Fontaine, 1842). He also contributed a section on Tuscany to Chateaubriand's two-volume guide on *L'Italie, la Sicile, les îles Écoliennes, l'île d'Elbe, la Sardaigne, Malte, l'île de Calypso, etc* (Paris, 1834-1837).

JOHANN GEORG KOHL (1808-1878) was a travel writer and geographer. His *Reisen in Irland* (1843) was the most detailed German travel account about Ireland in the nineteenth century. Its translation into English just one year later brought it to the attention of the English and Irish reading public where it received several positive reviews.

KNUT JONGBOHN CLEMENT (1803-1875) was born on the north Frisian island of Amrum and expressed Frisian patriotic sentiments in many of his writings. His journey through western European countries was made possible by grants from the King of Denmark. He lost his professorship at the University of Kiel after the Danish-German war of 1863/64.

AMÉDÉE PICHOT (1795-1877) was a director of *La Revue Britannique,* a prolific author and early translator into French of Byron, Scott, Dickens and Lytton.

LOUIS ÉNAULT (1824-1900), lawyer, literary specialist and prolific writer. He contributed to many of the leading newspapers of his day such as *Le Figaro, La Constitution, La Gazette de France, Le Nord* and *L'Illustration.* He translated Harriet Beecher Stowe's *Uncle Tom's Cabin* into French. He also wrote in Latin.

NAPOLÉON CHAIX (1807-1865) founded the L'Imprimerie Centrale des Chemins de Fer in Paris in 1845 which brought out the *Bibliothèque du Voyageur,* a series of popular travel guides in the nineteenth century of which our Ireland guide is one.

FREDERIK KREBS (Denmark). No biographical details available.

ALFRED DUQUET (1842-1916) was a military historian specialising in the wars of the Second Empire. He edited *La Nouvelle Revue* and contributed to other publications such as *La Revue Bleue, La Revue Militaire* and *Le Moniteur de l'Armée.*

JEAN CANIS was a lawyer at the Paris bar. He wrote at least one other monograph, *Histoire de la République Française depuis 1870 jusqu'en 1873* (Paris: Ghio, 1884).

A GERMAN PRIEST. The identity of this Catholic priest remains obscure.

PAUL VILLARS (1849-1935) was London correspondent of the newspapers *Le Figaro* and *Le Journal des Débats*.

MARIE-ANNE DE BOVET (born 1855) was the pen name of the Marquise de Bois-Hébert. She was a prolific author of novels, literary criticism, chronicles and exotic travel accounts. She also translated extensively from English. An anecdote tells of her meeting with Oscar Wilde. 'Come confess, Mr Wilde, that I am the ugliest woman in France,' she is supposed to have said to Wilde, to which the latter bowed low and said with smiling courtesy, 'In the world Madame, in the world'.

JIŘÍ GUTH (LATER JIŘÍ GUTH-JARKOVSKY (1861-1943) was a Czech prose writer, journalist and sports official. He was a collaborator of Pierre de Coubertin and founding member of the International Olympic Committee. After the foundation of Czechoslovakia in 1918, he became Master of Ceremonies to its first President, Tomás Garrigue Masaryk. Guth-Jarkovsky wrote a number of articles on his travels around Europe.

CHARLES LEGRAS (born 1872) was a journalist with *Le Journal des Débats* and Paris correspondent of *The Westminster Gazette*.

CHARLES SCHINDLER, in this account of his visit to the 1902 International Exhibition in Cork, describes himself as a journalist for a Paris newspaper. He also wrote a practical account of the preparation of food in wartime, *L'Alimentation du soldat en campagne. La Ration de guerre et la préparation rapide des plats en campagne* (Paris: Charles-Lavauzelle, 1887) as well as a statistical study of the forests of the Austro-Hungarian Empire (1864).

The *HACHETTE GUIDES-JOANNE* were mainstream guides – a sort of forerunner of *Le Guide Bleu* – for the burgeoning tourist industry in the nineteenth and early twentieth centuries.

RICHARD BERMANN (1883-1939) was born in Vienna and published in Expressionist periodicals, also under the pen name of Arnold Höllriegl. He had to emigrate to the USA in the 1930s and died in Saratoga Springs.

HENRI BÉRAUD (1885-1958) was a prolific novelist, winning France's main literary prize, le Prix Goncourt, in 1922. He reported from Cork on the

hunger strike there in 1920. A polemicist, he was condemned to death for anti-French activities in 1944 and was pardoned by de Gaulle.

ANTÓN LOSADA DIÉGUES (1884-1929) had a degree in Law and a PhD in Philosophy. He played an important role in the development of Galician nationalism in the 1920s. He wrote one play, and also published short stories and poems in journals, but his main achievement as a writer were his political essays, collected in *Obra Completa* (1985). He exerted a decisive influence among the members of Galicia's first major unified intellectual grouping: the Xeración Nós.

SIMONE TÉRY (born 1897) wrote novels, plays and studies of countries she visited. Many of these were published by leading Paris publishing houses such as Flammarion. A friend of Picasso, she was associated with the philanthropic work financed by banker, Albert Kahn.

J. GUST. RICHERT (1857-1934) grew up in a prosperous home in Gothenburg, as the son of a civil engineer. He became an engineer himself and established a highly successful consulting company, which soon became one of Europe's largest firms, working with the generation of water power. He travelled widely in his work and in the text describes a visit made to Cork at the beginning of the 1920s.

JOSEPH KESSEL (1898-1979) was a leading novelist, journalist and member of the Académie Française. For decades, he reported from all corners of the world on political turbulence: in his early twenties, he reported from Cork on the hunger strikes there in 1920. He dedicated his novella, *Mary de Cork*, to his fellow French reporter in Cork at that time, Henri Béraud (see above).

LUÍS AMADO CARBALLO (1901-1927) was born in Pontevedra, and worked as a teacher and a journalist. Although he started his literary career as a fiction writer, his reputation as a writer lies in his poetry, which had a great influence on the subsequent twentieth-century Galician poetry. He published the poetry collection *Proel* (1927); another collection *O Galo* (1928) was published posthumously.

PIERRE FRÉDÉRIX (1897-1970) was a novelist and prolific writer on wide ranging topics of historical, political and literary interest from Swift, Descartes, Goya, Melville and Hitler, to Rome and China. Many of his

works were published by leading Paris publishing houses such as Gallimard.

MARIO BORSA (1870-1952) was a well-known Italian journalist who worked in London in the 1930s and took up the position of director of the important Italian newspaper, *Corriere della Sera*, following the fall of fascism.

ALFONSO DANIEL RODRÍGUEZ CASTELAO (1886-1950) is one of the most outstanding figures of Galician culture. A member of the Xeración Nós, he was known as a writer, an artist, a dramatist and a politician. He published several works of fiction, a play and volumes of essays. He also worked as a cartoonist and illustrator. He died in Buenos Aires, Argentina.

KEES VAN HOEK was a Dutch journalist who spent the war years in Ireland and wrote regularly for *The Irish Times*. He also wrote the biography of Pope Pius XII (1939).

HENRIK TIKKANEN (1924-1984) was a Swedish-language Finnish author and artist, best known for his novels and memoirs. He also wrote travel books from his wide journeys in Europe and illustrated many books and short stories. His drawings use a fine touch, with a few hesitant strokes to build up his sketches. He was married to Märta Tikkanen, one of Finland's most-read contemporary authors, who published a well-known bitter account of their stormy life together in *Århundradets kärlekssaga (The Love Story of the Century)* in 1978.

HILDING FAGERBERG (*1913) The legendary evangelist and preacher from Småland in southern Sweden spent his youth working as farm hand and was 'saved' by a travelling Bible woman who came to his village in the early thirties. During his long and eventful life he has travelled to many countries, including Kenya, India, England and USA. His description of Cork is from a book recounting an eighteen-day car trip through Ireland and Scotland, at the beginning of the 1960s

HANS CARL ARTMANN (1921-2000) was one of the most important Austrian writers of the twentieth century. His huge oeuvre includes numerous volumes of poetry and prose, as well as a long list of translations, among the latter a collection of Celtic religious verse, *Der Schlüssel des Hl. Patrick (The key of St Patrick)* published in 1959.

KARL GUSTAV GEROLD (1909-1988) was a German diplomat and one-time Cultural Attaché at the Embassy of the Federal Republic of Germany in Dublin until his retirement in 1974. Before he joined the diplomatic service he worked as a journalist, author and editor.

GILLES ROSSET is a French senior civil servant and a prolific novelist.

HANS CHRISTIAN KIRSCH was born in 1934 in Breslau/Wroclaw. The work of this very prolific author who also publishes under the pen-name Frederik Hetmann, shows a particular emphasis on fairy tales, fantasy literature, biographies and children's books. His strong interest in Ireland is documented by this travel book, as well as translations and editions of Irish folk and fairy tales and books on Irish history, largely for younger readers.

OLLI JALONEN (*1954) has a Masters degree in Political Science and undertook postgraduate studies in Trinity College Dublin. He has written nineteen books, mainly novels but also plays and short stories and has won numerous literary prizes. RIITTA JALONEN was also born in 1954, and has an MA from the University of Tampere. She writes both children's and young people's literature as well as fiction for adults. The travel book *Matkailijan Irlanti* (1980) written together with her husband was her first book. She has written ten books to date.

MARC GIANNESINI is a journalist with the French daily *Le Monde*.

JYRKI JAHNUKAINEN is a Finnish translator of cartoon literature, the famous Snoopy books among them, and a writer on fishing and wilderness pursuits.

ROBERT MALLET (1915-2002) was a journalist, publisher, writer as well as university professor, and one-time Président of the Université of Paris VII. His literary output spans all genres – poetry, prose and drama – and he won many literary prizes and accolades. In 1975 he was elected member of the Belgian Académie royale de langue et de littérature française.

MANFRED SCHEWE (*1954) is Statutory Lecturer in German at University College Cork. He has been living in Ireland for over twenty years.

REINHARD ULBRICH is a former lecturer in Celtic Studies at the East Germany Humboldt University in Berlin, and one-time Lektor in German at Dublin City University. He is now a prolific travel writer.

CHRISTOPH POTTING and ANNETTE WEWELER, two German journalists and authors, teamed up in 1984 to bring out one of the best known and most widely read critical and alternative travel guides about Ireland. Subtitled, *Ein Reisebuch in den Alltag*, (A travel guide to everyday life), it was intentionally far removed from the romanticised images one finds in much German book publishing about Ireland.

SABINE BOEBÉ (*1925) studied history, psychology and art education in Berlin and Göttingen. She published on the history of art and travelled Western Europe often retracing the footsteps of famous personalities. Her book *Eines Fürsten Irland* follows the same route Prince Pückler-Muskau (also in this volume) took when he visited Ireland in 1828/29.

ALESSANDRO BARICCO, born in Turin in 1958, is a novelist and playwright as well as an arts journalist. He won the Prix Medicis Étranger in 1995.

RALPH GIORDANO was born in Hamburg in 1923. Half-Jewish on his mother's side, a significant part of his considerable output of journalistic and documentary work focuses on the legacy of National Socialism in Germany. He has worked extensively for broadcasting and TV stations in the north and west of Germany. Travel writing also features frequently in his work.

MARTÍN VEIGA born in Noia, A Coruña, in 1970, is Lector in Galician and Assistant Director of the Irish Centre for Galician Studies, University College Cork. A poet and a translator, he is currently completing a PhD in Hispanic Studies at UCC.

MARÍA DO CEBREIRO (*1976) was born in Santiago de Compostela, A Coruña and is a writer and a researcher in the field of Comparative Literature. She has published three poetry collections and has edited anthologies of poetry by women.

CHRISTOPHE BOLTANSKI is a journalist with the major left of centre daily French newspaper, *Libération*.

FABIENNE DARGE is a journalist with *Le Monde*.

PIERO CALÌ was Professor of Italian at University College Cork for over 30 years. He helped to set up the Dante Alighieri Society in Cork and promoted

the Italian Language in the city. On his retirement he returned to Italy with his wife Renata.

ALLESSANDRO GENTILI is the director of the James Madison University in Florence. He worked in the Italian Department in University Collge Cork in the early 1980s and has published extensively on recent Irish poetry, translating many important Irish poets into Italian.

THOMAS KABDEBO (*1934) is of Hungarian extraction. Until his retirement, he was librarian of NUI Maynooth university library. A prolific writer, eg. on Irish-Hungarian connections, poet and translator, he lives in Dublin.

JUAN CASAS RIGALL is a lecturer in English at the University of Santiago de Compostela.

VLAD MURESAN was born in Uriu, Bistrita-Nasaud, Romania. He holds a B.A. in English and Romanian Literature from the Universitatea de Nord, Baia Mare, Romania, and an M.A. in Canadian Studies from the University of Bucharest. He lived in Ireland for four years, in Westmeath, Dublin and Cork, where he qualified as a Cambridge English Language Trainer, and is currently teaching English in Yemen.

ELENA TONIATO is a native of Padua in Italy. She came to Cork in 1999 as part of the ERASMUS programme to study English in University College Cork. She worked in the Italian Department in Galway for a number of years and completed a Masters degree in Irish Studies in 2004.

MARTIN ALIOTH, born 1954 in Basel, Switzerland holds a Ph.D. in Medieval History from the University of Basel. Together with his wife, the novelist Gabrielle Alioth, he moved to Julianstown, Co. Meath, in 1984. He reports on British and Irish affairs for German-speaking public radio and newspapers, the Swiss *Neue Zürcher Zeitung* among them.

Introduction

A MEDIUM-SIZED port city on the southern coast of a small island some 450km adrift off mainland Europe: what hope did Cork city ever have of being mentioned in continental European writings throughout the centuries? The question is a fair one, and yet, the present volume is just the tip of an enormous iceberg, the size of which we ourselves never imagined when we embarked on this project. Their memorable experiences of Cork encouraged many visitors to immortalise their recollections in writing. In a profusion of texts from a wealth of countries and a multiplicity of languages, the name of Ireland's Rebel City (Corcagia, Korq, Karke, Corke, Corcke, Cork, Corcaigh, Corca, Corcakh, Corcava …) swims into view again and again across the ages, from the twelfth century down to last week: a striking reminder that, at no stage in its development, was Cork ever anything *other* than a European city. Words, images and texts are not enough to capture its charms and, it must be said, its failings: for centuries, visitors remember the 'Venice of the North' for its spectacular scenery, its spectacular hospitality … and its spectacular poverty.

Almost all accounts presented here are by eye-witnesses; the foreign eye sees things which native citizens often overlook, at times even deliberately. As the comments on the title page of Marie-Anne de Bovet's book in the Cork City Library proves, some Corkonians were none too pleased when foreign visitors criticised their city! 'A bigot,' an annoyed reader wrote in pencil underneath the author's name, 'an enemy of the Irish people. She is a revenger because she could not get the better of us.' But let us be more tolerant and welcome the fresh new look at the past as well as the present of the city, provided by these outsiders; their comments help us understand more fully the reality of life in Cork, and for this reason alone they are worth collecting. Surprisingly, perhaps, this is the first time that European views of the city have been systematically collected and presented.

Plus ça change ... One of the earliest texts in this volume, a Latin text, dating from 1149, recounts power struggles, in-fighting and deep dissension around the election of Cork's bishop: an indication, perhaps, that Cork's reputation as the Rebel City, if not the Independent Republic, goes back at least as far as the twelfth century. The most recent text included, an article from one of Switzerland's most prestigious newspapers, the *Neue Zürcher Zeitung*, features an interview with one of this volume's co-editors about this current work: a nod in the direction of post-modernist intertextuality, perhaps! In between, patterns of observation can be detected.

Many of the earlier texts concern mapping and measuring: key activities in the colonial enterprises of various ambitious Continental European powers. In trying to capture Cork in words and images, visitors frequently reveal as much of themselves as of the object of their attention: we see the viewer as much as the viewed. Eighteenth and nineteenth-century visitors, in particular, often viewed Cork through the lens of a particular ideology. As true children of the French Revolution (a revolution deemed by historian, Eric Hobsbawm, to be the greatest revolution of them all), French visitors of the nineteenth century are repeatedly appalled, astounded and angered at the depths of poverty and deprivation everywhere on view in the southern city. Leading French writers like Charles de Montalembert and Alexis de Tocqueville interpret what they see as proof that Ireland is, indeed, a failed colony, with the added piquancy of affording them an irresistible opportunity of lambasting France's ancestral enemy, *le perfide Albion*, into the bargain. They, and visitors from other countries, scour the city for any scraps of evidence of progress: some find it in the prisons ('admirably organised'), the orphanages or the barracks!

In the nineteenth century the 'Irish question' and the consequences of British rule move into the foreground. With more than a few German visitors, the burgeoning Romantic stereotype of Ireland, a result of the popularity of James MacPhersons' fake, pseudo-Celtic epic *Ossian* of the 1760s, informs their perception. With some visitors, religious bias is clearly discernable and determines their judgements. The inclusion of Cork in travel guides points to the beginnings of mass tourism to Ireland. To be sure, Cork was often not the main reason why the visitors came to Ireland: for many tourists, journalists and visitors on business, Dublin and

the west of Ireland in general proved more attractive and/or more important. Indeed, it must be admitted that a certain dissatisfaction with the lack of attractions in Cork rings through not a few texts in this volume.

Of all Irish cities, it could be argued that Cork most keenly fits historian Pierre Nora's concept of a *lieu de mémoire*: a place on the landscape charged with emotional meaning and soaked in memories. Simone Téry's graphic description of Cork as '*une ville martyre*' recalls the city's fate during the euphemistically-called 'Troubles' when, before the Civil War erupted, the death on hunger strike in Brixton Prison in 1920 of its first citizen, the Lord Mayor, Terence MacSwiney, made front page headlines throughout the world and attracted to Cork some of Europe's leading reporters.

The history of Cork is a history of change and the texts recorded here trace the economic and social development of Cork through the ages: its flourishing port, the central importance of import and export activities, the pre-Celtic Tiger days of emigration and unemployment. As recently as the 1980s commentators like Marc Giannesini in *Le Monde* are shocked by the obvious financial hardship of many of its citizens. With the much analysed Celtic Tiger come further transformations. A salutary note of warning is sounded by Christophe Boltanski, a Paris journalist in the left-of-centre newspaper, *Libération*, when he observes changing mentalities in Cork towards the needy: this time the huddled masses are non-nationals, and the hospitality celebrated in Cork's proud, age-old motto: *Statio bene fide carinis* (a safe harbour for ships) seems significantly less in evidence than in previous generations. The Germans Christoph Weweler and Annette Potting similarly cast a cold and critical eye over casual Irish ways of protecting the environment in Cork harbour.

By sheer coincidence, though quite appropriate for the food capital of Ireland, the earliest and the latest texts in this anthology are linked by food and eating, while poor Thugdal has a near-death experience after finishing his meal in Cork, journalist Martin Alioth, visiting Cork eight centuries later, enjoys a box of Turkish Delight, the latter in itself a powerful reminder of Cork's multi-cultural heritage. These two bookended incidents mark opposite ends of the spectrum of culinary experience. This is what the reader will find again and again: stark contradictions, at times even in the same text, vastly differing accounts, which make it difficult to

state clearly what the image of Cork among our visitors from over 750 years has been. Rather than one coherent picture, we encounter many images; the book is a mosaic, a collage, a kaleidoscope, a hall of mirrors from which readers are free to draw their own conclusions. The beauty of any book is the freedom it affords readers to take from it what they want, to dip in, skip, read and ignore whatever they choose, nowhere more so than in an anthology of bits and snippets like ours. We intend to encourage this creative reading by presenting a multitude of shortish pieces rather than a few longer ones.

The two eating experiences further recall our aim to pay particular attention to the foreign visitors' perceptions of everyday life. This brings us to our selection criteria. Our main goal was to convey the wide variety of texts there are: we have included extracts from novels, history books, travel accounts, newspaper articles, lives of the saints as well as poems, short stories and humorous sketches. We have also tried to represent as many centuries, countries, languages and social and political backgrounds of the authors as possible. The noticeable preponderance of texts in French and German does not contradict this aim nor is it the result of our own scholarly backgrounds: rather is it a reflection of the reality that most continental European texts about Ireland and Cork are in these two languages. It should also be noted that there are clear indications, for instance in Alfred Duquet's text, of a particularly strong affinity between Cork and France among the citizens of Cork. Ultimately our main criterion was that a text was interesting to a modern reader; in some instances outrageous, quirky or downright ludicrous passages were preferred to well-founded and scholarly ones. We wanted the personal perspective to shine through, mediated by the writers' cultural and national backgrounds. The aesthetic quality of the texts was generally less of a decisive factor, and while only few of the authors represented here would have had high literary ambitions, some of the texts are nevertheless of a high stylistic and aesthetic standard.

We are conscious that many readers will wonder about the absence of British texts in this anthology. This has nothing whatsoever to do with a view frequently held in these isles which equates 'European' with mainland Europe (a view we as lecturers in modern languages are highly critical of). Of course Britain is part of Europe. But the inclusion of British

texts would have fundamentally changed this project. In sheer number alone they may match all our mainland European texts taken together. Many of them are very well known and easily accessible. More importantly, these texts tend to take a perspective, which we are all too familiar with: that of a (former) colonial master towards a (former) subordinate race or country. Our aim was to broaden out the debate and to refract the image of the city of Cork through the lens of foreign language visitors from more distant parts. This is not only a new, wider (and often more objective) perspective, it also highlights the reality that Europe is multilingual and that only a minority speak English as their mother tongue. As such we feel this book well deserves the word 'European' in the title, inaccurate as it may seem at first glance.

As editors of a volume which we could have filled two if not three times over, we are conscious there are still gaps in what is presented here. The new citizens of Cork, economic refugees, asylum seekers, migrant workers, many from Eastern Europe, are not present here. No doubt they have their own stories to tell. Many of these accounts may not be happy and will thus differ significantly from those of our generally well-to-do middle-class authors. These newer stories are hardly ever written down. Here is another book which needs to be written, as one hopes it will be. For this present collection, we restricted ourselves to written and printed sources. The book has a strong historical dimension, though the present day is also represented by a substantial number of texts, eight of them written especially for this volume.

From the beginning, it was vital to us that the original text, as well as the English translation, should appear in this book, because it makes the European and multi-cultural dimension which underlies our work so much more explicit. It also allows those familiar with the foreign languages in question to enjoy the original versions. Those interested in translation criticism can examine and evaluate the choices made by our translators. Ultimately, the multilingual nature of this publication will, we hope, enable the book to fulfil more fully the guiding idea behind the European Capital of Culture Year 2005 of which it is an integral part: to bring Europe closer to Cork and Cork to Europe.

JOACHIM FISCHER, Limerick   GRACE NEVILLE, Cork

Brother Marcus
(1149)

Latin original in: *Visio Tnugdali. Lateinisch und Altdeutsch.* Ed. by A. Wagner.
Erlangen: A. Deichert, 1882, pp. 5-9.

Incipit visio cujusdam militis Hyberniensis ad edificationem multorum conscripta

HYBERNIA IGITUR insula est in ultimo occidentali oceano posita, ab austra in boream porrecta, stagnis et fluminibus precipua, nemoribus insita, frugibus fertilissima, lacte et melle omnibusque piscationis et venationis generibus opulenta, vinearum expers, set vini dives, serpentium, ranarum, bufonum et omnium animalium venena ferentium ita inscia, ut ejus lignum aut corrigia aut cornu aut pulvis omnia vincere noscantur venena; religiosis viris et feminis satis preclara armis autem crudelis et inclita, cominus ad meridiem habens Angliam, ad ortum vero Scotos nec non et Brittos, quos quidam Galenses vocant, ad boream autem Catos et Orcades, ex adverso vero ad austrum Hispanos. Hec ergo insula civitates habet precipuas triginta quattuor, quarum presules duobus subsunt metropolitanis. Artimacha namque septentrionalium Hyberniensium est metropolis, australium autem precellentissima est Caselensis, de qua ortus est quidam vir nobilis nomine Tnugdalus, cujus crudelitas vel potius in eo quod egit dei pietas nostro huic opusculo materiam dedit.

Erat namque vir prefatus etate juvenis, genere nobilis, vultubilaris, aspectu decorus, curialiter nutritus, vestibus compositus, mente magnanimus, militari arte non mediocriter instructus, habilis, affabilis atque jocundus. Verum, quod ego non sine dolore possum dicere, quanto confidebat in forma corporis et fortitudine, tanto minus curabat de anime sue eterna salute. Nam, ut ipse modo sepius cum lacrimis solet confiteri, gravabat ipsum, si quis ei de salute anime aliquid licet breviter vellet dicere. Ecclesiam dei neglexerat, pauperes autem Christi etiam videre nolebat. Scurris mimis et joculatoribus pro vana gloria distribuerat quicquid habebat. Set cum tot malis divine misericordie finem dare placuit, eum, quando voluit, provocavit. Nam, ut plurimi Corcagensis civitatis testantur

Brother Marcus
(1149)

(Religious visions after a meal in Cork)

Beginning of the vision of an Irish knight written for the edification of the multitude

IRELAND IS an island situated at the extremity of the western ocean and stretches out from south to north. It is outstanding for its lakes and rivers, planted with woods, most fertile in cereals, opulent in milk, honey and all kinds of fish and game, lacking in vines but rich in wine. Snakes, frogs, toads and all venomous animals are unknown there, to the extent that its wood, leather thongs, horns and clay are known to triumph over all poisons. It is quite famous for its religious men and women but is also well known for its cruel battles. Near it, there is England on the south side; to the east are the Scots as well as the Britons who are called Welsh by some; to the north are the Shetlanders and the Orcadians and, on the opposite side, to the south, are the Spaniards. This island has 34 dioceses, the bishops of which are under two metropolitans. Armagh is the metropole of the northern Irish, but Cashel is the most eminent see in the south, and there a nobleman was born, called Tnugdal, whose wickedness – or rather the workings of God's mercy on him – are the subject of our little work.

This man was of a young age, of noble lineage, had a happy face and an elegant appearance; he had been brought up in the manner of the court, was carefully dressed, arrogant in spirit and not ill-trained in martial arts. But I cannot say this without pain: his confidence in his physical appearance and strength was matched by an equally bad neglect of the eternal salvation of his soul. As he himself confessed with tears on many subsequent occasions, he used to become angry whenever anyone mentioned, even briefly, the salvation of his soul. He did not care about God's Church and did not even want to see Christ's poor. He gave away whatever he had to jesters, players and jugglers. But when divine mercy chose to put an end to so much evil, he was challenged at the appointed time. For, according to the testimony

7

incole, qui ei tunc aderant, per trium dierum et noctium spatium jacuit mortuus, per quod spatium amare didicit, quicquid antea suaviter deliquid, nam vita ejus presens testatur, quecunque patiebatur. Passus est enim plurima incredibilia et intolerabilia tormentorum genera, quorum ordinem sive nomina, sicut ab ipsius, qui viderat et patiebatur, ore didicimus, nos ad augmentationem vestre devotionis vobis scribere non gravabit.

Hic igitur, cum multos haberet amicos sodales, inter eos unum habuerat, qui ei commutationis debito trium equorum debitor erat. Hic cum statutum prestolaretur terminum, suum transacto tempore convenit amicum. Qui cum bene receptus perendinaret tribus noctibus, cepit tractare de ceteris rebus. Cui cum ille responderet, se ad manum non habere quod petierat, multum iratus iter expetere disposuerat, quo veniebat. Debitor vero, mitigare cupiens amicum suum, rogabat eum, quatinus secum, priusquam recederet, dignaretur sumere cibum. Cujus cum precibus negare nequiret, resedit et securi deposita, quam manu tenuerat, cibos cum socio sumere cepit. Set prevenit divina pictas hunc appetitum. Nescio namque cita qua occasione percussus manum, quam extenderat, replicare non poterat ad os suum. Tunc terribiliter clamare cepit suamque securim, quam ante deposuerat, uxori socii sic commendavit: Custodi, inquiens, meam securim, nam ego morior. Et tunc verbotenus corpus exanime continuo corruit, ac si nullatenus spiritus antea ibi fuisset. Assunt signa mortis, crines candent, frons obduratur, errant oculi, nasus acuitur, pallescunt labia, mentum cadit et universa corporis membra rigescunt. Currit familia, tollitur cibus, clamant armigeri, plorat hospes, corpus extenditur, pulsantur signa, accurrit clerus, miratur populus et tota civitas cita boni militis morte turbatur.

Quid moramur? Ab hora quasi decima in quarta feria usque ad eandem ipsam horam in sabbato mortuus jacebat nullo in eo remanente vite signo, excepto, quod calor modicus in sinistro pectore ab his, qui diligenter corpus palpare studuerant, sentiebatur. Eapropter ipsum corpus

of many inhabitants of the city of Cork who were close to him at the time, he lay dead for a period of three days and three nights, during which he learned bitterly about all the sins he had previously committed with pleasure. His subsequent life bears witness to all the suffering he underwent. Indeed he suffered many kinds of unbelievable and intolerable torments, the order and name of which we have not been loth to write to you, for the sake of strengthening your devotion, just as we learned them from the mouth of the person who saw and suffered them.

Tnugdal had many cronies among whom one was his debtor in an exchange contract and owed him three horses. He waited for the final limit which had been set for repayment and, when the time had elapsed, he went to visit his friend. He was made most welcome and stayed there for three nights before he started discussing the matter outstanding. When the other answered that he did not have at hand what he asked, he fell into a rage and began to prepare to set off the way he had come. But the debtor, wishing to placate his friend, asked him to be so good as to agree to have a meal with him before leaving. As he found it impossible to refuse his pleas, he sat down again and, having laid down the axe he held in his hand, began to take food with his companion. But God's mercy forestalled his appetite. For, struck by I know not what sudden occurrence, he was not able to lift to his mouth the hand he had stretched in front of him. Then he started to shout dreadfully and entrusted his axe, which he had previously laid down, to his friend's wife, saying: 'Keep my axe, for I am dying'. And with these words, his body immediately collapsed unconscious, as if there had never been any spirit in it. The symptoms of death are present: the hair is white, the forehead numb, the eyes hazy, the nose becomes pointed, the lips go pale, the chin falls and all the limbs of the body become stiff. The household rushes around, the food is taken away, the squires shout, the host moans, the body is laid down, bells are rung, the priest comes running, the population is astounded and the whole city is overcome by the sudden death of the good knight.

But let us not linger! From about the tenth hour on Wednesday until the very same hour on Saturday he lay dead with no sign of life remaining in him except a slight warmth that was felt in his left side by those who conscientiously took the trouble to palpate his body. That is why

9

subterrare noluerant, eo quod calorem in ipsa ejus partiuncula sentiebant. Post hec autem presente clero et populo, qui ad sepeliendum illum convenerant, resumpsit spiritum et debili flatu quasi per unius hore spatium respirare cepit. Mirantur cuncti, etiam sapientes, dicentes: Nonne hic est spiritus vadens et non rediens? Tunc ille, debili intuitu circumspiciens, interrogantibus se, si vellet communicare, innuit afferri corpus domini, et cum illud sumeret et vinum biberet, cepit cum gratiarum actione deum laudare dicens: O deus, major est misericordia tua, quam inquitas mea, licet mea sit magna nimis. Quantas ostendisti michi tribulationes multas et malas et conversus vivificasti me et de abyssis terre iterum reduxisti me. Et cum hec dixisset, sub testamento omnia, que habuit, dispersit et dedit pauperibus, ipse vero signo se salutifere crucis signari precepit et pristinam vitam in antea se relicturum omnimodis vovit. [...]

they refused to bury him, precisely because they felt heat in this small part of him. But after this period, in the presence of the priest and the people who had gathered for his burial, he regained consciousness and, within an hour, began to breathe feebly. Everyone wondered, even though they knew the answer: 'Is it not so that when the spirit passes away it does not return?' Then he looked around with a weak gaze and, when they asked him if he wanted to receive communion, he indicated that the Lord's body should be brought to him, and when he had taken it and drunk the wine, he started to praise God with thanksgiving, saying: 'O God, your mercy is greater than my wickedness though it is quite great. You showed me so many cruel trials, but you restored me to life and you brought me back from the depths of the earth.' When he had said this, by written deed he gave away and distributed to the poor everything he had; as for himself, he ordered that the redemptive sign of the cross be put upon him, and he vowed to abandon in every manner and for ever his former life. [...]

English translation in: The Vision of Tnugdal. *Translated by Jean-Michel Picard. With an introduction by Yolande de Pontfarcy. Dublin: Four Courts Press, 1989, pp. 11-13,*

Bernard de Clairvaux
(Twelfth century)

Latin original in: *Éloge de la nouvelle chevalerie – Vie de Saint Malachie – Épitaphe, hymne, lettres.* Introduction, translation, notes and index by Pierre-Yves Emery. Paris: Les Éditions du Cerf, 1990, pp. 307-308.

CIVITAS HIBERNIAE, nomine Corcagia, vacabat episcopo. Tractatum est de electione: dissensere partes, quibusque, ut assolet, praesulem volentibus constituere suum, non Dei. Venit illuc Malachias, audita dissensione. Convocato clero et populo, etiam corda et vota discordantium unire curavit. Et persuasis illis totum negotium sibi debere credi, cui potissimum sollicitudo incumberet illius, sicut et aliarum per Hiberniam ecclesiarum, incontinenti nominat eis, non quempiam de nobilibus terrae, sed magis quemdam hominem pauperem, quem sciret sanctum et doctum; et *hic* erat *alienigena.*

Quaeritur ille: nuntiatur decumbere lecto, et ita debilis, ut nullo pacto exeat, nisi in manibus portatus ministrantium. Et Malachias: 'Surgat, inquit, in nomine Domini: ego praecipio; oboedientia salvum faciet eum.'

Quid faceret ille? Parere volebat, sed imparatum se sentiebat, quod, etsi possit ire, episcopari reformidabat. Ita cum voluntate oboediendi, pugnante gemino hoste, pondere languoris et metu oneris, vicit illa tamen, data sibi in adiutorium spe salutis. Itaque conatur, movet sese, tentat vires, invenit se solito fortiorem. Crescit pariter fides cum viribus et, rursum facta fortior fides, dat vicissim viribus incrementum. Iam surgere per se valet, iam meliuscule gradi, iam nec sentire in ambulando lassitudinem; demum expeditus et alacer pervenire ad Malachiam sine hominis adiutorio. Qui assumens eum, misit in cathedram, clero et populo collaudante.

Hoc ita in pace factum est, quia nec illi ausi sunt Malachiae voluntati in aliquo obviare, *videntes signum quod fecerat,* nec ille parere dubitavit, tam evidenti argumento factus securior de Domini voluntate.

English translation on page 13 in: Bernard of Clairvaux: The Life and Death of Saint Malachy, The Irishman. *Translated by Robert T. Meyer. Kalamazoo: Cistercian Publications, 1978, pp. 65-66.*

Bernard de Clairvaux
(Twelfth century)

(St Malachy performs a miracle cure and appoints a new bishop)

A CITY of Ireland called Cork was without a bishop. An election was called but the parties could not agree; as often happens each side had its own prelate in mind, not God's. When Malachy heard about the argument he came there. Having called together the clergy and the people, he made every attempt to bring into one the hearts and choice of the people. Once he had persuaded them that they should leave the entire decision to him since the special care of this as well as of the other churches throughout Ireland was especially incumbent on him, he named a candidate for them without delay. It was not one of the nobles of the country but rather a poor man whom he knew to be both learned and holy and he happened to be an outsider.

They sought him out, but he was reported to be lying abed and so weak that he could leave only if he were carried in the arms of his attendants. Malachy spoke up: 'Let him arise in the name of the Lord. I tell you, obedience will make him whole.'

What would he do? He was willing to obey, but he felt that even if he could go he was wholly unprepared and he dreaded being made a bishop. So along with the desire to obey there were twin enemies facing him: the weight of his weariness and the fear of the burden. But obedience won out; the hope of salvation was given to help him. So he tried, he moved, he tested his strength and found that he was stronger than usual. His faith increased with his strength and once faith became stronger in turn, it gave increase to his strength. He was now able to get up by himself and to walk a little better and he did not tire himself out by walking. Finally he was able to come to Malachy without hindrance and quickly, without everyone's help. Malachy took him in hand and enthroned him amid the applause of clergy and people.

This was done peaceably, for no one dared to oppose the will of Malachy in any way after seeing the sign he had done. Nor did the other man hesitate to obey since by so clear a proof he was quite certain of God's will.

Georg Braun / Frans Hogenberg
(1618)

Latin original in: *Civitates Orbis Terrarum. Teatri Praeciparum Totius Mundi Urbium. Liber sextus.* Cologne: Kempen, 1618, p. 3.

IN EADEM prouincia, sed longe diuersa parte, nimirum inter ortum & meridiem aliud opidum visitur, *Corcagia* Latinis, *Corcke* Anglis, & *Corcach* indigenis dictum; astrictiore quidem murorum ambitu inclusum, & vna quasi directa platea protensum, ciuibus tamen frequens, & opulentum. Seditiosis vero vicinis ita vndique cingitur, vt ciues perpetuas quasi excubias interdiu noctuque agere cogantur, nec filias in agrum elocare audeant. Vnde fit, vt contractis inter se nuptijs, omnes aliquo affinitatis gradu se contingant, ac tanto facilius, immo arctissime pacem et amicitiam inter se seruent, & communi tutelæ ac saluti intenti sint.

Hoc in oppido religiosus ille & sanctissimus vir Briocus, a quo Sanbriochiana in Britannia Aremorica Diœcesis (vulgo *Saint Brieu*) nomen sumpsit, natus & educatus fertur. Districtus ipse, vti & Limmericum, Comitatus dignitate censetur; qui quum Desmoniam quoque contineret, olim quoque Regni prærogatiua fuit insignis. Ita enim ab Henrico Secundo Rege in donationis diplomate, Roberto Stephani filio, & Miloni de Cogan factæ, nominatur his verbis: Sciatu me concessisse totum regnum de Corcke (excepta ciuitate & Oustmannorum Cantredo) tenendum, ipsis & hæredibus, de me & Ioanne filio meo, per seruitium sexaginta militum.

Georg Braun / Frans Hogenburg
(1618)

(Cork in general – St Brieu – Henry II)

IN THE same province, but in a far distant part, doubtless between the south and the east, another city is found. In Latin it is called *Corcagia*; the English call it *Corcke*, and the indigenous peoples call it *Corcach*. It is confined within narrower walls [than Limerick], and stretched out straight as if along one main street, but it is wealthy and thronged with citizens. Truly, it is bound on all sides by seditious neighbourhoods, so that the citizens have to keep almost constant guard, day and night, and they dare not farm out their daughters to the country. Whence it comes that, having contracted marriages among themselves, everyone is connected by some degree of affinity, and by so much the more easily, or rather most firmly, they maintain peace and friendship among themselves, and they are intent on common safety and welfare.

In this city that most devout and holy man Briocus is said to have been born and educated, from whom the diocese of Sanbriochiana (*Saint Brieu* in the vernacular) in Brittany took its name. This same district, as also that of Limerick, is considered worthy of an earldom, and, since it also contains the territory of Desmond, formerly it was marked with the prerogative of a kingdom. Hence it is mentioned in the following terms by King Henry II in a letter of donation made to Robert Fitzstephen and Milo Coggan: 'Know that I have conceded the whole kingdom of Corcke (excepting the city and the cantred of the Ostmen) to be held of me and my son John by these men [Robert and Milo] and their heirs through the service of 60 soldiers.'

English translation by Jason Harris.

François de la Boullaye-le-Gouz
(1644)

French original in: *Les Voyages et Observations du sieur de La Boullaye-Le-Gouz: gentilhomme Angevin*. Paris: F. Clousier, 1653.

Aun mille de Korq est une fontaine appellée par les Anglois Sundayspring, ou source du Dimanche laquelle les Irois tiennent estre beniste, et guarir plusieurs maux, i'en trouvay l'eau extrememement froide, vis à vis de cette fontaine au Midy de la mer sont les vestiges d'un Monastere fondé par S. Guillabé, il y a une cave qui va fort loing sous terre, où l'on dist que S. Patrice frequentoit souvent pour vacquer à l'Oraison. Dans un des fauxbourgs de Korq il y a une vieille tour, laquelle a dix ou douze pas de circuit, et plus de 100 pieds de haut, que l'on tient religieusement avoir esté bastie par S. Baril sans chaux ny sans pierre, pour prouver par ce miracle sa Religion, puis couppée, ou destruitte à moytié par le mesme Sainct, lequel sauta du haut en bas, et imprima la marque de son pied sur un caillou, où les vieilles vont en grande devotion faire leurs Oraisons.

François de la Boullaye-le-Gouz
(1644)

(Cork marvels: Sunday's Well – Gilabbey – St Finbarr's tower)

A MILE from Korq is a well called by the English Sunday spring, or the fountain of Sunday, which the Irish believe is blessed and cures many ills. I found the water of it extremely cold. Opposite this well to the south of the sea, are the ruins of a monastery founded by Saint Guillabé; there is a cave which extends far under the ground, where they say, that Saint Patrick resorted often for prayer. In one of the suburbs of Korq there is an old tower ten or twelve feet in circumference, and more than 100 feet high, which they conscientiously believe to have been built by Saint Baril [Fin Barr] without lime or stone, to prove by this miracle his religion; then it was lopped or half destroyed by the same saint, who jumped from the top to the bottom of it, and imprinted the mark of his foot on a flint stone, where the old women go with great devotion to say their prayers.

English translation in: The Tour of the French Traveller M. de la Boullaye de Gouz in Ireland, AD1644. *Ed. and translated by T. Crofton Croker. London: T. and W. Bonne, 1837, pp. 29-30.*

Jacques Nicolas Bellin
(1757)

French original in: *Essai geographique sur les isles britanniques*. Paris: Ministère de la Marine et des Colonies, 1757, pp. 212-13.

CORKE, CAPITALE de la Province et Siege d'un Evéché, est une jolie Ville bien peuplée et fortifiée; elle est située sur la Riviere de Lée, ou Leo, qui y forme un très bon Port, quoiqu'éloigné de la Mer de quatre lieues; mais avant que d'y arriver, il y a une très belle Baie, qu'on appelle le Havre de Corke, dans laquelle il peut tenir un grand nombre de Vaisseaux, à l'abri de tous vents. La plupart des habitans sont des Anglois, que le Commerce y a attirés, et des Réfugiés François. La meilleure partie de la Ville est bâtie dans les Isles que la Riviere forme en cet endroit.

Jacques Nicolas Bellin
(1757)

(Cork harbour – English and French inhabitants)

CORK, PROVINCIAL capital and bishopric, is a pretty, fortified town with a substantial population. It is situated on the River Lee or Leo which forms a very fine port there although it is at a distance of four leagues from the sea. But before one reaches it, there is a very beautiful bay which is called the Haven of Cork in which a great number of vessels can be accommodated and sheltered from all winds. Most of the inhabitants of Cork are English, trade having drawn them there, as well as French refugees. Most of the town is built on islands formed by the river there.

English translation by Grace Neville.

Philip (Filippe) Mazzei

(*c.* 1783)

Italian back-translation of 'Memoirs of Philip Mazzei'. In: *William and Mary Quarterly*, 2nd series, vol. ix, no. 4, October 1929, pp. 259-60.

D OPO QUELL'EPISODIO non successe niente di straordinario finché non arrivammo a Cork, in Irlanda, a quaranta giorni da New York.

Appena entrammo nel porto, un socio della compagnia di Pedder, Hamilton & Soci, che era considerata una delle migliori imprese di Cork e a cui apparteneva la nave, venne a bordo. Si chiamava Cotter e pareva sui trent'anni. Gli irlandesi erano, per lo più, dalla parte dei coloni americani, e il signor Cotter era estremamente ben disposto nei loro confronti. Ci trovò subito vitto e alloggio in una casa privata e ci procurò ogni possibile comodità e facilitazione [...]

Prima di lasciare l'Inghilterra, avevo dato a mia moglie un orologio d'oro, ne avevo dato un'altro alla mia figliastra a Parigi e me n'erano rimasti due per me. Ne diedi uno al padrone di casa, chiedendogli di venderlo senza dire a nessuno chi ne fosse il proprietario. Ma Cotter venne a saperlo – non so come – e venne a protestare perché non gli avevo rivelato le mie ristrettezze. Criticava fortemente la ragione per cui vendevo gli orologi proprio in quel momento, poiché avrei percepito poco più del valore dell'oro stesso.

Ero commosso della sua generosità, e osservai che non potevo approfittarmi di lui, soprattutto date le condizioni, non solo delle mie finanze, ma anche della mia salute. Mi rispose esattamente così: 'Senta, non sono un uomo ricco. Ero un giovane impiegato in questa impresa, senza nessun capitale personale, quando i signori Pedder e Hamilton – che sono benestanti e che desiderano passare tre quarti dell'anno in campagna – mi imposero di gestire la loro impresa nella sua interezza, condividendo con me una parte dei profitti. Ripeto, non sono ricco, ma la somma di ottanta o di cento sterline, per permetter Le di andare a Nantes, non mi rovinerà, e mi procurerà un grande dispiacere se non accetterà quello di cui ha bisogno.'

Mi fece accettare otto ghinee che aveva in tasca, ma quando volle darmi il resto per arrivare fino a cento sterline, gli dimostrai che me ne

Philip (Filippe) Mazzei
(*c.* 1783)

(Sympathy with American revolutionaries – a political activist on the run –
Cork generosity)

NOTHING REMARKABLE happened after this incident until we arrived in Cork, Ireland, forty days out of New York.

As soon as we entered the harbour, a partner of the firm of Pedder, Hamilton and Company, owners of the ship and rated one of the best firms in Cork, came aboard. His name was Cotter, and he appeared to be about 30 years old. The Irish, as a rule, were in sympathy with the American colonists, and Mr Cotter was exceedingly in favour of them. He at once found good board and lodging for us in a private house, and he gave us every comfort and advantage possible [...]

Before leaving England, I had given a gold watch to my wife, another one to my step-daughter in Paris, and I had two for myself. I gave one of them to my landlord, asking him to sell it and not to tell anybody who was its owner. But Cotter found out – I do not know how – and he came to remonstrate with me because I had not told him of my necessitous circumstances, decrying strongly my purpose of selling my watches at that critical time, since I could get only a little more than the value of the gold.

I was touched by his generosity, and I observed to him that I could not take advantage of him, especially because of the predicament in which I was, not only as to my finances, but also as to my health. He answered me exactly as follows: 'Listen, I am not a wealthy man. I was a young clerk in this firm, without any capital of my own, when Mr Pedder and Mr Hamilton – who are very well fixed, and who, desiring to pass three-fourths of the year in the country – thrust upon me the entire management of their business, sharing a part of the profits with me. I repeat, I am not rich, but a sum of £80 or £100, enabling you to go to Nantes, will not ruin me, and you will cause me deep sorrow if you do not accept what you need'.

He forced me to take eight guineas that he had in his pocket; but when he wanted to give me the balance making up the £100, I showed

bastavano cinquanta per giungere a Nantes, soprattutto dal momento che mi aveva già procurato l'alloggio su una nave portoghese che sarebbe salpata dopo qualche giorno.

Quando mi diede le cinquanta sterline, gli misi in mano una tratta a vista per la stessa cifra, pagabile a Nantes. Dimenticai, comunque, le otto ghinee che mi aveva dato prima delle cinquanta sterline.

Salimmo a bordo durante la notte, per evitare il rischio di essere scoperti, in quanto sarei stato arrestato e chiuso nella Torre di Londra finché la pace non fosse stata dichiarata, se qualcuno avesse minimamente sospettato che io eseguivo una missione pubblica.

Translated by Louise Sheehan.

him that £50 were sufficient to bring me to Nantes, especially since he had already arranged for my accommodations on a Portuguese ship that was sailing in a few days.

When he gave me the £50, I put in his hands a sight draft for the same amount against me, payable in Nantes. However, I forgot about the eight guineas he had given me before the £50.

We went aboard during the night, in order to avoid the risk of being discovered, because any suspicions that I was performing a public mission would cause me to be arrested and to be put in the Tower of London until peace had been declared.

Translated by E.C. Branchi; for source see page 20.

Jacques Louis de Latocnaye
(1797)

French original in: *Promenade d'un Français dans l'Irlande*. Dublin: Graisberry, 1797. This version in: *Promenade d'un Français dans l'Irelande* [sic] 2nd ed. Brunswick: P.F. Fauche, 1801, pp. 104-08

JE RETOURNAI à Cork, par la rivière, et j'eus lieu d'observer que les bateliers ont à-peu-près le même ton goguenard que ceux des grandes rivières de France. Le peuple semblait animé, et des bandes d'ouvriers couraient les rues en criant; je m'informai de ce que ce pouvait être, et l'on me dit que les garçons cordonniers avaient d'un commun accord, tous quitté leurs maîtres ce jour-là et qu'ils couraient les rues afin de les forcer à augmenter leurs gages. Je les suivis et les vis plusieurs fois s'arrêter à la maison de quelques maîtres cordonniers et avoir de chaudes altercations avec eux. Les magistrats à la fin cependant, crurent devoir faire cesser le trouble; un d'eux, à la tête de quelques soldats, courut les rues pour les disperser: mais les ouvriers se moquèrent de lui, et surent si bien faire, qu'il était toujours dans les endroits où ils n'étaient pas eux-mêmes; la nuit, comme en Angleterre, fit cesser le tumulte, et envoya tout le monde se coucher.

J'étais recommandé à l'Evêque qui me reçut fort bien, et ce qui me fit grand plaisir, (parce que cela prouve que toutes animosités entre les deux religions sont finies,) il m'adressa à l'Evêque Catholique, Dr. Moylan, qui est un homme instruit et respecté dans le pays.

Au sujet de je ne sais quelle fête, les enfans firent un feu d'ossemens (ce qui est un usage commun en Irlande, pour les jours de réjouissance) et ils s'amusèrent à danser autour et même à le traverser pieds nuds. Ceci me donna lieu de faire réflexion sur l'étymologie du *bone fire*[1] en

---

1. Feux d'ossemens; c'est ainsi qu'on appelle les Feux de joye que l'on fait aux réjouissances publiques, dans la Grande Bretagne.

Jacques Louis de Latocnaye
(1797)

*(Strike of Cork shoemakers – bonfires – 'characters' –
trade and commerce)*

I RETURNED to Cork [from Cove] by the river, and was able to observe that the boatmen here adopt the same bantering air of those working on the great rivers of France. The people seemed animated, and groups of workers were rushing shouting through the streets. I asked what was going on and was informed that the apprentice-shoemakers had, by common accord, all downed tools that day and that they were hurrying through the streets in order to force their masters to increase their wages. I followed them and saw them stop several times in front of the houses of some master-shoemakers where they exchanged heated words with them. The magistrates finally intervened in the belief that they were duty bound to bring the disturbance to an end. One of them at the head of some soldiers ran through the streets in order to disperse them, but the workers only made fun of him, and arranged matters so well that wherever he was, there was no sign of them. Night, as in England, brought the tumult to an end and sent everyone home to bed.

I had a recommendation to the Bishop who received me very well. Something that gave me great pleasure (because it proves that all animosities between the two religions are no more) was the fact he sent me on to the Catholic Bishop, Dr Moylan, an educated man much respected in the country.

On the occasion of I know not what celebration, the children made a fire of bones (a common practice in Ireland on days of rejoicing) and they amused themselves by dancing around the fire and even by running over it in their bare feet. This brought me to reflect on the etymology of *bone*

1. Bone fires: this is the term given to fires of celebration that mark public celebrations in Great Britain.

25

Angleterre, qui m'a tout l'air de venir de ces feux d'ossemens, plutôt que du français forcé, de *bon feu* pour feu de joye.

Le climat à Cork est pluvieux à un point extrême: il y pleut tous les jours de la vie; la température de l'air a peut-être influé sur le caractère des habitans: on pourrait avec quelque raison appeler ce pays *the land of whim and spleen* [...] Il y a ici grand nombre de personnes, qu'on appelle gens à caractère, et qui tous ont des fantaisies fort singulières: l'un ne se met jamais à table, crainte d'être suffoqué par l'odeur des viandes, et mange tout seul dans le vestibule: l'autre dépense son revenu en animaux favoris, ou *pêts* comme on les appelle: un troisième (assez, bon enfant chez lui) après vous avoir enchanté par une belle voix et une musique charmante, finira par vous boxer. Il y en a un qui court les rues au grand gallop avec un bonnet rouge, et entre à cheval dans les boutiques, quand il a besoin de quelque chose; j'ai vu un joueur de cornemuse, qui aima mieux être déshérité de près de deux mille livres sterlings de rente, que de quitter sa musette, qui est à présent son seul gagne-pain. Il y a un homme qui croit que toute la terre veut l'empoisonner; aussitôt qu'il voit quelqu'un entrer chez un boulanger, il le suit et saute avec avidité sur le pain qu'il a acheté, parce qu'il est sûr, dit-il, que les boulangers n'en veulent qu'à lui: il fait de même à la boucherie, etc. Je pourrais bien citer d'autres caractères mais c'est assez.

Il n'y a point de loge pour les fous à Cork: c'est un spectacle hideux de les voir courir les rues: la plupart, il est vrai, sont très-tranquilles, mais il est si cruel et si humiliant de voir la nature humaine dégradée à ce point, qu'on devrait penser à les séparer de la société.

Au surplus, la ville de Cork, a fait dans ces derniers temps des progrès immenses dans le commerce, l'augmentation des maisons et des habitans, et en quelque point dans leur amélioration. La ville est située sur différentes petites îles marécageuses au milieu de la rivière: c'est de cette situation qu'elle a tiré son nom, (car *Corcakh* signifie '*bourbeux*' en Irlandais, et elle est passablement bien nommée.)[2] Les canaux

---

2. On fait aussi venir le nom de Cork, de *Cuirky*, qui veut dire 'avoine': il est sûr que les paysans l'appellent encore à présent comme cela; mais cela ce fait rien, l'ancien nom de Cork, est *Corca*.

fire[1] in England, which seems to me to come from these bone fires, rather than from the forced French of *bon feu* for 'feu de joie'.

The climate in Cork is rainy in the extreme. It rains there every single day, and the air temperature has perhaps influenced the character of the inhabitants. It would not be incorrect to call it 'The Land of Whim and Spleen'. There are a great number of people here who are called 'characters', all of whom have all sorts of strange whims. One of them will never sit down at table for fear of being suffocated by the smell emanating from the meats, and so he eats alone in the hallway; another spends his income on his favourite animals or its as they are called; a third (a fairly inoffensive creature in his own home), having bewitched you with his beautiful voice and charming music, ends up by boxing you. There is another with a red cap who gallops through the streets and enters shops on horseback when he needs something. I saw a bagpipe player who preferred to lose out on an annual inheritance of nearly £2,000 sterling from rent rather than to give up his pipes which are at present his sole source of income. There is a man who believes that everyone is out to poison him. As soon as he spots someone going into a baker's shop, he follows him and eagerly seizes the bread he has just bought, because he is sure – as he has said – that every baker has it in for him alone. He acts the same way in butchers' shops, etc. I could easily mention other examples of these characters but I have said enough.

There is no place of shelter for mad people in Cork. It is a hideous sight to see them out in the streets. It is true that most of them are very quiet, but it is so cruel and humiliating to see human nature so degraded that consideration should be given to separating them from the rest of society.

Yet it is true that the city of Cork has recently made great progress in commerce and with a growing population, in the increased provision of housing, along with some improvement in its overall standard. The city stands on different little marshy islands in the middle of the river. From this it takes its name (as *Corcakh* means *muddy* in Irish, the city is thus fairly accurately named).[2]

---

2. The name of Cork is also said to come from *Cuirky*, which means 'oats'. It is certain that the peasants still use that name for it. No matter: Cork's former name is *Corca*.

The narrow canals that separate the islands are filled with water only at
étroits qui séparaient les îles n'étant remplis d'eau qu'à la marée,
nuisaient considérablement à la salubrité de l'air: on les a voûtés tout le
long de la ville [...]

La principale exportation est à présent en viandes salées; on tue les
différens bestiaux par milliers dans la saison, et ensuite on n'a plus
rien à faire; j'ai connu un marchand qui m'a dit, *occire* tous les ans, entre
vingt et vingt-cinq mille cochons; aussi je me permis de lui dire, qu'il
était *the greatest murderer of hogs, that I ever knew.*

high tide, and so considerably worsen the quality of the air. They have been paved over throughout the entire length of the city [...]

Salted meat is the main export at present. Thousands of different types of animals are killed in the season, after which there is nothing further to be done. I knew a merchant who told me that he kills between twenty and twenty-five thousand pigs every year, and so I was able to tell him that he was 'the greatest murderer of hogs I ever knew'.

English translation by Grace Neville.

Charles Baron Baert-Duholand
(1800)

French original in: *Tableau de la Grande Bretagne et de l'Irlande*. Paris: Jansen, 1800, pp. 328-30.

Il s'est tué à Corke en 1783, dans la saison qui dure octobre, novembre et décembre, vingt-quatre mille quatre-vingt-sept bœufs, vingt-deux mille cent soixante-une vaches, et douze cent quatre-vingt-cinq jeunes taureaux ou génisses; en tout quarante-sept mille cinq cent trente-trois têtes de gros bétail, non compris les cochons qui se tuent au printems et dont le produit monte à une valeur à peu près égale à celle du bétail rouge[1]; mais soit l'augmentation de l'agriculture, qui diminue nécessairement le produit des pâturages, soit la sortie du bétail vivant, soit que l'exportation par d'autres ports s'accroisse, soit que la cherté excessive des bestiaux fasse tirer des salaisons d'ailleurs, les demandes y sont depuis beaucoup diminuées. On n'y a tué l'année dernière, 1786, que de trente-cinq à quarante mille têtes de gros bétail, et pour une valeur à peu près égale de cochons. Le lord Sheffield dit que le *galeage* de Corke, impôt *d'un penny* par tête de bétail qui y entre, monte à 610 liv. st. par an; ce qui feroit cent quarante-quatre mille têtes de bétail gros ou petit. Il s'est tué l'année dernière à Waterford, m'ont assuré les principaux négocians de cette ville, environ quinze mille têtes de gros bétail et cinquante mille cochons. Limmerick passe pour tuer le tiers de ce que tue Corke, et Dublin le quart; Belfast fait aussi beaucoup de salaisons, mais exporte une bien plus grande quantité de bétail vivant. Il est sorti l'année dernière par le nord, de trente à trente-cinq mille têtes de bétail rouge, venant presque tous du Leinster et du Munster, et allant en Ecosse. On commence aussi à exporter des chevaux.

Il paroît évident que l'exportation du bœuf salé diminue, et j'ai ouï des négocians, à Corke, se plaindre qu'il en restoit beaucoup dans les

---

1. En tems de guerre il s'y étoit tué jusqu'à soixante-dix mille têtes de bétail rouge dans une saison.

Charles Baron Baert-Duholand
(1800)

(Meat production and meat trade)

IN CORK were killed in 1783, in the season that lasts from October to December 24,087 steer cattle, 22,161 cows, and 1,285 young bulls or heifers; in all, 47,533 heads of cattle, not counting the pigs that are killed in the spring, and whose rough value is equivalent to that of the red livestock.[1] However, whether it is due to factors such as the increase in agriculture resulting in an inevitable reduction in pasturage production, or whether it is due to the export of live cattle or because the increase in exports through other ports or their exorbitant price leads to them being salted elsewhere, demand for them has fallen considerably. Last year, 1786, only between 35 – 40,000 heads of cattle were slaughtered, along with pigs of an equal value. Lord Sheffield says that the Cork levy, the penny tax on each head of cattle entering Cork, amounts to £610 sterling per year; this would result in 144,000 heads of small or large cattle. The main Waterford dealers assured me that last year in that town about 15,000 head of livestock along with 50,000 pigs were slaughtered. Limerick is said to kill a third of what Cork kills, and Dublin a quarter; Belfast also carries out a significant amount of salting but exports considerably more live cattle. Last year, between 30 – 35,000 heads of red cattle were exported through the North, almost all of them originating in Leinster and Munster, and bound for Scotland. Horses are also beginning to be exported.

There is clearly a slump in the export of salted beef, and I have heard dealers in Cork complaining that much of it remains unsold in the

---

1. In war time as many as 70,000 head of red cattle were killed in just one season.

magasins, et que la France, qui en tiroit autrefois une grande quantité, commençoit à en faire venir d'Archangel où il étoit à meilleur marché. Mais la sortie des bestiaux vivans et l'exportation du porc salé et du beurre ont beaucoup augmenté; j'ai ouï porter par des gens très-instruits du commerce d'Irlande, ce dernier article seul à un million sterling. L'exportation des cuirs diminue nécessairement en raison de celle du bœuf salé, et presque tous s'exportent crus ou salés, faute de tan; ce qui a occasionné, en 1786, beaucoup de pétitions de tanneurs au parlement.

Les salaisons sont tirées en grande partie par l'Angleterre, les îles angloises et surtout par Terre-Neuve; il en passe aussi en France, en Espagne, en Portugal, et quelque peu en Hollande et dans le nord. Le beurre s'exporte en Angleterre, aux îles, en France et beaucoup en Portugal. Les cuirs salés ou crus passent en Angleterre, dans les Pays-Bas et en Espagne.

stores, and that France, which used to take a significant amount of it, was starting to have it brought from Archangel where it is cheaper. But the export of live cattle and of salted pork, along with butter, has risen sharply; I have heard the amount in question for the latter product alone put by Irish commercial experts at £1,000,000 sterling. The export of hides is falling inevitably as a result of the export of salt beef and it is almost all exported untreated or salted for want of tan. In 1786, this led to numerous petitions by tanners to parliament.

The salted meat is taken mainly by England, the English islands and especially Newfoundland; some also goes to France, Spain, Portugal, with a small amount bound for Holland and the north of Europe. The butter is exported to England, the islands, France and, especially, Portugal. The salted or raw hides go to England, the Low Countries and Spain.

English translation by Grace Neville.

Cornelius de Jong
(1802)

Dutch original in: *Reizen naar de Kap de Goede Hoop, Ierland en Noorwegen in de Jaren 1791 tot 1797[...] met het, onder zijn bevel staande, 's lands fregat van oorlog, Scipio. Eerste Deel.* Haarlem: François Bohn, 1802, pp. 236-65.

ZES-EN-TWINTIGSTE BRIEF

Cork den 25 October 1793

HET ZOU voor u, lieve Vriend, ruim zoo vervelend, als voor mij lastig zijn, wanneer ik thans met passer en winkelhaak de openbare gebouwen intrad en zeer omslagtig de onderscheidene bouwordc der kerken, beurs, *Customhouse* of de Douane, liefdadige gestichten en anderen beschreef. Het geen mij ten aanzien van de laatsten het meest voldaan heeft, is vooreerst een spinschool, waarin jonge meisjes beneden de vrij-ster-jaren uit de laagste klassen van menschen, dagelijks haar werk afspinnen, en de eerzucht voelen aangespoord door prijzen, die aan de beste spinsters door fatzoenelijke vrouwen in de hoedanigheid van regentessen worden uitgedeeld. Ten anderen een vondelinghuis, waarin ik de goede orde en uitstekende zindelijkheid moest bewonderen; de slaapvertrekken zelve waren zoo luchtig en schoon, dat men geene de minste benauwde lucht bespeurde; en hetgeen mij inzonderheid voldeed, was, dat, na alles nauwkeurig te hebben laten zien, de opzichters van dit huis verpligt zijn, een boek aantebieden, dat altoos op de vergaderkamer der Regenten open ligt, waarin ieder vreemdeling ernstig verzocht wordt, zijne aanmerkingen te willen opteekenen, die dan vervolgens maandelijks door Regenten onderzocht worden. Voor het overige, heb ik tot heden in deze stad weinig aanmerkenswaardig gevonden. De vleeschhal evenwel verdient gezien te worden. Dit is een groot, langwerpig, vierkant gebouw onder één dak, verdeeld in een aantal gaanderijen, waarin ieder slagter zijne vaste plaats heeft en zijn geslagt vee, dat men weinig beter vinden kan, ten toon stelt. Een gedeelte dezer hal is de vischmarkt, die meesttijds wel voorzien is.

Cork, eene koopstad zijnde, was voorheen, even als onze Hollandsche

Cornelius de Jong
(1802)

(*Canals and houses – public entertainments – character of the Irish –
eating and drinking – women – poverty – local government – Irish music – the
Irish language – a girl sailor*)

TWENTY-SIXTH LETTER

Cork, 25th October, 1793

MY DEAR Friend, it would be as boring for you, as it would be awk-
ward for me, were I now, armed with a compass and a set square,
to enter the public buildings and to elaborately describe the typical
building style of the churches, the Exchange, Customhouse, charities –
and other buildings. What pleased me most concerning the latter, was
firstly, a spinning school, where young girls under courting age and
from the lowest social classes, spend each day at the spinning wheel,
and whose pride in their work is encouraged through prizes given to
the best spinsters by respectable women, and distributed by the gov-
ernesses. Secondly, I was pleased by an orphanage, where I had to
admire the good order and excellent cleanliness; the sleeping quarters
were so airy and clean that no stuffiness whatsoever was apparent; and
what particularly satisfied me was the fact that after meticulously having shown everything, the supervisors of this house were obliged to
bring my attention to a book, that always lay open in the meeting
room of the Governors, and into which every stranger is strongly
requested to write down his remarks. Apart from this, I have so far
found little in this city that is remarkable. The meat hall, however,
needs to be seen. This is a big elongated rectangular building under one
roof, divided into several corridors, where each butcher has his own
spot where he exhibits his butchered meat, which is hard to find better
anywhere else. Part of this hall is a fish market, which is well stocked
most of the time.

Cork, a city noted for commerce and trading, was previously, like
our Dutch cities, intersected by canals, but these were in a short time for

steden, doorsneden met grachten, die thans voor het meerder gedeelte binnen korte jaren tot meerdere voorkoming van besmettelijke ziektens gedempt zijn. De straten vindt men, op die weinige na, welke door de demping der tusschen beide gelopen hebbende grachten verbreed zijn, smal en slecht, en de huizen over het algemeen tamelijk; enkelen evenwel zijn zeer goed; doch dezen, ofschoon alle nieuw en binnen weinige jaren gebouwd, verdienen, in vergelijking van die in andere Europische steden, den naam van prachtig niet, en zijn zoodanig met de oude en gemeene, in de onderscheidene straten, dooreengemengd, dat het geheel een verward voorkomen heeft. Dan daar nog dagelijks aangebouwd en de stad vergroot wordt, zal misschien alles welhaast eene andere gedaante aannemen.

De Paradeplaats is ruim, lang en breed; en in dezen tijd van het jaar de gewoone morgen-wandeling der fatsoendelijkste viouwen, vooral des zondags. Hier heeft men de voornaamste winkels, waar onder die van Parfumeurs en Galanterien, naar evenredigheid der stad, in te groote menigte zijn. Op het midden der plaats ziet men de beeltenis van den vorigen Koning levensgrootte te paard met de staf van kommando in de rechte hand; daar ik niet weet, dat deze Vorst iets in het bijzonder, ten voordeele van Ierland, veel min van Cork, gedaan heeft, verwonderde het mij hem hier aantetreffen. Eene andere statue, meer in het klein, vindt men in een nis op de beurs, verbeeldende George Lawton, een man nog in leven, die in vorige jaren Major zijnde, zoodanig in goed bestier, inzonderheid in het zindelijk, en schoon houden der straten, uitmuntte, dat zijne stadgenoten, door's mans beeltenis op hunne beurs te plaatzen, de deugden van dezen eersten Magistraats-persoon bij het nageslacht vereeuwigd hebben. Boven deze beurs, die naar evenredigheid van koophandel en kooplieden vrij klein is, heeft men het voornaamste Koffijhuis, alwaar alles, wat men gewoonlijk in den voormiddag gebruikt, te krijgen is. Gaarne evenwel, had ik 'er allerhande soort van Nieuwspapieren gezien; de eenigen, die men 'er vindt, zijn Engelsche en Iersche, waar door vreemdelingen, die deze taal niet verstaan, verstoken zijn van het voornaamste genoegen, dat een koffijhuis voor hun oplevert.

Van openbare vermaaklijkheden is *Cork* schaars voorzien; men heeft 'er een Schouwburg, waarin, in sommige zomer-maanden, juist de tijd van het jaar, het minst daar toe geschikt, door een troep uit Dublin gespeeld wordt;

the greater part filled in, in order to further prevent contagious diseases. The streets are narrow and bad, apart from a few which were widened as a result of the filling in of the canals, and the houses in general are in bad shape; some, however, are very good; nevertheless, although these are new and recently built, in comparison with those in other European cities, they do not deserve to be called 'beautiful', and they are so mixed in with old and ordinary houses in the different streets that it looks disorderly overall. But maybe, seeing that there is still daily building going on and the city is growing, everything will look different eventually.

The Parade is spacious, long and wide; and is used this time of the year by the most respectable women for their regular morning walks, particularly on Sundays. The main shops are found here, with, considering the size of the city, too many perfumeries and shops selling luxuries. A life-size representation of the previous king on horseback holding a commando sceptre in his right hand, can be seen in the centre of this place; as I am not aware of anything special this monarch has done in favour of Ireland, let alone in favour of Cork, I was surprised to come across him here. Another, smaller statue, to be found in an alcove on the Exchange, represents George Lawton, a man still alive, who in previous years so excelled while governing as mayor, particularly in the up-keep of order and cleanliness in the streets, that his citizens have eternalised the virtues of this first Magistrate for future generations, by placing this man's image in the Exchange. Above this building, which is quite modest, considering the extent of trade and the number of tradesmen, is the Coffeehouse, which offers everything that one normally would use in the morning. However, I would like to have seen a greater diversity of newspapers here; one can only find English and Irish ones, which means that foreigners who do not understand these languages are deprived of the most important pleasure that a Coffeehouse has to offer.

Public entertainment is in short supply in Cork; there is a Theatre where during some of the summer months, predominantly during that time in the year least suitable for it, a group of actors from Dublin give

maar deze toneel-spelers, aan den Schouwburg van de Hoofdplaats verbon-
den, vertrekken, zoo dra de herfst de menschen van hunne landgoederen in
de stad terug roept. Het zijn meest Engelschen en waarschijnlijk de beste
niet; ten minsten de derde of vierde dag, dat ik hier binnen kwam en toen
zij voor het laatst speelden, heb ik zulks moeten denken. Behalve de
Schouwburg is 'er eene liefhebberij-comedie, die in geen aanmerking komt.
Openbare concerten vindt men weinig, maar *private ones* of zulke, die aan
bijzondere huizen gegeven worden, zijn 'er meer, en over het algemeen schijnt 'er vrij veel liefhebberij voor de musiek te wezen. Bij het eindigen van
mijn laatsten brief noemde ik de *Drum*. Dit is eene openbare danspartij, die
alle agt of veertien dagen plaats heeft. Ieder persoon betaalt twee Engelsche
schellingen voor den toegang. Ik kwam 'er met drie vrouwen mijner kennis
en dacht het pligtmatig ieder een lootje aantebieden; maar men antwoordde, dat zulks hier in het geheel niet gebruikelijk was; en elke vrouw
telde hare eigen schellingen toe, en niet alleen die vrouwen, welke ik bij mij
had, maar ook zij, die naderhand met hare mans en broeders inkwamen.
Het gezelschap was niet talrijk; de danzen Menuets en Engelsche
Contradanzen. De zaal is volmaakt geschikt tot eene danszaal, ruim, breed,
lang en koel, vrij wel verlicht; doch het orchest kan nauwlijks den naam van
taamljjk dragen: trouwens deze partij wordt zoo schaars bezocht, dat misschien meerdere kosten niet zouden kunnen goedgemaakt worden. De reden
hier van doet weinig eer aan de vrouwen. Hoe dan? vraagt gij; geduld, mijn
vriend, zoodra ik u over de schoone sexe onderhoude, zal die nieuws-
gierigheid voldaan worden.

Zeven-en-Twintigste Brief

Cork den 3 November 1793

Zijn 'er weinige openbare vermaken te Cork, met de wandelingen is het
niet veel beter gesteld. Men heeft 'er de Mall de *Dijke* of *Mardijke*, met een
of twee anderen, doch geen eene van aanbelang. De *Dijke* heeft dit bijzon-
ders,dat het een natuurlijke bank is, door de rivier de Lee gevormd, thans
aan beide zijden bedijkt, die zich meer dan een kwartier uurs westwaards
uitstrekt, en het werk van zekeren Heer WEBBER in het begin dezer eeuw.
Aan het eind derzelve wordt een huis gevonden, waar achter men de rivier, die hier met veel vaart van hooger land naar beneden stroomt, over

performances; but these actors who are attached to the Theatre in the capital, leave as soon as autumn calls people back from their country residences to the city. The actors are mostly English and probably not the best ones; at least that was my opinion when I had seen them for the third or fourth time and when I saw them when they had their final performance. Apart from the Theatre, there is an amateur comedy, which does not really need any mention. Public concerts are rare, but private concerts, which take place in special houses, are more plentiful and in general there seems to be quite a lot of interest in music. At the end of my last letter I mentioned the 'Drum'. This is a public dance event which takes place every week or every fortnight. Every person pays two English shillings admission. I came with three female acquaintances and felt it my duty to offer each a ticket; but they told me that this was not the custom here; and each woman paid their own shillings and not only the women who accompanied me, but also those who arrived later with their husband or brothers. Not many people were there; the dances comprised of Minuets and English Contredances. The space is perfect for a dance hall, spacious, wide, long, airy, quite well lit; however, the orchestra could not even be called mediocre: anyway, this event is so badly attended that perhaps one could not afford more expense. The reason for this is not very flattering for the women. Why is that so? You ask; patience, my friend, as soon as I tell you about the fairer sex, your curiosity will be satisfied.

TWENTY-SEVENTH LETTER

Cork, November 3rd, 1793

Public entertainment is poor in Cork and likewise opportunities for walks are not much better. There is the Mall, the Dyke or the Mardyke, with one or two others, but none are of importance. The Dyke is specialas it is a natural bank shaped by the River Lee which has at present a dyke on both sides, stretching more than a quarter of an hour westwards and which was built by a certain Mister Webber at the start of this century. At the end of the Dyke is a house behind which one can observe how the river, streaming very fast here from higher ground downwards, falls, after

kleine muurtjes lage vallen ziet maken; hetwelk iemand, die van ruischend water houdt en genoegen vindt in het schuimend voor bij zich heen te zien bruischen, hier met vermaak eenige oogenblikken kan doen doorbrengen. Doch daar Mardijke wat ver uit het midden der stad gelegen is en het lastige heeft, dat men denzelfden weg terug moet, blijft de Paradeplaats de begunstigde wandeling der vrouwen, die men 'er meesttijds slecht weer uitgezonderd, van 's middags twaalf of een uur af tot drie of half vier uren in de namiddag vindt.

De kleeding voor dit gedeelte van den dag bestaat in het zelfde *Negligé,* dat men de Engelsche vrouwen ziet dragen; welke natie, sedert dat Grootbritannien, *Schotland* en *Ierland* tot één Rijk vereenigd zijn, hare kleeding, gewoontens en zeden aan die volkeren heeft medegedeeld; alles is Engelsch. Evenwel de Ieren, een volk op zichzelve, waarvoor de Engelschen, die hun wreed, hardvochtig en valsch noemen, over het algemeen weinig achting toonen, hebben een karakter op zichzelve en enkele gewoontens hun bijzonder eigen. Van de laatsten zal ik u het een en ander melden, doch ten aanzien van het eerste mij wel wachten om 'er een oordeel over te vellen. Zou het niet vermetel zijn, omtrent menschen, wier taal men niet in den grond verstaat, in wier land men nog geen volle twee maanden doorbragt, en met wie men niet leeft op dien gemeenzamen vriendschappelijken voet, die allen afstand verwijdert, en die volstrekt noodzakelijk is, om min of meer sommige trekken van het karakter met grond te durven beoordeelen, eene beschrijving te willen doen? Dit alleen kan ik over het algemeen zeggen, dat de Ier mij meer vleijend voorkomt, dan de Engelschman; dat de natie minder beschaafd schijnt, maar echter meer oplettendheid, meer *égards* heeft voor vreemdelingen, en dat, zo de beschuldiging van wreed en hardvochtig gegrond is, zulks mogelijk nog als overblijfsels van de vorige woedende binnenlandsche oorlogen zou kunnen beschouwd worden, waarin zekerlijk de verschrikkelijkste wreedheden hebben plaats gehad.

De manier van leven der fatsoenlijkste lieden, derzelver kleeding, tafel en verdeeling van den dag, is, met weinige uitzonderingen, voor het overige geheel op zijn Engelsch. Om negen uren staat men op; om tien of elf uren, ook wel op den middag, ontbijt men met koffij en thee beide, nemende eerst een kop koffij en vervolgens thee, waarbij brood,

flowing over some low walls; anyone who likes rushing water and enjoys the sight of seeing it foaming and speeding by, can spend some time here with pleasure. However, as the Mardyke is situated a bit far removed from the centre of the city, and because of the annoying fact that one has to walk the same route back, the Parade remains the favourite walking place for women, who, except when the weather is bad, are to be found there from twelve or one o'clock in the afternoon till three or half three in the evening.

The clothes for this part of the day consists of the same *negligé* as one sees English women wear; which nation, since Great Britain, Scotland and Ireland are united in one Monarchy, has given her dress sense, habits and traditions to these people; everything is English. However, the Irish, a nation in their own right, for whom the English, who call them cruel, hard and mean, show little respect in general, have their own unique character and their very own typical habits. Concerning the latter I will tell you some things, but concerning the former I will stay well away from giving a judgement. Would it not be bold to try to give a description concerning people whose language one does not fully understand, in whose country one has not even stayed yet for two full months, and with whom one does not live on such a level of friendship that it bridges the distance to them? All this would be absolutely necessary, were one to make a well-founded judgement about some character traits. In general I can only say that I find an Irish person more agreeable than an English person; that the nation seems less civilised, but has more concern and respect for foreigners. If the accusation of cruelty and roughness is justified, this could be seen as the remains of previous nasty internal wars, where undoubtedly the most terrible cruelties would have taken place.

The way of life of the most respectable people, including clothing, table manners, daily routines, is, with few exceptions, totally English. One rises at nine o'clock, at ten or eleven o'clock, but also at noon, one has breakfast with both coffee and tea; firstly the coffee is drunk and then afterwards the tea, with which bread, butter, toast (which is baked white

boter, *toast,* hetwelk gebraden wittebrood is, daar veel boter is inge-
trokken, eijeren en ook somtijds gebak wordt voorgezet. Niet voor zes
uren gaat men aan het middagmaal, en al wat voor die tijd is wordt
voormiddag genaamd; in welken tijd kooplieden en anderen hunne zaken
doen. Om drie uren begint de beurs, waarbij men, om de maag in het
lang wachten wat te gemoet te komen, veelal in een koffijhuis een kom
bouillon met gebraden brood gebruikt. Aan tafel vindt men een
Engelsche maaltijd; ook hebben daar dezelfde gewoontens plaats; eerst
verzoekt men aan de vrouwen om de eer te mogen hebben van een glas
wijn met haar te drinken, vervolgens doet men dit aan de mans, die het
ook tevens aan u vragen, en op het desert, na het drinken van het eerste
glas wijn, staan de vrouwen op. Dit is meesttijds om agt uren, wanneer de
thee in hare kamer gereed staat. De mans intusschen, die meest welgemaakte, sterke menschen zijn, blijven zitten tot negen, zomtijds tot elf uren en
komen dan (maar *gij* begrijpt, dat dit niet dagelijksch werk is*)* dikwijls vrij
vrolijk, hetwelk zij *half tipsi,* noemen, bij de vrouwen. Gij ziet dus, dat hier
omtrent dezelfde levenswijs plaats heeft, welke ik u in mijne brieven uit
Engeland beschreven heb. Evenwel hier drinkt men meer, en de Ieren, die
weleer den naam hadden van sterke drinkers te zijn, geloof ik niet, dat die
reputatie nog verdienen te verliezen. Met middernacht gaat men weder aan
tafel; welk avondmaal in ligtere spijzen bestaat; en om twee uren scheidt
men. Deze verdeeling van den dag, kan ik niet zeggen, dat aangenaam is
voor vreemdelingen. In de lange voormiddagen geene bezigheden
hebbende, verveelt men zich, en *Cork* levert weinig op, om deze lastige ziek-
te voortekomen of te verdrijven. De vrouwen, die men om twaalf uren kan
gaan zien en noodigen om te wandelen of te paard te rijden, zijn daartoe het
eenige middel; de mans zijn alle op hunne kantooren. Maar gij, die zelf
gereist hebt, weet, vooreerst, dat vreemdelingen in hun kort verblijf zelden
op dien vrijen voet in de huizen komen, welke diergelijke partijtjes aangenaam maakt; ten anderen, dat daarbij zekere jaren en smaak vereischt worden, om hierin op den duur genoegen te vinden.

De vrouwen, weder over het algemeen gesproken, munten hier niet uit
in schoonheid noch opvoeding, maar wel in het schrijven van een goede
hand, hetwelk ik zelfs in vele burgervrouwen bewonderd heb. De weelde,
die in deze eeuw haren zetel alom schijnt gevestigd te hebben, maakt ook

bread with much butter soaked into it), eggs and sometimes cake is offered. Not before six hours later the afternoon meal starts. All that comes before it is called early afternoon, during which time tradesmen and others do their business. The market starts at three o'clock, during which one often has a cup of bouillon with baked bread in the Coffeehouse, to bridge the long gap until the next meal. At table English meals are offered; also, the same manners prevail; firstly one asks the women whether one may have the honour to drink a glass of wine with them, then one requests the same of the men, who also in turn ask you; after the desert, having finished the first glass of wine, the women get up. This is mostly at eight o'clock, at which time tea is prepared and ready to be drunk in the lady's room. Meanwhile the men, mostly strong and well built, remain seated until nine, sometimes till eleven o'clock (but you understand this is not a daily occurrence); afterwards they join the women, at which point they are quite jolly, what they call 'half tipsy'. You see here more or less the same way of life as I described in my letters from England. However, one consumes more drink here, and I do not think that the Irish, who have the name of being heavy drinkers, deserve to lose this reputation. At midnight one eats again; this evening meal consists of lighter food and at two o'clock one parts company. I cannot say that this daily schedule is pleasant for strangers. As one has nothing to do during the long early afternoons, one gets bored and Cork offers little to prevent or to fight this annoying situation. The women whom one may visit from twelve o'clock on and whom one may invite for a walk or a horse ride are the only antidote to this boredom; the men are all in their offices. But those of you, who have travelled themselves, know that strangers during a short stay can seldom feel enough at ease while visiting house parties for these to be a pleasure; furthermore it will take some years and a certain taste for these occasions to enjoy them.

The women, again speaking in general, do not distinguish themselves by their beauty or culture, but by their beautiful handwriting, which I admired even with ordinary womenfolk. The prosperity, which in this century seems to be present everywhere, even here, means that there is little difference in the way people dress. Shopkeepers' wives and others

hier, dat men weinig onderscheidt in kleeding vindt. Vrouwen van winke-
liers en anderen gaan op feestdagen gekleed, als die van den eersten rang.
Onder de tweede en derde klasse vindt men 'er, die zeer gezet en trotsch
zijn op lange welgemaakte nagels, welke zij zeer zindelijk houden en volstrekt niet toelaten, dat afgeknipt worden. Ik heb zulks schertzende meer
dan eens getracht te doen, maar altoos gezien, dat ik veel eer de gunst dier
schoonen zou verloren hebben, dan in dien stouten toeleg gelukken. De
vrouwen van den eersten rang, ja bijna de geheele sexe, het spijt mij geene
uitzondering te kunnen maken, vindt men hier zoodanig overgegeven aan
het kaartspel, dat ik schier twijfel, of 'er ergens een voorbeeld van is. En
bepaalde zulks zich nog tot dezulken, die den naam van bejaard moeten
dragen en dus langzamerhand ongevoelig worden voor andere vermaken;
maar neen, vrouwen in het beste van haar leven, in het bloeijendst van de
jeugd, ongehuwde meisjes beneden de twintig jaren, alle zijn zoodanig verzot op dit tijdverdrijf, dat dans, musiek-comedie, ja alles voor de kaarten
wijken moet. Zie daar de reden, dat de *Drum* zo schaars bezocht wordt, en
dat geen tooneelspelers het hier houden kunnen. De begunstigde spelen
zijn Casino en Whiest, en daar 'er vrij hoog gespeeld wordt, verliezen de
vrouwen, in weerwil van hare geslepenheid, somtijds aanmerkelijke som-
men. Zo u dit nu wederom een denkbeeld geeft van rijkdom, reekent gij
kwalijk, lieve Vriend! *Cork* bevat weinige rijke lieden; de grootste fortui-
nen, en die zijn enkel, zijn 2000 pond Iersch of omtrent 20000 Guldens 's
jaars; en het meisje, dat 5000 pond of 50000 Guldens mede ten huwelijk
brengt of maar te wachten heeft, wordt voor zeer gegoed gehouden.

Als een gevolg der Engelsche manieren, vindt men hier veel liefhebberij voor het paardrijden, waarin verscheiden meisjes uitmunten. Velen heb
ik 's morgens gantsch alleen met een knecht achter zich gantsche toeren
van twee en drie uren zien doen. Ik beklaagde dikwijls die ongelukkigen,
want *Cork* is omtrent in de juist omgekeerde omstandigheid als *Rome,* toen
Romulus niets anders wist uittevinden dan eene Sabijnsche Maagdenroof;
hier zijn bijna geen jongelingen. Niet alleen worden 'er doorgaans meer
meisjes geboren; maar daarbij heeft de oorlog reeds 20000 man naar het
vaste land doen trekken, en nog telkens komen 'er transportschepen om
'er meer te halen, waardoor de guarnizoenen der steden reeds alle uit
militie bestaan. Als eene andere reden zou men 'er kunnen bijvoegen,

go similarly dressed on special days, as those of the upper classes. Some women of the second and third classes are very keen and proud of their long, well-cared-for fingernails, which they keep very clean and absolutely do not allow to be cut. More than once I have jokingly attempted to do just that, but always realised that I would more easily lose the favour of the belle than to ever succeed in my plan. The women of the upper ranks, indeed almost the whole sex, and regrettably I am unable to make an exception, are here so hooked on card games that I doubt that there is a similar example anywhere else. It would be different if this was limited to those who we call 'aged' and who therefore slowly become uninterested in other enjoyments; but no, women in the best years of their lives, in the height of their youth, unmarried girls under twenty years of age, are all so mad for this activity, that dance, music, comedy, very well everything, has to make way for the cards. Here you have the reason why the Drum was so badly attended and that no actors can survive here. The most favourite games are 'Casino' and 'Whist', and as one plays for quite high stakes, women, despite being cunning, sometimes lose substantial sums. In case this should give you an idea of wealth, you have it wrong, dear friend! Cork has few rich people; the biggest fortunes, and they are unique, are 2,000 Irish pounds or about 20,000 Dutch guilders yearly; and the girl that brings 5,000 pounds or 50,000 guilders into her marriage is considered a very good catch.

As a consequence of the English lifestyle, horse riding is a well-loved pastime, and several girls excel in it. I have seen many in the mornings, on their own with a servant behind them, going on treks of two to three hours. I often felt sorry for these unfortunates, because Cork is in this sense the opposite of Rome where Romulus had to resort to the robbery of the Sabine Virgins; here there are hardly any young men. Not only are generally more girls born here; but the war has also caused the departure of 20,000 men to the Continent, and still transport ships keep coming to take more, which means that the armies in the cities already all consist of militia. Another reason, one could say, is the fact that many men of higher rank go and live in England, which they prefer to own motherland; but more about this soon. This and other circumstances are the

dat vele mans van den eersten rang zich met 'er woon in *Engeland* neerzetten, alwaar zij het veel verkiezelijker vinden, dan in hun Vaderland; doch hierover nader. Dit een en ander maakt, dat vele meisjes uit den middelstand met vreemde schepelingen trouwen en zich met eene onbegrijpelijke gerustheid en spoed in de armen werpen van een man, dien zij nauwlijks kennen; trouwens hoe vreemd zulks ook schijnen moge, het is ruim zoo vreemd aan de zijde der ouders, eene dochter, voor welke ik vertrouw dat zij die genegenheid hebben, welke men aan een rechtschapen kind verschuldigd is, een man te doen volgen, van wiens karakter, fortuin, familie en landaard veeltijds niemand hunner het minste denkbeeld heeft; en met dat al ziet men velen dezer huwelijken goed gaan. Dan daar ik, dus voortgaande, geen bloot beschouwer en eenvoudig verhaler blijven zoude, zal het best zijn te eindigen na &c.

AGT-EN-TWINTIGSTE BRIEF

Cork den 15 November 1793

[...] Nergens vindt men het gemeen armer. Geen voet kan men in *Cork* verzetten zonder omringd te zijn door een troep bedelaars, die op de onbeschaamdfte wijze een aalmoes afvorderen, en u bij weigering, in hunne ontevredenheid, schelden en laagheden zeggen. Zij verzellen een vreemdeling overal, gaan met hem binnen in de winkels, en hem hier nog geen rust gunnende, noodzaken zij de Kooplieden hen te verzoeken uit het huis te gaan, welk verzoek altoos met veel bescheidenheid geschiedt, waarop echter de bedelaar bij zijn weggaan altijd zeer onbescheiden andwoordt. De groote menigte en onbeschaamde vrijpostigheid dezer menschen van onderscheiden kunne en jaren geeft voorzeker een reiziger, bij wien zulks een ongewoon verschijnsel is, geen voordeelig denkbeeld van eene regeering, die niet instaat is, deze ledige handen werk te geven, en die duldt, dat vreemdelingen en inwooners, zoodra zij zich maar op straat vertoonen, op eene zeer onaangename wijze, worden lastig gevallen.

De regeering (niet die van geheel *Ierland,* dat door een Onderkoning, door het Engelsche Hof gekozen, en een Parlement geregeerd wordt, maar van *Cork,* de eenige stad, welke ik gezien heb)

reasons why many girls from the middle classes marry strangers from the ships and why they throw themselves with an incomprehensible ease into the arms of a man they hardly know; no matter how strange this all seems, it is even stranger that the parents of a daughter, whom as any good child can expect I would presume they feel sympathy for, should allow their child to follow a man of whose character, fortune, family or nationality they often have not the slightest knowledge; and in spite of all this, many marriages work well. As it becomes more difficult to remain a neutral observer and a simple storyteller, I better finish up here.

TWENTY-EIGHTH LETTER

Cork, November 15th, 1793

[...] Nowhere does one see poorer people. One cannot move in Cork without being surrounded by beggars, who shamelessly demand money, and who, when one refuses, express their dissatisfaction by cursing and name-calling. They keep walking at the side of a stranger, enter shops with him and as they keep pestering him there, they compel the shop-keeper to ask them to leave the place, which they do, although reluctantly, all the while brazenly talking back while leaving. The great number and shamelessness of these people who are all different in ability and age, does not instil in a traveller, unaccustomed to such an experience, a favourable image of a government that is unable to provide work for people who have nothing else to keep them occupied and that permits strangers and inhabitants to be hassled in this very unpleasant way as soon as they appear on the streets.

The government (not that of the whole of Ireland, which is governed by a Viceroy, who is chosen by the English Court and Parliament, but the local government of Cork, the only city I have seen) consists of

bestaat uit een Major, Sherifs en een *Commun Council* of Raad. De Major is Burgemeester en Hoofdofficier, de Scherifs zijn de Schepenen. Deze eerste Magistraats-persoon gaat gemeenlijk in een zwarten mantel, in den smaak als die der Engelsche Predikanten, met een dun stokje, omtrent als een teentje, in de hand, een zware gouden keten om den hals, en heeft tot gevolg twee geregtsdienaars. De Scherifs hebben een dergelijke keten, doch kleiner en ligter. De eerste dag, dat deze Major met zijne medeverkozene Magistraats-personen in bediening treedt, heeft hier de bijzondere gewoonte plaats, van hen met zemelen te bestrooijen. Meer dan eens is dit reeds verboden geworden; maar het gemeen is 'er, als zijnde een voorouderlijk gebruik, dat zekerlijk eeuwen heugt en bij hun beschouwd wordt, als een zinnebeeld van overvloed, niet wel van aftebrengen en doet het nog plaats hebben.

Hier boven heb ik gezegd, dat het gemeen nergens armer is dan hier. [...]

Over het algemeen gaat de gemeene man en arbeider van de beide kunne barrevoets, en hebben tot hunne gewoone spijs aardappelen met karnemelk, die hun tot saus verstrekt. Het ontbijt bestaat in gekookte aardappelen, waarbij een kom gekarnde melk is gesteld, waarin de aardappel van tijd tot tijd gedoopt wordt. Het middagmaal is als het ontbijt, en het avondmaal als dat op den middag, en dus volgt de eene dag de andere. Vleesch komt zeldzaam en dan nog spaarzaam op hunne tafel, en brood bijna nooit. Daar nu koorn en vleesch, hier ten minsten, een vierde goedkooper dan bij ons is, en echter nog niet door hun kan bekostigd worden, geeft u zulks denkbeeld genoeg van den ongelukkigen toestand dezer menschen. Evenwel ik heb 'er ook gezien, die het iets beter hadden, en de aardappelen aan stukjes in zoetemelk sneden, zoo als bij ons melk en brood gegeten wordt.

In weerwil van dit magere voedsel vindt men deze menschen sterk en oud. De ouderdom van 75 en 80 jaren beletten niet, dat het land nog door hunne stramme, maar niet krachteloze armen bebouwd wordt, dat zij lange en vermoeijende bewegingen uithouden en op het oog zeer gezond zijn. In *Cork* daarentegen vindt men onder meer gegoeden en rijken weinigen van hooge jaren, en de meesten van die weinigen zijn nog uitgeleefd. Zo nu het beter leven, de wijn en het veel voedsel uit het dierenrijk van dit laatste verschijnsel een oorzaak kan zijn, en dan ook het voedsel uit het rijk der planten de reden van de betere welvaard der

a Lord Mayor, Sheriffs and a Common Council. The Lord Mayor is the first citizen and Chief Officer, the *Elders* are the Sheriffs. The Chief Magistrate, normally appears in public clad in a black cape, quite similar to that of an English preacher; he is holding a little stick, a bit like an osier, wears a heavy golden chain around his neck and is followed by two police officers. The Sheriffs have similar chains but they are smaller and lighter. On the Mayor's and his co-elected Magistrates' first day in office, a peculiar custom of throwing bran at them takes place. More than once this has been banned, but the ordinary people see it as a tradition which goes back generations and centuries, as a symbol for abundance, and they cannot be made to give it up.

I have already told you that over all, people here are poorer than anywhere else. [...]

The ordinary people and workers of both sexes in general go barefoot and have as their daily food potatoes, with buttermilk as gravy. Breakfast consists of boiled potatoes with a bowl of buttermilk to dip the potato into every now and then. The midday meal is the same as the breakfast and the evening meal the same as the midday meal, and so it goes on day after day. Meat gets seldom on the table and even then only in small quantities; bread almost never features. The fact that, here at least, corn and meat is only a quarter of our price and still cannot be afforded, gives an idea of the miserable situation these people are in. However, I also saw people who were slightly better off, and who cut the potatoes in cream, the same way as we eat milk and bread.

Despite this meagre food, people here are strong and old. Even at 75 and 80 years of age they work the fields with stiff but still powerful arms, work long hours, do tiring work and look very healthy. In contrast to this, one finds amongst the better off and wealthy people of Cork few elderly people, and most of these few have hardly any energy. Thus, if it is true that a good life, wine and much food from the animal kingdom are the cause of this last phenomenon, and if it is also true that the diet based on plants is the reason for the better health of the poor, this possibly contradicts the theory of the great naturalist Buffon.

armen is, zou misschien de groote Natuurkundigen BUFFON hier min of meer eene tegenwerping tegen zijne aangenomene stelling vinden.

De aardappel, dat groote vervulsel voor den gemeenen man, van wien het bijna het eenig voedsel is, wordt hier verkocht voor 26, 28 en ook 20 Hollandsche stuivers de 100 pond, en is in zoo grooten overvloed, dat 'er sterke drank van gestookt wordt onder den naam van *Whieskij.* Men drinkt deze enkel, of ook met water gemengd en tot pons gemaakt; doch de reuk en smaak is 'er zeer onaangenaam van; voor het overige heeft hij veel overeenkomst met den Westindischen kilduivel en de *aqua riento* van *Sint Jago.* Het bier van het land is mede vrij slecht, kan niet lang duren, en komt in geene vergelijking bij het Engelsche. De wijn is 'er ongemeen duur; gemeenlijk drinkt men dien van *Port à Port,* doch ook worden de Bourdeaux- en Madera-wijnen op alle fatsoenelijke tafels gevonden. [...]

NEGEN-EN-TWINTIGSTE BRIEF

[...] Tot dus verre schreef ik heden morgen, wanneer mijn paard voor de deur kwam, en ik niet een mijner Corksche kennissen een toer maakte. Wij namen den weg langs de rivier, en sloegen langzamerhand links af naar een klein dorp *Glanmire* genaamd. Dit ligt in een aardig plantzoen, omtrent een uur van de stad, aan een rivier van denzelfden naam, die zich in de *Lee* ontlast. Men heeft hier een koornmolen, die door het water der rivier bewogen wordt, en die men wil, dat de eerste is, in dezen smaak in dit gedeelte te van het Koningrijk gebouwd. Zonder stilhouden reedden wij door en vervolgden onze toer langs een zeer aangenamen weg onder nog aangenamer gesprekken, die echter welhaast gestoord wierden door het geluid van een doedelzak. 'Dáár hebt gij nu', zeide mijn Vriend, 'het rechte, oude Iersche speeltuig, waar ook mijn Vaderland op roemen mag. Dit echt voorouderlijk muziek is ons onbetwistbaar eigen. Gij lacht, en ik wil gaarne gelooven, dat aan uw gehoor, hetwelk niet Iersch is, de toonen onaangenaam en het geluid wanklankig moet voorkomen; doch ons gemeen is 'er zoodanig op verzot, dat de meesten van hun het bespelen, en de landjeugd 'er op ten dans geleid wordt.' De speelman, dat een oude arme boer scheen, behandelde het instrument met zoo vele vaardigheid, dat hij mij voorkwam een meester in de kunst

The potato, that staple diet for the ordinary man, for whom it is more or less the only food, is sold here for 20 Dutch *stuivers* (five pence) for 100 pounds and is so plentiful, that one distils a strong drink from it which is called Whiskey. This is drunk neat, with water or as a punch; the smell and taste are very unpleasant, however; apart from this, it has much in common with the West Indian 'kilduivel' and the *acqua riente* from Santiago. Beer here is also quite bad, does not keep long and is no comparison to the English beer. Wine is incredibly expensive; in general the *Port à Port* is drunk, but in respectable circles one also finds Bordeaux and Madeira wines. [...]

TWENTY-NINTH LETTER

[...] I have been writing this morning until I went out for a horse ride with one of my Corkonian acquaintances. We took the road along the river and turned left towards a little village named Glanmire. It is situated in nice parkland, within an hour of the city, and built at the bank of a river of the same name, which flows into the Lee. One finds a mill here which is powered by the water of the river, and is reputedly the first one built in this particular style in this part of the kingdom. Without stopping we rode on and continued along a very pleasant road while engaged in an even more pleasant conversation. This was disturbed, however, by the sound of bagpipes. 'Here,' my friend said, 'you have the quintessential Irish instrument, which my homeland can be proud of. This genuine music, passed on through generations, is without any doubt, ours. You laugh and I can understand that for you, not being Irish, the tunes sound unpleasant and the sounds appear unmusical; but we are so fond of it that most can play the instrument and the young ones in the country dance to its music.' The musician who looked like an old poor farmer played the

te zijn. Ik sprak hem aan in het Engelsch; maar wij verstonden elkander zoo weinig, als de Muselman den Hottentot, en mijn vriend, die zoo min als ik, de taal van zijn land sprak, kon voor geen tolk dienen. Na dus een kleinigheid gegeven te hebben, reedden wij weder stadwaards.

In dit terug rijden kon ik niet nalaten mijne verwondering te kennen te geven, dat een Ier, in *Ierland* geboren, opgevoed en woonende, geen Iersch verstond. Hij antwoordde, dat de taal zoo hard, zoo barbaarsch en daarbij zoo weinig noodzakelijk was, dat alleen het gemeen ze onder malkander sprak, van welke ze van vader op zoon overging, en dat geene fatsoenelijke lieden zich ooit moeite gaven van ze te leeren; te meer, daar de meeste gemeene menschen, behalve het Iersch, Engelsch spraken, en alle publieke afkondigingen in het Engelsch gedaan wierden. Ook schrijft men, vervolgde hij, het Iersch niet of ten minsten zeer zeldzaam. Schaars kan men 'er een Woordenboek of Spraakkunst van vinden, en waarschijnelijk, zal in weinige jaren de Iersche taal het zelfde lot ondergaan, als het Corniesch en Wallisch, en geheel verloren zijn. Ik dorst den goeden man, daar hij gereisd had, geen zoodanig antwoord geven als mij voor den geest kwam, uit vrees voor de tegenwerping, dat bij ons de welopgevoede meisjes zeer na aan de Iersche grenzen, daar 'er slechts weinigen Hollandsche boeken lezen en velen geen brief in haar eigen taal schrijven kunnen , en 'zij spreken even- wel Hollandsch', zou alles geweest zijn, dat ik 'er op had kunnen zeggen.

Gij vraagt mij in uw laatsten, of ik alle vrouwen in *Ierland* gezien heb, om de sexe zoo algemeen en stout te durven beoordeelen? Maar, mijn Vriend! vergun mij u weder te mogen vragen, of gij dien brief met aandacht gelezen heb? Ik spreek in denzelven over de Corksche en niet over de Iersche vrouwen. De eersten behooren alleen tot ééne stad, de anderen tot het gantsche Rijk; en in *Cork,* heb ik zeker de meeste vrou- wen van rang gezien; zie hier, hoe. In het begin mijner komst in deze haven had de Heer JAMESON, die thans onze Consul geworden is, een man, van wien de koophandel zich alles goeds kan belooven, de vrien- delijkheid, mij ter maaltijd te noodigen. Aan tafel wierd ik tusschen Mevrouw JAMESON en Mevrouw SEALY geplaatst; zijnde de laatste een lieve, jonge, aardige en mooije vrouw, gehuwd aan een Doctor in de Theologie, die een zeer hupsch mensch is en ook aan tafel was. Onder degesprekken merkte Mevrouw SEALY mijne begeerte om vrouwen van

Beautiful.

instrument so skilfully, that to me he seemed a master in the art. I addressed him in English; but we understood each other as little as a Muslim and a Hottentot, and my friend, who did speak the language of his country as little as I, could not act as an interpreter. After we had given the man a little money, we proceeded towards the city.

On the way back, I could not resist to express my surprise at the fact that an Irishman, born in Ireland, educated and living in Ireland, could not understand Irish. He answered that the language is so difficult, so crude and furthermore so seldom needed that it was only spoken by ordinary folk amongst themselves, who passed it on from father to son; no respectable persons ever bothered to learn the language; all the more so, as most ordinary people spoke both Irish and English and all public announcements were done in English. He added that Irish is only rarely if ever written. It is difficult to find an Irish dictionary, and in the coming years it will probably suffer the same fate as Cornish and Welsh and completely disappear. As the man was well travelled himself and I feared an objection, I did not dare togive the answer that I had in mind, as the only answer I could give, which was, that our well-educated girls are like the Irish, in the sense that few read books and many are not able to write a letter in their own language, but 'they speak neverthless Dutch'.

You asked in your last letter if I have truly seen all women in Ireland to be able to give such general and bold judgements? But my friend! Forgive me to ask you again if you read my letter carefully? I speak about the women of Cork and not Irish women in general. The former belong to one city, the latter to a whole country; and in Cork I definitely saw most women from the upper classes. I tell you how this came about. After I had just arrived in this port, Mr Jameson, who is now our Consul and a very good man for commerce, was so kind to invite me for a meal. During dinner I was seated between Mrs Jameson and Mrs Sealy; Mrs Sealy was a gentle, young, pleasant and pretty woman, married to a doctor in theology, the latter a very cheerful person who was also present. During our conversation Mrs Sealy became aware of my

het land te zien, waarvan zij in haar persoon, een allervoordeeligst denkbeeld gaf, en oogenbliklijk beloofde zij, ten onzen gevalle in de volgende week een *assemblée* te zullen geven. Hier vond ik de halve wereld vergaderd; drie zalen waren opgepropt met menschen en vergunden nauwlijks de ronde te doen. Zoo zeer als het klein getal van manspersonen mij verwonderde, even en nog sterker trof mij het groot aantal van vrouwen, daar men nooit had kunnen denken, dat Cork een zoo groot getal zoude hebben kunnen opleveren. Blijft 'er nu, daar dit *assemblée* thans verscheiden malen is rond geweest, geene mogelijkheid, om een enkele aanmerking te maken, die gegrond is?

Naar buiten ben ik nog niet geweest. De Heer Grave VAN BYLAND, die met het schip Gelderland van 64 stukken en een kotter voorgisteren hier binnen gekomen is, om het konvooi te versterken, is oorzaak dezer vertraging en misschien wel van het geheele vervallen van dit uitstapje.

DERTIGSTE BRIEF

Cork den 17 December 1793

[...] Zoo even gaat de Kapitein HENGST, het bevel voerende over den Kotter de Snelheid van mijn boord. Voorleden week heeft hij van ons een Ierschen jongen gekregen, die, wetende dat men menschen noodig had, op Scipio kwam om dienst te nemen. Hij was knap, vlug, doch zeer beschaamd en angstig, en had de houding als van iemand, die gejaagd wordt, hetwelk maakte, dat de Officieren, daar ik aan wal was, hem wegzonden en wel naar de *Snelheid,* die men wist dat niet voltallig was. In de agt dagen, die deze jongen aan boord geweest is, deed hij zijne wapenoefeningen en scheepswerk vlijtig en gewillig; alleen het klimmen stond hem tegen, en reeds bij herhaling had hij den bootsman trachten overtehalen, om aan de Officieren voortestellen, of 'er geen mogelijkheid was om hiervan bevrijd te zijn. En, op het gedurig weigerend antwoord, dat hij hierop ontving, had hij van morgen bekend, tot de schoone sexe te behooren, en is nu een aardig lief meisje van negentien jaren, hetwelk de Heer HENGST in de matrozen plunje weder aan wal doet zetten. Ware deze ontdekking later gedaan, of had de bootsman ze voor zich gehouden, wie weet, welk eene netelige krijgsraad dit geval veroorzaakt had?

desire to meet some women of the area; she quite liked the idea and promised to organise a gathering on our behalf for the following week. Half the world was gathered here; three rooms were so thronged with people that one could hardly move around. As much as I was surprised by the small number of men, I was more taken aback by the amazing number of women present, as I could not have thought that so many women could come from Cork. Don't you think that, since several such gatherings have taken place since, it is possible to make well-founded observations?

I have not been to the country yet. The reason for this delay, and possibly for the complete cancellation of the trip, is the arrival yesterday of Count van Byland on the *Gelderland*, a ship with 64 cannons, and a cutter, as reinforcement for the convoy.

THIRTIETH LETTER

Cork, December 17th, 1793

[…] Captain Hengst, commander of the cutter, the *Snelheid*, has just left my ship. Last week we provided him with an Irish boy, who, realising that we needed people, arrived on *Scipio* to offer his services. He was clever, fast, but very shy and anxious and had a haunted demeanour. It was because of this demeanour that, while I was ashore, the Officers sent him to the *Snelheid*, as it was known that they did not have a full crew. The boy, during the eight days that he was on board there, did all his weapon-exercises and shipwork very well and willingly; only, he did not like climbing and he had repeatedly tried to persuade the boatswain to ask the Officers to exempt him from it. As this was refused all the time, he admitted this morning to belong to the fairer sex, and is now a nice sweet girl of nineteen years of age, whom Mr Hengst had to put ashore again, sailor's garb and all. Who knows what a tricky court-martial this could have caused, if it had not been discovered till later, or if the boatswain had not been so insistent?

English translation by Romanie van Son.

Hermann von Pückler-Muskau

(1830)

German original in: *Briefe eines Verstorbenen. Ein fragmentarisches Tagebuch aus England, Wales, Irland und Frankreich, geschrieben in den Jahren 1828 und 1829.* Munich: F.G. Franckh, 1830.

Cork, 6 October

[...] DAS LAND wird jetzt sehr fruchtbar, voll reicher Feldfluren; hie und da sieht man stattliche Landsitze. Cork selbst liegt in einer tiefen Schlucht höchst malerisch am Meer. Es hat ein altertümliches Ansehen, welches noch origineller durch die Bekleidung vieler Häuser über und über mit schuppenartigen Schieferpanzern wird. Prachtvolle Gebäude sind die beiden neuen Gefängnisse, das der Stadt und das der Grafschaft, wovon das eine im antiken Geschmack, das andere im gotischen Stil aufgeführt ist und einer großen Festung ähnlich sieht.

Nachdem ich gefrühstückt und mehrere kleine Häuslichkeiten besorgt hatte, mietete ich ein sogenanntes Walfischboot (schmal und spitz an beiden Enden und daher sicherer und schneller als andere) und segelte bei gutem Winde in der Bay, welche *The River of Cork* genannt wird, nach Cove, wo ich mir vornahm, zu Mittag zu speisen. Ein Teil dieser ohngefähr eine Viertelstunde breiten Bucht bildet für Cork, von der Meerseite, eine der schönsten Entreen in der Welt! Beide Ufer bestehen aus sehr hohen Hügeln, die mit Palästen, Villen, Landhäusern, Parks und Gärten bedeckt sind. Auf jeder Seite bilden sie, in ungleicher Höhe sich erhebend, die reichste, stets abwechselnde Einfassung. Nach und nach tritt dann, in der Mitte des Gemäldes, die Stadt langsam hervor und endet auf dem höchsten Berge, der den Horizont zugleich schließt, mit der imponierenden Masse der Militärbaracken. So ist der Anblick von der See aus. Nach Cove zu verändert er sich öfters, nachdem die Krümmungen des Kanals die Gegenstände anders vorschieben. Die eine dieser Aussichten schloß sich ungemein schön mit einem gotischen Schloß, das auf den hier weit hervorspringenden Felsen mit vielem Geschmack von der Stadtkommune erbaut worden ist. Durch die vortreff

Hermann von Pückler-Muskau
(1830)

(Romantic views in Cork harbour – Cove – food – philosophical reflections)

Cork, Oct. 6th, [1828]
[...] THE COUNTRY was now very fertile, full of rich meadows, with, here and there a stately mansion. Cork lies most picturesquely in a deep valley on the seashore. It has an air of antiquity, which is rendered more peculiar by the roofs of scale-like slates with which many of the houses are covered. The two new prisons are magnificent buildings: they are erected, the one by the city, the other by the county: the former is in an antique taste, the latter in the perfectly Gothic style, and has the appearance of a great fortress.

After I had breakfasted, I hired what they call here a whale boat, narrow and pointed at each end, and thence safer and swifter, and sailed with a fair wind along the bay, which is called the 'river of Cork,' to Cove, where I intended to dine. A part of this bay, which is about three quarters of a mile broad, forms one of the most beautiful harbours in the world. Both shores consist of high hills, covered with palaces, villas, country seats, parks and gardens. On either side, rising in unequal height, they form the richest and most varied boundary. By degrees the city advances into the middle of the picture, and terminates on the brow of the highest hill, with the imposing mass of the barracks. This is the view from the sea. Towards Cove it frequently changes, as the windings of the channel present objects in different positions. One of these pictures was finely bounded by a Gothic castle, which has been built with great good taste by the city on a bold projecting rock. Its admirable site not only gives it importance, but it appears, if I may say

liche Lage gewinnt es nicht nur an Bedeutung, sondern es erscheint, wenn ich mich so ausdrücken darf, wie natürlich dort, während dergleichen an andern Orten so oft nur als ein unangenehmes Hors-d'oeuvre auffällt. Obwohl ich glaube, daß wir den Engländern in der edlern Baukunst überlegen sind, so fehlen wir doch darin, daß wir bei unsern Gebäuden viel zu wenig die Umgebung und die Landschaft umher berücksichtigen. Diese aber ist es grade, welche größtenteils für den zu wählenden Stil entscheiden sollte.

Die Burg hier schien für irgendeinen alten Seehelden bestimmt, denn der Eingang war bloß vom Meer aus angebracht. Ein kolossales Tor, mit Wappen verziert, in das die Fluten bis an den Fuß der Treppe drangen, wölbte sich über der schwarzen Öffnung. Ich dachte mir Folko mit den Geierflügeln, wie er eben von einem gewonnenen Seetreffen hierher zurückkehrt, und belebte mir das Meer mit Phantasiebildern aus Fouqués 'Zauberring'.

Wir segelten hierauf mit gutem Winde bei Passage, einem Fischerdorf, und Monkstown vorbei, das seinen Namen (Mönchsstadt) von einer im Walde darüber liegenden Klosterruine herschreibt. Hier fing der eine Zeitlang unterbrochne Regen wieder an, gab aber diesmal Gelegenheit zu einer herrlichen Naturszene. [...]

Ich etablierte mich nun sehr vergnügt am Fenster des kleinen Gasthofs, in der Hoffnung, eine vortreffliche Fastenmahlzeit mit den delikatesten frischen Fischen zu machen. Es blieb aber bloß beim *Fasten,* denn auch nicht *ein* Fisch, noch Auster oder Muschel war zu bekommen. In den kleinen Fischerorten am Meer begegnet dies häufiger, als man glaubt, weil alles Disponible sogleich zum Verkauf in die großen Städte gebracht wird. In dieser Hinsicht war also mein Zweck schlecht erreicht, und ich mußte mich mit den gewöhnlichen, in englischen Gasthäusern unsterblichen 'Mutton-chops' begnügen. Doch ließ ich mir meine Laune dadurch nicht verderben, las ein paar alte Zeitungen, deren ich lange nicht gesehen, zum kärglichen Mahle und trat nach schon eingebrochner Dunkelheit meinen Rückweg zu Lande an. Ein offner Karren mit Strohsitz war alles, was ich mir verschaffen konnte; der Wind blies kalt und heftig, und ich war genötigt, mich dicht in meinen Mantel zu hüllen. Wir cotoyierten das Meer in ziemlicher Höhe, und die vielen Lichter der Schiffe und Marinegebäude unter uns glichen einer reichen

so, as if it grew there naturally; while buildings of this kind in ordinary situations so often strike one as unpleasant 'hors d'oeuvres'. Though I think we excel the English in the higher sorts of architecture, we are very deficient in attention to the objects and the scenery which surround our buildings; and yet these are the circumstances which ought generally to decide the style. This castle seemed built for one of the sea kings, for the only entrance is from the sea. A colossal gate, adorned with a coat of arms, beneath which the waves wash the steps, overarches the dark entry. I thought of Folko with the vulture's wings returning hither after a successful sea fight; and peopled the deep with fantastic beings from Fouqué's *Magic Ring*.

We sailed with a fair wind past Passage, a fishing village, and then past Monkstown, which takes its name from a ruin of a monastery in a wood above. The rain, which had ceased for a time, here began to fall again, but I was requited by a splendid effect. [...]

I now established myself very agreeably at the window of the little inn, in the hope of an excellent fast-day dinner of the most delicate fresh fish. No part of my scheme was verified but the fasting; not a fish, not an oyster was to be had. This happens oftener than you would think in the little fishing towns on the coast, everything 'disponible' being immediately carried to the great cities. In this point of view therefore I attained my end but badly, and I was forced to content myself with the eternal 'mutton-chops'. However, I did not suffer this to disturb my equanimity. I read an old newspaper or two, not having seen one for a long time, and took my way homewards by land, when it was nearly dark. An open car, with a bundle of straw as a seat, was the only carriage I could get. The wind blew cold and gusty, and I was obliged to wrap myself closely in my cloak. We skirted the shore at a considerable elevation, and the numerous lights of the ships and marine buildings below us were like an illumination. Five flickering flames danced like Will-o'-the-wisps on the black convict ship, and the report of a cannon from the guard ship

Illumination. Fünf flackernde Flammen tanzten wie Irrwische auf dem schwarzen Schiffe der Deportierten, und ein Kanonenschuß, der vom Wachtschiff gefeuert wurde, donnerte dumpftönend durch die Stille der Nacht.

Als diese Aussicht verschwand, wendete ich meine Aufmerksamkeit erst auf den ungemein klaren Sternhimmel. Wer kann lange in die hehre Pracht dieser flimmernden Weltkörper blicken, ohne von den tiefsten und süßesten Gefühlen durchdrungen zu werden! Es sind die Charaktere, mit denen Gott von jeher am deutlichsten mit den Menschenseelen gesprochen hat. Und doch hatte ich der himmlischen Lichter nicht gedacht, solange noch die irdischen glänzten! Aber so geht es immer auf der Erde – erst wo diese uns verläßt, suchen wir den Himmel auf. Sie liegt uns ja auch näher, und ihre Autorität bleibt für uns die mächtigste – grade wie der Bauer mehr von der Person des Amtmanns als der des Königs in Zaum gehalten wird; der Soldat sich mehr vor seinem Lieutenant fürchtet als dem General en chef; der Hofmann mehr dem Günstling als dem Monarchen die Cour macht, und endlich der Fromme ... doch wir wollen darüber nicht weiter philosophieren, liebe Julie, denn Dir brauche ich es ja nicht zu wiederholen: *qu'il ne faut pas prendre le valet pour le roi.*

thundered through the stillness of night.

As this view disappeared, I turned my eyes to the unusually clear firmament. Who can look intently on the sublime and holy beauty of those glittering worlds, and not be penetrated by the deepest and the sweetest emotions? They are the characters by which God has from all time spoken most clearly to the soul of man; and yet I had not thought of these heavenly lights so long as the earthly ones sparkled before me! But thus is it ever. When earth forsakes us, we seek heaven. Earth is nearer, and her authority more powerful with us; just as the peasant stands more in awe of the justice than of the king; the soldier fears the lieutenant than the general; the courtier is more assiduous to please the favourite than the monarch; and lastly, the fanatic – but we won't philosophise further about it, dear Julia; for I need not repeat to you, *'qu'il ne faut pas prendre le valet pour le roi'* [that one should not take the servant for the king].

English translation in: Tour in England, Ireland, and France, in the years 1828 & 1829 […] in a Series of Letters by a German Prince. *2 vols. Vol. II. London: Effingham, Wilson, 1832, pp. 14-21.*

Charles de Montalembert
(1830)

French original in: *Charles de Montalembert. Journal Intime Inedit.* Ed. by
Louis Le Guillou and Nicole Roger-Taillade. Paris: Editions du CNRS, 1990,
vol. II, pp. 80-83.

Vendredi 24 Septembre. Tems atroce. Course de Fermoy à Cork, en
diligence, par Rathcormick et Watergrass Hill; 18 milles d'une fort
jolie route, dont je n'ai rien vu, sauf le voisinage de Cork, qui est charmant à partir du village de *Glenmore,* au-dessus duquel se trouve le beau
parc de *Punketcle* [*sic*] appartenant à je ne sais quel riche marchand de
Cork. Puis la vue s'ouvre sur le magnifique bassin de la baie de Cork,
bordé de tous les côtés par les *villas* et les *parcs* de négocians: c'est un
coup d'œil admirable, qui rehausse l'effet pittoresque de la tour crénelée
et gothique de *Blackrock* sur la rive opposée.

Cork est une très belle ville, à rues larges et spacieuses sur la *Lea,* qui
forme plusieurs îles et qui est surmontée par de fort beaux ponts. Il y a
100.000 habitans, pas d'édifices remarquables, beaucoup de commerces,
mais peu de vaisseaux dans le port. A en juger par le grand nombre d'institutions littéraires et scientifiques, les habitans de cette grande cité sont
à la fois entreprenans et intelligens. Les femmes des classes un peu élevées
y sont charmantes: je n'ai jamais rencontré de plus belles tailles, des visages plus expressifs qu'à Cork, pas même à Bruxelles ni à Dublin.

Course inutile chez l'évêque [...] Visite au Lieutenant *Clements,* du
37e de Ligne, fils de Lord Leitrim; charmant garçon qui m'a comblé
d'amitiés. Course avec lui à la *prison du Comté,* assez bel édifice, divisé en
deux parties, la *geôle* où l'on enferme les accusés, et la maison de correction, où l'on astreint au travail du *tread-mill* les condamnés. Le tout est
assez bien organisé, sauf l'usage dégoûtant qui oblige les détenus à se
laver la figure dans leurs pots de chambre.

Dîner au mess du 37e régiment sur l'invitation de Clements; luxe
inconcevable. Ennui. Peu satisfait [...]

Samedi 25 Septembre. [...] Courses fatigantes pour faire ma visite à l'évêque

Charles de Montalembert
(1830)

(Prison – Fr Francis Mahony – mass in Irish – religiosity – salary of Protestant clergy – a wake)

Friday, 24 September. Atrocious weather. From Fermoy by coach, through Rathcormac and Watergrass Hill; eighteen miles on a very pretty road but I saw nothing of it apart from the neighbourhood of Cork. These outskirts are charming from the village of *Glenmore* onwards, above which lies the beautiful *Dunkettle* estate which belongs to some rich Cork merchant or other. Then the view widens to take in the magnificent area of Cork harbour bordered all around by merchants' *villas* and *large gardens*: an admirable vista which sets off the attractiveness of the crenellated gothic tower in *Blackrock* on the opposite bank.

Cork is a very beautiful city, with wide, spacious streets on the *Lee* which forms several islands and is crossed by some very fine bridges. It has a population of 100,000, no notable buildings, many thriving businesses but few vessels in the port. Judging by the large number of literary and scientific institutions, the inhabitants of this large city are both enterprising and intelligent. The upper-class women are quite charming: never, not even in Brussels or Dublin, have I encountered any more shapely, nor have I seen more expressive faces than in Cork.

Fruitless visit to the bishop [...]. Visited Lieutenant *Clements* of the 37th League, son of Lord Leitrim; a charming young man who showered me with his friendship. Accompanied him to the *County Prison*, a fairly handsome building, divided in two: the jail where the accused are locked up and the penitentiary where the condemned are forced to work the *treadmill*. The whole enterprise is fairly well organised, apart from the disgusting practice of forcing the prisoners to wash their faces in their chamber pots.

Dined at the mess of the 37th regiment on Clements' invitation; unbelievable luxury. Bored. Not really satisfied.

25 September [...] Tired from rushing around trying to visit Bishop

Murphy que j'ai enfin trouvé; c'est un petit homme gros, réjoui et fort intelligent, qui parle français à merveille, et qui m'a étonné par son approbation, je dirai presque son admiration, de ce qui vient de se passer en France. Il m'a consigné aux soins du Dr Castillon, médecin catholique, qui m'a comblé d'attention, m'a mené à l'*exhibition* des artistes indigènes (pitoyable) et m'a fait passer la soirée chez lui, avec le père Francis *Mahony*, jeune prêtre élevé à St Acheul, plein d'âme et d'esprit, *Richard Dowden*, chef des Presbytériens de Cork et un Mr Corbet, gros et bon Catholique. Thé, souper et chansons: mélodies irlandaises et autres airs nationaux et comiques, tels que les *Groves of Blarney* et le *Wedding of Ballypoureen* – Soirée amusante et pour moi fort intéressante et instructive. Accord merveilleux des Catholiques et des Presbytériens contre les Episcopaux. Mahony surtout m'a intéressé; il a bien l'ardeur et le patriotisme du clergé irlandais; il est, comme je l'ai su depuis, on ne peut plus populaire à Cork; il m'a déclaré qu'il pourrait armer 40.000 hommes d'un seul mot. Tous quatre m'ont reçu à merveille.

Dimanche 26 Septembre. Course avec le bon petit Docteur *Catillon* [*sic*] et l'intelligent et enthousiaste *O'Mahony* dans les environs de Cork. Tems atroce mais excursion néanmoins charmante: d'abord le long des bords verdoyans et accentués de la Lea, jusqu'au vieux et imposant château de *Carring-rohan,* situé au sommet d'un rocher qui domine la Lea, anciennement séjour de la puissante tribu des *Mc Carthy* More, aujourd'hui abandonné […]

[A] la chapelle catholique de Blarney […] le prêtre y disait la messe. J'arrivai au moment de l'élévation et toute cette fervente population se prosterna le front contre terre. J'imitai presqu'involontairement ce touchant exemple et m'agenouillai parmi eux; puis je m'efforçai de pénétrer sous le toit de l'étroite chapelle qui regorgeait de monde. Pas d'ornemens, pas même de siège, un toit à peine complet. J'entendis le prêtre annoncer en irlandais, dans l'antique et poëtique langage du peuple persécuté, que tel jour il irait, pour abréger le chemin de ses paroissiens, dans telle cabane qui deviendrait pendant un tems la maison de Dieu, qu'il y distribuerait les sacremens de la Pénitence et de l'Eucharistie, et qu'il y recevrait le pain dont le nourrisent ses enfans. Je sortis de l'église où la chaleur m'étouffait, et je retrouvai la foule prosternée dans la boue. Bientôt

Murphy whom I eventually found: a fat little man, joyful and very intelligent, and who speaks French admirably. He astonished me by expressing his approval – admiration, almost – of what has just happened in France. He recommended me to Dr Castillon, a Catholic doctor who could not have been more attentive to me, bringing me to the *exhibition* of local artists (pitiful) and who had me spend the evening in his home, with Father Francis *Mahony*, a young priest full of life and spirit educated at St Acheul, *Richard Dowden*, head of the Presbyterian community in Cork and a certain Mr Corbet, a fine large Catholic. Tea, supper and songs: Irish airs and other national and comic ones like the 'Groves of Blarney' and the 'Wedding of Ballypoureen' – an enjoyable evening, both interesting and instructive for me. Marvellous agreement between the Catholics and Protestants against the Episcopalians. Mahony especially was of interest to me; he definitely possesses the passion and patriotism of the Irish clergy. He could not, as I later discovered, be more popular in Cork. He assured me that it would take just one word for him to arm 40,000 men. All four received me marvellously well.

Sunday, 26 September. Excursion with goodly little Dr *Catillon* [*sic*] and the intelligent and enthusiastic *O'Mahony* in the Cork area. Atrocious weather but charming excursion nonetheless: first of all along the undulating green banks of the Lee, as far as the impressive old castle in *Carringrohane*, perched on top of a rock looking out over the Lee, the former seat of the powerful *McCarthy* More clan, now abandoned, however [...]

[At] the Catholic chapel in Blarney, the priest was saying mass. I arrived there at the consecration and the entire fervent crowd prostrated themselves, their foreheads touching the ground. Almost involuntarily I followed their touching example and knelt amongst them; then I tried to go into the narrow chapel that was packed to the doors. No ornaments, not even a seat, a roof barely whole. I heard the priest announcing in Irish, in the ancient and poetic language of this persecuted people, that on such and such a day, in order to shorten his parishioners' journey, he would go into such and such a cabin which would become the house of God for the duration, that he would distribute the sacraments of Confession and the Eucharist, and that there he would receive the bread with which his children nourish him. I left the church where the heat was suffocating me and returned to the

le Saint Sacrifice fut terminé; le prêtre monta à cheval et partit; puis chacun se mit lentement en route pour ses foyers; les uns, laboureurs itinérans portant avec eux leurs faux de moissonneurs, se dirigeaient vers la chaumière la plus voisine pour y demander une hospitalité qui est un droit; les autres, prenant leurs femmes en croupe, regagnèrent leurs lointaines demeures à travers le pays. Mais peu de femmes obtiennent de leurs maris la permission de faire la longue course du dimanche: cette tâche virile est le privilège et l'imprescriptible devoir du père de famille.

Mon émotion fut profonde; jamais je ne sentis plus complètement ce que valait la dévotion et ce qu'était une population vraiment pieuse. Jamais mon cœur ne fut tellement maîtrisé par l'influence de la religion; jamais ses pompes ne me parurent plus augustes, plus touchantes.

En revenant je vis une belle église bien entretenue avec un haut clocher, et tout à côté un vaste domaine qui entourait une maison des plus confortables; et je demandais [*sic*] et l'on me dit que c'était l'église *anglaise* de la paroisse dont je venais de quitter la chapelle *irlandaise;* et que cette demeure était celle du recteur protestant. Et je demandais combien il y avait de fidèles, et l'on me répondit qu'il y en avait 5 ou 6 sur 4 000 Catholiques. En en rentrant dans la ville, je m'informai du revenu de ce pasteur de six âmes et j'appris que sa cure lui valait 2 000£, cinquante mille francs! […]

Enfin, entre Blarney et Corke, nous avons rencontré une procession funéraire, le cercueil déposé sur un char peint de toutes les couleurs excepté de noir, et surmonté de plumes rouges: une foule d'hommes et de femmes suivaient en poussant le fameux hurlement connu sous le nom de *Irish Howl.* Un mouchoir blanc suspendu à un bâton et placé à la porte de la maison du défunt indique au public que la mort y a fait sa visite.

De retour à Corke, après avoir visité mes deux excellens guides, le *North Chapel,* sorte de cathédrale catholique, orné de détails gothiques un peu trop fleuris où je vis le tombeau de l'illustre évêque *Moylan* qui empêcha Cork de se révolter en 1798 et où plus de mille enfans apprenaient et récitaient leur cathechisme; après avoir admiré dans les rues quelques charmantes jeunes personnes, et après avoir fait mes paquets, je suis parti à 4 heures pour *Skibbereen* en diligence. Il faisait un tems abominable et la nuit est bientôt survenue, de sorte que je n'ai rien vu de la route qui est cependant assez pittoresque, et passe par des endroits assez intéressans […]

crowd prostrated in the mud. Soon the Holy Sacrament was over; the priest got up on his horse and left; then people all started on their journey home; some, wandering labourers carrying with them their harvesters' sickle, headed for the nearest cottage to ask for hospitality which is a right; others, with their wives on horseback, went back to their homes far off across the countryside. But few women get permission from their husbands to go on this long Sunday trip: this virile task is the privilege and the inalienable right of the father in the family.

An emotional experience for me; never had I felt so completely just what religious devotion means and just exactly what a really pious population was. Never had my heart been so overcome by the influence of religion; never had its pomp seemed more noble or more touching to me.

On the way back, I saw a fine, well-maintained church with a tall spire, and right alongside a vast domain surrounding a very comfortable house; when I asked, I was told that it was the *English* church of the parish whose *Irish* chapel I had only just left, and that the house belonged to the Protestant rector. When I asked how many faithful there were, the answer was that there were five or six for every 4,000 Catholics. Back in Cork, I enquired as to the salary of this pastor with his six followers, and discovered that his appointment is worth £2,000: 50,000 francs! [...]

Between Blarney and Cork, we met with a funeral procession. The coffin had been placed on a cart painted in every colour except black and surmounted with red plumes. A crowd of men and women followed, letting out the well-known cry known by the name of *Irish Howl*. A white kerchief hanging from a stick and placed at the door of the deceased person is a sign for the public that death has visited this place.

Back in Cork, having visited both of my excellent guides, the *North Chapel*, a sort of Catholic cathedral, adorned with somewhat extravagant Gothic details, where I saw the tomb of illustrious Bishop *Moylan* who prevented Cork from rising up in 1798 and where over one thousand children were learning and reciting their catechism. Having admired several charming young persons in the street, and having packed my affairs, I left by coach at four o'clock for *Skibbereen*. The weather was appalling and night soon fell, which meant that I saw nothing of the route that is, however, quite attractive and passes through fairly interesting places [...]
English translation by Grace Neville.

Alexis de Tocqueville
(1835)

French original in: *Voyage en Angleterre et en Irlande de 1835.*
Paris: Gallimard, 1958, pp. 135-36.

L'ENTRÉE DE Cork est très belle. Les quartiers marchands sont beaux. Dans les faubourgs se trouvent d'infames demeures et une population plus horrible encore, telle qu'on ne peut en rencontrer qu'en Irlande.

C'est au milieu de ce quartier que demeure dans une petite maison l'éveque catholique. Le berger au milieu du troupeau …

Nous avons avec nous dans notre diligence découverte deux jeunes gens ayant chacun une très forte pointe de vin. Ces jeunes gens adressaient la parole et faisaient des plaisanteries à presque tous les passants. Tous, hommes ou femmes, répondaient en riant et par d'autres plaisanteries. Je me croyais en France.

Cork *(28 juillet 1835)*

Détresse de presque tous les propriétaires irlandais, qui les empêche de porter aucun secours à la population, quand meme ils en auraient envie, de rien améliorer de peur de mettre dehors du capital, et [les force] de pressurer le pauvre afin d'accroître leurs revenus, ce qui rend le pauvre encore plus incapable de se passer d'eux.

Nouvelle complication, spéciale à ce malheureux pays, et qu'il ne faut pas perdre de vue, lorsqu'on veut en parler. Une de causes principales de l'état actuel est là. Mais cette cause elle-même n'est qu'un effet de la cause plus générale qui a rendu l'aristocratie irlandaise étrangère au pays, et l'a portée à se ruiner en voulant imiter l'aristocratie anglaise, sans avoir son esprit viril et sans savoir comme elle tirer de la liberté et de l'aisance des classes inférieures des sources nouvelles de richesses.

Le duc de *Bridgewater* a doublé sa fortune en ouvrant un canal, le duc de *Newcastle* en ouvrant des mines de charbon de terre.

Que servirait d'ouvrir un canal en Irlande, où personne n'a de *goods* à transporter? De produire du charbon de terre, que nul ne peut acheter?

Alexis de Tocqueville
(1835)

(Conviviality – economics)

THE ENTRANCE to Cork city is very attractive. The business areas are beautiful. In the suburbs you can find filthy houses and an entire population even more awful, of a kind to be found only in Ireland.

It is in the middle of this district that the Catholic bishop lives in a small house. The shepherd is in the midst of his flock …

With us in our open carriage were two young men, both quite merry after drinking much wine. These young people talked to almost all the passers-by and joked with them. Everyone – men and women – replied with laughter and other jokes. I thought I was in France.

Cork *(28 July 1835)*

The financial straits of almost all Irish landlords prevent them from helping the population, even if they so wished, or from improving anything, for fear of expending money. These financial difficulties force them to bring pressure on the poor in order to increase their revenues. This makes the poor all the more incapable of doing without them.

There is a further complication particular to this misfortunate country, one that should never be lost sight of when one wishes to speak about Ireland. Therein lies one of the main causes of this present state of affairs. But this cause is itself merely the consequence of a wider cause that has made the Irish aristocracy a stranger in its own country, and has resulted in it ruining itself by wishing to imitate the English aristocracy without possessing its virile spirit or its ability to extract from the freedom and money of the lower classes new sources of wealth.

The Duke of *Bridgewater* doubled his fortune by opening a canal, as did the Duke of *Newcastle* by opening coalmines.

What use would it be to open a canal in Ireland, where no one has goods that need to be transported, or to produce coal that no one could buy?

English translation by Grace Neville.

Pierre Etienne Denis Saint Germain-Leduc
(1838)

French original in: *L'Angleterre, l'Ecosse et l'Irlande. Relation d'un Voyage Récent dans les Trois Royaumes*. Paris: Levrault, 1838, pp. 284-85.

Cork 30 septembre

CORK EST bâtie dans un profond ravin sur le bord de la mer et dans un site très-pittoresque. Elle est d'une architecture ancienne, et qui le paraît davantage encore par la toiture originale de beaucoup de maisons, où les ardoises sont disposées de manière à imiter les écailles d'un poisson. Deux nouvelles prisons, celle de la ville et celle du comté, la première dans le style grec, l'autre dans le style gothique, sont de magnifiques édifices: le second ressemble à une grande forteresse. Voilà de ces présents dont l'administration anglaise est libérale envers l'Irlande, surtout en les faisant construire aux frais des indigènes.

La vente et les salaisons de viande sont pour la ville de Cork, comme pour tous les ports de l'Irlande, un objet important de commerce. Aussi ce commerce est-il soumis à une législation spéciale. Les bœufs destinés à l'engrais doivent avoir quatre ans, et ne peuvent etre achetés à la distance de plus de quatorze de nos lieues d'une foire. L'abattage des bestiaux se fait surtout en novembre et décembre. Une fois le bétail dépecé en morceaux de quatre à douze livres, les saleurs s'en emparent, et par une préparation fort simple mettent la viande en état de voyager jusque dans l'Inde. Des hommes robustes, armés de gantelets garnis de fer, frottent de sel les morceaux et les entassent ensuite dans des tonneaux d'une capacité prescrite. Au bout de dix ou douze jours on rouvre les tonneaux pour couvrir la viande d'un nouveau sel. Vingt-deux tonneaux de sel sont nécessaires pour saler vingt tonneaux de viande.

On sale également les peaux pour les exporter dans les pays qui ont de grandes tanneries; l'Irlande même n'en tanne qu'une faible partie. On sale aussi, pour les envois aux Indes, les tripes et le cœur. Les boyaux s'exportent pour Livourne, les vessies pour la Hollande et l'Écosse; les cornes vont jusqu'en Afrique.

Pierre Etienne Denis Saint Germain-Leduc
(1838)

(Prisons – meat trade)

Cork, 30 September

CORK IS built in a deep ravine by the sea in a very picturesque setting. Its architecture is old, and the unusual roofing of many of its houses, with the slates arranged in a pattern reminiscent of fish scales, makes it seem all the more so. Two new prisons, the city prison and the county prison, the former in the Greek style and the latter in the Gothic style, are magnificent edifices: the second building resembles a large fortress. Both are fine examples of the gifts which the English government has bestowed so generously on Ireland, especially as it has them built at the expense of the natives.

The sale and salting of meat is an important commercial activity in Cork, as it is in all Irish ports. This trade is regulated by special legislation. Cattle raised for slaughter must be four years old, and cannot be bought at a distance of more than fourteen miles from a market. The cattle are slaughtered mainly in November and December. Once the carcasses have been carved into cuts of meat weighing between four to twelve pounds, the salters take over, and prepare the meat, following a very simple procedure so that it is in a fit state to be transported as far away as India. Sturdy men, wearing metal gloves, rub salt into the cuts of meat and then place them in barrels of a prescribed capacity. After ten or twelve days the barrels are opened and the meat is treated with fresh salt. Twenty-two barrels of salt are needed to salt twenty tons of meat.

The hides are also salted for export to countries equipped with large tanneries; Ireland itself tans only a very small quantity. Tripe and the hearts of the animals are also salted for export to the Indies. The innards are exported to Livorno, the bladders to Holland and Scotland, and the horns are exported as far away as Africa.

English translation by Gearóid Cronin.

Johann Georg Kohl

(1843)

German original in: *Reisen in Irland*. 2 Tle. Dresden and Leipzig: Arnoldische Buchhandlung, 1843, pp. 344-53.

*D*IE *KERRY-MEN* SIND, wie gesagt, gelehrt, aber arm und in ihrer Sitte etwas bäuerlich, die Limerick-*people* sind schöne und artige Menschen, die Dublin-*people* sind besonders zuvorkommend und gastfreundlich und die höflichsten und feinsten von allen Irländern. – 'Und wie sind die Cork-*people*?' fragte ich meinen Reisegefährten, der mir dieß Alles im Commercial-Hotel, in welchem wir abgestiegen waren, des Breiteren auseinandersetzte. '*Rather sharp!*' (mehr oder weniger etwas spitzig!) antwortete er. 'Sie machen sich gern über Andere lustig und sind vor allen Irländern durch ihren eigenthümlichen moquanten Witz ausgezeichnet. Sie merken schnell die schwachen Seiten anderer Menschen und verfolgen sie oft unbarmherzig mit feinen, aber schneidenden Sticheleien.' – 'Haben denn die Cork-*people* selbst keine schwache Seite?' – 'O ja! hm!' – indem mein Freund noch darüber nachsann, was er mir darauf antworten wollte, brach unter unserem Fenster eine der furchtbaren Musiken los, welche die Temperance-Banden, die des Abends in den Straßen von Cork herumziehen, zu machen pflegen, und es folgten ihnen, da es gerade ein Sonnabend war, so viele Menschen nach, daß ich wohl einsah, wie eine der schwachen Seiten der Cork-people in die Nähe des Ohres fallen müßte, da bei ihnen so schreckliche Ohrenschmäuse von ihrer Polizei nicht unter die das ganze Publicum beleidigenden Katzenmusiken gerechnet werden.

Und als ich den anderen Tag auf die Gemälde-Ausstellung der guten Stadt ging, bemerkte ich wieder, daß eine andere schwache Seite sich bei dem Cork-people in der Nähe des Auges befinden müsse, da auf den verschiedenen Leinwandstücken, die hier ausgestellt waren, so viele mißfällige Formen und Farben zusammengebracht waren, daß ihre Disharmonie mich fast eben so verletzte, wie den Abend vorher die Temperance-Banden-

Johann Georg Kohl
(1843)

(Preservation of provisions – county gaol – fever hospital – barracks – Catholic Emancipation – collections in Catholic churches – customs of mourning)

IT IS SAID the Kerry people are learned, but poor, and somewhat boorish in their manners; the Limerick people handsome and polite; the Dublin people extremely complaisant and hospitable, and the most refined of all the Irish. 'And what are the Cork people?' inquired I of my travelling companion, who was giving me all this information at the Commercial Hotel, where we had alighted. 'Rather sharp!' replied he; 'they like to make merry at other people's expense, and are distinguished from all the other natives of Ireland by their peculiar and witty mockery. They are quick at remarking the weak sides of others, and often mercilessly persecute them with delicate yet cutting sarcasms.' 'Have the Cork people themselves, then, no weak side?' 'Oh yes!' – But while my friend was meditating a suitable reply, there burst forth beneath our window one of those most frightful attempts at music which the temperance bands, who march through the streets of Cork in the evening, are in the habit of making; and as it was Saturday night, they were followed by so many persons, that I clearly perceived that one of the weak sides of the Cork people must be somewhere in the region of their ears, since, were it otherwise, their police would not suffer the ears of the entire public to be annoyed by sounds more detestable than even the catterwauling of cats.

The following day, on visiting the picture exhibition of this good city, I imagined I had discovered another of the weak sides of the Cork people, in a neighbourhood not very remote from their eyes, since upon the various pieces of canvas which were here exposed to view, so many displeasing forms and colours were brought together that their want of harmony annoyed me almost as much as the music of the evening before. As, however, I had come to this exhibition not to criticise the works of the Cork artists, nor to delight myself with perfect creations of

Musik. Da ichaber weniger deßwegen, um die Gemäldeproduction von Cork zu kritisiren oder mich an vollkommenen Schöpfungen zu ergötzen, als vielmehr um etwas aufzusuchen, was mich über das Land belehren könne, hingegangen war, so fand ich doch meine Rechnung dabei.

Die Maler jenes Landes – besonders jetzt, wo die Genremalerei so sehr an der Tagesordnung ist, – stellen doch so viel Ethnographisches, Geographisches, Klimatisches, Sitten und Volkswesen Charakterisierendes in ihren Gemälden dar, daß Jemand, der dieß zu seinem Studium gemacht hat, die Gemäldegalerien überall als eine Hauptquelle benutzen muß und selbst die unbedeutendsten Ausstellungen nicht verschmähen sollte.

So erschienen auf der Corker Ausstellung die Büsten des Corker Bürgermeisters, des vorjährigen Dubliner Ober-Bürgermeisters (Daniel O'Connell's), des Vaters Mathew. Alsdann sah man eine Auswanderungsscene von armen Irländern aus dem geliebten Erin nach Amerika, ferner irische Fischer und einige wilde Gebirgs- und Torfmorastscenen.

Es ist das Beßte, was die Maler thun können, die Scenen und Vorfälle ihres Landes darzustellen. Denn dann sind selbst die geringsten Talente sicher, daß sie etwas haben, was sie verstehen, und daß sie etwas produciren, was, wenn es nur einigermaßen erträglich ist, doch etwas vorstellt und einigen Nutzen in der Welt stiften kann. Ja selbst die größten Genies vielleicht können nur innerhalb des Horizontes ihrer Nationalität das Höchste leisten und nur, wenn sie nationale Dinge oder nationale Anschauungsweisen verkörpert darstellen, zu etwas Außerordentlichem gelangen. Die größten Maler wie die größten Dichter sind immer ächt patriotisch geblieben, und ihre Schöpfungen sind aus dem tiefsten Innern ihrer eigenen Seele und aus der Psyche ihrer Nation oder der Natur ihres Vaterlandes hervorgegangen.

Cork hat in anderen Dingen als in den Künsten seine Hauptstärke. Die Stadt ist bekanntlich der Hauptverschiffungshafen für die rohen Producte des ganzen südlichen Theiles von Irland, und ich eilte daher in die Waaren-Magazine, in die Schlacht-, Pack- und Provisionshäuser der Stadt, in ihre Butterwaagen, Einsalzungsinstitute, Einmachungsmanufacturen etc , um Einiges über die eigenthümlichen Industriezweige zu lernen, in denen hier der größte Theil der Bevölkerung beschäftigt ist.

In der Nähe von Cork giebt es die größten Meiereien oder Schweizereien

art, but to search for something that would give me information concerning the people and the country, I found that I was not disappointed in my expectations.

The painters of every country, especially at present, when *tableaux de
genre* are so much the order of the day, represent in their pictures so
much that is descriptive of their nation, of the geography and the climate
of their country, and so much that is characteristic of the manners and
habits of its people, that any one who has made these his study must
everywhere use picture galleries as one of the chief sources from whence
to draw his information, and should not despise even the most insignificant exhibitions. Thus, at the Cork exhibition were displayed the busts
of the Mayor of Cork, of last year's Lord Mayor of Dublin, Daniel
O'Connell, and of Father Mathew. Then there was an emigration scene,
of poor Irish leaving their beloved Erin for America; besides various Irish
fishermen, and several views of wild mountains and turf-bogs. The best
thing a painter can do is to represent the scenes and incidents of his own
country, for in them men of the slightest talent may be certain they have
a subject they understand, and that they will produce a picture which, if
it is at all tolerable, possesses the merit of being a copy of something, and
therefore likely to be of some use to the world. Even the greatest genius
can, perhaps, only produce a masterpiece when he remains within the
horizon of his nationality, and can only attain extraordinary excellence
by embodying in his pictures the national scenes or national habits characteristic of his country. The greatest painters, like the greatest poets,
have ever been eminently patriotic, and their best creations have invariably sprung from the inmost depths of their own souls, and illustrate the
life of their nation or the nature of their fatherland.

But the chief strength of Cork lies in other things than the fine arts.
This city is well known as the principal port for the exportation of the
raw produce of the whole south of Ireland. I therefore hastened to the
store-houses of the town – to the slaughter houses, packing cellars, and
to its butter weigh house, salting establishments, &c., in order to acquire
information respecting those particular branches of industry in which
the greater part of the population is employed.

In the neighbourhood of Cork are some of the greatest dairies of Ireland.

(*dairies*) von Irland. Auch sind Kerry und einige andere Viehzucht betreibende Gegenden nicht fern. Daher werden denn die größten Quantitäten von Butter, Speck, Schinken, Fleisch und Vieh hier zusammengeführt, so wie Dublin von den vorzugsweise ackerbauenden Districten umgeben ist und daher meistens Getreide ausführt. Butter ist einer der Hauptartikel, und Cork's Buttermarkt oder Butterwaage (*firkincrane*) ist beinahe eine Merkwürdigkeit der Stadt. Die Butter kommt hier in kleinen Fässchen (*firkins*) an, deren Gewicht und Butterqualität auf der Waage durch ein Gericht von Butteraufsehern untersucht und bestimmt wird. Diese Butterinspectoren entscheiden darüber unter der Leitung eines General-Waagemeisters. Auf jedes Faß wird die durch richterliche Entscheidung bestimmte Qualität eingebrannt und auf diese Weise der Butterhandel von Cork, der sehr weit verzweigt ist, in gutem Credite erhalten. Da die Corker Butter oft für sehr entfernte Plätze bestimmt ist, so wird sie sehr stark gesalzen. Die Kerry'sche Gebirgsbutter (*mountainbutter*) wird als besonders *firm in body* (fest in ihrem Körper) gelobt.

Bei den großen Provisionshändlern sieht man ungeheure Vorräthe von Lebensmitteln (*life-store*) aufgehäuft. Schinkenmassen von schönen Speckseiten, alle wie Octavbände und Folianten in langen Räumen rangirt. In den Vorstädten giebt es große Schweineschlächtereien, in denen jährlich Tausende von den irischen Cabin-Bewohnern und Rentenbezahlern ihr Leben aushauchen. Ich möchte wissen, mit welchen Gefühlen und Augen der hungrige Paddy jene Speckfolianten durchstudirt. Es ist schrecklich zu denken, daß der arme Irländer das, was er selbst oft in so großem Maße entbehrt, in so reicher Fülle an andere Menschen abgeben muß. Irland ist zum Theil für die Engländer, was Sicilien für die Römer war und zum Theil auch jetzt noch für die Neapolitaner ist. Diese schöne Insel wurde ebenfalls immer von Italien tyrannisirt und ausgebeutet.

Wäre Paddy nur etwas industriöser, so könnte er gewiß manche Speckseite in seinem eigenen Rauchfange sich für die Festtage aufbewahren. So muß er sich aber oft erst zum Soldaten ihrer Majestät machen lassen und den Speckseiten, die er in seiner Hütte fett machte, Tausende von Meilen nachsegeln, bis er in Ost-oder Westindien eines Stückchens davon wieder habhaft wird. Die Ausrüstungen vieler Truppensendungen finden nämlich auch hier in Cork statt.

Kerry, and other cattle-grazing districts, are also not very distant; so that here the largest quantities of butter, bacon, hams, meat, and cattle are brought together. In the same manner, the principal export of Dublin is grain, the produce of the arable districts by which it is surrounded. Butter is one of the chief articles of export from Cork, and the butter market and firkin crane is almost a curiosity. To this the butter is brought in little barrels or 'firkins', and the weight and quality of each firkin is ascertained by an inquest of butter inspectors, who are under the direction of a general weighing-master. The quality thus determined is branded on every firkin; and in this way the butter trade of Cork, which is very extensive, is kept in good repute. As Cork butter is often intended for very distant markets, it is made very salty. The Kerry mountain butter is praised as being particularly 'firm in body'.

At the cellars of the provision merchants are to be seen immense quantities of 'life stores'. Masses of hams and sides of bacon are arranged in long rows, like octavo and folio volumes. In the suburbs are extensive slaughter houses for pigs, in which thousands of the inmates of the Irish cabins and rent payers yearly lay down their lives. I would like to know with what feelings hungry Paddy studies these folios of bacon! It is lamentable to think that the poor Irishman must hand over to others such vast quantities of what he himself so much stands in need. Ireland is to the English, in some measure, what Sicily was to the Romans, and is to the Neapolitans at the present day. That lovely island was always, in like manner, tyrannised over and plundered by Italy.

Were Paddy only a little bit more industrious, he could, I am certain, keep a flitch in his own chimney for festive days. As it is, however, he must first become a soldier of her Majesty, and sail away thousands of miles after the bacon he has fattened in his cabin, and then, in the East or West Indies, he may perchance be allowed to partake of it, as large quantities of provisions are made up in Cork for troops on foreign service.

CONSERVIRUNG DER VICTUALIEN

Sehr interessant sind in dieser Stadt die Etablissements der Kaufleute, welche mit frischen Lebensmitteln handeln und diese durch eigene Processe, die sie erfunden haben, in ihrer ursprünglichen Frische zu erhalten wissen. Man nennt diese Kaufleute *preserved-fresh-provision-merchants.* Dieser Handels- und Manufacturzweig des *preserved fresh provision trade* ist erst seit 20 Jahren in Irland etablirt und in letzterer Zeit zu besonderer Ausdehnung gekommen. Man kann so etwas nur in Großbritannien sehen, weil es das einzige Land ist, das ein so ungemeines Interesse daran hat, alle Arten von Vorräthen in unverdorbenem Zustande in alle Weltgegenden schicken zu können.

Ich besah das größte Etablissement dieser Art, das des Herrn Gamble, '*Patent preserved fresh provision merchant to Her Majesty's navy and to the Hounorable the East-India-Company*' (patentirten frisch erhaltener Lebensvorräthe Kaufmann der Flotte Ihrer Majestät und der Ehrenwerten, der ostindischen Compagnie). In den Etablissements dieses Hauses sieht man fast alle erdenklichen eßbaren Dinge in blecherne oder zinnerne Büchsen so vortrefflich verpackt, daß sie sich zum Theil Jahre lang vollkommen frisch erhalten. Sogar Milch und Rahm wissen die Leute so gut zu verpacken, daß, wenn man die Büchsen auf eine Reise um die Welt mitnimmt und sie in der Südsee oder im ostindischen Meere öffnet, man den Inhalt so süß und frisch findet, als käme er so eben von der Kuh. Die Hauptsache dabei ist nur die vollkommen luftdichte und feste Zubereitung des Gefäßes, die Auswahl einer guten Qualität der Waare und die vollkommene Entfernung der Luft aus den Vorräthen selbst sowohl, als aus den Gefäßen. Auch frische Gemüse, Erbsen, Wurzeln, Champignons, kurz alle möglichen Dinge werden auf diese Weise conservirt.

Wie weit es die Leute in dieser Kunst gebracht haben, beweist das Zeugniß, welches Capitän Roß der besagten Handlung ausgestellt hat. Er bezeugt ihr, daß er im Jahre 1824 verschiedene Büchsen mit *vegetables* (Gemüse) von ihr für seine nordwestliche Expedition gekauft habe. Mehrere dieser Büchsen blieben in dem gestrandeten Schiffe *Fury* steckenund wurden erst im Jahre 1833 im August, also nach 9 Jahren, wieder aufgefunden und geöffnet. Und obgleich sie während dieser Zeit alle Unbill der Einwirkung jenes nördlichen Klimas, im Winter einer Kälte von 52

PRESERVATION OF PROVISIONS

Very interesting in this town are the establishments of those merchants who deal in fresh provisions, which they know how to preserve in their original freshness by some peculiar process of their own. These merchants are called 'preserved fresh provision merchants'. This branch of trade has been established in Ireland within the last twenty years, and has lately been considerably extended. Things of this kind can only be seen in Great Britain, because it is the only country which has so great an interest in being able to send all kinds of provisions to every quarter of the globe in an uninjured condition.

I visited the largest establishment of this description, that of Mr Gamble, 'patent preserved fresh provision merchant to her Majestys navy, and to the Honourable the East India Company'. In this establishment is to be seen almost every kind of food you can think of, packed up in so wonderful a manner, in tin or pewter cases, that most of them will keep perfectly fresh for years. Even milk and cream are so well preserved that if one were to take the cases with him on a voyage round the world, and open them in the South Seas or the Indian Ocean, he would find the contents as sweet and fresh as if just milked from the cow. The principal points to be attended to are the preparation of vessels perfectly close and air-tight, the selection of articles of the best quality, and the complete exhaustion of the air, as well out of the provisions themselves as from the vessels in which they are contained. Fresh vegetables of every description are also preserved in this way.

The perfection which this art has attained is best proved by the testimony which Captain Ross has presented to this establishment. He certifies that in the year 1824 he bought here various cases of vegetables for his north-western expedition. Many of these remained in the stranded ship *Fury* till August, 1833, nine years afterwards, when they were again found and opened; and although during this time they had been exposed to all the injurious influences of that northern climate – in winter to a cold 52 degrees below zero of Fahrenheit, and in summer to a heat 80

Graden Fahrenheit unter 0 und im Sommer einer Hitze von 80 Graden über 0 ausgesetzt waren, so wurden doch alle Gefäße unzerstört und ihr Inhalt in vollkommenem Zustande der Erhaltung und völlig genießbar gefunden.

Dieser ganze Handelszweig ist auf eine bewundernswürdige Weise vollkommen eingerichtet. So findet man z. B. eine große Quantität von Büchsen vorräthig, deren jede so viel Rahm enthält, als für 12 Tassen nöthig ist, andere, die für 24 oder 36 Tassen berechnet sind. Der Schiffscapitän, der sich hier versehen will, hat mithin nur die Anzahl seiner Offiziere oder Passagiere anzugeben, und findet dann Büchsen, die für seine Verhältnisse gerade die gemessene Tagesportion enthalten, und da für jeden Tag nur so viel geöffnet wird, als für jeden Tag nöthig ist, so verdirbt nichts, und es ist sogar eine geregeltere Sparsamkeit möglich als hätte man Kühe an Bord. Eben so sind auch Fleisch- und Gemüseportionen in jede Büchse für eine gewisse Anzahl von Personen bemessen, wozu noch der Vortheil kommt, daß die meisten der Dinge schon gekocht sind, und daher auf diese Weise dem Schiffskoch Mühe und Feuerung erspart wird. Auch Saucen und Suppen aller möglichen Art werden auf diese Weise, nach den Regeln der beßten Kochkunst zubereitet, verpackt, und man kann nachher die Sache nur von dem ersten beßten Matrosen aufwärmen lassen und von seiner Hand Delicatessen empfangen, als wäre er der beßte Koch.

Der Hafen von Cork bietet aller dieser eigenthümlichen Waaren, besonders der Verpackung der lebendigen Waare, der Schweine, Ochsen, Kühe wegen ein besonderes Interesse dar. Das Einschiffen der Schweine ist das interessanteste, und es giebt Hunderte von Zuschauern dabei. Dem komischen Paddy, diesem *'queer fellow'* (närrischen Kerl), wie er sich selbst nennt, der bei allen seinen Beschäftigungen so viel Geschrei macht, und der, wie mir eine 'ready witted' (witzige) Corker Dame sagte, *'always allowed to say everything twice'* (dem man immer die Erlaubnis giebt, jedes Ding zwei Mal zu sagen), diesem lärmenden, schreienden, gesticulirenden Irländer zuzusehen, wie er seinen *rent-payers* (den Schweinen) Lebewohl sagt und mit ihnen sich zum letzten Male abmüht und sie endlich in das Schiff, in dem sie von dem Boden Erins scheiden, hineinprakticirt, gewährt ein unerschöpfliches Amusement, an dem die müßigen Spaziergänger Cork's beim Vorübergehen gern Theil nehmen.

degrees above zero – yet all the cases were found uninjured, and their contents in a state of perfect preservation, and fit for use.

Everything connected with this branch of trade is remarkably complete. Thus, for instance, a quantity of cases are in readiness, each of which contains as much cream as is requisite for twelve cups, and others for 24 or 36 cups. The captain of a ship who wishes to supply himself here has therefore only to state the number of his officers or passengers to be provided with cases containing exactly the portions required for his daily consumption. Thus he wastes nothing, and even more regular economy is practicable than if there were cows on board. In like manner, the portions of meat and vegetables in each case are suited for a certain number of persons; and there is this further advantage, that most of the articles are already cooked, and both trouble and fire are alike saved. Sauces and soups of every possible kind, prepared after the best rules of cookery, are also packed up in the same way, so that it is only necessary to give the article to the nearest sailor to warm, and receive from his hands delicacies as excellent as if he were the best of cooks.

The quays of Cork present much that is interesting in the shipping of all these varieties of merchandise, especially the embarkation of the live stock, pigs, oxen, cows, &c. The shipping of the pigs is the most amusing, and hundreds of the idle strollers of Cork stand looking on, delighted with the scene. It is an inexhaustible source of entertainment to behold this humorous Paddy, this 'queer fellow' as he calls himself, who makes so much noise in whatever occupation he may be engaged, and who, as a 'ready-witted' Cork lady said to me, 'is always allowed to say everything twice' – this talking, shrieking, gesticulating Irishman, bidding farewell to his 'rent payers', and busied about them there for the last time, and at last hoisting them into the ship which is to waft them away from Erin's soil. One ship is being laden with firkins of butter for foreign lands, where Ireland must be thought one of the richest countries in the world,

Ein Schiff wird mit Butterfässern beladen und kommt in fremde Länder, die dann dieses von ganzen Schiffsladungen von Fett triefende Irland für eines der reichsten Länder der Welt halten müssen. Ein anderes nimmt Mehlsäcke ein, und die armen Porters sinken fast nieder unter einer Last von Mehl, von dem ihnen nie ein Körnlein zu Theil wird. Ein drittes versieht sich mit Schiffszwiebäcken, die in den großen *steammill-bakeries* (Dampfmühlen-Bäckereien) von Cork gebacken, getrocknet und für eine Aufbewahrung von Jahren zubereitet werden. Wunderbar ist es, daß das arme hungrige Irland, in dem jährlich so und so viele Menschen geradezu vor Hunger sterben oder in Folge von Hunger ums Leben kommen und in dessen Totenlisten und Hospitälern *starvation* (Hungerleiden) eine eben so regelmäßige Rubrik ist, wie andere Todesursachen, vor allen Dingen so viele Menschen sattzumachen bestimmt ist.

Als es mir vergönnt war, an diesem Hafen zu spazieren, lagen hier gerade drei der schnellsten englischen Dampfschiffe am Quai: the *Princess royal*, der *Prince of Wales* und der *Feuerkönig* (*the fire-king*). Das schnellste von allen ist das erste, die Princess royal, die überhaupt als das schnellste aller der englischen Dampfschiffe, die zwischen den britischen Inseln hin und her gehen, betrachtet wird. Es macht im Durchschnitt, schlechtes und gutes Wetter eingerechnet, 13$\frac{1}{2}$ Meilen in einer Stunde. Sonst wurde der Prince of Wales als das schnellste betrachtet. Doch bleibt dieser jetzt gegen die Princess royal auf 36 Meilen um 2 Minuten zurück. Es ist hier indeß nur von Seeschiffen die Rede, und auf der Themse giebt es Dampfschiffe, die sogar 20 Meilen in einer Stunde zu machen vermögen.

Ich besah mir jenes interessante Schiff. Es war in seinen Salons und Cajüten ganz im Rokoko-Style ausgeschmückt. Sonst rann es (*she run*) [sic] zwischen verschiedenen Häfen. Jetzt aber hat es seine Station in Cork genommen (*she has taken her station*) und arbeitet nun für die Verbindung Irlands mit England. Alle diese für Irland arbeitendenSchiffe müssen vor allen Dingen auch auf animalische Passagiere gefaßt sein, und so hat denn selbst diese elegante Prinzessin auf ihrem Vorderdeck eigenthümliche Vorrichtungen getroffen, um Ochsen, Kühe und Schweine auf eine bequeme und zweckmäßige Weise stallen zu können.

Durch diese raschen Verbindungsmittel Irlands mit England fällt nun Irland immer mehr in die Hände Englands. Es ist, als wenn sich die

or she would not export these whole cargoes of fat. Another is receiving sacks of flour, and the poor porters are almost sinking beneath a load of bread stuff, of which not a morsel will fall to their share, a third is being provided with ships' biscuits, which have been baked in the great 'steam-mill bakeries' of Cork, dried and prepared to keep for years. Strange it is that this poor hungry Ireland, in which so many actually die of hunger every year, and in whose bills of mortality and hospital books 'starvation' is as regular a heading as any other cause of death; – strange it is, I say, that this country should, above all things, be destined to feed so many strangers to her soil.

During my stroll about these quays, I saw lying at them three of the quickest of English steamboats – the *Princess Royal*, the *Prince of Wales*, and the *Fire-King*. The *Princess Royal* is generally allowed to be the swiftest of all the steamboats which ply between the British Isles. On average, including good and bad weather, she proceeds at the rate of twelve miles and a half per hour. The *Prince of Wales* was once considered the quickest, but its speed is now exceeded by the *Princess Royal* by two minutes in six and thirty miles. I am here speaking of sea boats only, for on the Thames there are steamboats which can make twenty miles an hour.

The *Princess Royal* is a beautiful vessel, and her saloons and cabins are fitted up quite in rococo style. She has now taken her station in Cork, and aids in bringing Ireland into closer connection with England. All the vessels in this trade must, above all things, be constructed for animal passengers, and accordingly this elegant *Princess* has on her deck peculiar arrangements for the reception of oxen, cows, and pigs.

By these rapid modes of conveyance Ireland is ever falling more and

Inseln, die sich ohnedieß schon nahe liegen, noch um 100 Meilen genähert hätten. Jetzt wo die Dampfschifffahrt und die Eisenbahnen es möglich machen, in weniger als 24 Stunden beinahe aus jedem beliebigen Theile Englands Truppen nach Irland hinüber zu schicken, ist Irland noch weit mehr als früher an England gefesselt.

DAS GRAFSCHAFTSGEFÄNGNISS
Einen der interessantesten und lehrreichsten Besuche machte ich in Cork in dem dortigen *county-gaol* (Grafschafts-Gefängnisse), welches hier vor einigen Jahren sowohl für criminelle Verbrecher, als auch für Schuldner gebaut worden ist. [...]

Das Corker Grafschaftsgefängniß ist ein schönes und großes Gebäude, und es ist für Verbrecher sowohl, als auch für Schuldner eingerichtet. Es giebt sowohl *master-debtors* (Meister-Schuldner), die sich selbst unterhalten, als auch *pauper debtors* (arme Schuldner), die unterhalten werden, darin. Ich finde es sonderbar, daß man selbst in dieser neuesten Zeit noch nicht zu einer besseren Logik gekommen ist. Denn offenbar hat doch ein Mensch, der einem anderen nicht seine Schuld bezahlen kann, gar nichts mit einem Verbrecher gegen die Gesellschaft gemein. Und es heißt doch den armen Schuldnern offenbar Unrecht thun, wenn man sie mit den Verbrechern durch die selbe Pforte in ein Haus gehen läßt, auf dem eine so große Ehrenrührigkeit ruht. Sonst steckte man auch noch die Wahnsinnigen dazu, überhaupt alle Personen, die irgend einer Ursache wegen angehalten werden mußten. Die Wahnsinnigen hat man endlich von den Verbrechern unterscheiden gelernt. Die Schuldner wird man vielleicht auch noch einmal davon sondern.

Ein *Captain of the Navy* (Seecapitän), der vor einigen Jahren hier Gouverneur war, hatte in diesem Gefängnisse manche Verbesserungen eingeführt, die vielleicht der Erwähnung werth sein möchten, da man sieauch anderswo nachahmen könnte. Erstlich hatte er, wenigstens in einem Theile des Gefängnisses, statt der Betten Hängematten eingeführt, offenbar diejenigen Schlafstätten, welche die größte Reinlichkeit und Raumersparung möglich machen. Alsdann hatte er Speisetische erfunden ohne Füße. Mittels eines sehr einfachen Mechanismus werden nämlich die Tischplatten an 4 Balken von der

and more into the hands of England, the two islands being thus, as it were, drawn 100 miles nearer to each other. Now that the railroads and steamers render it possible at any moment to transport troops from any part of England to Ireland in less than 24 hours, the latter is chained to the former more firmly than ever.

THE COUNTY GAOL

One of my most interesting and instructive visits in Cork was to the county gaol built here some years ago, both for debtors and criminals. [...]

The Cork County Gaol is a large and handsome building, and is appropriated for debtors as well as for criminals. There are 'master debtors', who support themselves, and 'pauper debtors', who are supported at the public expense. In these enlightened modern times, it is strange that people have not yet learned better logic, than to compel the man whose only offence is that he cannot pay his debts, and who has nothing whatever in common with criminals, to become their companion. It is also an evident injustice to the poor debtor to thrust him through the same gate with malefactors, and into a place which entails upon him so much disgrace. Formerly the insane were also confined there; its [*sic*], all who on any account were required to be kept in custody. As the necessity for a distinction between lunatics and criminals has at length become apparent, the debtors may probably hereafter be also separated.

A captain of the navy, who some years since was governor here, has introduced into this prison many improvements, which are deserving of notice, and may perhaps be thought worthy of imitation elsewhere. In the first place, instead of beds he introduced hammocks, as being that description of sleeping accommodation which unites the most perfect cleanliness with the greatest saving of room. He next invented dining-tables without legs, which are lowered from the ceiling by very simple machinery, and drawn up again when no longer required for use. Thus they completely disappear, and leave the dining-room quite unencumbered. For seats in those eating rooms they have round, smooth blocks of wood, painted

Zimmerdecke heruntergelassen, und nach gemachtem Gebrauche zieht man die wieder in die Höhe, und sie verschwinden so also völlig, indem sie unter der Decke des Zimmers hängen bleiben, und lassen nachher unten den Raum des Eßzimmers völlig frei. Als Stühle dienen bei diesen Speisetischen runde Holzblöcke, die recht glatt bearbeitet und recht hübsch schwarz angestrichen sind. Diese Art von Stühlen sieht erstlich in einem Gefängniß gar nicht schlecht aus, und zweitens sind sie unverwüstlich, und drittens können sie ohne Umstände in einem Winkel aufgehäuft werden, ohne viel Raum einzunehmen.

Das ganze Gefängniß besteht aus Eisen und Stein, und insofern Paddy's Wohnung gewöhnlich nur aus Erde oder Schmutz besteht, kann man gewiß ohne Uebertreibung sagen, daß der Irländer eines argen Verbrechens wegen aus einer Höhle in einen Palast versetzt wird. Eben so wird auch seine Kost gewöhnlich ganz außerordentlich verbessert. Denn während er als ehrlicher Mann zu Hause nur wässerige Kartoffeln hatte, bekommt er im Gefängnisse als Sünder täglich zwei Pfund Brod und süße Milch dazu. Es ist aber schwer, es dem Paddy im Gefängnisse nicht besser zu geben, als er es bei sich zu Hause gewohnt ist. In diesem Gefängnisse befindet sich sogar ein *hot-closet* eine heiße Kammer, in welche die Wäsche der Gefangenen wie Brod in einen Backofen hineingeschoben wird, um vollkommen getrocknet zu werden. Wo hat Paddy wohl in seiner Hütte ein solches *hot closet?* Ja hat er überhaupt nur Wäsche auf seinem Leibe? Aber freilich ist eben die goldene Freiheit doch selbst in den Augen des Hungrigen ein so schönes Ding, daß im Allgemeinen durch das bessere materielle Leben in den Gefängnissen eine Sehnsucht nach ihnen nie zu befürchten sein wird, und daß man im Allgemeinen wegen gut eingerichteter Gefängnisse eine Vermehrung der Verbrechen nie besorgen sollte.

Aber allerdings wird dadurch eine eigenthümliche gemeine Classe von Verbrechen producirt, die das Gefühl für Freiheit völlig verloren haben und die, weil sie es in dem Gefängnisse eben so gut und besser haben, sich nichts daraus machen, nach ihrer Freilassung wiederum ein Verbrechen zu begehen und wiederum ins Gefängniß gesteckt zu werden. Es giebt genug solche Leute in England, die ihr ganzes Leben hindurch zuweilen frei, zuweilen im Gefängnisse verbringen.

Dieß sind indeß, wie gesagt, nur Ausnahmen, und die meisten gehen

black. These seats are not unsightly; and whilst they are indestructible, they may also be piled up in a corner without ceremony, and without taking up much room.

The entire prison is built of iron and stone; and as Paddy's dwelling is usually constructed of earth or mud, it may be said, without exaggeration, that for the commission of a wicked crime an Irishman is removed from a hole to a palace. His diet is also, in general, very much improved; for while he remained at home, with unimpeached honour, he had only watery potatoes; but as an offender in prison, he receives daily two pounds of bread, and an allowance of milk along with it. It would, indeed, be difficult to make Paddy more uncomfortable in gaol than he is at home. In this prison there is even a 'hot closet', or heated chamber, into which the washed clothes of the prisoners are put, like bread into an oven, to dry them thoroughly. Where has Paddy in his cabin such a 'hot closet'? Nay, has he even clothes on his body? But golden freedom is so fair, even in the eyes of the hungry, that with all the better living in the gaols, no longing after them is to be feared, and in general one need never apprehend an increase of crime on account of well-arranged prisons.

There is, however, certainly thereby produced a peculiar and numerous class of offenders, who have entirely lost their love of freedom, and who because they live as well or better in gaol, do not scruple, after being set free, to offend again, and again to be imprisoned. There are plenty of such people in England, who pass their whole lives, sometimes free, but oftener in gaol.

But these, as I have said, are the exceptions; and the greater proportion quit such a prison as that of Cork with at least better habits. This is

doch wohl aus einem solchen Gefängnisse, wie es das *Cork-County-gaol* ist, mit besseren Gewohnheiten wieder heraus. Bei der Jugend, die hier fleißig zur Arbeit angehalten und auch im Gefängniß unterrichtet wird, ist dieß gewiß. Selbst von den alten Verbrechern lernen in der Gefängnißschule noch viele das Lesen und Schreiben. Die gewöhnlichen Arbeiten, welche man in den englischen Gefängnissen im Ganzen findet, sind folgende: Aufzupfen von alten Tauenden zu Werg zum Auskalfatern der Schiffe, das Verfertigen der in England so nöthigen Fußdecken, die man vor die Kamine legt, aus Stricken, und das Treten in der Tretmühle, was sie hier *working by the cubbitt* (Arbeiten mit dem Cubbitt) nennen, weil Cubbitt der Mann war, der die Tretmühle hier einführte.

FIEBERHOSPITAL

Ein anderes interessantes Institut von Cork ist sein *Fieberhospital*. Es ist eines der beßten in Irland, und es rühmt sich, daß die Sterblichkeit in seinen Betten geringer sei als in irgend einem anderen Fieberhospitale der ganzen vereinigten Königreiche. Es werden in diesem Hospitale im Durchschnitt jährlich nicht weniger als 1500 bis 2000 Fieberkranke behandelt.

Es giebt fast in der Hauptstadt jeder irischen Grafschaft ein Fieberhospital, und zuweilen sieht man ein solches auch in den kleineren Städten. Dublin hat bekanntlich das größte und schönste Fieberhospital in der Welt. In diesen Hospitälern werden in der Regel bloß Fieberkranke, an denen Irland einen so großen Überfluß hat, aufgenommen. Doch behandelt man darin zuweilen gelegentlich auch andere Kranke. Unter 1970 Kranken waren in dem Corker Fieber-Hospital im Jahre 1839 1856 Fieberkranke und nur der Rest bestand aus mit anderen Krankheiten Behafteten [...]

Wahrscheinlich sind das Elend, die Noth, die schlechte Nahrung, der Mangel an Brennmitteln und dabei das feuchte Klima die Hauptursachen dieser Erscheinung. Aus den Berichten des Corker Fieberhospitals geht hervor, daß es im April und Mai und alsdann im November und December die meisten Fieberkranken aufnimmt. April und Mai sind diejenigen Monate in welchen die Noth der Armen in Irland im Laufe des Jahres am höchsten steigt, und November und December wieder diejenigen, in welchen der meiste atmosphärische

certainly the case with the young, who are kept at hard work, and also educated; even many of the old prisoners learn reading and writing in the prison school. The common employments to be found in English prisons are, picking old ropes into oakum for caulking ships, making rope doormats, and working on the treadmill, which is termed 'working by cubbitt', because it was by a person named Cubbitt that the treadmill was first introduced here.

FEVER HOSPITAL

Another interesting institution in Cork is the fever hospital, which is one of the best in Ireland, and boasts that the mortality of inmates is less than in any other similar establishment in the United Kingdom. No fewer than from 1,500 to 2,000 patients are annually received into this hospital.

There is a fever hospital in the principal town of almost every Irish county, and sometimes one in the smaller towns also. Dublin, it is well known, has the largest and best in the world. Fever patients, who are so very numerous in Ireland, are by the rules alone admissible into those hospitals, yet other patients are also occasionally received. In 1839 out of 1,970 patients in the Cork fever hospital, 1856 were fever cases, and the remainder people affected with other diseases. [...]

Misery, want, bad food, scarcity of fuel and the moist climate, are probably the origin causes of this disease. The records of the Cork fever hospital inform us that the greatest number of patients is received in April and May, and in November and December. The former are the months in which the distress of the poor in Ireland is at its greatest height; and the latter months are those in which the greatest quantity of rain falls. It is also remarked that in years of extreme wetness or scarcity the typhus fever is most prevalent. The increased humidity of a year works not only directly on the constitution, but also increases disease indirectly, by preventing the preparation and drying of the turf,

Niederschlag stattfindet. Auch bemerkt man, daß in besonders nassen und besonders hungrigen Jahren das Typhusfieber besonders stark grassirt. Die größere Feuchtigkeit eines Jahres wirkt nicht nur direct auf die Körperconstitution ein, sondern sie vermehrt auch noch indirect die Krankheit, indem sie die Bereitung und Trocknung des Torfes unmöglich macht und den Preis dieses so nothwendigen Materials so sehr steigert, daß er für die Armen unerschwinglich wird. Wie oft ereignet es sich in Irland, daß diese dann gezwungen sind, ihre Tische oder Bettstellen oder andere nothwendige Materialien zu zerbrechen und, um sich etwas Wärme zu schaffen, zu verbrennen. [...]

DIE BARRAKEN

Wie bei vielen irischen Städten, so befinden sich auch bei Cork bedeutende *barracks* (Casernen). Sie liegen auf einer Anhöhe vor den Thoren der Stadt, wie denn in ganz Großbritannien die Soldaten immer aus den Städten hinausquartirt werden. Die Corker Barraken sind besonders interessant, weil Cork einer von denjenigen Häfen ist, in welchen die Truppen für die Colonieen eingeschifft und verproviantirt und auch wieder ausgeschifft werden, wenn sie nach drei Jahren von den Colonieen zurückkommen, um dann durch das ganze Königreich hindurch, durch Irland, Schottland und England die Quartiere zu wechseln und nach dem Ablauf von zehn Jahren wiederum in die Colonieen verschifft zu werden, wo man sie auch oft von einem Punkte zum anderen verlegt. Diese Circulation der Regimenter durch das Mutterland und seine Colonieen wiederholt sich beständig. Und wenn man nun bedenkt, wie lange die Truppen auf den weiten Meereswogen immer unnütz unterhalten und besoldet werden müssen, so ist es wahrscheinlich, daß auch aus diesem Grunde die englische Armee eine der kostspieligsten der Welt ist. Von jedem in die Colonie gesandten Regimente bleibt ein Theil, ich glaube, zwei Colonnen, im Mutterlande zurück, um daselbst das Interesse des Regiments wahrzunehmen, hauptsächlich aber, um Rekruten anzuwerben, einzuexerciren und dem Regimente in die Fremde nachzusenden. Diese zurückbleibenden Colonnen werden das Depot des Regiments genannt. Die Perioden der Circulation sind für die Artillerie anders als für die Infanterie. Und ganz von dieser Circulation

and increasing the price of this necessary article so much that it is unattainable by the poor. How often does it happen, in Ireland, that they are compelled to break up and burn their tables, bedsteads, and other furniture, to produce a little warmth! [...]

THE BARRACKS

Cork, like most towns in Ireland, has its barracks, which stand on a hill in the suburbs of the city. These barracks are more interesting than usual, as Cork is one of those harbours in which troops are embarked and provisioned for the colonies, and where they also disembark on their return home. The usual period of foreign service is three years, after which, for ten years, the regiments are continually changing their quarters throughout the entire kingdom – Ireland, Scotland, and England – when they are again shipped for the colonies, where also they are frequently moved from one place to another. When it is considered how long, according to this system, the troops must be maintained and supported unprofitably on the wide waves of the ocean, it is evident that on this account alone the English army must be one of the most expensive in the world. Of every regiment sent to the colonies, a part (two companies, I believe) remains behind in the mother country, to attend to the interests of the regiment, but principally to collect recruits, train them, and send them to the regiment on the foreign station. Those companies which remain behind are termed the depôt of the regiment. The periods of circulation for the artillery and infantry are different; and the troops destined for the East Indies have also their own peculiar regulations. The latter have no depots in Cork, being all equipped and embarked from English harbours.

ausgenommen sind die Truppen, welche für Ostindien bestimmt sind. Diese haben wieder ihre eigenen Vorschriften. Auch haben diese ostindischen Truppen keine von ihren Depots in Cork. Sie werden alle von den englischen Häfen ausgerüstet und eingeschifft.

Einer meiner ersten Spaziergänge in Cork war zu jenen Barraken. Das große Thor, welches zu ihren inneren Höfen führt, war von oben bis unten mit Aufrufen und Einladungen an junge Leute beklebt, in den Dienst Ihrer Majestät zu treten. Diese englischen Aufrufe, welche von den Depots der Regimenter ausgehen, sind in ihrer Abfassungsweise etwas ganz Eigenthümliches, und wir auf dem Continente, wo Jeder von Haus aus zum Soldatendienste verpflichtet ist, kennen so etwas gar nicht mehr. Sie sind ungefähr eben so abgefaßt, wie prahlerische Comödienzettel. Ueber dem einen steht z. B. das Bild eines hübschen Reiters, der in voller Parade dahin galoppirt, darunter mit großen Buchstaben: 'GOD SAVE THE QUEEN!' Dann liest man weiter: '12 der schönsten Regimenter Ihrer Majestät von der größten *respectability* (Ansehen) und von der anerkanntesten *gallantry* (Hochherzigkeit) stehen jetzt zur freien Auswahl den Söhnen Erin's offen. Es ist jetzt gerade die beßte Zeit für tüchtige junge Leute, sich in einem derselben für den Dienst ihrer *gracious Majesty* einroliren zu lassen. Es ist der leichteste Dienst, und man hat die beßte Beköstigung. Die, welche Rekruten bringen, bekommen 7 Schilling 6 Pence Belohnung per Kopf!' – Ueber dem anderen steht:

'EAST INDIA COMPANY FORCES!'
'Es werden noch einige *spirited young men* (muthige Jünglinge) verlangt für den *service of the Honourable the East-India-Company*.
Bounty (Prämie)   3 Pfund 6 Schilling.
Paiement (Sold) 1 Schilling 6 Pence täglich.
Belohnung für Rekrutenbringer: 17 Schilling.
Unter besseren Bedingungen wird ein junger Mann seine Arbeit nirgends verdingen können!'

Ich hatte leider nicht Muße genug, einen solchen Anschlag in seiner ganzen Länge mir zu merken. Viele Ausdrücke waren noch viel stärker und schreierischer als die wenigen, welche ich behielt, und die ich hier wiedergab. [...]

One of my first walks in Cork was to these barracks. The great gate which leads to the inner court was placarded from top to bottom with advertisements, inviting young men to enter her Majesty's service. These English invitations are, in their composition, of a very character-istic nature; and we on the continent, where every one is compelled to serve as a soldier in his turn, can form no idea of them. They are gen-erally got up like attractive playbills: for instance, at the top of one is placed the representation of a dashing horseman galloping in full uni-form, and underneath, in large letters, 'GOD SAVE THE QUEEN!' It then proceeds to say, that 'twelve of the finest of her Majesty's regi-ments, of the greatest respectability, and of the most acknowledged gal-lantry, are now open to the free choice of the sons of Erin. Now it is the very best time for active young men to enrol themselves in one of them for her Majesty's service. It is the most easy service and the best pay. Those who bring recruits will obtain seven shillings and sixpence for each!' Another runs thus:

'EAST INDIA COMPANY'S FORCES.'
'Some spirited young men are still wanted for the service of the Honourable the East India Company.

Bounty   3£ 6s.
Pay   1s. 6d. a day.
Bounty to those who bring recruits   1/s.
A young man can no where turn his labour to better account.'

My time would not permit me to copy these announcements ver-batim; but many of them were of a much more alluring character, and offered still greater advantages than those I have mentioned. [...]

Die Barraken von Cork sollen die größten und beßten Englands sein, und während wir in ihren Schlaf- und Speisezimmern, in ihren *canteens* (so heißen die Marketenderbuden oder Schenken in den englischen Barraken), in ihren *mess-rooms* (so heißen die Speisezimmer der Offiziere) und ihren ausgedehnten Höfen umherspazierten, ereignete sich Allerlei darin, was unsere Aufmerksamkeit und unser Interesse fesselte. Zuerst defilirte das 10. Husarenregiment, das von einem Manöver zurückkehrte, herein. Lauter ausgezeichnet schöne Leute! die herrlichsten Pferde von der Welt! Die Sättel waren alle mit Tigerfellen bedeckt, die meisten mit ächten. Die Ausrüstung der englischen Soldaten ist, da sie in der Regel Alles von der beßten Qualität haben, wahrscheinlich die kostspieligste auf der Welt. [...]

Einer der Offiziere erzählte mir, daß sie einen Deutschen als Musikdirector bei ihrem Regimente hätten. Es ist dieß sehr häufig bei den englischen Regimentern der Fall, eben so wie bei den russischen. Die Besoldung eines solchen deutschen Musikdirectors ist vortrefflich. Sie beläuft sich täglich auf 12 Schillinge, nebst Diät und Kleidung. Man findet überhaupt von allen fremden Nationen die Deutschen am häufigsten in dem englischen Militärdienste, insbesondere auch in der Navy, und die Franzosen von allen am seltensten. Ja in der Navy soll es sogar gar keine Franzosen geben *dürfen*. (Giebt es Engländer im französischen Dienste?) Höchstens in dem militärischen Küchendepartement scheint man hie und da eine Ausnahme von jener den Franzosen ungünstigen Regel zu machen. Denn in dem Meßroom des 45. Regiments, das nach dem mittelländischen Meere eingeschifft werden sollte, fand sich ein Koch dieser Nation. Ein deutscher Schneider, den ich ebenfalls dort traf, und der die Güte hatte, mir viel Interessantes zu zeigen, versicherte mir, daß es der einzige Franzose sei, der ihm in der englischen Armee vorgekommen sei. Er konnte ein gutes Stück von dieser Armee kennen, deren Regimenter er schon seit Jahren immer durch Cork passiren sah und bekleiden half.

Unsere deutschen Landsleute sind sonst etwas selten hier in Cork. Ich lernte drei Fünftel aller dortigen Deutschen kennen, nämlich drei, eben jenen Schneider, einen Lehrer der Musik und einen jungen Musiker, die alle viel Güte für mich hatten. Es gibt hier keine deutschen Kaufleute, auch keine jungen Deutschen an den Comptoiren, auch sonst keine deutschen Künstler und Handwerker. Wie gesagt, ich habe da-

Cork barracks are said to be the largest and best in the kingdom; and as we wandered about in the sleeping rooms and eating rooms, the canteens, (as the sutlers' shops or alehouses in English barracks are called,) the officers mess rooms, and the extensive squares, we everywhere saw much to excite interest and attract our attention. The 10th hussars, returning from exercise, defiled before us. The regiment was composed of remarkably fine men, and the noblest horses in the world. The saddles were all ornamented with tiger skins, most of them genuine. The equipment of the English soldiers is indeed the most costly in the world, for everything is of the best quality: thus the hussar jackets worn by the officers in this regiment alone cost about £40 each. [...]

One of the officers informed me that the band master of his regiment was German. This is very frequently the case, in English as well as in Russian regiments. These band masters are very well paid, receiving as much as twelve shillings a day, besides diet and clothing. Of all foreigners, Germans are most frequently found in the English service, especially in the navy; whilst Frenchmen are most rarely met with. It is said, however, that no Frenchman is permitted to enter the British navy. (Are there any Englishmen in the French service?) It is only in the cooking department that the exception to this rule, so unfavourable to the French, is apparent; for in the mess room of the 45th regiment, which was about to be embarked for the Mediterranean, I found a cook of that nation. A German tailor, whom I also met here, and who was kind enough to direct my attention to many things worthy of notice, assured me that this was the only Frenchman he had ever known in the English army, and he must have seen a large portion of it, during his long residence in Cork, where he had assisted in clothing most of the regiments that are constantly passing through that city.

Germans are somewhat scarce in Cork. I could only hear of five, and three-fifths of these I saw, that is to say – the tailor above mentioned, a teacher of music, and a young musician – all of whom showed me much kindness. There are no German merchants, no young Germans at the counter, nor,

selbst durch Erkundigung nicht mehr als fünf auffinden können. Ich dieß besonders hervor, weil man sonst gewohnt ist, in den englischen großen Städten immer eine Fülle von Deutschen zu finden. Ich glaube, daß Cork in den britisch-europäischen Dominien unter den Städten, die mehr als 100,000 Einwohner haben, diejenige ist, welche die geringste Anzahl von Deutschen aufzuweisen hat. [...]

[KLÖSTERLICHE ERZIEHUNGSANSTALT FÜR MÄDCHEN]
Schon auf meinem Wege nach Cove hatte ich am Ufer ein großes Gebäude liegen sehen, das man mir als ein Kloster und Erziehungsinstitut für junge Damen bezeichnete. Am anderen Morgen fuhr ich, von einigen freundlichen Corker Gönnerinnen mit Introductionsbriefen versehen, dahin, um mir diese Anstalt zu besehen. Es werden daselbst 40 junge Mädchen aus den ersten Ständen in allen schönen Künsten und Wissenschaften unterrichtet und zu gleicher Zeit einer klösterlichen Erziehung theilhaftig gemacht. Die Erzieherinnen sind Nonnen von der Congregation von Paris. Das Gebäude ist höchst geräumig und elegant. Die Vorsteherin der Stiftung, eine höchst gebildete Dame, hatte die Güte, mich mit allen Theilen des Gebäudes bekannt zu machen und mir darin eine Anstalt zu zeigen, deren Ausstattung in der That allen Ansprüchen genügt. Ich hätte nicht geglaubt, daß das Irland unserer Tage, dessen alte berühmte Schulen in Ruinen liegen, solche Erziehungs-Anstalten besäße. Manche irländische Familien schicken ihre Töchter nach Frankreich hinüber, damit sie in dortigen klösterlichen Stiftungen ihre Erziehung erhalten. Auch in diesem irischen Stifte war die Erziehungsweise halb französisch, und die Damen sprechen mit Vorliebe diese Sprache, so wie sie auch mit Vorliebe von jenem Lande redeten. Die Franzosen haben ihrerseits eine außerordentliche Vorliebe für die Irländer, die sie sowohl wegen ihres Katholicismus als wegen ihres Celtismus als ihre von den Germanen unterdrückten Brüder betrachten. Es ist kein französisches Buch über Irland erschienen, das nicht den O'Connell in die Wolken erhöbe, das nicht voll Bewunderung für den irischen Nationalcharakter wäre, und ebenso voll Abneigung gegen die Engländer und nicht nur voll von Abscheu gegen ihre Tyrannei, sondern auch voll Verblendung gegen die Wohltaten, die Irland wirklich doch noch wie Rosen zwischen Dornen

with the above exceptions, no German artists or tradesmen. I mention this more particularly as a great many Germans are always to be found in the large towns and cities of England; whilst I believe there are fewer resident in Cork than in any other city of equal population in the British-European dominions. [...]

[A CONVENT SCHOOL]

On my way to Cove I had observed on the shore a large building, which I was informed was a nunnery, and also a place of education for young ladies. Next day, provided with letters of introduction by some kind lady-patronesses at Cork, I visited this institution. It contains 40 young ladies of the higher classes who are here instructed in all the fine arts and sciences, and at the same time partake of the discipline of the cloister. The building is very spacious and elegant, and the teachers are nuns of the congregation of Paris. The principal of the institution, a lady of most polished manners, was so obliging as to conduct me over the entire building, and thus made me acquainted with an educational establishment which left nothing to be desired. I could scarcely have believed that Ireland, whose ancient renowned schools lie in ruins, now possessed such a seminary. Many Irish families send their daughters to France to be educated in the convents there; and even in this institution the education was half French, the ladies preferring to converse in that language, and taking much pleasure in speaking of France. The French have also, on their side, an extreme partiality for the Irish, because they regard them as having been oppressed by their Germanic conquerors, aswell on account of their Catholicism as of their Celtic origin. No French book appears respecting Ireland that does not laud O'Connell to the sky, that is not full of admiration for the Irish national character, and equally redolent of denunciations of the English and their tyranny, as well as of blindness to those benefits which, like roses among thorns,

in seiner Union mit England findet. [...]

Die Emancipation der irischen Katholiken hat freilich in neuerer Zeit ungemein Vieles an jenen Gesetzen gemildert und verbessert. Denn in Folge derselben sind die Katholiken nicht nur ins Parlament gekommen, sondern auch im Innern des Landes haben sie überall ihr Haupt erhoben und erfreuen sich in allen inneren Angelegenheiten des Landes und der Städte, desselben einer größeren Gleichstellung mit den Protestanten, was ein protestantischer Menschenfreund nur mit Freuden bemerken kann.

Katholik und Armer waren sonst in Irland ziemlich gleichbedeutend – (arme Katholiken) – jetzt werden die Katholiken überall wohlhabender. Katholik und Serviler waren auch ungefähr dasselbe. Der Katholik, selbst wenn er nicht zu den gemeinen gehörte, spielte immer gegen den Protestanten, der schon als solcher vornehm war, den Bescheidenen und Unterthänigen. Jetzt fangen sie an, sich mehr zu fühlen, ja es ist bemerkenswert, daß schon hie und da manche, wie dieß mit allen Freigelassenen der Fall zu sein pflegt, sich ihrer Macht überheben und mit Stolz und Anmaßung auf die Protestanten hinabzusehen affectiren. Katholik, Papist und Antichrist waren sonst gleichfalls ungefähr dasselbe. Jetzt haben sich die Protestanten allmählig darein gefunden, auch die Katholiken als Christen neben sich existiren zu lassen, und es scheint auf ihrer Seite eine größere Duldsamkeit sich Raum zu schaffen.

Die Durchsetzung der Emancipation selbst ist ein Zeichen der größeren Duldsamkeit dieser Zeit, und manche lehrt schon ihr Interesse duldsamer zu sein, da die Katholiken mehr Gewalt in Händen haben und hie und da diese Gewalt die Protestanten fühlen lassen können. Der jetzige Bürgermeister von Cork war ein Katholik, und als sein Nachfolger wurde ein sehr gemäßigter Protestant bezeichnet.

Zu hoffen ist es, daß in Folge der allgemeinen Emancipation der Katholiken und der Reformirung ihrer ganzen Stellung man bald auch dahin kommen werde, ihre Priester anders zu situiren, damit solche Aergernisse, wie man sie noch jetzt bei ihren Kirchen sieht, beseitigt werden. Ich meine die Collecten, die zu Gunsten der Priesterschaft an den Thüren der katholischen Kirchen in Irland veranstaltet werden. Die geringen Einkünfte, welche die irischen Priester besitzen, haben sie nämlich

Ireland actually finds in her union with England. [...]

The emancipation of the Irish Catholics has, indeed, greatly moderated and improved their condition. Not only are Catholics now admitted into Parliament, but everywhere throughout the country they enjoy a much greater equality – a result which cannot fail to be gratifying to every humane and right-minded Protestant.

A Catholic, and a poor man, were formerly in Ireland almost synonymous terms. The Catholic, even if he did not belong to the lower orders, was ever obsequious and humble to the Protestant, who, on his part, was haughty and exclusive. Now, they are everywhere in improved circumstances, and are beginning to respect themselves more; nay, it is worthy of remark, that here and there many of them (as is usually the case with all people freed from slavery) are already elated with their power, and affect to look down on the Protestants with pride and arrogance. Catholic, Papist, and Antichrist were also at one time synonymous names. Now the Protestants have found themselves by degrees permitting the Catholics to live with them as Christians; and this appears to prepare the way for a still greater degree of toleration.

The Emancipation Act is itself a proof of the increased tolerance of the present age; and many have lately discovered that the practice of this virtue is more conducive to their interests, as the Catholics have now more power in their hands, and occasionally make the Protestants feel that they possess it. The present Mayor of Cork is a Catholic, and a very liberal Protestant is appointed his successor.

In following up the complete emancipation of the Catholics, and the reforming of their situation, it is to be hoped that the position of their priests may speedily be altered, so as to do away with the contemptible practices which still prevail in their churches. I allude more especially to the collections which are made at the doors of Catholic churches for the benefit of the priesthood. The small income of the Irish priests has compelled them to collect a tribute from church goers, for

dazu vermocht, beim Gottesdienste einen Tribut von den Kirchengängern zu erheben, wie er auf diese Weise in keinem einzigen anderen katholischen Lande erhoben wird. Ich sah dieß an mehreren Orten in Irland mit an, unter anderem auch in Cork. Der Tribut wurde an zwei Thüren der Kirche erhoben, an der großen Hauptthüre, wo die Unbemittelten eingingen und à Person einen Penny erlegen mußten, und an einer Seitenthüre, wo die Reichen eingingen und nach Belieben mehr bezahlten. Hier stand mit großen Buchstaben angeschlagen: 'A SILVER COLLECTION IS EXPECTED' (heute wird eine Silber-Collection erwartet), d. h. daß man wenigstens einen Sixpence bezahle. Ein Priester war selbst dabei gegenwärtig, um die Geldeinnahme zu beaufsichtigen und auch, wie man mir sagte, um durch seine Gegenwart auf den Geldbeutel der Leute einen wirksameren Eindruck zu machen. Er bedankt ich bei jeder Gabe, die in das vor ihm stehende Becken fiel. Vor der Hauptthüre der Kirche, die geöffnet war, und auf den Stufen der Treppen drängten sich viele Arme und Bettler, welche zu arm waren, um den geforderten Pfennigtribut bezahlen zu können. Sie lagen mit gefalteten Händen und kniend auf den Steinen und horchten den entfernten, aus der Kirche zu ihnen heran dringenden Tönen. 'Sie sind zufrieden, wenn sie nur das Glöcklein des Dieners des Priesters, der vor dem Altare den Gottesdienst verrichtet, vernehmen,' sagte mir mein Begleiter, 'haben sie nur dieß Glöcklein von innen gehört und dabei sich verbeugt und bekreuzigt, so nehmen sie dieß als eine angehörte Messe und als eine Mitmachung des Gottesdienstes an.'

Ich und viele Andere, die daran gewöhnt waren, sahen dieß mit an, ohne eben viel Arges darüber zu äußern. Aber wenn man dieß Verfahren mit derjenigen Fackel, welche Christus uns in die Hände gegeben hat, nahe, hell und scharf beleuchten wollte, könnte man sich dann einer Sprache bedienen, welche zu heftig und zu hart wäre, um einen Zustand der Dinge zu beklagen, in welchem die Priester, um ihre leibliche Existenz zu sichern, zu solchen Mitteln zu schreiten genöthigt wären. Man sagt, daß die katholischen Priester in Irland ihre Haupteinkünfte aus diesen Kirchen-Collectionen beziehen. Die Protestanten tadeln diese Beziehungsweise der Einkünfte am meisten, mehr noch als die katholischen Laien selbst, obgleich sie nicht diejenigen sind, welche hier etwas

the service of God, such as is not raised in a similar manner in any other Catholic country. I witnessed these collections in several places, among others in Cork. The tribute was gathered at two entrances – at the principal gate where the poor went into the church, and were obliged to pay a penny each; and at a side door, where the rich entered, and paid as much more as they pleased. At the latter was posted up, in large letters, 'A SILVER COLLECTION IS EXPECTED'; that is to say, you are expected to pay at least sixpence. A priest attended in person to receive the money, and also, as I was told, to produce by his presence a still more effectual impression on the purses of the people. He returned thanks with a bow for every gift that was deposited on the plate. Before the principal door of the church, which was open, and on the steps leading to it, were crowded many poor people and beggars – too poor to pay the required tribute. They lay with folded hands and bended knees upon the stones, and listened for the far-off sounds that reached them from the interior of the church. 'They are satisfied,' said my companion, 'if they but hear the little bell of the assistantof the priest who officiates at the altar; when they have heard that little bell from within, and bowed and crossed themselves, they think they have heard mass, and participated in the worship of God.'

I, and many others who were accustomed to the matter, looked on this scene without perceiving in it anything very disgraceful; but if we examine it narrowly, clearly and sharply with the torch which Christ has placed in our hands, can we find language too strong in which to reprobate a state of things which forces the priest to resort to such measures in order to support his existence? It is said that the incomes of the Catholic priests in Ireland are chiefly derived from these collections, which are censured by the Protestants still more than by the Catholic laity, although the former are not called on to pay anything, but are in reality those by whom this scandal was originated, since it was by the Protestants that the Irish Catholic church was deprived of

bezahlen, wohl aber diejenigen, welche die eigentliche ursprüngliche Veranlassung zu diesem Scandale gaben, da sie der katholischen Geistlichkeit alle anderen Einkünfte entzogen. Die völlig *armen* Irländer sind auf diese Weise fast ganz vom Gottesdienste ausgeschlossen und auf jenes Meßglöckchen reducirt. Hätten sie nicht so viel religiösen Sinn von Haus aus in dem tiefsten Herzensgrunde ihrer Seele, so sähe es wohl höchst schlimm um den Zustand ihres Seelenheiles aus.

Für diejenigen Irländer, welche die alte irische Sprache als ihre Muttersprache betrachten, ist noch schlimmer gesorgt. Denn in der großen Stadt Cork, die in einer Gegend von Irland liegt, wo das Irische noch viel gesprochen wird, wird nur von zwei Predigern in dieser Sprache gepredigt. Und doch ist es wohl eher natürlich, daß die armen Leute das-jenige, was ihnen das Höchste ist, in derjenigen Sprache ausgedrückt zu hören wünschen, welche ihnen die theuerste ist. Noch vor Kurzem richteten die irischen Gefangenen im Corker *County-Gaol* eine Petition an ihren Prediger, daß er ihnen des Sonntags wenigstens zuweilen die Predigt statt in englischer in irischer Sprache halten möchte – so erzählte mir in jenem Gefängnisse der Prediger selbst.

Der Bischof von Cork hat eine der interessantesten Büchersammlungen, die man sehen kann. Dieser gelehrte und fleißige Mann hat sein ganzes Haus in eine Bibliothek verwandelt. Nicht nur seine Wohn- und Speisezimmer hat er in Büchersäle verwandelt, sondern auch in seinem Schlafzimmer hat er jeden benutzbaren Raum mit Büchern ausgefüllt. Seine Bedienten und sogar seine Magd schlafen in kleinen Bücherzimmern. Die Treppen seines Hauses sind auf den Seiten mit Büchern bestellt, und die Corridors, welche die Zimmer verbinden, haben gefüllte Bücherrepositorien an den Seiten. Sogar bis in die Dachstübchen hinauf sind die Bücher aufgestapelt. Seine Bibliothek ist die größte Privatbibliothek, welche in Irland existirt, und es befinden sich in ihr die interessantesten und kostbarsten Werke.

Ich führe dieß nur an, weil ich nicht gewiß bin, ob man überall weiß, daß es unter den katholischen Geistlichen Irlands noch jetzt solche Männer giebt, die mit so außerordentlichem Eifer alle Erscheinungen auf dem Gebiete der Literatur berücksichtigen und sammeln. Es gab eine Zeit, wo Europa um Irland besser Bescheid wußte als um manches

its ancient revenues. The utterly destitute Irish are thus entirely excluded from the worship of God, except what pertains to the tinkling sound of the mass-bell; and were the inmost recesses of their hearts less deeply imbued with religious feeling, the result would be most unfavourable to their spiritual welfare.

Those who deem the ancient Irish language as their mother tongue are still worse provided for. In the great city of Cork – around which Irish is still much spoken – two preachers only deliver sermons in that language; and yet it is very natural that the people should wish to hear what they hold most sacred in the language they love the best. A short time since, as I was informed by the chaplain himself, the prisoners in the Cork County Gaol petitioned him occasionally to preach his sermon in Irish instead of English.

The Roman Catholic bishop of Cork has one of the most interesting collections of books I have anywhere seen. This learned and industrious man has turned his whole house into a library: not only has he converted his sitting-rooms and dining-rooms into book-rooms, but even in his bedrooms every available space is filled with books: his attendants, even his maid-servants, sleep in little libraries; the staircases are lined with books along the walls; and the corridors which lead from room to room have full bookcases at their sides; everywhere books are literally piled up, even to the garrets. This is the largest private library in Ireland, and contains many interesting and costly works.

I mention this because I believe it is not generally known that there are still such men among the Roman Catholic clergy, who regard and collect everything relating to literature with such extraordinary zeal. The time

andere Land und wo von der 'heiligen Insel' (diesen Namen hatte Irland schon im höchsten Alterthume) mehr Licht zu uns ausströmte, als wir der Insel je wieder vergolten haben. [...]
   Die Zeiten haben sich gewaltig verändert. *'Felix Hibernia!'* fällt selbst einem Dichter nicht mehr ein die Insel anzureden. Alle Erzeugnisse der irischen Dichter haben etwas Melancholisches, und Haydn, als ihm ein irisches Musikstück vorgespielt wurde, ohne daß er wußte, woher es käme, sagte, es müsse dieß die Musik eines unglücklichen und unterjochten Volkes sein. Und die großen Geister und Sprößlinge, die aus der Insel hervorgehen, absorbirt alle England in seinem Staatsdienste. Der Litteratur und Gelehrsamkeit wegen gehen jetzt die katholischen Irländer, die erst in neuerer Zeit wieder eine katholische Schule zu Maynooth in ihrem Vaterlande haben, häufig nach dem Continente. Der würdige Prälat von Cork erzählte uns, er selber habe seine Bildung in Frankreich erlangt. Und dieses Land ist es eben, welches die irischen Geistlichen mit besonderer Vorliebe wählen. Es ist sehr häufig und war früher noch häufiger, daß sie dorthin wandern, um die ihnen nöthigen Kenntnisse zu erlangen. Und ich traf selbst zwei Mal auf meiner Wanderung durch Irland arme Aeltern, die mir sagten, daß sie hofften, so viel zu ersparen, um im Stande zu sein, ihren Sohn, der sich dem geistlichen Stande gewidmet, wenn er das gehörige Alter erreicht, zu seiner völligen Ausbildung nach Frankreich zu schicken.
   Nirgends sah ich so viele schwarz beflorte traurige Herren als in Cork, wie man denn überhaupt in keinem Lande mehr Trauer erblickt als in den vereinigten Königreichen. Es kommt dieß theils daher, weil man hier in sehr vielen Fällen Trauer anlegt, wo wir es nicht thun, und dann, weil man sie später als wir abzulegen pflegt. Man trauert für nahe Verwandte Jahre lang. Selbst aber auch für sehr entfernte Anverwandte legt man schwarze Kleidung an. Ja man trauert sogar um Freunde, und was noch mehr ist, es kommen Fälle vor, daß Leute deswegen Trauer anlegen, weil ihre Freunde Trauer haben, selbst wenn sie die hingeschiedenen Lieben derselben gar nicht gekannt haben.
   Die englische Trauer ist länger als die unsrige, dann ist sie auch tiefer. Man geht dabei so weit, daß man nichts Farbiges an sich sehen kann. Alles bis zum Geldbeutel muß schwarz sein. Es giebt Trauerringe,

once was, indeed, when Ireland was better known in Europe than many other lands, and when more light streamed to us from the 'Island of Saints' (as Ireland was anciently designated) than we have ever repaid. [...] But those times are now much changed. This island can no longer be styled, even by a poet, 'Felix Hibernia'! All the productions of Irish poets are somewhat melancholy; and Haydn, when an Irish melody was played before him, without his knowing from what country it came, said that such music must belong to an unhappy and enslaved people. The great and promising spirits which frequently arise in the island are speedily absorbed by England in the various services of the state. For study and literature, the Irish Catholics mostly resort to the continent; but they lately obtained a Roman Catholic seminary at Maynooth, in their fatherland. The worthy prelate of Cork informed me that he had received his education in France, which country is generally preferred by the Irish clergy for acquiring the knowledge requisite for their vocation; and in my wanderings through Ireland I twice met with poor old men who expressed a strong wish to save enough to enable them to send thither their sons (who had devoted themselves to the priesthood) when they reached the proper age.

In no country that I have visited is mourning so general as in the United Kingdom, and nowhere have I seen so many black craped, mourning gentlemen as in Cork. Mourning is not only usual in very many cases where it would not be thought of in Germany, but is also of longer duration. For near relations it continues an entire year; even for very distant relations, or intimate acquaintances, black clothes are worn; and there are cases where people assume the garb of woe merely because it is worn by their friends, although the deceased is utterly unknown to them. In England, during the period allotted to mourning, nothing coloured must be seen about the person. Everything, even to the purse, must be black. They have mourning rings, brooches and earrings;

Trauerbroschen, Trauerohrringe, Traueroblaten, Trauerbriefpapier mit schwarzem Rande etc Bei dem Briefpapier ist der schwarze Rand anfangs sehr breit, wird aber nach und nach schmäler, zuletzt hört er ganz auf, und nur noch mit dem schwarzen Siegellack wird fortgefahren. Auch ist die Trauer für verheirathete und für unverheirathete Personen verschieden. So tragen in Irland wenigstens die Herren, wenn sie dem Begräbnisse eines unverheiratheten Mädchens folgten, einen schwarzen Flor mit weißen Streifen. Auch tragen die Witwen nach dem Tode ihres Mannes eine eigene Witwenhaube, deren Form in ganz England genau bestimmt ist. Bei dem Tode eines Hausherrn oder der Hausfrau versetzt man nicht allein die ganze Dienerschaft, sondern auch die Bewohner der Hütten an der Gränze des Parks auf ein Jahr in tiefe Trauer, so daß ein wahrer Trauermantel über dem ganzen Orte hängt.

Auch ist die Trauer allein nicht bloß in der Kleidung tiefer, sondern die Trauernden nehmen lange an keiner Art von Vergnügung Theil, und man hütet sich sehr, ihren Schmerz mit Besuchen zu unterbrechen. Ich wollte einst Herrn F.... besuchen. 'Sie würden, glaube ich, besser thun, dieß zu unterlassen,' sagte mir Herr P..., 'F.... hat vor einem Jahre seinen jüngsten Sohn verloren, und wir wollen ihn lieber nicht in seinem Schmerze stören.' – Dazu kommt, daß alle die, welche am Morgen bei einem Begräbnisse gewesen sind, den Flor den ganzen Tag über nicht wieder ablegen. Und dieser Begräbnißbegleiter sind immer, besonders in Irland, eine außerordentliche Menge.

'*When they plume a hearse*' (wenn sie einen Leichenwagen mit Federn schmücken), d. h. nach irischer Weise, wenn sie einen Todten haben, so werden zu seinem Begräbniß allen nahen und fernen, selbst die fernsten Freunde eingeladen, und der Wagenzug, der der Leiche folgt, ist gewöhnlich ohne Ende, um so mehr, da auch unterwegs sich noch viele Bekannte oder Unbekannte anschließen. Selbst wenn sie zu Wagen einem Leichenzuge begegnen, lassen sie wohl ihren Kutscher eine Zeit lang dahinter herfahren. Dieß Alles macht den Trauerpomp in Irland überall sehr groß.

Ich sagte oben, daß die Katholiken jetzt mächtiger und reicher und die Protestanten gemäßigter wurden. Es ist dieß auch unzweifelhaft wahr, jedoch nur so weit, daß eine gemäßigte und tolerante Protestantenpartei

black-bordered mourning letter paper, sealed with black wax or wafers. This black border on the paper is at first very broad, but becomes gradually narrower, and at length it entirely disappears, along with the black sealing-wax. There is also a difference, in Ireland at least, between the mourning for married and unmarried persons. In attending the funeral of an unmarried maiden, black crape tied with white ribbons is worn by the gentlemen. At the death of the head of a wealthy family, not only are all the servants, but the inhabitants of every cottage within the bounds of the park, clad in deep mourning for a year, so that a true mantle of sorrow seems to overhang the entire place.

Nor is this mourning confined to dress alone: during its continuance the mourners take no share in any kind of amusement, and people carefully avoid intruding on their grief with visits. Having once expressed a wish to visit an individual, a friend said to me, 'I think it would be better not to do so. F— lost his youngest son a year ago, and we should only disturb his sorrow.' Moreover, those who have been at a funeral in the morning, do not lay aside the crape for the remainder of the day; and the number of persons who attend funerals, especially in Ireland, is very great.

'When they plume a hearse' (as it is expressed in Ireland when a corpse is to be buried) 'all, far and near, even the most distant friends, are invited to the funeral, and the train of carriages which follow the bier seems almost endless, especially as many individuals, friends as well as strangers, are continually joining it on the road. Even when travelling in a carriage, should a funeral be met or overtaken, the travellers permit their coachman to drive after it for some distance. All this makes the pomp of funerals in Ireland everywhere very great.

nie so groß war als jetzt, und daß die Katholiken seit Cromwell's und Wilhelm's III. Zeiten nie auf so gutem Wege waren als nun. Daß im Großen und Ganzen genommen aber einstweilen noch die alten Verhältnisse fortbestehen, hatte ich oft genug Gelegenheit zu bemerken. Mir wurde einige Mal in Irland verboten, meinen Hut so häufig abzunehmen, weil das die *armen* Katholiken thäten. Und ich wohnte in dieser Stadt in einem Wirthshause, dessen Wirth es mit den Protestanten hielt, ein Tory war und nur Protestanten als Gäste bei sich empfing. Ein zweites Hotel der Stadt wurde auf dieselbe Weise ausschließlich von Whigs und Katholiken besucht. Es giebt in mehreren Städten Irlands eben solche protestantische und katholische Wirtshäuser. Ja man hat mir sogar gesagt, daß es Fahrgelegenheiten und Diligencen gäbe, mit denen Protestanten am meisten führen, und andere, welche in der Regel von Katholiken vorgezogen würden.

Die schönen und guten Erfolge, welche die Temperance-Sache über die Heftigkeit und Gewaltthätigkeit des Volkes erlangt hat, darf man zwar beklatschen, aber man muß auch wieder nicht sofort glauben, daß nun schon Alles gewonnen sei. Noch kurz vor meiner Anwesenheit in Cork war eine merkwürdige Gewaltthat so recht im irischen Style verübt worden. Ein Kaufmann hatte mit einem anderen in Compagnie einen Modewaarenladen eröffnet. Da er sich aber nicht mit dem anderen vertragen konnte, so wollte er sich wieder von ihm trennen und ihn mit Geld abfinden, da er zum Besitze des Ladens sich selber berechtigt hielt. Der andere aber glaubte seinerseits, daß er den Besitz des Ladens in Anspruch nehmen und seinen Compagnon mit Geld abfinden könne. Da sich beide nun nicht darüber vereinigen konnten, und da durcheinen Proceß die Sache zu entscheiden in Irland sehr langwierig ist, so rüsteten sich beide zum Kampf. Der eine ging hin und wiegelte eine Partie Volks auf, die mit *shelalas* (den eigenthümlichen gefürchteten irischen Knüppeln) bewaffnet, mit ihm den Laden seines Gegners überfielen und bestürmten. Dieser war zwar nicht ganz unvorbereitet und vertheidigte sich, allein der Angreifer waren zu viele, und der Laden wurde erobert. Nur *ein* Menschenleben ging dabei verloren. Auf solche Weise setzt man sich in Irland also noch jetzt zuweilen in Besitz und Avantage.

I have before remarked, that the Irish Catholics are now more powerful and wealthy, and the Protestants more liberal. This is undoubtedly true, inasmuch as the liberal and tolerant Protestant party was never so great as now; and never, since the times of Cromwell and William III, were the Catholics in so prosperous a state as at present. I had, however, frequent occasion to remark that they still sometimes stand in their old relative positions. I was once recommended not to take off my hat so often, as that was only done by the poor Catholics; and in Cork I lodged at an hotel, the landlord of which was a Protestant and a Tory, and received Protestants only as his guests. Another hotel in the city was, in like manner, exclusively frequented by Whigs and Catholics. In many other towns of Ireland these exclusively Protestant or Catholic hotels are to be found; and I have been told that there are even public conveyances in which Protestants chiefly travel, and others regularly preferred by the Catholics.

Whilst recognising the beneficial influence of the temperance movement on the passions and violence of the people, we must not at the same time imagine that everything is already accomplished. This will be clearly exemplified by the relation of a remarkable deed of violence, which was perpetrated in true Irish style, a very short time before my arrival in Cork. A trader, already engaged in business, had entered into partnership with another individual; but finding that they could not agree, a separation was decided upon. Each party was anxious to buy the other out, and retain possession of the shop. As, however, no satisfactory agreement could be made on the subject (and the arrangement of such matters by process of law is very tedious in Ireland) one of them collected a party of his friends, who, armed with shillelaghs (the terrible Irish cudgel) attacked and stormed his opponent in his shop. The latter was not altogether unprepared, and stoutly defended himself; but the attacking party was too powerful, and the shop fell into their possession. Only *one* man was killed in this affair! But such is the mode by which people in Ireland sometimes obtain possession, even at the present day.

English translation in: J. G. Kohl, Travels in Ireland. *Translated from the German. London: Bruce and Wyld, 1844, pp. 162-88.*

Knut Jongbohn Clement
(1845)

German original in: *Reisen in Irland in historischer, statistischer, politischer und socialer Beziehung.* Kiel: Bünsow, 1845, pp.143-164.

UNGEFEHR 27 DEUTSCHE Meilen oder 124 englische und 96 irische Südwest von Dublin und etwa 11 deutsche [im] Süden von Limerick liegt Cork, die glänzende Haupstadt von Munster. Sie ist, die Lage mitberücksichtigt, die schönste Stadt in Irland. Ihr Haupthandel ist Ausfuhr von Speck, Butter, Vieh u.s.w., und sie ist neben Limerick die wichtigste Seestadt in der Westhälfte Irlands. Sie hat eine Wollen-Factorei, viele Gießereien, ungeheure Kornmühlen am Lee, eine bedeutende Glasfabrik, viele große Brennereien und Brauereien und daneben Pater Mathew, einen schönen Hafen und Kanäle, Schiffswerfte und Segeltuchfabriken, einen bischöflichen Palast, ein großes Zuchthaus (für die ganze Landschaft), eine sogenannte Institution mit Bibliothek und Museum, das modernste Seebad (Cove) in Irland, ein ganz großstädtisches Leben, ungeheuer viele Fuhrwerke, prächtige Häuser, jammervolle Bettler und einige reiche Kaufleute.

Den Hang zum Großthun und Prahlen haben die Kelten von jeher mit einander gemein gehabt. Eine Probe davon ist die Arthussage, das *non plus ultra* keltischer Großprahlerei. Auch die Irländer haben eine sehr starke Neigung dazu, und sie macht sich vielfach bemerklich. Daß der Irländer gern den Großen spielt, merkt man auch an dem Dubliner und Corker Kaufmann, welcher sich Fuhrwerk und Landhaus anschafft, sobald er etwas mehr erworben hat, als er auf einmal verzehren kann. Dann setzt er sich ruhig nieder, wie gewöhnlich auch in unserm Continent geschieht, und lebt von seinem Gelde. Dann aber fängt der Engländer oder Schotte erst recht an, sein Geschäft im Großen zu treiben. Wer in Cork so weit gekommen ist, daß er reiten, jagen, am Comtoir sein Pferd besteigen, und dann auf seiner Villa den Sommer verleben kann, der ist in Cork ein vornehmer Mann. Diese

Knut Jungbohn Clement
(1845)

(Character of Cork people – appearance of the city – Cork hotels – intelligence of Cork people – politics – visit to the Protestant bishop of Cork)

THE CITY of Cork is approximately 27 German miles (that is about 124 Imperial or 96 Irish miles) southwest of Dublin and just under 11 German miles south of Limerick. The glamorous capital of Munster, it is perhaps the most beautiful town in Ireland, not least because of its location. Its chief source of revenue is the export of bacon, butter, cattle etc., and it is the most important trading port in the western half of Ireland. It also has a woollen mill, several foundries, some huge grain mills on the River Lee, as well as important glassworks. It may have Fr Matthew, yet it also possesses a number of breweries and distilleries. The harbour is quite impressive, as are the various canals, the shipyards and sail-making businesses. Furthermore, there's the Bishop's palace, a huge gaol (serving the whole county), a so-called 'Institute', complete with a library and museum, and the most modern seaside resort in all of Ireland (Cove). With its prodigious number of vehicles, palatial buildings and the most miserable beggars living side by side with some extremely wealthy merchants, it has the ambiance of a big city.

A common trait shared by all Celtic peoples is their penchant for bragging, as is exemplified in the legend of King Arthur, which must surely be the epitome of Celtic boastfulness. The Irish are no exception, and their inclination to show off surfaces in many different ways, such as a tendency among Dublin and Cork merchants to acquire country houses and carriages as soon as they have a few pennies to spare. Scarcely have they made some money than they retire from business to live off their profits, just as people are wont to do on the continent. A Scot or an Englishman on the other hand would avail of such an opportunity to expand his operations. Those who can afford to ride home from the office on horseback and spend the summer on a country retreat,

Beschränktheit des Geistes ist dem irischen Nationalcharacter nicht ausschließlich eigen, sondern zieht ihre reichliche Nahrung aus Staatsformen, welche Ländern nicht entsprechen. Aber doch ist der keltische Mensch mehr als der ursprünglich germanische zur Großthuerei geneigt. In unfreien Ländern ist der Mensch am meisten geneigt, groß zu thun oder sich wichtig zu machen, und die Ursache davon ist ein Übel, dem er nicht entgehen zu können scheint. Nebst dem Menschen der Hauptstadt Irlands ist der Bewohner Corks der prunksüchtigste im Lande. Alles will glänzen, reiten, fahren, jagen, der Irländer überhaupt ist auf Pferde und Jagd verpicht.

Cork ist reizend belegen, und von Cork her strömt groß wie eine Seebucht der stattliche Lee an seinem lieblichschwellenden und mit zahlreichen prangenden Villas und Landhäuschen wie mit Kunstblumen besäeten Ufern 2¹/₂ deutsche Meilen weit nach seinem hübschen Cove hinab, dem vielbesuchten und modernsten Badeort, und weil die Irländer außerdem viel vergnügungssüchtiger sind, als die Bewohner Großbrittaniens, so sieht man in den Sommertagen Alles auf und an dem Strom zwischen dem prächtigen Cork und seinem reizenden Cove mit Lustbooten und Staatswagen bedeckt. In solchem Galla tritt Cork auf, und doch ist Cork so voll von schmutzigen Gassen, Ecken und Winkeln, Menschen und Eseln, Lappen und Lumpen. Es stank und stob in Cork entsetzlich, als ich da war. Die Stadt sei reich, heißt es dort, und doch ist es auf allen Straßen voll von Bettlern und bedauernswürdigen Eckenstehern ohne Arbeit.

Die Städte auf dem europäischen Continent machen sich bemerkbar durch ihre Thürme, manche durch viele und hohe Thürme, welche das Ansehen haben, als möchten sie über halb Europa hin gesehen werden. Die großbrittanischen Städte zeichnen sich eben nicht durch Thürme aus, wohl aber durch thurmhohe Denksäulen, deren Zahl so groß ist, daß man an ihre[n] denkwürdigen Erinnerungen verzweifelt. Das Säulenwesen dieser Art hat sich von England aus auch nach Irland verpflanzt. Cork, welches herrlich liegt auf einem sehr unebenen Boden, hier am Strome, dort in hohen Bäumen, bald hoch, bald niedrig, ist im Thurmbau recht bescheiden, obwol es, seiner eigenthümlichen Gestalt sich bewußt, da keine Straße der anderen gleicht und fast kein Haus dem anderen, hübscher sein will in der Nähe, wie von Ferne, als es wirklich

indulging in equestrian sports and in the hunt, are revered as gentlemen by the citizenry of Cork. This kind of narrow-mindedness is not specific to the Irish, but rather comes about as a direct result of inadequate forms of government. Having said that, I would still argue that the Celtic peoples are more prone to bragging than the genuinely Germanic ones. The need to exaggerate and to boast is more commonly encountered in oppressed nations, and it is triggered by an ill that few people seem immune to. The citizens of Cork represent the most pompous class of Irishmen, such as are to be found in the capital. They crave glamour, and they all want to go a-hunting or a-riding, either on horseback or in carriages. The Irish generally have a great passion for horses and for hunting.

Set on the gently flowing River Lee, its banks planted with stately mansions and country homes that are as pretty to behold as artificial flowers, the environs of Cork city are truly charming. As it journeys 2½ German miles towards the neat little town of Cobh, the portly river, which is almost as big as a fjord, comes alive with pleasure boats; for, unlike the British, the Irish have an irrepressible urge to spend the summer months carousing. During the season, the road from the magnificent city of Cork to Cobh bustles with carriage upon carriage of revellers, anxious to make merry in Ireland's most fashionable seaside resort. Such are the decadent allures of Cork, and yet it is full of rags and scraps, grimy nooks and crannies, not to mention filthy laneways crawling with paupers and shabby donkeys. During my stay there, I had to endure lots of dust and stench, and although the city is reportedly a wealthy place, its streets were full of beggars and the most pathetic loafers without employ.

The cities of continental Europe are conspicuous by their many tall spires, some of which appear as though they are to be visible across half of Europe. The British cities mostly make do without spires, and in their stead one encounters such a vast number of towering memorial pillars that one cannot help wondering if the initial cause of their erection merits any remembrance at all. Naturally enough, this British tradition of pillar building has been carried over into Ireland. Built on hilly terrain ranging from soft riverbanks to wild wooded slopes, Cork does not require spectacular spires to make an impression, but I should add that the city's beautiful setting has induced its architects to indulge their vanity, for

ist, es hat nur ein paar Thürme und ist doch beinahe so groß als Hamburg. Aber die ganze Stadt rauscht und prasselt von wilden klappernden Karren, diesen oft einspännigen, echt irischen und vielleicht urkeltischen Nationalwagen, auf welchen man zweireihig sitzt, beide Reihen von einander abgewendet, und mit dem Rücken an den Bagagekasten angelehnt, welcher der Länge nach die Karre durchschneidet und manchmal auch Menschen zur Bagage hat, unten aber die Füße festgestellt, während man vorn ohne Halt und darum in größerer Gefahr ist beim Umwerfen. Noch außer seinen unzähligen herrschaftlichen Fuhrwerken soll Cork mehrere hundert von solchen Lohnwagen besitzen, und wer weiß wie ungeheuer viele Dublin hat, wo der Fußgänger oft garnicht über eine Straße kommen kann, wenn er auch schnell liefe [...] Dublin ist glänzend und arm, vielbewegt und geschäftslos, gelehrt und unwissend, voll von Leben und dennoch todt. Etwas besser ist Cork. Wer Cork und Dublin mit unparteiischen Augen gesehen hat, wird derselben Meinung sein.

Vor Engeln und vor Kronen (*Angel-Inns* und *Crown-Hotels*) hat mir auf meinen Reisen in Großbrittanien und Irland oft gegraut. Auch zu Cork gerieth ich in das *Crown-Hotel*. Bei meiner Ankunft vor diesem Hotel ward die Kutsche von hundert zerlumpten Personen umringt. Sie rissen und schlugen sich um etwas, wovon ich kaum wußte was, merkte aber bald, daß es mein alter Koffer war, der einsam und hoch auf der Kutsche stand. Alle erwarteten mit eifrigen Fäusten und Augen seine Niederkunft. Zehn zugleich griffen zu, als er herankam, und ich dachte, nun zerfetzen sie ihn. Da ist keine Polizei unter den wilden Massen, allein man hat Mitleid mit so armem Volk, welches des Lebens Last bitter trägt. Ein starker Kerl ward endlich der Beute allein habhaft und stieß brüllend und zuweilen mit den Fäusten ausschlagend damit fort durchs Gedräng hindurch wie ein Stier. Ich sprang alsbald ihm nach, da ich nicht wußte, wohin sein Curs gerichtet sei, glücklicherweise der 'Krone' nicht vorbei, er schoß zur Thür hinein, schmiß

there's hardly a house in Cork that resembles the next. Each street is unique in character, and everything is calculated to look more imposing than it actually is, either from afar or at close quarters. As for spires there are but a few, though the city is almost as big as Hamburg. The whole place is shaking with the mad roar of those rickety one-horse contraptions that may well have been the national mode of transport since the days of the ancient Celts. They consist of two benches mounted back-to-back and separated by a luggage box running the length of the vehicle which is often employed to carry extra passengers. Except for a footrest, there is nothing to support or protect the travellers should the car topple over. On top of scores upon scores of private carriages, Cork is said to possess several hundred omnibuses of this kind, and who knows how many are to be found in Dublin, where a man cannot cross the street at any pace for fear of being flattened by one of the thousands of carriages and hackneys thundering along at full speed. [...] Dublin is glamorous yet poor, always in motion yet without industry, learned yet ignorant, lively yet dead. Cork is somewhat better. Those who have observed both Dublin and Cork with unbiased eyes will no doubt be of the same opinion.

On my travels through Britain and Ireland, the notion of angels and of crowns often made me shudder with disgust. I'm talking of the famous 'Crown Hotels' and 'Angel Inns'. Upon arriving at Cork, I once again ended up in a Crown Hotel. As I alighted in front of the hotel, my carriage was immediately surrounded by hundreds of ragged persons, and there was a great tussle and fighting over something which I failed at first to make out, until I realised that the whole commotion concerned my old suitcase, sitting lone and forlorn high on top of the coach roof. With keen eyes and ready fists, they awaited its descent, and when it arrived no less than ten people lunged for it at once, and I was sure it would be ripped to pieces. There are no police to be seen about those wild hordes, but the burdensome existence these poor people are condemned to lead cannot fail to rouse one's pity. At last, a strong looking young lad made off with the booty and pushed his way through the crowd, occasionally wielding his fists and roaring like a bull. I scampered after him, for I wasn't sure whither he was bound, and found to my relief that he was indeedheading for the 'Crown'. Having dumped the suitcase in the foyer,

den Koffer hin, und stand nun da vor mir so grade wie eine Mauer und forderte Zahlung. Das war der Einzug in[s] *Crown Hotel*. Hier war man wieder wie gewöhnlich, in allen Dingen unwissend. Die Unwissenheit geht durch das ganze Volk hindurch. Des *Waiters* (Aufwärters) Antworten waren die alten hergebrachten: 'Ich weiß es nicht.' 'Das kann ich nicht sagen.' 'Das mag sein.' 'Das ist möglich.' 'Ich will mich erkundigen.' '*Yes Sir.*' '*No Sir.*' Und doch lebt man hier unter einer Krone. Da muß einem wohl das *damn* auf die Zunge kommen. '*Waiter!* Wieviele Einwohner hat Cork?' 'Das kann ich Ihnen nicht sagen, Sir.' 'Warum nicht?' 'Ich habe nie daran gedacht.' 'Woher sind sie gebürtig?' 'Aus dieser Stadt.' 'Aus dieser Stadt?' '*Yes Sir.*' 'Schämen Sie sich.'

Ich hatte ein Empfehlungsschreiben von einer Freundin in Dublin an ihre Schwester, welche auf Vosterberg bei Cork wohnt. Hundertmal habe ich gefragt, und keiner wußte von diesem alten wohlbekannten Orte. So ging es mir auch in Limerick, wo Hunderte und Tausende, welche in der Stadt leben und geboren sind, nicht einmal wissen, daß hier ein Dom ist, obwol sie den Thurm tagtäglich mit den Augen sehen können. Endlich traf ich einen Krüppel, der mit Zuversicht behauptete, er könne mir den Weg nach Vosterberg zeigen. Wir gingen also aus der Stadt. 'So! Nun grad aus etwa eine *Mile*, dann rechts durch den Thorweg gegangen.' Gut, dann werd' ichs wohl finden. Der kleine Mensch war nicht aus Gefälligkeit mitgegangen, sondern aus Eigennutz. Man verzeiht solchen armen Irländern das, vor allem einem Krüppel, dessen Lumpen bei jedem Schritt gegen seine Krücken aufschlugen. Ich gab ihm 3d (2½ Sgr.), womit er nicht zufrieden war, denn er dankte nicht und machte ein saures Gesicht. Ich kam am Thorweg an. Der Eingang zum Garten war verschlossen. Ich läutete. Eine alte Frau that auf. 'Wohnt hier Mrs R?' 'O yes.' 'Heißt dieser Ort Vosterberg?' '*No Sir, it is called Treamore.*' (Nein Sir, er heißt Treamore.) 'Treamore!' '*Yes Sir.*' Ich ging zu dem Hause und traf sehr freundliche Leute hier, die Söhne eines reichen Kaufmannes. Sie bedeuteten mir, ich sei nicht am rechten Orte, Vosterberg liege in der entgegengesetzten Richtung von Cork. So war ich denn über eine halbe deutsche Meile von Vosterberg und mußte unverrichteter Sache wieder zu meinem Logis zurück. '*Waiter!* Vosterberg klingt dänisch.' '*Yes Sir.*' 'Wissen Sie, wie Dänisch klingt?' '*No Sir.*' 'Hat man hier

he suddenly loomed before me like a wall and demanded pay. Such was my entry at the 'Crown Hotel'. The staff were utterly uninformed as usual. The entire populace seems to be without any education whatsoever, and the waiter treated me to the well-worn replies of, 'I don't know', 'I couldn't tell you', 'That may be true', 'It's possible', 'I'll endeavour to find out', 'Yes, Sir' and 'No, Sir' – and yet my lodgings were emblazoned with a crown! Small wonder I could not suppress the odd 'damn!' 'Waiter! How many citizens has Cork?' – 'I couldn't tell you sir!' – 'Why ever not?' – 'I've never thought about it!' – 'Where are you from then?' – 'I was born in this very city.' – 'This city!' – 'Yes Sir!' – 'Shame on you!'

I had in my possession a letter of introduction from a lady friend in Dublin, addressed to her sister who lived at Vosterberg near Cork. I must have asked about a hundred people, but nobody could tell me where the well-known place in question was to be found. I had the same experience in Limerick, where hundreds and perhaps thousands of natives are ignorant of the fact that their town boasts a cathedral, although they have its spire in front of their very eyes each and every day! Finally, I came across a cripple who was confident he could direct me to Vosterberg, and thus I followed him out of town. 'Now,' said he, 'Keep on straight for about a mile and then go through the gateway on your right.' Well, in that case I will surely find it. However, the little fellow had not acted out of kindness but with selfish designs, which are forgivable enough in an Irish beggar, especially a cripple whose rags are flapping against his crutches with every step he takes. I gave him 3d (equivalent to $2^1/_2$ Sgr.), but he did not seem to think it adequate, for he scowled and would not thank me. When I arrived at the garden gate, I found it locked. I rang the bell and an old woman answered it. 'Does Mrs R. reside here?' – 'Oh yes.' – 'Is this Vosterberg?' –' No, Sir, it is called Treamore.' – 'Treamore?' – 'Yes, Sir!' I walked up to the house and was greeted with great civility by the sons of a wealthy merchant, only to be told that I'd come to the wrong place and that Vosterberg was on the opposite side of Cork. So here I was, half a German mile away from my destination, and I had to return to my lodgings, without having achieved my objective. – 'Waiter, Vosterberg has a Danish ring to it!' – 'Yes, Sir.' – 'Are you familiar with the sound of Danish?' – 'No, Sir.' – 'Do you have such things as points of

auch Himmelsgegenden in Cork?' *'No Sir.'* 'Ich meine Westen, Osten, Norden, Süden.' *'Yes Sir.'* 'Oder hat man so viele als man will?' *'Yes Sir.'* 'Vosterberg liegt wohl nach allen Himmelsgegenden?' 'Nach allen Sir?' 'Ja nach allen.' 'No Sir, es liegt noch eine Strecke von hier.' *'Waiter!* Wie heißt ein Krüppel auf Irisch?' 'Auf Irisch Sir?' 'Irisch kann ich nicht.' 'Und sind ein Irländer?' 'Yes Sir, so halb und halb.' 'Und das in Cork?' *'Yes Sir.'* Das war zum Verzweifeln. Ich dachte oben wieder an den Krüppel. Ein solcher heißt auf Irisch *bacach* oder *creimjoch*, als hätte man beim ersteren Namen eine Bagage zu suchen und beim letzteren ein Joch.

In dieser 'Krone' lernte ich zwei eifrige Alterthumsfreunde kennen, Mr. Abraham Abell und Mr. John Windele aus Cork. Sie forschen sehr nach den alten irischen Buchstaben, welche man *Ogham* (sprich Ahm) nennt. Es sind nichts als Striche und Puncte. Eine zweite Bekanntschaft, welche ich hier machte, war ein junger Lord Gambier, ein naher Blutsfreund von dem in Dänemark wohlbekannten Lord Gambier, wenn ich nicht irre, war es sein Sohn. Er bot mir eine Cigarre an, sein Benehmen im Hause war artig.

Aber wenn man nun so allein da sitzt in solchem Hause, Allen wildfremd, mitten in der öden Zeitungsstille, in dem kalten Wirtshausleben, wo alle Gastfreundschaft ausgezogen ist, so kann das für einen Beobachter anziehend werden, welcher eine Ferienreise macht, auf langen Reisen wird es einem ekelhaft. Alles steif wie Puppen, stumm wie Bildsäulen. Da sitzt man bei den Zeitungen stundenlang, ohne aufzusehen, und liest sich ein ganzes Irland in den Kopf hinein, andre schreiben Briefe, Rechnungen, und was zum Zahlenleben mehr gehört, andre essen, andre trinken, andre schlafen oder schlummern, andre sehen nur, andre hören nicht einmal, weil nichts zu hören ist. Alle heißen Gentlemen. Die einzige Maschine, welche sich hier bewegt, hin und her, auf und nieder, aus und ein, rasch und unwandelbar, ohn' Ende, ist der stumme Waiter mit saurer Miene. So währt es bis zur Mitternacht vom frühen Morgen an. Und wenn die Gentlemen nun fertig sind zur Rück- oder Weiterreise, so stehen sie da mitten im Zimmer, stumm wie bei der Zeitung. Der Beutel wird ausgezogen, es wird geschellt. Der Waiter fliegt heran. *'The Bill* (Rechnung), *Waiter.'* *'Yes, Sir.'* Die Bill kommt. Flüchtig wird hineingeblickt, denn das ist die *rule* (Weise), gezahlt, und nebenbei dem Waiter auch das Seine zwischen

the compass here in Cork?' – 'No, Sir.' – 'I mean, west, east, north & south?' – 'Yes, Sir.' – 'Or do you have as many as you like?' – 'Yes, Sir.' – 'It seems Vosterberg lies in every direction!' – 'In every direction, Sir?' 'Yes, in every direction!' – 'No Sir, it's a fair stretch away.' – 'Waiter, what's the Irish for "cripple"?' – 'The Irish? I can't speak Irish.' – 'But you are Irish, are you not?' – 'Yes, Sir, half and half.' – 'And this in Cork!' – 'Yes, Sir.' It was enough to drive a man demented. My thoughts strayed back to the cripple. The Irish for cripple is *bacach* or *creimjoch* [*creimeach*], the former sounding more as if it had something to do with baggage, while the latter with a yoke [Germ. *Joch*].

At the 'Crown' I made the acquaintance of two keen antiquarians, a Mr Abraham Abell and a Mr John Windele of Cork, who are doing extensive research on those ancient Irish letters called 'Ogham', which consist of nothing but dots and straight lines. Furthermore, I met a young Lord Gambier, a blood relative of the elder Lord Gambier, who is well known in Denmark. If I'm not very much mistaken, this was his son. He offered me a cigar, and his behaviour in the house was very civil.

However, it is not much fun staying in such cold, inhospitable establishments as a complete stranger and having to sit there in dank silence, with nothing to be heard but the dull rustle of newspapers. This ambiance might seem intriguing to those on a brief holiday, but when you're on a protracted journey it eventually becomes a bane. Everyone stiff as dressmaker's dolls, and dead silent. So one starts to read the paper and to cram one's skull with Irish affairs. Some busy themselves with bills, letters and other forms of paper work; others may be seen eating, drinking or sleeping, and a few may be observed just staring blankly into space, there being nothing to listen to. And such people are known as Gentlemen! The only thing with any visible life in it is the surly dumb waiter, forever pacing back and forth like some grumpy clockwork toy. That's the routine from morning till midnight, and whenever a gentleman is ready to continue on his way, he will position himself in the foyer in perfect paper-reading silence. Flicking out his wallet he will ring the bell, and a waiter will come running swiftly to his assistance. – 'Waiter, the bill.' – 'Yes, Sir'. The bill will be brought and, after a fleeting glimpse at the figures, as is the 'rule', the guest will then settle, handing the waiter

zwei Fingern seitwärts hingereicht. Das alles gehört mit zur *rule*, und kein Wort wird häufiger, vor allen von Wirthen, gebraucht, als *rule*, und das linkische Irland hat auch manches Stücklein von der englischen rule abgekriegt, sieht aber darin aus wie in einem fremden abgetragenen Rock, welcher zu lang in den Ärmeln und zu weit am Leibe ist. Wenn du in Großbrittanien und auch in Irland, welches England nachbetet, gegen hohe Forderungen Einwendungen machst, so heißt es jedesmal -als ob alle Wirthe des Reichs den Satz auswendig gelernt hätten: '*It is the general rule, every Gentleman pays so much*' (Es ist ganz in der Regel, jeder Gentleman zahlt so viel.) Wer aber nicht so viel zahlen will, ist kein Gentleman. In England, und sogar in Irland, sind mehr Gentlemen als bei uns Fräulein, welches auf gut Deutsch Jungfer heißt. Und dennoch ist es ein englisches Sprichwort: '*It is nature and not art that makes the Gentleman*', (Es ist die Natur und nicht die Kunst, welche den Gentleman macht).

Rauchen im Wirthshause ist nicht die *general rule*, und in *Crowns* und *Angels* und dergleichen Instituten mehr ist es ganz dagegen, außer in aparten Rauchzimmerchen. Eine Cigarre kostet mindestens 3 Schilling. Die Lord Gambier'sche war verraucht unter einer kurzen anziehenden Unterhaltung. Was nun zu thun? Einen Augenblick in die stille Lesewelt. Da lag ein Corker Blatt *The Constitution* auf dem Tisch. Ich nahm es in die Hand und las aus einem Auszug aus den *Times* Folgendes:

[*original quote in English, see page 121, 123*]

Laß uns sehen, wie die verschiedenen Kräfte, wodurch die Gesellschaft zusammengehalten und geleitet werden soll, jetzt zu einander stehen in Irland. Eigenthum – Erziehung – Geisteskraft – Anhänglichkeit an der brittischen Alleinherrschaft – Eifer für religiöse Freiheit – Ordnungsliebe – Alles was politische Einsicht und allgemeine Gesittung begründet, ist auf Seiten des protestantischen Volks jenes Landes zu finden. Bei der entgegengesetzten Partei finden sich wilde Haufen – dicke, tiefe, undurchdringliche Unwissenheit – die ärgste Armuth – greuliche Leidenschaften – wüthende Gewaltthätigkeit – Verachtung gegen das Gesetz – Unbekümmerniß um die Zukunft – ein Glaube, welcher die Menge in Hörigkeitsverhältniß zu einer

his due sideways between two fingers. This is all part of the 'rule', and everything in England is subject to the 'rule'. In fact, 'rule' seems to be one of the most common words in the English language, especially for innkeepers. Clumsy old Ireland is included in the English 'rule', but it looks like a worn coat on her, the sleeves too long and a wide fit. Whosoever dares to dispute an exorbitant bill while travelling in England or Ireland (parotting England), will invariably be told 'It is the general rule. Every gentleman pays so much!', as though all the innkeepers on the British Isles had learnt that formula off by heart! If you're not prepared to pay the sum in question, you cannot be considered a gentleman. There are more gentlemen in England and indeed Ireland than there are maidens, i.e. virgins, at home and yet, according to an English proverb 'It is nature and not art that makes the gentleman'.

At most inns, smoking goes against the general rule, and hotels in the 'Crown' or 'Angel' category will not tolerate it, except in designated smoking salons. A single Cigar costs at least 3 Shill. Lord Gambier's cigar lasted the length of a short, if pleasant, conversation, and thereafter I could not think of anything better to do with myself than to return to the silent world of reading. There was a Cork paper lying on the table called *The Constitution*. I picked it up and read the following extract from *The Times*:

Let us see how the several forces by which society ought to be held together and directed, now stand towards each other in Ireland. Property – education – power of mind – attachment to the British monarchy – zeal of religious liberty – love of order – whatever constitutes political intelligence or general civilisation, are to be found on the Protestant side of the people of that country. With the opposite party are to be found brute numbers – thick, deep, impenetrable ignorance – extreme poverty – atrocious passions – outrageous violence – contempt for law – recklessness of the future – a creed which-places the multitude in vassalage to a body of well organised, artful and aspiring teachers, who regard the Protestant state no otherwise

Gesammtschaft von wohl organisirten, listigen und emporstreben-
den Lehrmeistern stellt, welche den protestanti schen Staat für
nichts Anderes als für einen Feind ansehen, mit welchem ihre
Interessen, wenn nicht ihre Pflichten, sie verbindlich machen,
ewigen Krieg zu führen, bis sie am Ende seine Mittel ganz bewältigt
und sich selbst zugewandt haben werden.

Die Worte hat ein Tory geschrieben. Doch es sind nicht allein torystische
Worte, sondern überhaupt englische, die meisten Engländer werden so
sprechen. Und es ist im Ganzen Wahrheit darin. Mit dem Glauben hat es
wohl seine Richtigkeit, mit allem Übrigen mehr oder weniger auch. Die
wilden Haufen sind da, eine solche Unwissenheit sicherlich, jene Armuth,
jene Leidenschaften, jene Gewalthswuth, jene Gesezverachtung, jene
Sorglosigkeit, Alles ist da in Irland. Die Priester wirken im conse-
quentesten Zusammenhalten, das ist der erstes Vorsatz des Papstthums vor
der protestantischen Kirche, sie sind listig und viel listiger, als der protestantische Klerus, sie streben immerdar nach Oberherrlichkeit, und so ist es
in der römisch-katholischen Welt immer gewesen. Aber dieses Lob auf der
einen Seite und dieser Vorwurf auf der anderen werden ohne
Berücksichtigung der Verhältnisse einseitig. Das Eigenthum in Irland ist
zwar auf Seiten der protestantischen Macht, wie es aber erworben war, ist
bekannt genug, und wer das zeitliche Vermögen hat, kann auch leicht
erziehen; unter einem Volk von Bettlern, dem Hab und Gut genommen,
ist wenig Erziehung möglich. Die Geisteskraft geht unter, wo das Volk in
Dürftigkeit, Schmutz und Läusen vergeht. Übrigens ist dem Irländer, den
der Engländer *stupid* nennt, und welcher gar zu oft auch stupid genug ist,
Geistesanlage nicht völlig abzusprechen, und einzelne Irländer, wenn
freilich nicht immer von reinkeltischem Blut, haben große Geisteskraft
bewiesen. Übrigens ist Geist vorzugsweise dem Germanen eigen, und der
Kelt ist wenig geschickt, sich Eigenthum zu erwerben und das erworbene
zu erhalten. Anhänglich an die Monarchie Englands werden diejenigen
immer sein, welche in Besitz irländischen Eigenthums gekommen sind,
solange diese politische Tugend nicht politisch gefährlich ist. In
Anhänglichkeit an der [*sic*] brittischen Alleinherrschaft hat der eigentliche
Irländer im Ganzen weder Trieb noch Veranlassung. Religiöse Freiheit

than as a foe against whom their interests, if not their duties, bind them to wage everlasting warfare, until they shall have finally overturned and transferred its resources to themselves.

These words were penned by a Tory, but the views expressed therein are typical not just of Tory attitude, but of English opinion in general. Most Englishmen would say exactly the same thing, and they have a point, particularly in relation to the religious issues, but also in a broader sense: everything mentioned above, be it the brute numbers, the undeniable ignorance, the poverty, the atrocious passions, the outrageous violence, contempt of the law and recklessness – all these things are indeed to be met with in Ireland. The priests work closely together in perfect collusion. In this regard the Protestant church stands no chance against Papism, for in their eternal quest for worldly power, the Catholic clergy are far more astute and cunning than any Protestant minister. These are the ways of the Roman world, and that is unlikely ever to change. Still, such damning praise would be rather one-sided without taking into consideration the mitigating circumstances. The Protestants may own most of the property, but we are all aware of how they got hold of it in the first place. Those who possess material wealth may extol the virtues of education as much as they please, but it is not so easy to instruct a nation of paupers who have had everything taken away from them. The intellect cannot thrive amongst the needy, who must put up with filth and lice throughout their lives, and while it is true that many Irish people are as stupid and ignorant as the English will have them, some display considerable mental faculties. Ireland has, in fact, produced a few men of great genius, but some of them clearly do not have purely Celtic ancestry. On the whole, however, true genius and wit is more commonly to be met with among Germans. The Celts on the other hand find it hard to acquire property and struggle to retain it. Those who have taken possession of Irish property will always be attached to the English monarchy, so long as such political diligence does not pose a political threat to their existence. The indigenous Irish as such have no desire to oblige the Crown, and why should they? One cannot expect papists to embrace religious freedom, nor can one hope to foster a love of order, where chaos and mayhem

läßt sich bei einem papistischen Volk nicht erwarten, und Ordnungsliebe noch weniger da, wo Alles aus den Fugen geraten ist. Die Wildheit und halbspanische Art liegt schon in dem irischen Nationalcharakter; der römische Glaube als verderblicher Glaube der großen Masse in seiner untergeordneten Stellung zu dem herrschenden oder quasi-herrschenden und der Haß gegen die Engländer macht die Irländer noch wilder, leidenschaftlicher und wüthender. Etwas sorgloses und Gedankenloses liegt zwar in der irischen Natur, allein diese Unbekümmerniß um das Künftige ist häufig Muthlosigkeit. Die Lust vergeht dem Menschen, wenn er sieht, daß seine Mühe ihm nichts hilft, daß er nicht weiter kommt, als eben seinen Hunger stillt und auch das nicht einmal. Ein träges und schlenderndes Volk, welches durch fremde Ungerechtigkeit bis auf das Hemd ausgezogen ward, wird auch dieses verlieren. Und nun die Verachtung gegen das Gesez, welche an den Irländern getadelt wird. Man hat ihnen ihre eigenen Rechte gewaltsam entrissen und fremde aufgedrängt. [...]

Der Irrweg mit dem Krüppel verdarb mir vieles, denn in der Zwischenzeit war ich vom Lord Bischof von Cork, den ich den Morgen, als ich Besuch im Palais machte, nicht getroffen hatte, zu Tafel geladen worden. Ich konnte leider die Einladung nicht annehmen, weil ich noch immer nicht auf Vosterberg gewesen. Sie lautete so: der Bischof bedaure nicht zu Hause gewesen zu sein, als ich ihn mit meinem Besuch beehrt. Im Fall meine Essenszeit heute frei stände, sollte es den Bischof sehr verpflichten, wenn ich um halb 7 im Palais mein Mahl hielte. Vom Crown Hotel war ich nach Lloyds Hotel gezogen, und hier war der Brief abgegeben worden. Sobald man im Palais erfahren, daß ich nicht zu Tisch käme, erschien – so artig ist man gegen den Reisenden – eine zweite Einladung von der Lady folgenden Inhalts: der Bischof von Cork und sie entbieten ihre Grüße und bedauern so unglücklich zu sein, mich vor meiner Dinnerstunde nicht angetroffen zu haben; vielleicht aber, da des Bischofs Zeit eine so späte sei, als halb 7, könnte ich ihnen doch noch den Gefallen erweisen, dann hinzu[zu]kommen und ein *Lookeron* (Zuschauer am Tisch) zu werden, oder falls solches unbequem sein sollte, der Lady darin zu willfahren, daß ich ihr das Vergnügen machte, mich beim Kaffe im Palais zu sehen um halb 9 Uhr. Palais, Cork, Sept. 27. So etwas abzuschlagen, war unmöglich. Ich ging also hin.

rule supreme. Wildness, combined with quasi-Spanish intensity, are an integral part of the Irish national psyche; the Roman religion of the masses becomes particularly destructive when subordinated to the powers that be or at least purport to be. This only serves to render the Irish even more furious and emotive, and, on top of everything else, it keeps their hatred of all things English burning bright. While it is true that the Irish are inclined to be a trifle careless and unheeding of their destiny, at least some of these allures may be put down to utter discouragement. If he sees all his endeavours come to nought, and if his efforts barely suffice to ward off hunger, man must lose heart. Stripped down to their last shirt by foreign injustice, a cumbersome, slothful people such as these eventually stand to lose even this last shred of human dignity. As for the much-vaunted lawlessness the Irish stand accused of, one should bear in mind that they were forcefully deprived of their own laws, henceforth being expected to abide by foreign legislation which had been imposed upon them against their will. [...]

My fool's errant at the side of the cripple spoilt much of the day, for in the meantime I had been invited to dine with the Lord Bishop of Cork who had not been at home when I'd called at his palace that morning. Unfortunately, I was unable to accept the invitation because I still had not been to Vosterberg. The bishop's invitation read: The bishop regretted not having been at home when I'd honoured him with my visit. Should I happen to be free at mealtime, he, the bishop, would be much obliged if I would care to come and dine at the palace at half past six o'clock. I had since moved from the *Crown* to Lloyd's Hotel and the invitation had been delivered to the former address. However, once it was known at the palace that I would not come to dinner that night, I was promptly issued a new invitation by the lady of the house, which goes to show the great kindness with which travellers are treated. It read: The Bishop of Cork and her Ladyship send their regards, and regret very much not finding me before my dinner time. Since it was so late now, half past six, I might still favour them with my visit and be a 'looker Das on' at table. Should this arrangement be disagreeable to me, however, I could always do her Ladyship the pleasure of coming to coffee at 9 o'clock. [Bishop's] Palace, Cork, Sept. 27th. This was an offer I could hardly refuse and I decided to go.

I was gracefully received into sumptuous surroundings by very dear

war ein höchst feiner und angenehmer Empfang in einem glänzenden Local von allerliebsten Leuten. Die Gesellschaft war nicht groß, aber anziehend, die Lady ein sehr gebildetes Weib bei ansprechendem Aeußeren und feinem ungekünstelten Wesen, der Lord Bischof ein stiller Mann von ernstem anscheinlich schottischem Character (auch sein Name, welcher Kyle heißt, weist auf Schottland hin), er sprach wenig. Ohne Auszeichnung ist er nicht Bischof von Cork, Cloyne und Ross geworden. Vorhin war er Professor der Theologie in Trinity College (der protestantischen Universität zu Dublin). Seine Kleidung war die gewöhnliche bischöfliche, schwarzseidene kurze Hosen, schwarzseidene Strümpfe und Schuhe mit goldenen Schnallen. Hier lernte ich auch Mr S— kennen und Mr B— (Prediger in Cork), beide menschenfreundliche und sehr unterrichtete Männer. Des Lord Bischofs Töchter sind gar liebe Wesen, mehr englisch von Wuchs und Aussehen, als irisch. [...]

Dem lieben Mr. Lindsay (Verfasser der *Coinage of Ireland by John Lindsay Esq. Barrister at Law* zu Cork) und seiner netten Frau hatte ich auf ihrer Sommerwohnung bei Blackrock, etwa zwei *Miles* von Cork, Lebewohl gesagt, am folgenden Morgen nahm ich mit der Hand Abschied – denn das ist die herrliche Sitte überall im englischen Reich, auch in der vornehmen Gesellschaft – von der angenehmen Familie im Palais zu Cork. Die Lady bat mich, ihnen zu schreiben, wenn ich wieder in England angekommen, und das habe ich auch gethan. Ich bin ein armer Fremdling und meine Reise ist dieses Leben, *'our little life is rounded with a sleep, and we are such stuff, as dreams are made on'*, [sic] ein kleiner Fleck im Meer, den fast Niemand kennt, war mein Anfang, das ist meine einzige irdische Heimath; lang schon von ihr getrennt, trage ich ihr Bild immer in mir, bis die rechte Heimath kommt, wenn der Weg vollendet ist. In einer schönern Absicht ist mir kein Buch geschenkt worden, als *Pilgrim's Progress* von meinen Freunden Isabella und John Gordon in Edinburgh beim letzten Abschied. Es ist eine Prachtausgabe, und sie haben ihre Namen vorn eingeschrieben, und einen innigen Wunsch hinzugesagt. Das ist eine allgemeine Sitte in Großbrittanien. O wie schön ist es um Cork herum, ich wäre gern länger geblieben, allein die Reise lag noch endlos vor mir.

people. There were few people present, but they were all very appealing. The lady of the house was a most refined woman. Educated and attractive, she did not seem in the least artificial. Her husband was a quiet man with a serious, seemingly Scottish character (even his name, Kyle, would seem to indicate Scottish connections), and he spoke but little. He would hardly have become Bishop of Cork, Cloyne and Ross without some form of distinction, and indeed he had formerly held the chair of theology at Trinity College Dublin (which is the Protestant university of Dublin). He was dressed after the usual episcopal fashion in short trousers of black silk, stockings made of the same material and black shoes with gold buckles. I met Mr S— and Mr B— [Rev George Burrowes] (a preacher in Cork), both well-informed men of a philanthropic disposition. The Lord Bishop's daughters are very dear creatures, more English in appearance and in breeding than Irish. [...]

I called upon the kind Mr Lindsay (author of *Coinage of Ireland* by John Lindsay Esq. Barrister at Law in Cork) and his kind wife at their summer residence at Blackrock about two miles out of Cork, to bid them farewell, and in parting we shook hands. This delightful gesture is practiced throughout the British Empire, even among the gentry, as I was to discover when paying my respects to that pleasant family in the palace the following morning. The Lady asked me to write to them upon my return to England, and this I duly did. I am only a poor stranger and my journey resembles life itself, for 'our little life is rounded with a sleep, and we are such stuff as dreams are made of.' My travels began on a little speck of land in the middle of the sea, which few people have even heard of; yet it is the only home I have upon this earth. Even now, after a long, long absence, I still carry its image around in my heart and always will, until I reach the home of homes when the journey comes to an end. Upon my last encounter with my Edinburgh friends, Isabella and John Gordon, I was presented with a copy of *Pilgrim's Progress*, and I have never been given a book with nobler intentions. It is a luxury edition, signed by the Gordons themselves and adorned with their best wishes. Such is the custom in Great Britain. The environs of Cork are so beautiful! I would dearly have liked to wile a little longer, but I still had an endless road ahead of me.

English translation by Sebastian Stumpf.

Amédée Pichot
(1850)

French original in: *L'Irlande et le Pays de Galles*. Paris: Guillaumin, 1850, vol. 1, pp. 328-36

Q UELQUES PARTICULARITÉS du mobilier de la prison de Cork rappellent la ville maritime: ce sont des couchettes en hamac, des tables à manger sans pieds, qui descendent magiquement du plafond, au lieu de sortir d'une trappe du plancher, comme dans les pièces féeriques. Avant le gouverneur actuel, l'établissment fut administré par un capitaine de batiment au long cours, qui introduisit ces inventions. Quand je dis que les prisonniers sont classés par la conduite, ce mot comprend quelque chose de plus que le bon caractère. Ils *travaillent*, et les plus laborieux sont naturellement ceux qui se procurent le plus de douceurs.

Les casernes de Cork sont encore plus séduisantes que la prison: tout y est admirablement tenu. Quelle propreté! Les soldats sont superbes. Comment le pauvre paysan qui passe à Cork peut-il resister à la tentation de se transformer de mendiant en héros! Ceux qui savent lire sont d'ailleurs avertis, par de nombreuses affiches, que sa Majesté la reine a toujours besoin du courage de Paddy; car ce n'est pas elle qui démentira O'Connell, répétant si volontiers que ses compatriotes ont gagné seuls toutes les batailles de lord Wellington. Tout Irlandais qui s'engage à Cork aura un *shelling* [*sic*] six *pences* par jour; plus, une prime de trois livres six shellings [...]

La veille de mon départ de Cork, en traversant la rue de Saint-Patrick, j'aperçus sur le trottoir une pancarte portée par un homme affiche, qui se contentait de montrer du doigt indicateur les gigantesques lettres de cette espèce de bannière parlante: c'était le sommaire des nouvelles apportées par le dernier courrier, et contenues avec tous leurs détails dans une des feuilles périodiques de la ville. On y lisait: PROBABILITÉS D'UNE GUERRE PROCHAINE AVEC LA FRANCE. INSULTE FAITE AU CONSUL ANGLAIS DE TAÏTI PAR LES OFFICIERS FRANÇAIS HUMILIATION DE L'ANGLETERRE ETC.; enfin le résumé des incidents qui émurent tout à coup Londres et Paris à la fin du mois de

Amédée Pichot
(1850)

(Prisons – army barracks – French/English antagonism)

SOME OF the special features of the furniture in Cork Prison under-line the city's maritime character: berths in the form of hammocks, dining tables without legs, that are lowered from the ceiling, instead of rising up from a hatch in the floor, as if by magic or in some fairy tale play. Before the arrival of the present governor, the establishment was administered by a naval captain who introduced these inventions. When I say that the prisoners are classified according to their behaviour, this word covers more than simply good character. They *work*, and the hardest workers are naturally those who earn the most preferential treatment.

The barracks in Cork are even more attractive than the prisons: everything is very well maintained there. Such cleanliness! The soldiers are superb. How could any poor peasant passing through Cork resist the temptation to change from being a beggar into a hero! In any case, those who can read are informed by numerous posters that Her Majesty, the Queen, still needs Paddy's courage; for it is not she who will refute O'Connell as he repeats so willingly that his compatriots, on their own, won all of Wellington's battles. Every Irishman who joins up in Cork will get one shilling and six pence per day, as well as a bonus of three pounds and six shillings [...]

The day before I left Cork, as I crossed St Patrick's Street, I noticed on a footpath a sandwich man carrying a placard, who was simply pointing to the huge letters on this sort of talking banner: it was a summary of the latest news brought in by the latest post, and contained in detail in one of the city's news sheets: On it could be read: LIKELIHOOD OF AN IMPENDING WAR WITH FRANCE: ENGLISH CONSUL INSULTED IN TAHITI BY FRENCH OFFICERS. ENGLAND HUMILIATED, ETC.: the summary of the incidents that suddenly shook London and Paris in late July 1844. I

juillet 1844. Je remarquai facilement l'animation de tous ceux qui s'arrêtèrent avec moi devant l'affiche. Quelques-uns affectaient de lire assez haut la phrase de *probabilité d'une guerre prochaine*, puis se regardaient avec un sourire qui exprimait clairement tout le plaisir qu'ils éprouvaient. Avant la fin du jour, l'affaire Pritchard avait provoqué dans toute la ville une polémique assez vive; car le lendemain, dans la cour du bureau de la diligence, où je fis transporter mon bagage une heure avant le départ, ma qualité de Français me valut d'être abordé cordialement par plus d'un honnête bourgeois, qui croyait devoir me complimenter des nouveaux lauriers dont la France allait se parer le front. Mes compagnons de route, depuis Cork jusqu'à Skibereen, discutèrent maintes fois les chances que la guerre allait offrir à l'Irlande.

could easily observe the excitement of all those who were stopping with me in front of the notice. Some were affecting to read out rather loud the phrase 'likelihood of impending war'; then they would look at each other with a smile clearly indicating all the pleasure they were feeling. Before the day ended, the Prichard affair had provoked a fairly lively polemic across the entire city; because, the following day, in the yard of the coach service where I had my luggage brought an hour before departure, the fact that I am French meant that I was greeted cordially by more than one honest bourgeois who felt it imperative to compliment me on the fresh laurels with which France was about to adorn her brow. My travelling companions from Cork to Skibbereen repeatedly discussed the opportunities that the war would represent for Ireland.

English translation by Grace Neville.

Louis Énault
(1859)

French original in: *Angleterre, Ecosse, Irlande: Voyage Pittoresque.*
Paris: Morizot, 1859, pp. 463-66, 470-75.

Moi-même, pendant le cours de ce voyage, j'ai été témoin, dans la baie de Cork, d'un de ces départs d'émigrants qui vont, par delà les mers, demander à des continents nouveaux le droit de vivre en travaillant. Pour rendre la solennelle et morne tristesse de ces grandes scènes, il faudrait la sombre énergie des prophètes bibliques pleurant sur les malheurs d'Israël.

Le paysan irlandais aime son pays, il aime sa terre; il a pour elle cette sorte d'adoration que les nobles races auront toujours pour une patrie opprimée. Chez eux cet attachement est presque une religion.Que de misères et que de douleurs, avant que de tels liens ne soient rompus! Que de combats vaillamment combattus, avant la défaite suprême! Que de luttes contre le désespoir! ... Enfin, épuisés de larmes, d'émotions ... et de faim, ils signent un traité – à terme – avec *l'Australian Emigration Society,* qui se charge des enrôlements de travailleurs. Le terme arrive, un terme arrive toujours! ... il faut partir ... Ce jour néfaste entre tous, c'est vraiment pour l'Irlande le

Dies iræ, dies illa

de la colère divine.

J'approchais des quais de Cork, – déjà la vapeur sifflait, les ancres dérapaient, les aubes du *Vultur* frémissaient le long de ses flancs noirs. La cloche d'appel tintait lugubrement ... À bord! à bord!!! criaient les matelots en parcourant la foule. – La foule, c'était peut-être trois mille personnes entassées sur le quai. De cette masse compacte et serrée sortaient des lamentations et des sanglots.

Les émigrants, au nombre d'environ trois cents, étaient accompagnés par leurs parents et leurs amis jusqu'à la planche fatale. Tous avaient voulu prolonger jusqu'à la dernière minute cette joie maintenant si douloureuse de

Louis Énault
(1859)

(Emigration scenes – poetic character – cityscape – trade – customs – drinking habits)

During this journey, I myself witnessed in Cork harbour one of these scenes of departure with emigrants going beyond the seas to other continents in search of the right to work for a living. The sombre energy of biblical prophets weeping over the misfortunes of Israel would be needed in order to convey all the solemn and gloomy sadness of these dramatic scenes.

The Irish peasant loves his country, his land. He has for her the sort of adoration that noble races will always have for an oppressed homeland. This feeling borders on religion for them. What misery and suffering before such links can be sundered! What courageous battles before the supreme defeat! What struggles against despair! ... Finally, exhausted from crying, from emotions ... and from hunger, they sign an agreement with the *Australian Emigration Society* which organises the recruitment of workers. The deadline arrives, a deadline always arrives! ... it's time to go ... For Ireland, this most calamitous of days is truly the

Dies iræ, dies illa

of divine anger.

As I was approaching the quays in Cork, the steamship's whistle could be heard, the anchors were being aweighed, the *Vultur*'s paddles were quivering along its black flanks. The bell called, chiming dismally. 'On board! On board!!!', shouted the sailors scouring the crowds. There were perhaps 3,000 people crowded onto the quay. Sobs and lamenting rose from this solid, compressed throng.

The emigrants, about 300 in all, were accompanied by families and friends as far as the fatal gangplank. They had all wanted to prolong to the very last minute the joy – now turning to sorrow – of being in their

la présence, et savourer jusqu'à la dernière goutte l'amère douceur des adieux … ils sentaient bien que c'étaient des adieux éternels... Aussi semblait-il que les bras ne se pussent dénouer des étreintes suprêmes. Parmi ceux qui partaient, il y avait des hommes au teint hâlé, aux bras robustes, dont l'œil était trempé de larmes; il y avait des jeunes filles qui se tordaient les bras. – Une ne disait rien, – elle était belle; mais la douleur avait sculpté son empreinte sur ce visage de marbre vivant; elle tenait entre ses mains un rameau d'if coupé sur une tombe. On voyait bien qu'elle laissait son cœur en Irlande. Des groupes d'enfants pleuraient, parce qu'ils voyaient pleurer leur mère. La cloche d'appel sonna pour la troisième fois, – un long gémissement lui répondit. C'était l'Irlande qui pleurait ses fils. – L'uniforme du constable se mêla à la foule et poussa le troupeau vers le navire. Mille adieux s'échangèrent … toutes les mains, tous les yeux, toutes les lèvres se cherchaient. – Un jeune homme, que personne n'avait accompagné, se jeta la face contre terre, et baisa le sol sacré de la patrie … Seul ici! seul là-bas! pouvait-on lire sur la morne austérité de son front … – On retira la planche. Un roulement de tambours couvrit les dernières clameurs. – La musique joua l'air national de Saint-Patrick; tout le monde s'agenouilla: un vieux prêtre découvrit sa tète blanche et murmura des prières. – Puis le sifflet du capitaine déchira l'air, le bateau s'ébranla, partit, disparut.

La foule se dispersa, triste, mais résignée, pleurant les siens, mais bénissant Dieu.

Si de telles calamités ne sont point vraiment inévitables, de quelle responsabilité se chargent devant le juge suprême ceux qui ont le pouvoir en main, s'ils ne font point TOUT pour les détourner d'un peuple aussi digne d'intérêt!

CORK

Il faut bien le reconnaître: l'Irlande est le pays du monde où les yeux sèchent le plus vite. Dieu a donné aux Irlandais une facilité d'oubli proportionnée à leurs malheurs. – Ou, plutôt, le malheur est devenu chose si commune, qu'il laisse à peu près indifférènts ceux qu'il n'a point personnellement touchés.

Une heure après la scène lamentable dont j'avais été témoin sur les quais

company, and to taste down to the last drop the bitter sweetness of farewells … they well knew it was forever … And so it seemed that their arms could not unclench these supreme embraces. Among those leaving were men with tanned complexions and strong arms, their eyes drenched with tears. There were young girls wringing their hands. One was saying nothing – how beautiful she was, but sorrow had sculpted itself on this face of living marble. In her hands she held a branch of yew cut from a grave. It was clear that she was leaving her heart in Ireland. Groups of children were crying because they saw their mothers crying. The bell rang out a third time – more lamentations answered it. It was Ireland mourning her sons. A constable in uniform in among the crowd pushed the herd towards the ship. A thousand adieux were exchanged … hands, eyes, lips were all looking for each other. A young man, who had come there unaccompanied, threw himself on the ground and kissed the sacred soil of his homeland … 'All alone here, all alone over there!', could be read on the sad bleakness of his face. The gangplank was taken away. A roll of drums drowned out the final clamour. The national air of St Patrick was played; everyone knelt down: an old priest took off his hat to reveal his white head. He prayed in a low voice. Then the captain's whistle split the air, the boat shook, set off and disappeared.

The crowd dispersed, sad but resigned, mourning its lost ones but blessing God.

If such calamities are not really inevitable, what responsibility, in the presence of the supreme judge, have those who hold the power in their hands taken on, if they do not do EVERYTHING to protect a people so worthy from such catastrophes!

CORK

It must be admitted that of all the countries in the world, Ireland is the one in which tears are most quickly dried. God gave the Irish an ability to forget commensurate with their sorrows. Or rather, sorrow has become so common that it does not move those whom it did not personally touch.

One hour after witnessing this woeful scene on the quays of Cork,

de Cork, j'entrais dans la ville. On n'y gémissait point: on y chantait; on y travaillait aussi, et beaucoup! Dans les promenades sur les places, dans les cafés, dans les hôtels, dans tous les lieux publics, c'était une agitation affairée, turbulente, bien éloignée de l'activité silencieuse et presque morne des Anglais. D'une boutique à l'autre, à travers la rue, mille lazzi s'échangeaient, pardessus les passants, qui ne dédaignaient point de saisir la balle au bond et de se mêler à ces bruyantes gaietés ... Je me serais cru à Naples ou à Livourne, si, au lieu d être doucement caressé par le bel idiome où résonne le si

Dove il si suona,

mon oreille, à chaque minute, ne s'était sentie heurtée par l'accent guttural d'un patois tout bardé de mot d'origine danoise, anglaise ou gaélique, entremêlés bizarrement.

Nulle part plus qu'ici l'imagination irlandaise ne se donne libre carrière. – Le peuple est poëte: il s'exprime en images ainsi que la nature, et fait, entre le déjeuner et le diner, une dépense de métaphores à ruiner un rhétoricien.

Cette vivacité d'impression – et d'expression – qui, à la longue et dans la familière habitude de la vie, pourrait devenir une fatigue et un ennui, est un charme, au contraire, chez ceux que l'on ne voit qu'en passant: elle rend les relations plus faciles, et improvise des amitiés de rencontre qui se dénouent aussi facilement qu'elles se sont nouées. On a des intimes à Cork au bout d'une heure; il est vrai qu'au bout d'un jour vos intimes vous ont oublié. C'est à vous d'en prendre votre parti, et de jouir, sans vous y trop attacher, de cette hospitalité empressée à vous souhaiter la bienvenue dans la *cité*. Les habitants de Cork appellent leur ville la *cité*, avec une sorte d'affectation que, du reste, – le patriotisme fait excuser [...]

Grâce à leur aptitude au commerce, à leur génie industrieux, et à l'admirable position de leur ville qui justifie et les emblèmes et la devise de son blason, (un navire à l'ancre, dans un port fermé par deux tours crénelées, avec cette légende virgilienne: *Statio bene fida carinis)* les habitants de Cork ont pu réparer les désastres de leurs longues guerres civiles et religieuses. Cork est donc entré depuis longtemps dans une ère de

I went into the city. No one was lamenting: people were singing, and working hard too! Crowds thronged the promenades, squares, cafés, hotels and all public places, boisterous and busy, so different from the English who, when active, are nonetheless silent and almost dismal. From one shop to another, across the street, a thousand gibes were being hurled over the heads of the passers-by who were in no way reluctant to catch the ball on the hop and to participate in the noisy fun … I could have thought that I was in Naples or Livorno if, instead of being gently and pleasantly caressed by that idiom in which the

Dove il si suona

resonates, my ears were not constantly assailed by the guttural sound of a patois larded with words of Danish, English and Gaelic origin in a bizarre jumble.

Nowhere more than here is Irish imagination given full reign. These people are poets: they express themselves in images just as nature does, spending between lunch and dinner a fortune in metaphors that would ruin a rhetorician.

This lively impression that they make, along with their liveliness of expression, could eventually become tiresome and boring through over-exposure. On the contrary, however, it is quite charming among people met only in passing: it facilitates contact between people and improvises passing friendships that are undone as easily as they are made. In Cork you make close friends in just one hour; it is true that after just one day these close friends have forgotten you. It's up to you to make the best of this, and to enjoy the intense welcome you get in the city without becoming too attached to it. The inhabitants of Cork call their town a *city*, with a kind of affectation that patriotism forgives in any case […]

Thanks to their flair for trade, their aptitude for hard work, and the fine location of their city which justifies both the emblems and motto of their crest (a ship at anchor in a port closed by two crenellated towers with this Virgilian inscription: *Statio bene fida carinis!*), the inhabitants of Cork have managed to set right the disasters of their long years of civil and religious wars. Cork has thus long since embarked on an era of rising

prospérité ascendante qui ne semble point devoir s'arrêter de sitôt.

La ville de Cork, qui est la seconde cité du royaume d'Irlande, n'a guère de monuments remarquables, – ou, pour mieux dire, elle n'en a pas. Il faut se contenter d'une vue d'ensemble, et, après un coup d'oeil jeté sur les bureaux de la compagnie des paquebots de Saint-George, ornés d'un fronton et d'un péristyle et couronnés d'un beau groupe en marbre représentant le guerrier au moment où il terrasse le dragon, on n'aura plus à voir que de grandes maisons blanches et carrées, telles que la banque les bâtit, que la bourgeoisie les envie et que le peuple les admire. [...]

Ceci est le vieux Cork, le Cork des étroites ruelles et des maisons obscures et surplombantes. Plus loin s'élève la ville neuve, pleine d'air, d'espace et de lumière, avec ses belles rues dignes d'une capitale; la Grande-Parade, dont les constructions défient toutes les prescriptions de l'alignement municipal; South-Hall [*sic*], encombrée de marchandises et de passants; Saint-Patrick, un immense bazar où le luxe, sous toutes les formes, étale ses tentations derrière les vitrines étincelantes.

Les grands négociants, ceux qui se livrent aux hautes spéculations de l'exportation du bétail, du blé, du wisky, du beurre, des viandes salées, du cuir tanné, n'ont en ville qu'un comptoir et un magasin. Ils ont leur *Ingouville* sur les bords de la Lee, et le long de cette rade magnifique, abritée de collines rocheuses, que Thomas Moore appelait, sans trop d'emphase, tant elle est grande, *la mer de Cork*.

La ville de Cork est une de celles qui gardent le plus fidèlement le culte et les coutumes du passé. Ainsi, le jour de l'élection du nouveau maire, les enfants jouissent du privilège de lui jeter du son ou de la farine au visage. A sa sortie de l'hôtel de ville, au moment où il vient d'être proclamé, c'est à qui saura l'assaillir des quolibets les plus piquants. Il sourit, en roi débonnaire, à ces saturnales d'un jour qui seront suivies d'une année d'obéissance.

Pendant les derniers jours de l'Avent, qui précède les fêtes de Noël, toute la population se répand dans les campagnes, battant les haies, fouillant les buissons, jusqu'à ce qu'elle se soit emparée d'un certain nombre de roitelets. Puis, le 26 décembre, jour de Saint-Étienne, les pauvres volatiles sont attachés en guirlandes à des branches de houx fixées à l'extrémité

prosperity which does not look like ending any time soon.

Cork, the second city in the kingdom of Ireland, has few notable monuments or, to be more accurate, it has none. A general overview must suffice, and after glancing at the offices of the Saint George steamships, decorated with a pediment and a peristyle and crowned with a handsome group scene in marble of the warrior on the point of striking down the dragon, all that remain to be seen are large square white houses, just as the bank built them, desired by the bourgeoisie and admired by the people [...]

[Old Cork is full of] narrow streets and dark, overhanging houses. The new town rises up further on, full of fresh air, space and light, with its fine streets worthy of a capital city; *Grand Parade* whose proportions defy all rules regarding the organisation of urban space; South Mall, packed with goods and passers-by; St Patrick's [Street], a huge bazaar where every form of luxury spreads out its temptations behind sparkling windows.

The leading merchants, those involved in advanced speculation on the export of cattle, corn, whiskey, butter, salt meat, tanned hides, have just one counter and one shop in the city. They have their *Ingouville** on the banks of the Lee, and all along this magnificent harbour, sheltered by rocky hills that Thomas Moore called, with no exaggeration, given its immense size, *the Sea of Cork*.

The city of Cork is one of those that preserve most faithfully the beliefs and customs of the past. Thus, on the day on which the new mayor is elected, children enjoy the privilege of throwing bran or flour at him in the face. As he leaves the City Hall, just after his inauguration, people vie with each other to find the sharpest jibes with which to assault him. Like a good-natured king, he smiles on these day-long shenanigans that are followed by a year of obedience.

On the last days of Advent just before the Christmas celebrations, the entire population spreads out into the countryside, beating the hedges and combing the bushes until it catches a number of wrens. Then, on 26 December, the Feast of St Stephen, the poor birds are attached in wreaths to holly branches that are secured to the ends of

---

* *Editor's Note:* Ingouville, a village that became part of Le Havre in the nineteenth century, was where the merchants of that city built their mansions.

d'une perche. Une sorte d'Hercule, le plus fort parmi les forts, porte cette bannière d'un nouveau genre, et suivi d'une foule bruyante qui chante à tue-tête et à pleins poumons les quarante couplets de la ballade du Roitelet:

The wran, the wran, the king of all birds!

Il va faire des stations plus ou moins longues à la porte de tous les riches, – avec le désintéressement des garçons bouchers qui promènent le bœuf gras devant nos ministères. – Après quoi on lapide les pauvres oiseaux. […]

Les habitants de Cork se sont surtout distingués, à toutes les époques et à travers toutes les vicissitudes de leur histoire, par leur habileté à bien boire. Bons vivants et fortes têtes, on les citait comme les modèles accomplis des francs buveurs. Pour un habitant de Cork qui s'enivre, vouloir c'est pouvoir. Ils ont fait en ce genre de véritables tours de force! Un gentleman, qui tenait à publier lui-même son autobiographie panta-gruélique, a raconté dans de complaisants détails tous les énormes paris qu'il a faits à table; pendant trente années, il a bu chaque jour vingt-cinq grands verres de *toddy,* une sorte de punch assez virulent, né du wisky, et qui ferait pâlir un Suisse! […]

Seigneurs et valets, maîtres et domestiques, bourgeois et artisans, tout le monde cultivait homériquement le wisky à Cork. […]

La classe inférieure, à Cork et dans toute l'Irlande, s'était adonnée toutefois en ces derniers temps à une ivrognerie qui n'avait plus rien de poétique; quand on descend au trivial, le lyrisme s'en va.

sticks. A kind of Hercules, the strongest of the strong, carries forth this new-style banner, followed by a noisy crowd singing the wren's song – all 40 verses of it – at the tops of their voices.

'The wran, the wran, the king of all birds!'

they chant, singing their heads off. Then, he stops for a period long or short at the doors of all the rich folk – as disinterested as the apprentice-butchers who parade the fat bullock in front of our ministries [in France], following which the unfortunate wrens are stoned to death [...].

The inhabitants of Cork have, at all times and through all the ups and downs of their history, distinguished themselves mainly by their skill at drinking. Tough and full of life, they are seen as the very models of serious drinkers. It is no problem for a Cork man to get drunk. Indeed, they have excelled themselves at this activity. A gentleman who was keen to highlight his Rabelaisian autobiography recounted in great detail all the enormous bets he had made at table: every day for 30 years, he drank 25 large glasses of *toddy*, a sort of fairly powerful punch derived from whiskey, and which would make a Swiss man turn pale! [...]

Lords and servants, masters and domestic servants, bourgeois and artisans, all Cork people devote themselves to whiskey in Homeric proportions [...]

The lower class, in Cork as in the whole of Ireland, has in recent times become addicted to the kind of drunkenness that no longer has anything poetic about it, for when people sink into coarseness, lyricism disappears.

English translation by Grace Neville.

Napoléon Chaix
(1862)

French original in: *Nouveau Guide à Londres dans ses Environs: en Angleterre, Ecosse, Irlande.* Paris: Guide-Chaix, 1862, pp. 339-40

CORK: ASPECT général de ce comté est assez varié; malheureusement le manque d'arbres lui donne quelque chose de triste. Le chemin de fer arrive à Cork après avoir traversé un tunnel d'un demi-mille de long. Cette seconde grande ville de l'Irlande est située sur la Lee, au fond d'un petit golfe et d'un port superbe. C'est une ville mal bâtie cependant, remplie de rues étroites et sales, sans édifices publics remarquables. Sa cathédrale est moderne, excepté la tour près d'une ancienne église qui n'existe plus; le collège de la Reine est encore un beau bâtiment gothique; il fut ouvert en 1849, lors de la visite de la reine dans cette ville. Outre les établissements du même genre, citons un *mont-de-piété*, imité des nôtres, établi sur le même principe.

Le jardin botanique de Cork a été converti en cimetière public par un capucin du nom de père Mathieu, qui fut l'apôtre de la première société de tempérance fondée en Irlande. Une société s'était formée, à l'instar de celles d'Amérique, pour essayer d'opposer une digue aux débordements de l'ivrognerie; les premiers importateurs du système américain s'étaient déjà réunis à Cork, à Belfast, à Dublin […]

Il est à Cork quelques verreries, coutelleries et brasseries; les grains, le bétail, le whisky et surtout le beurre sont exportés en grande quantité. Nous ne parlons pas de ces fameux gants de Limerick, si délicats, si fins qu'on en vend une paire pliée et renfermée dans une coquille de noix.

Napoléon Chaix
(1862)

(Entry in a popular French tourist guidebook)

CORK: County Cork is quite varied to the eye; unfortunately, the lack of trees makes it look somehow sad. The railway arrives in Cork city through a tunnel half a mile long. Ireland's second city is situated on the River Lee, deep in a small bay with a superb port. However, the city is badly built and full of dirty narrow streets without any notable public buildings. Its cathedral is modern, except for its tower built near an old church that no longer exists. The Queen's College is a fine Gothic building; it was opened in 1849 when the queen visited this city. Apart from other similar establishments, a pawnshop should be noted, an imitation of those in France and established on the same principle.

The botanical garden in Cork was converted into a public cemetery by a capuchin priest of the name of Fr Mathew who was the apostle of Ireland's first temperance society. An organisation was set up along the lines of those in America in order to try to combat the excesses of drunkenness; the first importers of the American system had already met in Cork, Belfast and Dublin [...]

In Cork there are a few glassworks, knife manufacturers and breweries; grain, cattle, whiskey and butter are exported in great quantities. I won't even mention those famous gloves made of Limerick lace so delicate and fine that a pair can be sold folded and enclosed in a nutshell.

English translation by Grace Neville.

Frederik Krebs
(1864)

Danish original in: *Efter et Besøg i Storbritanien og Irland i Sommeren 1863.*
Copenhagen: Reitzel, 1864, pp. 333-37.

VED MALLOW dreier man pludseligt imod Syd, naar man vil til Cork. Veien mellem Mallow og Cork er uden Sammenligning langt skjønnere end den hele Strækning imellem Dublin og Mallow. Man gjennemskjærer paa dette Strøg den Bjergkjæde eller een af de Bjergkjæder, som, mere eller mindre nær Kysten, næsten uden Afbrydelse omkrandse Irland. Det er det samme Høidedrag, som noget længere imod Vest omslutter de deilige Killarney-Søer.

Cork er som bekjendt en stor Handelsby med en udmærket Havn og man træffer selvfølgelig der Alt, hvad der hører til et livligt Handelsrøre og en udstrakt Skibsfart. Men om Betydningen og Udstrækningen heraf faaer man den bedste og sikkreste Underretning ved at slaae op i de herom affattede Tabeller. Den Fremmede faaer snart at vide, at han er i en stor Søstad, thi han tituleres hvert Øieblik 'Captain', forudsat han er nogenlunde velklædt. Om det var min mørke Ansigtsfarve, der gav mig et særligt Krav paa denne Titel, skal jeg ikke kunne sige, men det lød bestandigt 'yes Captain', 'this way Captain', 'how do you do Captain?' Irlænderens livlige, meddeelsomme Charakteer fornægter sig ikke. Han er strax paa rede Haand med en Passiar og søger enhver Leilighed til at komme ikast med den Fremmede. Her er naturligviis kun Tale om den lavere Classe. Byen selv er en Søstad, som saa mange andre Stæder. Den har sine pene og sine stygge Gader, sine rige og sine fattige Quarterer, men i alle Gader og Quarterer er stor Overflødighed af Butikker. Jeg tilbragte den meste Tid med at gaae Gade op og Gade ned for ret at iagttage Folkelivet; thi her er et Gadeliv, som ikke overgaaes af det, der træffes i nogen sydeuropæisk By. Det, som var mig det meest Paafaldende, var Pjaltebefolkningens og Dagdrivernes talløse Mængde. Jeg har aldrig seet Noget, der kommer dette nær. For hver velklædt Person, man mødte, mødte man en halv Snees mere eller mindre pjalt-ede

144

Frederik Krebs
(1864)

(Street life – clothes – beggars)

A T MALLOW, one suddenly turns towards the south, if one wants to go to Cork. The road between Mallow and Cork is without doubt much more beautiful than the entire distance between Dublin and Mallow. On this road, one cuts through the mountain range, or one of the mountain ranges, that close to the coast more or less encircle Ireland without a break. It is the same range of hills that further west surround the wonderful Killarney lakes.

Cork is, as is widely known, a large commercial town with a very good harbour where one obviously finds everything that belongs to a lively trading area with extensive shipping. However, for the importance and the extent of this, one gets the best and most reliable information by looking it up in the relevant, composed tables. The stranger will soon know that he is in a large seaport as he is repeatedly addressed as 'captain', provided he is fairly well dressed. Whether it was my dark facial complexion that gave me a special right to this title, I cannot say, but it rang out constantly 'yes captain', 'this way captain', 'how do you do captain?' The lively, communicative Irish character surfaced again and again. The Irishman instantly has a chat at his fingertips and seeks any opportunity to get into a conversation with the stranger. This, naturally, only relates to the lower classes. The town itself is a seaport like so many other places. It has its nice and its ugly streets, its rich and poor quarters, yet in all streets and quarters is a superfluity of shops. I spent most of my time walking around the streets to observe the street life; for there is a street life here that is not surpassed by what one comes across in some southern European cities. What was most striking to me was the ragged population and the endless number of loafers. I have never seen anything that comes close to this. For every well-dressed person

Subjecter. Jeg kom til den Overbeviisning, at ikkun en saare ringe Deel af denne Befolkning bar Klæder, der fra Nyt af var syet til dem. Den store Masse af Befolkningen, der mylrer paa Gaden, baade af den lavere og laveste Classe, bærer aflagte Klæder. Arbeidsmandens grove, slidte, lappede eller bullede Klædning er et net og propert Stykke i Sammenligning med den fine, afjadskede Selskabskjole, der vandrer fra Ryg til Ryg, alt efter dens forskjellige Stadier af Lurvethed, indtil den omsider som et fryndset Drapperi venter sin sidste Opløsning paa Kroppen af et ynkeligt Væsen, der staaer allerlavest i det irske Samfund, og dybere kan man vel ingensinde og intetsteds komme. At bøde og lappe synes man ikke at forstaae. Man lader Lasen hænge og sveie for Vinden, saa længe den vil. Vil et Ærme eller et Kjoleskjød tage Afsked, saa lader man det fare og gjør sig slet ingen Uleilighed med at reklamere Flygtningen og knytte den til sig ved en Rempning. Der var en Mand, som var tre Gange gift, den ene Gang mere uheldigt end den anden; thi hans Koner overbøde hinanden i Ladhed og Sjudskeri. Den første rempede hans hullede Strømper, den anden stoppede Hullet ved Hjælp af en Burre, den tredie lod ham gaae med bare Been. Naar han da saa tilbage paa sit ægteskabelige Livs Gjenvordigheder, udbrød han klagende: 'Gud signe Rempe, Burre bedre end bare Been.' – I Irland synes det virkeligt, at man har passeret Rempningens og Burrens Stadium og er kommen til de bare Been i de fleste Retninger. Pjalterne falde bogstavelig af Folk her, Folkets store Masse hjælper sig og har i en lang Aarrække maattet hjælpe sig med aflagte Klæder og Pjalter, med Affald og Smuler i alle Retninger. Besiddere og Erhververe vare ikkun faa, og til disse klyngede den store Hob sig, for af den at forsynes med Pjalter og Smuler i materiel og aandelig Forstand. Det irske Folk kom aldrig ud over det oprindelige Clans-eller Septvæsen. I sin sletteste Skikkelse har dette bevaret sig derved, at Folket ikke kan faae et rigtigt Blik paa Ejendomsret og Erhvervspligt. I en tidlig Alder standsedes dette Samfund i sin naturlige Udvikling og blev derved en vanfør Krøbling. – Ved Qvindernes Pragt var der foruden Pjalterne og de bare Been en Ejendommelighed, som tiltrak sig min Opmærksomhed. Til den nationale qvindelige Dragt i Irland synes at høre en lang Kaabe med Hætte af mørkeblaat eller sort Klæde. Uagtet det var smukke varme Augustdage, saae man dog de fleste Fruentimmer

one meets, one also meets, give or take, half a score of ragged subjects. I came to the conclusion that only a small part of this population was wearing clothes that had been sewn specially for them. The biggest part of the population that swarm the streets, both the lower and the lowest classes wear discarded clothing. The unskilled labourers' rough, worn clothing, patched or full of holes, is still neat and tidy compared to the fine, bedraggled evening apparel that changes hands according to the different stages of its shabbiness until at last, as a frayed drapery, it awaits its final state of disintegration on the body of a pathetic creature at the absolute bottom of Irish society, where presumably, one can sink no further. It appears that repairing and patching are not comprehended. One merely allows the rag to hang and sway in the wind as long as it wants to. Should a sleeve or evening-tail want to resign then one abandons it and one does not take any trouble to advertise the removal or get attached to it by tacking it. There was a man who was married three times; one time more unfortunate than the other, for his wives surpassed each other in laziness and sloppiness. The first mended his holey socks, the other mended the hole with a burr, the third simply let him go out barelegged. When he looked back on the tribulations of his married life, he whined, 'God bless tacking, burrs are better than barelegged'. In most respects in Ireland, it really appears as though one has passed the tacking and the burr stages and has reached the barelegged stage. Here the rags literally fall off people, the huge majority of the population has helped themselves, and for many years has had to help themselves, to discarded clothes and rags, to rubbish and bits in all regards. The propertied class and businessmen are a small group to which the masses cling so that they can be supplied with rags and bits, in the material and the spiritual sense. The Irish people never progressed from their original clannishness or sectarianism. At their worst, these character traits have prevented the people from being able to fully understand private ownership or their duty to work. At an early period, the society stopped its natural development and therefore became like a disabled cripple. In relation to women's clothing, in addition to the ragged and bare-legged appearances, one peculiarity attracted my attention. The national women's dress in Ireland seemed to consist of a long cape with a hood of dark blue or black cloth.

slæbe omkring med en saadan Kaabe og – bart Hoved. Det maa imidlertid herved bemærkes, at ikkun meget Faa bare dette Klædningsstykke i dets nationale Skikkelse. Det var nemlig ikkun dem, der havde havt Raad til at lade Kaaben skjære og sye til dem selv. Den store Mængde trak derimod omkring i aflagte Damekaaber af alle mulige Snit og i alle mulige Stadier af Opløsning. Man kunde her see de sidste 10 Aars Moder hvad Damekaaber angaaer. Hvilken Rolle Pjalterne spille i Cork, derom fik jeg et tydeligt Begreb, da jeg gik igjennem en mere afsides Gade. Paa begge Sider af Gaden havde Handlende udspredt deres Varer paa Brostenene. Den største Deel af disse primitive Butikker indeholdt ikkun gamle Klæder. Man maa ikke troe, at et eneste af disse Udsalg lignede dem, vi kunne træffe i vore Smaagader i Kjøbenhavn. Det ringeste af de Stykker, der findes i disse vore Butikker, vilde være et Pragtstykke i disse Kludebunker, der i andre Lande for størstedelen vilde have været Kludesamlerens lovlige Eiendom. Men en vis Fuldstændighed charakteriserede dem alle. Her kunde begge Kjøn og alle Aldere lige ned til Pattebarnet blive forsynet – med Pjalter.

Dagdriveriet og Ørkesløsheden syntes at staae i et passende Forhold til Pjalternes Mangfoldighed. Man saa overalt en Mængde Mennesker, der dreve omkring uden Maal og Meed eller dannede sladdrende Klynger. Om enhver Omnibus, der kom eller gik fra Hotellet, samlede sig altid en Skare af Tilskuere, der syntes at være ubeskriveligt interesserede i denne vigtige Begivenhed. Men det Mærkeligste og Sørgeligste ved den hele Scene, som dette Gadeliv frembød, var dog den Sorgløshed, der var udbredt over den. Man var vant til Pjalterne og Dagdriveriet, det var ikke noget Nyt. De vare Alle glade og fornøiede. Man sladdrede og loe, loe og sladdrede, og bar sine Pjalter med en vis nonchalant Værdighed. Disse Herrer Vagabonder spankulerede omkring med en komisk Selvtilfredshed udbredt over deres hele Person. Disse Stoddere havde en Mimik og Gebærder, som man ellers ikke træffer hos nogen Almue i de nordlige Lande. I Spanien og i de tropiske Lande imellem Blandingsracerne kan man træffe noget Lignende. Da vi stege i Omnibussen for at tage ud til Jernbanen havde der som sædvanligt samlet sig en Hob af disse Lazaroner. Een Figur især var mærkelig. Det var

Despite the fact that the days in August were beautifully warm, most of the finer women lugged these capes around – bareheaded. It must, however, be noted that just a few wore this garment in its national form. That is to say that not many of them could afford to have the cape cut out and sewn for them personally. In contrast, the huge majority toiled around in discarded women's capes of every possible cut and in all possible stages of disintegration. Here, one could see the fashion of the last ten years in relation to women's capes. Of the role that the ragged people played in Cork, I formed a clear impression whilst walking through a more remote street. On both sides of the street, the tradesmen had spread out their wares on the cobblestones. The biggest part of what these primitive shops sold was only old clothes. One should not believe that even one of these shops was similar to anything we could find in our small streets in Copenhagen. The worst of the articles in our shops would be showpieces in these rag piles, and in other countries, most of it would be the legal property of rag collectors. Yet, a certain comprehensiveness characterises them all. Here, both sexes and all ages, all the way down to a baby, can be supplied – with rags.

Loafing about and futility seems to be in a suitable relationship for the ragged variety. One sees a quantity of people everywhere that wander aimlessly around or form gossiping groups. For every carriage that came to or left the hotel, a crowd of spectators flocked around and they appeared to be indescribably interested in this important event. Yet the oddest and most distressing thing about this scene, which the street life presented, was the carefree attitude that was prevalent amongst them. One was used to the ragged people and the loafers, nothing new there. They were all glad and content. They gossiped and laughed, laughed and gossiped and wore their rags with a certain nonchalant dignity. These gentlemen vagrants, however, strutted about with a comical complacency, pervasive throughout their whole person. These beggars had a facial expression and behaviour that one normally would not see in any common people in the northern countries. In Spain, and in the mixed races found in tropical countries, one can find something similar. As we boarded the carriage to travel to the train station, the usual group had gathered in a crowd of tramps. One figure in particular was strange. It

en Stodder med en skyggeløs, bulet Hat og saa pjaltet som vel Nogen i denne med Pjalter draperede Befolkning; men Hatten sad paa Snur, og. med Hovedet lidt heldende til den ene Side, korslagte Arme og den ene nøgne Fod lidt fremskudt betragtede han os med et ubeskriveligt Udtryk af Overlegenhed.

was a beggar with a brimless, dented hat and he was as ragged as most of this ragged, draped population, but his hat was cocked and with his head leaning slightly to one side, crossed arms and one naked foot a little projected, he regarded us with an indescribable expression of superiority.

English translation by Sharon Wilkins.

Alfred Duquet
(1872)

French original in: *Irlande et France*. Paris: Michel Levy, 1872, pp.120-37.

APRÈS UNE descente très-rapide, nous traversons sur un beau pont la rivière de la Lee, dont l'embouchure est à Cork, et suivons maintenant une route unie.

Les curieux commencent à affluer. Ils sont venus en avant de la ville, afin d'être plus libres de regarder les Français. Un des messieurs qui se trouvent dans notre voiture, l'ancien maire de Cork, me montre un grand bâtiment, fort bien placé, qui sert d'asile d'aliénés. Mais la foule augmente; Cork apparaît; nous allons entrer en ville, ou tout au moins dans le faubourg. De tous côtés flottent au vent les bannières des corporations: saint Crépin, saint Finbar, sainte Marie, saint Denis, saint Louis, saint Joseph, saint Luc, saint Patrick prennent l'air par suite de la circonstance. Les hommes, placés sur six rangs, poussent à notre arrivée des *cheers* retentissants.

Le cortège se met en marche. D'abord dans la première voiture les massiers de la ville, avec leurs masses et leur inévitable épée en croix; puis les bannières de la sainte Vierge et des autres bien-heureux; dans la seconde voiture M de Flavigny, ses deux filles et le maire. Les autres calèches suivent. Derrière elles les corporations s'étendent à l'infini. La foule devient si compacte que les chevaux ne marchent plus qu'au pas. Ainsi que je le disais tout à l'heure, je suis désolé, racontant toujours les mêmes choses, d'être obligé d'employer toujours les mêmes expressions; mais, franchement, je ne me sens pas le talent de ne pas retomber dans ce défaut. L'enthousiasme est donc immense. Les drapeaux tricolores trônent à toutes les maisons en compagnie de leurs frères les drapeaux verts. Un grand nombre d'habitations sont ornées de feuillage depuis le haut jusqu'au bas. Il est curieux de voir cette fourmillière humaine couverte de rubans verts, jaunes, bleus, blancs, rouges, s'agiter, se pousser et se précipiter sur les voitures des Français; hommes, femmes, enfants portent tous des branches d'arbres, et cette forêt mouvante, semblable à celle de *Macbeth*, produit un effet aussi beau que pittoresque.

Alfred Duquet
(1872)

(A pro-French demonstration during the Franco-Prussian War)

JOURNEYING AT great speed, we crossed a fine bridge over the Lee, whose estuary is at Cork, and then travelled along a level road.

Curious onlookers began to gather. They had come out of the town, so as to be able to get a better view of the French visitors. One of the gentlemen in our carriage, the former Mayor of Cork, showed me a large building, excellently situated, which houses the lunatic asylum. All the while the crowd was getting bigger; Cork city appeared; we were about to enter the town, or at any rate its suburbs. On all sides the banners of the various guilds fluttered in the wind: Saint Crispin, Saint Finbar, Saint Mary, Saint Denis, Saint Louis, Saint Joseph, Saint Luke and Saint Patrick were borne aloft in honour of the occasion. The men, six rows deep, burst into loud cheers as we arrived.

The procession set off. At its head, in the first carriage, were the town's macebearers, with their maces and the inevitable swords in the shape of crosses; then the banners of the Virgin Mary and the other saints; the occupants of the second carriage were M. de Flavigny, his two daughters and the Mayor. The other carriages followed after. Behind them stretched a whole host of guilds. The crowd became so dense that the horses could only trot along slowly. As I said earlier, I must apologise, as it befalls me to be always describing the same things, to be obliged to reuse the same expressions; but, quite frankly, I do not feel sufficiently talented to overcome this shortcoming. The wave of enthusiasm was immense. [French] tricolours were flown at every house, along with their counterparts, the green flags of Ireland. Many of the houses were bedecked with garlands from top to bottom. It was strange to see this mass of humanity, covered with green, yellow, blue, white and red ribbons, pushing and shoving against the carriages of the French visitors; men, women and children alike carried the branches of trees, and this moving forest, like the one in *Macbeth*, was as beautiful as it was picturesque.

Devant le Queen-Collège, on acclame M. O'Neill de Tyrone d'une manière formidable. Décidément la reine d'Angleterre n'a qu'à bien se tenir: M. O'Neill est un compétiteur redoutable.

Les cris de: 'Vive la République française!' retentissent de tous côtés. Il faut se faire une idée des grognements chaque fois que le nom de Bismarck ou de la Prusse est prononcé; cette foule qui acclame si bien sait également parfaitement huer. Ce qui m'a frappé dans ces manifestations auxquelles nous assistons depuis notre arrivée en Irlande, c'est le mélange des classes riches et pauvres. Tous, hommes en habits déguenillés et commerçants, à la mise soignée, tous sont confondus au milieu de la rue et sont unanimes pour faire aux Français une réception splendide.

Il est midi un quart; nous allons entrer véritablement en ville. Les fenêtres sont littéralement garnies de dames agitant leurs mouchoirs, des rubans tricolores et criant: 'Vive et vive la France!' c'est un délire. Les marches du Palais de Justice sont transformées en gradins vivants. Ces braves habitants de Cork se livrent à une véritable débauche d'acclamations. Comme ces excellentes gens sont heureux de pouvoir témoigner leurs sympathies à la France! Vive la France! Dieu, sauve la France! toujours, toujours la France!

Nous prenons South Man [*sic*] Street. L'enthousiasme augmente pour ainsi dire. Les dames ne se lassent pas d'agiter leurs mouchoirs. Je me repais, sans façon, du spectacle de ces jolies têtes d'Irlandaises qui sourient de toutes leurs belles dents blanches aux Français qui viennent leur faire visite. Quels beaux types! quelle douceur, quel velouté des yeux et quelle blancheur de teint! N'en parlons plus ... […]

Nous prenons South Mall, où se trouve notre hôtel. C'est là que la foule est le plus serrée. Je remarque de curieuses maisons le long cette rue. On dirait des habitations mauresques. Des cintres en cercles coupés, soutenus par des colonnettes de marbre à chapitaux fouillés; des balcons avancés avec des stores de couleur rouge ou bleue pour garantir du soleil ... ou de la pluie. En un mot, l'architecture de ces maisons est très-riche et très-originale.

Il est une heure quand nous descendons à l'hôtel Impérial, au milieu d'une tempête de *cheers*. Le maire et les conseillers municipaux, c'est-à-dire les fonctionnaires correspondant à nos conseillers municipaux, en robes

In front of Queen College, Mr O'Neill of Tyrone got a rousing reception. The Queen of England had better watch out: Mr O'Neill is a formidable rival.

Cries of 'Long live the French Republic!' rang out from all sides. You have to imagine the groans which greeted the names of Bismarck or Prussia every time they were mentioned; this crowd, who were so adept at cheering, were also well able to boo. What has struck me at these huge gatherings which we have witnessed since our arrival in Ireland, is the way in which the rich and poor classes of society freely intermingle. Everybody, men in rags and well-dressed shopkeepers alike, mingled in the middle of the street and unanimously gave the French a magnificent reception.

It was a quarter past twelve; we were about to enter the town itself. The windows were literally adorned with ladies waving their handkerchiefs and tricoloured ribbons and crying: 'Long live France!' The atmosphere was unbelievable. The steps of the Courthouse had been transformed into swarming terraces. The good citizens of Cork burst into rapturous cheering. How delighted these good people were to show their goodwill towards France! Long live France! God save France! France forever!

We went along South Main Street. The enthusiasm grew, so to speak. The ladies waved their handkerchiefs tirelessly. I enjoyed the sight of these pretty Irish women who smiled so dazzlingly with their beautiful white teeth at their French visitors. What fine looking women! What soft, velvety eyes and what fair complexions! Let me say no more … […]

We went along South Mall, where our hotel was. It was here that the crowds were at their most dense. I noticed strange-looking houses along this street. You would think that they were Moorish dwellings. Openwork arches supported by slender marble columns with finely-carved capitals; protruding balconies with red or blue canopies to give protection against the sunshine … or rain. In a word, the architecture of the houses was very rich and very original.

It was one o'clock when we arrived at the Imperial Hotel, to tumultuous cheers. The Mayor and the municipal councillors, that is to say the civil servants who are the equivalent of our own municipal

rouges et chaînes d'or, costume de cérémonie, sont réunis dans la grande salle de l'hôtel et offrent à M. de Flavigny une adresse dans laquelle ils le remercient, ainsi que ceux qui l'accompagnent, d'avoir bien voulu accepter l'invitation de la ville de Cork et témoignent de toutes les sympathies de l'Irlande pour la France, affirmant que notre pays ne tardera pas à reprendre son rang et à être salué comme le champion de la civilisation et du progrès. Elle se termine ainsi: 'Nous vous offrons l'hospitalité; nous désirons rendre votre séjour aussi agréable qu'il est possible, et nous regrettons que vos engagements nous empêchent de vous posséder très-longtemps parmi nous'.

Notre Président répond, toujours en excellent anglais et avec une facilité, d'élocution extraordinaire:

[…] 'La ville de Cork a été la première à adresser de l'argent et des provisions à notre Société, et l'Irlande envoya aussi une admirable ambulance pour soigner nos malheureux blessés. Il y avait le docteur Baxter et le docteur Maguire, deux chirurgiens distingués de ce pays. Cette ambulance était approvisionnée constamment d'Irlande, et lorsque d'autres nations nous négligeaient ou nous abandonnaient, celle-ci vint à notre aide de toutes les manières qu'elle put, tout en observant les lois de la neutralité; nous sommes ici pour lui en témoigner notre reconnaissance, et nous sommes reçus par un accueil royal. Ce sera pour nous une grande consolation de pouvoir rapporter à nos compatriotes les sentiments d'égards et de sympathie dont nous avons été l'objet'. (Applaudissements et hurrahs prolongés).

Je tiens à placer ici la courte adresse des corporations des métiers de Cork; on y verra le cœur de ces braves ouvriers irlandais non encore pourri par le sot orgueil comme celui de la majorité débauchée, ignorante et ridicule de nos ouvriers parisiens, lyonnais, marseillais, etc. […]

Après, la députation se retire et M. John Martin,[1] sur la demande du peuple, se présente à là fenêtre et prononce un discours fort applaudi dans lequel il dit que la France a toujours été l'amie de l'Irlande et que le peuple français est celui qui aime le plus et a le plus le droit d'aimer

---

1. J'ai eu tort de ne pas dire déjà que M. John Martin est un protestant très-aimé du clergé catholique, à cause de son caractère.

councillors, attired in red robes with gold chains, their ceremonial dress, were gathered in the foyer of the hotel and delivered a speech to M. de Flavigny in which they thanked him, as well as those who accompanied him for having been kind enough to accept the invitation from the city of Cork and expressed Ireland's profound affection for France, stating that it would not be long before our country reasserted its place among nations and was hailed as a champion of civilisation and progress. It finished thus: 'We offer you our hospitality: we wish to make your stay as pleasant as possible, and we regret that your engagements mean that we cannot enjoy your presence amongst us for longer.'

Our President replied, still in excellent English and with extraordinary fluency:

'[...] Cork city was the first to send money and provisions to our organisation, and Ireland also sent a fine ambulance to care for our unfortunate injured soldiers. There were Doctor Baxter and Doctor Maguire, two distinguished doctors from this country. Constant supplies for the ambulance were sent from Ireland, and at times when other nations neglected us or abandoned us, Ireland came to our assistance in every way that she could, while respecting the laws of neutrality; we are here to show our gratitude for this, and we have been given a royal welcome. For us it will be a great comfort to be able to go home and tell our compatriots of the demonstrations of affection and support which we have experienced here'. (*Prolonged applause and cheering*).

I wish to include here the short speech delivered by the trade guilds of Cork; it reflected the good heart of these decent Irish workers, which has not yet been corrupted by the idiotic arrogance that has sullied the majority of our Parisian, Lyons and Marseilles workers. [...]

Afterwards, the deputation withdrew and, at the request of the people, Mr John Martin[1] appeared at the window and delivered a speech to much applause in which he said that France has always been Ireland's friend and that the French are the people who love Ireland most and who have most right to love Ireland. He then complimented the people of Cork

---

1. I should have mentioned that Mr Martin is a Protestant who is much appreciated by the Catholic clergy thanks to his character.

l'Irlande. Il complimente ensuite les habitants de Cork pour l'admirable réception qu'ils ont faite à la députation, les engageant à ne se livrer à aucun désordre, non-seulement, à cause de l'honneur de l'Irlande, mais encore à cause de celuide leurs invités. Il les prie de ne troubler en rien ce jour qui fera époque dans l'histoire, et il dit qu'il a l'espoir que bientôt l'Irlande deviendra maîtresse d'elle-même et pourra alors agir comme une nation qui a ses revenus à elle et peut disposer à son gré de son armée et de sa marine. [...]

C'est ainsi que se termina, selon l'expression d'un journal irlandais, la plus grande démonstration dont Cork ait été le théâtre.

for the admirable reception which they had given to the deputation, urging them not to create any riots or disturbances, not just for the sake of Ireland's honour, but also out of respect for the guests. He asked them not to mar this historic day by any disorderly conduct and he said that he hoped that Ireland would soon become her own mistress and could then act as a sovereign nation in control of her own revenue and able to run her army and navy as she wished. [...]

Thus ended, to quote a phrase used by an Irish newspaper, the biggest demonstration that Cork has ever known.

English translation by Gearóid Cronin.

Jean Canis
(1881)

French original in: *Les Massacres en Irlande.* Paris: Dentu, 1881, pp. 149-50.

A Cork, grâce aux frayeurs que les émissaires du gouvernement ont su faire naître, la vie est en quelque sorte suspendue, le commerce est languissant, les rues presque désertes. Sur la devanture d'un grand établissement où se fait la vente du thé, on lit l'affiche suivante: 'Reçevant journellement des lettres contenant des menaces de mort et contre nous si nous fournissons du thé à d'autres personnes qu'aux membres de la Ligue agraire, et contre les personnes autres que les membres de la Ligue agraire qui entreront dans notre maison, nous nous sommes déterminés à fermer notre maison. Nous la rouvrirons lorsque la paix et la sécurité régneront de nouveau.'

La police de Cork a reçu de Londres de nombreux renforts. Aucun vaisseau ne peut entrer dans le port ni en sortir sans avoir été fouillé dans toutes ses profondeurs. Le nom et le signalement des passagers font l'objet d'un travail particulier. Tous les colis, sans exception, sont soumis à la formalité de la vérification. Aux stations intermédiaires des chemins de fer, des agents de la sûreté sont en permanence. Par le distributeur des billets, ils apprennent la destination des personnes suspectes, et aussitôt, par voie télégraphique, la font connaître à l'autorité. Partout l'inquisation, la terreur; les esprits sont soigneusement préparés.

Jean Canis
(1881)

(Oppressive measures – tense political situation in Cork)

IN CORK, due to the climate of fear that the emissaries of the government have managed to create, life seems suspended in a sense, business is slack and the streets are almost deserted. On the façade of a large tea merchant's shop, the following notice can be read: 'Having received letters daily containing death threats both against us if we provide tea to people other than members of the Land League, and against non-members of the Land League who patronise our establishment, we have decided to close down. We will reopen when law and order have been restored.'

Reinforcements to the Cork constabulary have arrived from London. No vessel can either enter or leave the harbour without having been searched from stem to stern. The names and particulars of passengers are subject to particular scrutiny. All parcels, without exception, are subject to checking procedures. All intermediate train stations are patrolled around the clock by the police. Through the ticket vendors, they obtain details regarding the travel destinations of suspects, and these are immediately communicated to the authorities by telegram. An atmosphere of inquisition and terror reigns; people have steeled themselves mentally.

English translation by Gearóid Cronin.

[Ein deutscher Pfarrer]
(1884)

German original in: 'Skizzen aus und über Irland'. In: *Historische Blätter für das katholische Deutschland* vol. 93. 1884, pp. 185-88

W ER CORK nicht gesehen, hat Irland nicht gesehen. Obgleich unter Irland's Städten die dritte an Größe, ist sie dem Irländer die erste und treueste Repräsentantin seiner Nation, eine Tochter reinern Geblütes – nicht nur als der fremde Eindringling im Norden, Belfast, sondern auch – als die Hauptstadt des Königreiches selbst. Durch die lebhafte Verbindung mit England, sowie durch die englische Beamtenwelt und die derselben assimilirten höheren Schichten der Bevölkerung ist Dublin in Physiognomie, Denk- und Lebensweise stark anglikanisirt. In Cork fühlt man sich so recht in Irland.

In einem leider nur flüchtigen Besuche kam ich am Nachmittage eines schönen Septembertages nach Cork. Der Bahnhof wimmelte von Fremden. Die Ausstellung irischer Industrie, welche schon seit ein paar Monaten eröffnet war, zog noch immer Schaaren von Fremden in die Hauptstadt des Südens. Bald waren die Wagen der glücklichen Lohnkutscher vergriffen und die Hotelomnibusse vollgepfropft. Wir fuhren eine kurze Strecke am Quai vorbei, dann über die schöne, sechzig Fuß breite St. Patrickbrücke und waren im Herzen der Stadt. Die sehr breite St. Patrickstraße bildet einen Halbkreis. Im geraden Gegensatze zu dem Einerlei der Straßen moderner, namentlich englischer Städte, reihen sich zu beiden Seiten Häuser vom verschiedensten Werthe, hohe und niedrige, in auffallender Unregelmäßigkeit aneinander. Gleich bei der Einfahrt in diese Hauptstraße empfängt uns das eherne Standbild des Father Mathew, des großen Mäßigkeitsapostels, dessen erhobene Hand uns vor den Gefahren geistiger Getränke warnt. In der Grafschaft Cork geboren, gab er in Cork den ersten Anstoß zu jener großen Bewegung, welche sich allen Ländern des britischen Weltreiches, sowie dem alten Coloniallande in Amerika mittheilte. Tausende von Familien, aus denen er den Teufel der Trunksucht austrieb, verdanken ihm Frieden und Wohlstand. Sein Schwager, ein Destillateur, welcher

[A German Priest]
(1884)

(Cork exhibition – Shandon bells – Catholic mass – religiosity of Cork Catholics)

A NYONE WHO has not seen Cork has not seen Ireland. Although third in size among Irish cities it is to the Irishman the foremost and truest representative of his nation; a daughter of purer pedigree not only than the foreign intruder in the north – Belfast – but even than the capital city of the kingdom itself. Because of its intense interaction with England and due to the English civil service and the higher echelons of society which have become assimilated to it, Dublin is noticeably anglicised in appearance, mode of thought and way of life. In Cork, however, one distinctly feels that one is in Ireland.

One beautiful September afternoon I arrived on a regrettably short visit to Cork. The station was abuzz with visitors. The exhibition of Irish industry which had been open for a few months was still drawing hordes of visitors to the capital of the south. Soon the carriages of the lucky cabbies were all occupied and the hotel omnibuses filled to capacity. We drove the short stretch along the quay, crossed the lovely 60 foot wide St Patrick's Bridge and reached the heart of the city. The very broad St Patrick's Street is semi-circular. In complete contrast to the monotony of streets in modern cities – especially in England – houses of the most varying value, high and low, stand side by side in eye-catching irregularity. Immediately one enters this main street one is greeted by the cast-iron statue of Father Mathew, the great apostle of temperance; his outstreched arm warning us against the dangers of spiritous liquor. Born in County Cork, he gave the initial impetus to that great movement which spread to all countries of the British Empire as well as to the old colonial territory of America. The peace and prosperity enjoyed by thousands of families are due to his driving out the demon of drunkenness. His brother-in-law, a distiller, supported his efforts and offers the rare example of an

ihn unterstützte, bietet uns das seltene Beispiel eines Industriellen, der vor dem Ankaufe und dem Genusse des Produktes seiner Industrie warnt, anstatt es zu empfehlen. Er verwendete den Ertrag seiner Branntweinbrennerei dazu, die Predigt totaler Enthaltsamkeit von Branntwein zu unterstützen. Das war edel, aber wenig kaufmännisch, und richtig fallirte er. Die englische Regierung zeigte sich großmüthig und belohnte seine Bemühungen um die Reformation des socialen und sittlichen Lebens durch Anweisung eines Jahrgehalts von dreihundert Pfund Sterling. [...]

Nachdem ich den Reisestaub abgeschüttelt, ließ ich mir den Weg zur Ausstellung zeigen. Das Lokal, vulgo Getreidemarkthalle, liegt auf dem südlichen Ufer des südlichen Armes des Leeflusses. Der Weg führt durch enge, unschöne Straßen und dann über die schöne – Parnellbrücke. Ich erstaunte, als ich die Brücke so benennen hörte. Wie O'Connell zu Dublin, so hat Parnell seine Brücke in Cork. Die Irländer sind etwas überschwenglich und voreilig in Austheilung von Lob und Tadel. Als Gladstone die bei der Wahlcampagne versprochenen Reformen nicht sogleich ausführte – sicherlich theilweise weil er nicht konnte – so hieß er gleich in irischen Zeitungen 'Judas-Gladstone'. Parnell hörte ich in maßgebenden Kreisen nennen 'a heavenly sent man'. Nun, Worte fliegen; Monumente, wie die Brücke mit ihrem Namen, bleiben und etwas gewagt ist es doch, dem Führer in einer Bewegung, deren Ende und fernerer Verlauf noch so sehr im Dunkeln liegt, ein solches dauerndes Monument zu setzen, bevor er sein Lebenswerk mit Ruhm vollendet. Sobald ich die Brücke erreicht, sah ich auf dem andern Ufer die in buntem Fahnenschmucke sich präsentirende Ausstellung und bald vernahm ich die Töne der Musik, durch welche im Innern des Gebäudes das Musikcorps eines englischen Regimentes die Besucher unterhielt.

Ich trat ein und wandte mich rechts zu den hier ausgestellten Antiquitäten. Mit größter Freundlichkeit kam sogleich ein Herr zu mir, welcher die Schlüsselgewalt in dem betreffenden Departement besaß; er machte mich auf einige uralte Gegenstände irischer Kunst aufmerksam, die in den Torfschichten gefunden worden. Eine kleine ovalförmige Glocke versetzte er in's fünfte Jahrhundert. Viele andere religiöse Gegenstände, wie Kreuze, Medaillons, Rosenkranzkörner waren aus der im Torfe gefundenen

industrialist not recommending his product but giving advance warning of its inherent dangers to the would-be purchaser. He used the profits from his brandy distillery to support the message of total abstinence from that very product. This was noble but not very businesslike and caused his business to fail completely. The English government demonstrated its generosity by rewarding his efforts at reforming the citizens' social and moral life with an annual pension of £300 Sterling. [...]

Having shaken off the dust of travel I asked for directions to the Exhibition. The venue, Cornmarket Hall in the vernacular, is situated on the southern bank of the south channel of the River Lee. The way leads through narrow, unattractive streets and then over the beautiful Parnell Bridge. I was astonished to hear the bridge thus called. Like O'Connell in Dublin, Parnell has his bridge in Cork. The Irish are somewhat extravagant and precipitous in apportioning praise and blame. When Gladstone did not proceed immediately with the reforms he had promised during the election campaign – partly, it is certain, because he was unable to – the Irish newspapers straightaway dubbed him 'Judas Gladstone'. I heard Parnell described in influential circles as 'a heavenly sent man'. Well, words fly but monuments like this bridge and its name remain, and it is certainly rather daring to erect such a permanent memorial to the leader of a movement whose end and further progress are still so very much in the dark, and before the life's work of that same leader has been completed and he himself has been crowned with the laurels of fame.

As soon as I reached the bridge I saw the colourful banners of the Exhibition on the other side of the river and heard issuing from the building the sounds of music played by the band of an English regiment for the entertainment of the visitors.

I entered and turned right to see the exhibition of antiquities. I was immediately approached by a most genial gentleman who appeared to be the person responsible for that particular area. He drew my attention to some specimens of antique Irish art that had been discovered in bogs. A small oval-shaped bell he judged to be fifth century. Many other religious items, such as crosses, medallions and rosary beads were carved from this black Irish bog

schwarzen irischen Eiche geschnitzt. Schon anderswo hatte ich Gelegenheit, dieses merkwürdige Holz, welches ein vortreffliches Material für Schmucksachen ist, kennen zu lernen. Es ist glänzend schwarz, fast wie Ebenholz. Die schwarze Farbe ist nicht die ursprüngliche, doch ist sie während der Jahrhunderte, welche das Holz in seinem schwarzen Grabe zugebracht, so von allen Fasern eingesogen, daß sie wie eine ursprünglich dem Holze eigene erscheint. – Außer den irischen Alterthümern fanden sich in dem Theile der Ausstellung, welchen mir mein freundlicher Führer erklärte, viele Gegenstände alt- und neuheidnischer Kunst aus dem Museum von South-Kensington, besonders solche, welche der Prinz von Wales aus Indien mitgebracht. Ich drückte mein Befremden aus, solche Gegenstände auf der Ausstellung zu finden, da sie ja eine Ausstellung irischer Industrie seyn solle und den Zweck habe, die Industrie in Irland aus ihrem Schlafe aufzurütteln.

'Dies ist freilich der Zweck der Ausstellung', antwortete der Herr, 'in der Haupthalle werden Sie auch nur Irisches finden. Aber aller Anfang ist schwer und wir haben, um mehr des Interessanten bieten zu können, die Hülfe fremder Museen in Anspruch genommen. Das Museum von South-Kensington hat sich besonders freigebig gezeigt.'

'Die Wiederbelebung der Industrie ist eine Kapitalfrage für Ihr Land?' frage ich.

'Ohne sie können uns die besten Gesetze, welche wir zur Lösung unserer Landfrage erlangen, nicht helfen. Das liegt ja auf der Hand. Die Zahl der Kinder in einer Familie ist durchschnittlich fünf. Wie sollen sich nun fünf Kinder mit den Familien, welche sie gründen, auf einer Farm ernähren, welche nur etwa für eine einzige oder für zwei Familien ausreicht? Gibt es außer Landwirthschaft keine Erwerbsquelle, so bleibt nichts übrig als Auswanderung.' [...]

'Das Volk scheint großes Vertrauen auf Parnell zu setzen?' fragte ich.

'Er besitzt das Vertrauen der großen Majorität im vollsten Maße.'

'Ich sehe, daß sie selbst die Brücke zu seiner Ehre umgetauft haben.'

'Es ist eine neue Brücke. Einige wünschten, ihr den Namen des hl Finbar, des Stadtpatrons, zu geben, andere drangen darauf, sie nach unserm Vertreter im Parlamente zu benennen.'

'Und Parnell schlug den Heiligen aus dem Felde', setzte ich hinzu.

oak. I had already had occasion elsewhere to become familiar with this remarkable wood which is a superb material for ornaments and articles of personal adornment. It is gleaming black, almost like ebony. Black is not the original colour but has been acquired over the centuries in its black, boggy tomb; the colour has been absorbed through all its fibres so that now it seems to be the original colour of the wood. – My genial guide pointed out that, apart from the Irish antiquities in this part of the exhibition, there were also examples of ancient and modern pagan art from the South Kensington Museum, in particular some pieces brought back from India by the Prince of Wales. I expressed my reservations about finding such items at the exhibition; an exhibition that was supposed to be of Irish industry and dedicated to shaking industry in Ireland from its slumber.

'Of course, that's the purpose of the Exhibition,' the gentleman replied; 'in the main hall you'll find only Irish exhibits. But getting started is always difficult and so we asked some foreign museums for help in order to be able to offer a wide range of interesting attractions. The South Kensington Museum was particularly generous.'

'Is the revival of Irish industry a key question for your country?' I asked.

'Without industry,' he responded, 'the best laws for solving this country's land question will be of little avail. It is clear to see why. The average family has five children. When these children want to start their own families, how can they live off a farm that could at best feed one or two families? If there is no source of income apart from agriculture, all that remains is emigration.' [...]

'The people seem to have great faith in Parnell,' I said.

'He enjoys the complete trust of the great majority.'

'I see that the bridge has been renamed in his honour.'

'It's a new bridge. Some wished to call it after St Finnbarr, the city's patron saint; others pushed for the name of our Member of Parliament.'

'And in the end Parnell got the better of the saint,' I said.

'Ich hätte die Brücke lieber nach dem Stadtpatrone benannt,' erwiederte er etwas verlegen; 'aber man machte geltend, daß andere Brücken schon den Namen von Heiligen trügen, und so ging der andere Vorschlag durch.'

Ich verabschiedete mich dankend von dem freundlichen Herrn und begab mich in die Haupthalle.

Wer die Ausstellung in der Erwartung besucht, mit neuen über-raschenden Erfindungen oder seltenen Weltwundern Bekanntschaft zu machen, hat sie enttäuscht verlassen. Sie war nicht eine Weltausstellung, wie die von London und Paris, sondern sie beschränkte sich nur auf ein Land und zwar auf ein Land, mit dessen Industrie es sehr schlimm steht. Ihre Aufgabe war es, das Beste von demjenigen, was trotz der Ungunst der Verhältnisse irischer Fleiß und irisches Talent geschaffen, vor Aller Augen zu stellen, zur Anregung und Ermuthigung und zugleich zum Beweise, daß das Volk gar Manches von den Dingen selbst schaffen könne, die es sich vom Auslande her verschreibt. Diese ihre Aufgabe hat die Ausstellung glänzend gelöst. Da standen in langer Reihe prächtige Fuhrwerke und Equipagen aller Gattungen, Eisenbahnwagen mit den Lokomotiven, Modelle von Dampfschiffen, herrliche Musikinstrumente der ver-schiedensten Art. Tuchlager waren aufgeschlagen, Kleidermagazine ein-gerichtet, Kurzwarenhandlungen eröffnet. Leben und Abwechslung brachten die Maschinen, deren wunderbar ineinandergreifende Räder durch Dampf oder Wasser vor Aller Augen in Betrieb gesetzt waren, und die Handwerker, welche von Schaaren von Besuchern umgeben, ihr Handwerk übten. Da wurde Mehl gemahlen, Wolle gesponnen, Tuch gewebt, Bürsten und Schuhe verfertigt, Ketten vergoldet, Karten gedruckt. Milch mußte vor den Augen der Besucher unter speciell Corker Behandlung alle Wandlungen durchmachen, bis sie zu dem eigentlichen Artikel Cork's, zu schöner goldener Butter geworden. Cork, so sagt man, liefert jährlich 28 Millionen Pfd. Butter auf den Markt.

Den schwächsten Punkt bildete die Ausstellung der Corker Zeitung *The Eagle*, welche an einem Pfeiler angeschlagen war. Wenn der Werth einer Zeitung mit der Elle zu messen ist, so verdiente sie ihren Platz auf der Ausstellung. Ihre Größe scheint ihr denselben in der That verschafft zu haben. Denn über ihr las man: 'Die größte Zeitung der Welt'. Es ist

'I would have preferred if it had been named after St Finnbarr,' he said, somewhat abashed, 'but it was pointed out that other bridges were called after saints, and so the other suggestion was adopted.'

Having expressed my gratitude I took leave of the courteous gentleman and betook myself to the main hall.

Anyone visiting the exhibition in the expectation of seeing new, astonishing inventions or rare wonders of the world will have gone away disappointed. It was not a World Exhibition like those in London or Paris, but one which focused on one country, a country, it must be said, whose industry is in a bad way. Its task was, despite the prevailing unfavourable circumstances, to present the visitor with the best of Irish industriousness and talent in order to stimulate and encourage the people while simultaneously proving that Irish people could manufacture many things themselves that are at present imported into the country. In this regard, the exhibition was a resounding success. There were long rows of magnificent horse carriages and equipage of all types; there were railway carriages with locomotives, models of steamships, wonderful musical instruments of every conceivable kind. Cloth stores were erected, clothes shops set up, haberdashery counters opened. Machines with wonderfully meshing wheels powered by water and steam brought life and diversion as they were set in motion for the public, as did the artisans who plied their trade, surrounded by onlookers. Flour was ground, wool spun, cloth woven, brushes and shoes manufactured; chains were gilt and cards printed. Before the onlookers' eyes, milk received its special Cork processing, undergoing all the steps in the transformation into that Cork speciality of beautiful, golden butter. Cork is said to supply the market with 28,000,000 pounds of butter annually.

The weakest point in the exhibition was the Cork newspaper *The Eagle*, which was affixed to a pillar. If size is the yardstick by which one measures the value of a newspaper, then it deserved its place at the exhibition. Its size alone would justify its presence there; the caption above it read: 'The biggest newspaper in the world'. English newspapers

überhaupt etwas Großes um eine englische Zeitung. Wer aber nicht die Arme eines Orang-Utang hat, der versuche es nicht, den *Eagle* von Cork zu entfalten. Abgesehen von dieser sonderbaren Schaustellung der größten Zeitung, an welcher weiter nichts gerühmt wird, als ihre Größe, schien mir, wie gesagt, die Ausstellung glänzend. Sie war stark besucht. Mit Staunen sahen die Irländer, wie mannigfach und herrlich doch noch die Dinge seien, welche ihr Volk zu schaffen vermöge. Auf allen Gesichtern glänzte Freude und von allen Lippen vernahm man: 'a great success, a great success'. 'Wir können nicht leisten, was London und Paris leistet; aber es ist doch ein bescheidener Anfang', sagte mir ein Irländer. Möge die Ausstellung Ideen anregen, Talente wecken, Vertrauen zur eigenen Kraft einflößen und ein mächtiger Anstoß zur Wiederbelebung der eigenen Industrie seyn, ohne die das arme, gedrückte Volk nicht zur Ruhe gelangt auf seinem heimathlichen Boden.

Ueber zwei Stunden hatte mich die Ausstellung festgehalten gegen meine Tagesordnung, in welcher nur ein Stündchen für den Besuch angesetzt war. Nun mußte ich aber nothwendig zur Besorgung eines kleinen Geschäftes in die Stadt zurück und nach manchen Irrfahrten fand ich meinen Weg, welcher über die Parnellbrücke, dann über die St. Patrickbrücke und endlich auf der Nordseite des Lee rechts den Hügel hinaufführte. Ein großer Theil der Stadt ist hier neu angebaut. Ein deutsches Wort fesselte meinen Blick, als ich durch diesen Theil dahineilte. Auf den vier Fenstern eines kleinen einstöckigen Hauses stand zu lesen: 'High School. For Ladies. Kindergarten. Mixed School.' Das deutsche Wort heimelte mich sofort an, aber nur so lange, bis die Reflexion über seine Bedeutung kam. Etwas beschämt lief ich von dem Hause weg, dieser traurigen Bescheerung, mit welcher ein Landsmann das harmlose irische Kind bedacht.

Die Sonne stand schon tief im Westen, als ich auf einen einsamen freien Platz gelangte. Wenn die Straßen, die ich durchwandert, der Mehrzahl nach mich nicht gerade angesprochen, so bot mir hier die Stadt, welche im Glanze der Abendsonne zu meinen Füßen lag, einen herrlichen Anblick. Zum Malen schön breiteten sich im Thale und auf Hügeln und Abhängen die Wohnungen der achtzig Tausend vor mir aus, um die hoch aufsteigenden Kirchen geschaart, durchschnitten von belebten Wasserstraßen und freundlich beleuchtet von den Strahlen der

generally tend to be large, but any person not provided with the arm span of an orangutan should not try to unfold *The Eagle* of Cork. Apart from this extraordinary exhibit of the largest newspaper, whose only claim to fame was its size, the exhibition was, as I have said, excellent. It attracted huge numbers of visitors. Irish people saw with astonishment the variety and excellence of the things that their fellow countrymen were capable of producing. Everybody's face glowed with pleasure and from their lips ran the words: 'A great success, a great success.' 'We can't compare with London and Paris,' one Irishman said to me, 'but at least it's a modest beginning.' May the exhibition stimulate ideas, awaken talent, create trust in native strength and be a powerful impetus for the revival of the country's industry without which that poor, oppressed people will never be at peace on their own native soil.

The exhibition had held me for two hours, whereas my plan for the day had foreseen a mere hour for the visit. Now, however, I had to return to the city to transact a little business and, having gone astray a number of times, found the way that led across Parnell Bridge, then St Patrick's Bridge and finally led up the hill on the north side of the River Lee. It is here that a large part of the city's new buildings are situated. A German word captured my attention as I hurried through this area. On the four windows of a small one-storey house was written: 'High School. For Ladies. Kindergarten. Mixed School.' The German word immediately made me feel at home but only until I came to reflect on its meaning. Somewhat shame-facedly, I moved swiftly away from the house, sad at what a fellow countryman of mine was inflicting on innocent Irish children.*

The sun was already deep in the west when I reached some isolated waste ground. The majority of the streets I traversed did not exactly appeal to me, but from here the city, nestling at my feet in the glow of the evening sun, offered me a magnificent view. Beautiful enough for a painter's brush, the dwelling places of the 80,000 inhabitants were spread out before me in the valley and on the hills and promontories, clustered around the tall churches, criss-crossed by busy waterways and lit by the

---

* Editor's Note: The concept of a 'kindergarten' was a controversial issue for this Catholic cleric.

untergehenden Sonne. Wie friedlich ist doch das Bild für den Betrachter auf der Höhe! Ist es, wie es zu seyn scheint? Wohnt unter den Dächern Friede? Stört kein Mißton die Harmonie der Herzen, die gesellig unter ihnen sich zusammengefunden? Nachdem ich mich dem Eindrucke, den das Gemälde auf mich machte, eine Zeitlang überlassen, schaute ich auf den Weg zurück, den ich gemacht, und mit Hülfe einer Karte der Stadt suchte ich mich mit der Topographie derselben bekannt zu machen.

Sie besteht aus drei Theilen. Der mittlere und ältere liegt auf einer Art von Insel zwischen dem südlichen und einem nördlichen Arme des Küstenflusses Lee, dessen beide Arme sich im Westen der Stadt von einander entfernen und unterhalb derselben im Osten zu einem mächtigen Strom vereinigen. Die Stadt verbreitet sich aber weit über die von den Flußarmen gebildete ovale Insel zu beiden Seiten hinaus, und die nördlich und südlich aufsteigenden Stadttheile sind durch mehrere Brücken mit dem Centrum verbunden. Im südlichen Stadttheile ragt unter den Gebäuden besonders die protestantische Kathedrale mit ihren drei Thürmen hervor, weiter rechts zeigt sich das Queens College, noch mehr rechts das Gefängniß der Grafschaft. *Cork, Corcagh* oder *Corroch* bezeichnet im Irischen Marschland oder Morast. Der Name war gewiß sehr bezeichnend, wie die irischen Namen gewöhnlich, als der hl. Finbar vor tausend Jahren durch Gründung einer Christengemeinde zwischen den beiden Flußarmen den Grund zur Stadt legte. Auch jetzt noch ist der im Thale gelegene Theil feucht.

Als ich nach Besorgung meines Geschäftes auf die freie Stelle zurückkehrte, war es schon dunkel. Im Wasser sich abspiegelnd bezeichneten Lichtreihen den Lauf der Flüsse. Ich ging den Hügel hinab zur Patrickbrücke, und von hier auf derselben Flußseite einen westlichen Hügel hinauf, um mich noch an demselben Abende eines andern Auftrages zu entledigen. Hier passirte ich die protestantische sog. Shandonkirche, deren Thurm anstatt eines Helmes eine Anzahl von Stockwerken hat, welche sich an Umfang abnehmend, übereinander lagern und so eine Art Thurmhelm bilden. Man läutete hier gerade die 'letzte Rose,' doch nur die beiden ersten Zeilen, die man beständig repetirte, und zwar mit Weglassung von ein paar Tönen, da die Glocken nicht für den vollständigen Lauf ausreichten. Die naturwüchsige

gentle rays of the setting sun. How peaceful a picture it is for the observer from this height! Is it as it seems? Does peace reside under the roofs? Does no jarring note disturb the harmony of the hearts that come together under them for social intercourse? Having surrendered to the impression that this painting had made upon me I looked back at the way I had come and, with the aid of a map of the city, I sought to acquaint myself with its topography.

The city consists of three parts. The older, central one is situated on a sort of island between the south and north channels of the Lee. These channels separate in the west of the city to be reunited again to form a mighty river below the city in the east. The city spreads on either side far beyond the oval island formed by the two channels, and the areas of the city located on the hills to the north and south are connected to the city centre by numerous bridges. Of the buildings in the southern part of the city, the protestant cathedral, with its three towers, is particularly distinctive. Queen's College lies further to the right and to the right of that again is the county prison. *Cork, Corcaigh* or *Corroch* means marshland or morass in Irish. The name, as most Irish names, was very apt when St Finnbarr founded the city as a community of Christians 1,000 years ago between the two arms of the river. Even today, the part of the city situated in the valley is damp.

It was already dark when, having transacted my business, I returned to the waste ground. Mirrored in the water, rows of lights marked the course of the river. I walked down the hill to St Patrick's Bridge and from there walked up another hill to the west to fulfill another obligation. Here I passed the Protestant church called Shandon. Its tower boasts not a single cupola but a number of storeys, which, decreasing in circumference, lie one on top of the other, thus creating a sort of cupola tower. Someone was playing 'The Last Rose of Summer' on the bells at that moment, and not getting past the first two lines, which were constantly repeated, while a few notes were omitted because the bells could not support

deutsche Glockenmusik, welche bei freien Schwingungen harmonisch zusammenstimmender Glocken feierlich über Stadt und Land erschallt, ist ebenso in Irland wie in England unbekannt. Der Läutende entlockt der Glocke, deren Seil ihm zugefallen, einen kurzlebigen Ton, fast als schlüge er mit dem Hammer auf die Glocke. Läutet man nur *eine* Glocke, so hört man nur die einförmigen, in gleichen Intervallen aufeinander folgenden Schläge. Läutet man mehrere, in der Regel sind es dann sechs, so haben die Glockenkünstler die Reihenfolge der Töne vorher bestimmt, und es gehört zur Kunst des Läutens, oft und ohne Unterbrechung die Ordnung der Töne zu wechsln. Selten spielt man eigentliche Melodien, und von der Schönheit einer solchen Musik kann man sich eine Vorstellung machen, wenn man sich ans Klavier setzt und, ohne Accelerando oder Ritardando, ohne Piano und Forte, mit *einem* Finger die Töne eines Liedes der Reihe nach abschlägt. Deutsches Glockengeläute gilt dem Engländer als ein ungeordnetes Durcheinander von Tönen; das einheimische begeistert ihn gerade so zu dichterischen Ergüssen, wie das deutsche Geläute den Deutschen. Es sind gerade die Shandonglocken, die von einem irischen Dichter, Franz Mahony, in einer Ode besungen wurden. Es folgen hier die Verse der ersten Strophe, deren vollen, den Glockenton nachahmenden Klang vielleicht mancher Leser der englischen Sprache nicht zugetraut hätte:

> With deep affection
> And recollection
> I often think on
> Those Shandon bells,
> Whose sound so mild would
> In the days of childhood
> Fling round my cradle
> Their magic spells.

Wie aus diesen Versen erhellt, stand die Wiege des Dichters nahe bei der Shandonkirche; obgleich katholischer Priester, ist er unter den von ihm besungenen Glocken im Thurme begraben.

Ich hatte nicht weit zu gehen, um von der Shandonkirche zur

the full melody. The natural German bell music which, combining the harmonies of freely swinging bells, wafts solemnly over town and country, is unknown in either Ireland or England. Here the bell ringer pulling on the rope coaxes a single short-lived note from the bell, almost as if he were striking it with a hammer. If only *one* bell is rung, one hears *only* the monotonous striking of one after the other in the same intervals. If several are rung, and as a rule, there are six bells, the ringers will have decided in advance on the sequence of the sounds. The art of ringing here requires a constant, uninterrupted changing of the sequence of sounds. Actual melodies are seldom played and the best method of describing the beauty of such music would be to sit at the piano and, using only one finger, play the notes of a song, one by one, without accelerando or ritardando, without piano or forte. To English ears the sound of German bells seems a random confusion of sounds. The sound of the native bells evokes poetic effusions, just as German bells awaken similar emotions in Germans. The Irish poet Francis Mahony celebrates these very Shandon bells in an ode. The following lines of the opening stanza imitate the full sound of the bells with a power that some readers might not have thought the English language possessed:

With deep affection
And recollection
I often think on
Those Shandon bells,
Whose sound so mild would
In the days of childhood
Fling round my cradle
Their magic spells.

As these lines demonstrate, the poet's cradle was close to Shandon church and, although a Catholic priest, he is buried under the tower that he celebrated in song.

I did not have far to go to get from Shandon to the Catholic cathedral. Here there was only the sound of *one* bell. It was calling the faithful

katholischen Kathedrale zu gelangen. Hier läutete man auch; doch nur mit *einer* Glocke. Sie rief die Andächtigen zum Abendsegen, welcher hier in der Octave von Mariä Geburt allabendlich Statt hat. Auf meinem Rückwege trat ich in die hohe, weite, im gothischen Stile erbaute Kirche. Draußen war mir Alles so fremd, hier war ich zu Hause. Eine große Menge von Gläubigen kniete in den Bänken und der Priester mit den Ministranten vor dem Altare, auf welchem, von vielen Kerzenflammen umgeben, das hochwürdigste Gut zur Anbetung ausgesetzt war. Als ich eintrat, stimmte die Orgel gerade das *Tantum ergo* zum Schlußsegen an. Die Andächtigen verneigten sich tief, als der Priester sich nach dem Hymnus mit der Monstranz zum Volke kehrte. Es herrschte lautlose Stille. Aber als das Glöckchen erklang, rauschte wie auf ein gegebenes Zeichen, von der Menge mehr geflüstert als gesprochen, ein Wort durch die Kirche; ein zweites und ein drittes Mal kehrte es wieder mit dem Zeichen des Glöckleins; es war der Name Jesus. Mir drang es durch Mark und Bein. Es war der Ausdruck des Staunens der versammelten Menge über die Gegenwart Gottes in ihrer Mitte und des Dankes für den mit ihrem lebendigen Glauben wie mit körperlichen Sinnen wahrgenommenen Gnadensegen, welcher sich in diesem Augenblicke über sie ergoß. Der Irländer hat einen tiefinnigen, lebendigen Glauben und zugleich das Bedürfnis, ihn zu manifestiren. Besteht bei Predigten die Zuhörerschaft aus ächten, vn 'höherer Cultur' noch verschonten Irländern, so werden die Zeichen der Zustimmung zu den Worten des Predigers und die Manifestationen der Herzensaffekte oft so vernehmlich, daß sie leicht einen Prediger, welcher an ein solches Echo seiner Worte nicht gewöhnt ist, aus dem Context bringen können. Solche Zeichen innerer Erregtheit schwinden in dem Maße, als man sich bewußt oder unbewußt den Engländern conformirt.

Nach Schluß der Andacht verweilte ich noch ein Viertelstündchen in der Kirche. Als ich zum Quai hinabeilte, stieß ich auf einen dichten Menschenknäuel. Von vielen Zuhörern umgeben standen auf einem etwas erhöhten Platze zwei Sänger, welche unter lebendigen Gestikulationen einen Dialog vortrugen und offenbar beim höchsten Pathos angelangt waren. Sobald sie mich mit den Abzeichen meines geistlichen Standes sahen, nahmen sie grüßend den Hut ab. Diese

to evening devotions which, during the octave of the feast of the Birth of the Blessed Virgin Mary, take place every evening. On my return journey I went into a church built in the tall, broad, Gothic style. Outside everything was strange to me, here I was at home. A large number of the faithful were kneeling in the pews and the priest and the acolytes were kneeling before the altar where, surrounded by burning candles, the Most Blessed Sacrament was exposed for adoration. As I entered, the organ was just striking up the *Tantum Ergo* for the final blessing. The faithful bowed low when, at the conclusion of the hymn, the priest turned to face them with the monstrance. Utter silence reigned. But as the little bell sounded, one word swept through the church as if at a given sign; more whispered than spoken by the congregation it was repeated a second and a third time at the sounding of the bell; it was the name: Jesus. It moved me to the core. It was the expression of the congregation's awe at the presence of God in their midst, and of their gratitude for the blessings which flowed over them at that moment; a blessing experienced as much through their living faith as through their physical senses. The Irish have a deeply internalised living faith and a matching desire to manifest it publicly. If the congregation listening to sermons consists of genuine Irish people who have been preserved from 'higher culture', then the signs of agreement with the words of the preacher and the external manifestations of heartfelt piety will be so marked that a preacher unaccustomed to such a response may well find himself distracted. Such signs of inner emotion diminish in accordance with how closely one has consciously or unconsciously conformed to the English.

After Benediction, I remained in the church for about a quarter of an hour. As I hurried down the quay I came across a tightly packed crowd of people. Two singers stood elevated above the surrounding listeners, reciting a dialogue accompanied by lively gesticulations and apparently reaching a climax of pathos. As soon as they saw me in my clerical garb, they doffed their hats in greeting. This public expression

Kundgebung ihrer Ehrerbietigkeit wirkte fast komisch bei ihrem Contraste mit der affektvollen Deklamation, die sie in der größten Erregtheit ohne Unterbrechung fortsetzten. Der Gruß zeigte indessen, wie die Achtung vor dem Priester dem Irländer zur zweiten Natur geworden. In die höchsten Regionen des Pathos entrückt, bezeugt sie der irische Acteur ebenso, wie wenn er auf dem Boden des gewöhnlichen menschlichen Lebens wandelt. Ehrfurcht für den Priester ist in der That ein charakteristisches Merkmal des Irländers. Sobald der Priester, von England kommend, den Boden Irlands betritt, liest er es auf den Gesichtern, daß er sich in einem katholischen Lande befindet. In England betrachtet man ihn mit Scheu, gewöhnlich mit großer Aufmerksamkeit, und in der Regel begegnet man ihm mit Achtung. In Irland leuchtet ihm Vertrauen und Ehrfucht aus den Augen entgegen. Männer und Kinder, sowie die Frauen, die keinen Hut tragen, grüßen meistens oder geben sonst ein Zeichen ihrer Hochachtung; so bemerkte ich z.B. mehreremale, daß Männer, welche rauchten, sobald sie mich sahen, augenscheinlich aus Ehrfurcht die Pfeife aus dem Munde nahmen.

Als ich auf meinem Wege zu einem Logis an den Quai kam, sah ich, wie zwei Mädchen im Vorübergehen mit zwei am Ufer stehenden jungen Männer ein paar Worte wechselten. Die letztern bemerkten mich und schienen den Mädchen zu sagen, daß ein Priester komme. Ohne aufzusehen, liefen diese in größter Eile davon. Bei der großen Sittenreinheit des irischen Volkes und seiner Feinfühligkeit im Punkte des sittlichen Anstandes und der Züchtigkeit, die sich in den eigentlichen Sitten dieses Volkes in seiner ganzen äußeren Erscheinung kund gibt, sahen sie in der Unschicklichkeit, mit Männern Abends auf der Straße gesprochen zu haben, ein Vergehen, mit dem befleckt sie den Blick eines Priesters nicht ertragen konnten. Zugleich fürchteten sie vielleicht eine Zurechtweisung. [...]

of reverence seemed almost comical in contrast with the emotional declamation that now continued without interruption and with great excitement. The greeting also demonstrated how respect for the priest in Ireland has become second nature. Even at the heights of pathos, the Irish actor stops to bear witness to what is also at the root of his normal, everyday life. Respect for the priest is, indeed, a characteristic of the Irishman. As soon as a priest travelling from England arrives in Ireland, the faces that meet him tell him that he is in a Catholic country. In England people are shy with him, normally paying him great attention and, in general, treat him with respect. In Ireland the sight of him causes people's eyes to light up with trust and reverence. Men and children as well as women, who do not wear hats, usually salute him and give some visible sign of their respect. I noticed, for example, that men who were smoking, on catching sight of me, instantly removed the pipes from their mouths as a sign of reverence.

On the way to my lodging on the quay, I saw two girls exchange a few words with two young men standing on the riverbank as they crossed the road. The young men noticed me and seemed to indicate to the girls that a priest was approaching. Without looking up, the girls hurried away. In light of the great moral purity of Irish people and their delicacy in matters of moral propriety and modesty – qualities which express themselves saliently in their native customs – the girls saw their conduct in speaking to men on the street in the evening as inappropriate and an offence and, conscious of the stain of that offence, the gaze of a priest would have been intolerable to them. Perhaps they also feared being reprimanded. […]

English translation by Kevin Power.

Paul Villars
(1885)

French original in: *L'Angleterre, l'Ecosse et l'Irlande.* Paris: Quantin, 1885, pp. 140-42.

CORK EST un curieux mélange de rues neuves et larges et de ruelles étroites et sales qui sont en majorité imposante; au lieu de gens affairés circulant à pas pressés, une foule insouciante se meut à loisir; les visages sont riants et vifs, la physionomie de ceux qu'on rencontre est éveillée, intelligente, spirituelle même; mais les Irlandais sont d'une nature passive et contemplative plutôt qu'énergique et résolue. Aussi tout s'en ressent. Qu'ont-ils fait de Cork? Une ville sans animation, sans commerce, dont la population décroît d'année en année. Et cependant, quelle admirable position que celle de cette cité assise au bord de la Lee et dont le port, Queenstown, un des plus vastes et des plus sûrs du monde, est assez spacieux pour que toute la flotte britannique y puisse manœuvrer à l'aise! Bien mieux, tous les navires en partance pour l'Amérique ou qui en viennent touchent à Queenstown et y débarquent et embarquent leurs sacs de dépeches; on pourrait donc donner un développement énorme au commerce avec les États-Unis. Au lieu de cela, il diminue annuellement. En 1878, Cork exporte des marchandises pour une valeur de 16,300 livres et en importe pour 2,200,000 livres. Cinq ans plus tard, les exportations ne sont plus que de 11,800 livres et les importations de 1,500,000 livres sterling! Chiffres officiels. A quoi cela tient-il? Affaire de tempérament, de race, disent les uns, tandis que d'autres soutiennent que si l'Irlande s'appauvrit et se dépeuple, cela tient à des considérations d'un ordre tout différent, et que, livrés à eux-mêmes, les habitants déploieraient des qualités de persévérance et d'énergie, ainsi que des ressources qu'on ne leur connaît pas encore. Soit. Mais n'est-il pas étonnant que Belfast prospère et que Cork décline, alors que l'un et l'autre sont soumis aux mêmes lois et que la présence et l'influence prépondérante de ceux auxquels on attribue la ruine du pays en général fassent précisément la richesse de la province d'Ulster? Grosse question, que les plus habiles n'ont encore pu résoudre et

Paul Villars
(1885)

(Trade – economic problems – Cork vs Belfast)

CORK IS a curious medley of new wide streets and narrow dirty lanes, the latter in a large majority. Instead of a hurrying and busy crowd, we find careless loungers with pleasant smiling faces – bright, intelligent, even clever features; but the Irish are of a passive and contemplative nature rather than energetic and resolute. The result is that everything suffers for it. What have they made of Cork? A city without animation or commerce, whose population is decreasing from year to year; and nevertheless, what a splendid position it stands on the banks of the Lee, whose harbour, Queenstown, one of the largest in the world, is spacious enough to admit the whole of the British fleet, which could manoeuvre there easily. Better still, all the main steamers from and to America call there to embark and trans-ship the mails, so the inhabitants could develop enormously their commerce with the United States. Instead of increasing, it diminishes year by year. In 1878, Cork exported merchandise to the value of £16,300, and imported goods to the value of £2,200,000. Five years later, the exports were only £11,800, and the imports £1,500,000 sterling. These figures are official. To what is this due? A question of temperament and race, say some; while others maintain that if Ireland is poor and depopulated, such results are referable to considerations of a totally different nature, and that if they were left to themselves the inhabitants would develop qualities of perseverance and energy, as well as other resources which people do not credit them with. All very well. But is it not surprising that Belfast is prospering, while Cork is declining, while both are amenable to the same laws, and that the presence and preponderance of those to whom Irishmen attribute the ruin of their country in general are making the fortune of Ulster? It is a big question, which the most skilful have not yet solved, and the solution of which appears always far off. [...]

dont la solution paraît toujours bien éloignée! [...]

Malgré tous ses avantages, sa situation exceptionnelle, Cork voit graduellement diminuer son importance et sa population, et rien ne saurait mieux faire ressortir, sans toutefois l'expliquer, la difference entre l'Irlande du Nord et l'Irlande du Midi que la vue de ces deux cités qui les personnifient, Belfast et Cork.

Cork est à peu de distance de la région la plus pittoresque et la plus agréable de l'Irlande, c'est-à-dire de la vallée de la Blackwater et des lacs et des montagnes de Killarney, que l'on atteint facilement par le chemin de fer.

Notwithstanding all its advantages and its exceptional situation, the importance and population of Cork is gradually diminishing, and nothing can more strongly accentuate, without explaining, the difference between the north and south of Ireland, than the sight of these two typical cities, Belfast and Cork.

Cork is within easy distance of the most agreeable and picturesque part of Ireland, the Valley of the Blackwater, and the lakes and mountains of Killarney, which are easily reached by railway.

English translation in: Paul Villars, England, Scotland and Ireland. *Translated by Henry Frith. London: Routledge, 1887, third part, pp. 140-42.*

Marie-Anne de Bovet
(1889)

French original in: *Trois Mois en Irlande*. Paris: Hachette, 1889.

NON LOIN de là [Monkstown], un caprice de la nature a taillé une soixantaine d'énormes marches au flanc d'une falaise rocheuse dont le pied baigne dans l'eau. L'imagination populaire y voit la main de l'homme, et on vous racontera que c'était l'escalier par lequel le géant O'Mahony descendait prendre son bain. À une distance d'environ six milles de Cork, on se trouve dans une seconde mer intérieure, arrière-rade qui porte le nom de lac Mahon. Laissant à droite deux jolies îles égayées de châteaux enfouis dans la verdure, on entre dans l'estuaire de la Lee, sur les rives plates duquel s'étendent des faubourgs fashionables, blanches villas et fraîches pelouses, dont l'un est affublé du nom de Tivoli, aussi bien approprié que celui de Rialto donné à un triste et froid canal de Dublin. Bientôt on accoste un pont Saint-Patrick [...]

Cork est absolument dénué de caractère. Aucun vestige d'antiquité, sauf une tour de l'abbaye Rouge et quelques fragments des anciens remparts. Disparus, les couvents de franciscains et de dominicains, disparues, la nonnerie de Saint-Jean-Baptiste et la léproserie de Saint-Stephen. Beaucoup d'établissements religieux et d'églises modernes d'un grec bâtard et glacé, ou d'un gothique richement fleuri. Les gens qui aiment la belle bâtisse neuve trouvent à se satisfaire dans la contemplation de la cathédrale consacrée à Saint-Finn Barr l'Albinos; elle est fort imposante, mais parfaitement ennuyeuse.

Le vieux Cork était fait d'un réseau de ruelles tortueuses dont deux seulement subsistent: Bridewell-lane, large de quatre pieds, où se trouvait le marché aux grains, et une autre à laquelle ses douze pieds avaient valu le nom de 'Grande Allée'. Aujourd'hui les voies principales sont très larges, mais fort mal tenues, les rues pauvres sordides à proportion. Les quais médiocrement animés ne sont ni assez monumentaux pour satisfaire le bourgeois, ni assez pittoresques pour plaire à l'artiste. La promenade appelée du nom à consonance flamande de Mardyke est fort belle avec ses grands

Marie-Anne de Bovet
(1889)

(The horrors of Cork architecture – the profession of begging)

NOT FAR from there [Monkstown], on the same side, a caprice of nature has carved out about sixty enormous steps in the side of a rocky, sea-washed, cliff. The popular imagination sees in it the hand of man, and they will tell you that it was the staircase by which the giant O'Mahony descended to take his bath. At about six miles from Cork you find yourself in a second inland sea, a kind of back water, which, bears the name of Lake Mahon – and, in fact, you must be there at low tide to understand that it is the sea which reaches so far. Leaving on the right, two pretty islets, brightened with residences nestling in foliage, you enter the estuary of the Lee, on the flat shores of which extend fashionable suburbs with white villas and green lawns, one of which is dignified with the name of Tivoli, about as appropriate as that of Rialto given to a melancholy canal in Dublin. Presently you reach St Patrick's Bridge in the middle of Cork [...]

Cork is a town, absolutely devoid of character and consequently of interest. There are no remains of antiquity except a tower of the Red Abbey, and some fragments of the ancient ramparts. There are plenty of brand new religious establishments and churches of the present century, of bastard Greek, or of a very modern Gothic, richly ornamented. People who admire modern architecture find satisfaction in gazing at the cathedral of St Finbar, the first stone of which was laid in 1868. It is very handsome, and perfectly uninteresting.

Old Cork was a network of narrow and tortuous alleys, two of which remain – Bridewell Lane, four feet wide, where is the corn market; and another, which, because it is twelve feet wide, is called the Great Alley. Today the principal streets are very wide, but very ill kept; the poorer streets are squalid in proportion. The moderately busy quays are neither sufficiently spacious to satisfy the man of business, nor picturesque enough to please the artist. The promenade, called by the Flemish-sounding name of Mardyke, is very fine, with its big elms, which, for the length of a mile,

ormes qui, sur une longueur d'un mille, entrelacent leurs branches hautes en dôme de verdure; mais elle est déserte. Le collège de la Reine, situé sur une des hauteurs qui bordent le bras sud de la Lee, est un magnifique monument moderne, de ce style d'une riche et élégante fantaisie dit le gothique Tudor, entouré d'un parc bien planté et d'un jardin botanique qui contient de vastes serres. Il ne console qu'à demi de la destruction de l'abbaye de Gill, sur l'emplacement de laquelle il a été érigé, vénérable édifice qui s'est subitement effondré en 1738, près de dix fois séculaire.

Cette platitude extérieure de Cork y rend la promenade d'autant moins attrayante que, comme partout, on ne peut s'arrêter une minute le nez en l'air sans être assassiné par les jérémiades de 'pauvres veuves' en loques et les importunités d'enfants en guenilles. Ici, on embrasse la mendicité comme un état: cela s'appelle 'prendre la route'. Outre que l'extrême détresse qui a de tout temps régné dans l'Ile Verte justifie dans une certaine mesure cette vocation. Les protestants accusent le catholicisme de l'encourager en faisant de la bienfaisance la première des vertus. Je m'explique. Il n'est nation plus charitable que la protestante Angleterre, où tous les hôpitaux et hospices, très nombreux, très magnifiques, sont entretenus par des donations et souscriptions privées. Mais la charité s'y exerce méthodiquement, administrativement, collectivement, l'aumône de la main à la main y est peu pratiquée et assez justement tenue pour immorale. Aussi la mendicité y est-elle sévèrement interdite. Elle l'est également en Irlande, nominalement du moins; mais elle passe à travers les mailles du filet, et si dans les villes elle se dissimule sous d'invraisemblables commerces, dans les campagnes elle s'étale sans déguisement. Il semble qu'en un pays aussi peu fortuné, le métier ne devrait guère être lucratif; mais il n'est d'aussi donnant que les pauvres, et, les exhortations du clergé aidant, l'honorable corporation des mendiants y vit à peu près aussi bien que la moyenne de la population rurale, moins le travail et le noir souci de la rente à payer au landlord, des taxes au fisc.

Puis la mendicité y est dans le sang. Outre les gueux de profession, il y a les femmes qui tendent la main par occasion, lorsqu'elles n'ont rien à faire – le cas est fréquent – que le passant a bonne mine et que le *policeman* de ronde a le dos tourné. Mais la pire engeance, ce sont les enfants, qui presque tous se livrent à la chasse aux gros sous jusqu'à ce qu'ils soient

interlace their lofty branches in a dome of verdure. But it is deserted; and serves for nothing but the Sunday walks of a few shopkeepers and their families. Queen's College, situated on one of the heights on the southern arm of the Lee, is a magnificent modern building, in the elegant style called Tudor-Gothic, and is surrounded by a well-planted park and a botanical garden, which contains immense greenhouses. But it only half consoles one for the destruction of the Abbey of Gill on the site of which it has been erected, a venerable edifice which suddenly collapsed in 1738.

Cork is all the less attractive, because there, as everywhere, you cannot stop for a moment without being pestered by the lamentations of 'poor widows' in rags, and the importunities of children in tatters. Here they follow begging as a trade; they call it 'taking the road'. Besides the extreme distress always prevailing in Ireland, and justifying this calling to some extent, the Protestants accuse the Catholics of encouraging it by making charity the first of virtues. I must explain myself. There is no nation more charitable than Protestant England, where all the hospitals and refuges, which are very numerous and very magnificent, are founded and maintained by private donations and subscriptions. But the charity is exercised methodically, administratively, and collectively; indiscriminate almsgiving is little practised, and justly regarded as immoral. Begging is also sternly forbidden. It is equally forbidden in Ireland, at least, nominally; but it passes through the meshes of the net; and if in the towns it is thinly disguised by the offer of impossible articles for sale, in the country there is no disguise attempted. It would seem that in a country so unfortunate the vocation ought not to be very lucrative, but the poor are the best givers, and, with the aid of the exhortations of the clergy, the honourable corporation of beggars lives almost as well as the average of the rural population, without the work and the worry of rent and taxes.

And then, begging is in the blood. Besides the professional beggars, there are women who beg occasionally, when they have nothing else to do; when the passer-by looks good-natured, and the policeman on his beat has his back turned. But worst of all are the children, who almost universally

en âge de gagner leur pain d'autre manière.

Nous nous reposions dans l'église catholique Saint-Pierre et Saint-Paul, un de ces riches édifices néo-gothiques dus à l'architecte Pugin, pour lesquels Érin trouve toujours de l'argent. Dans les coins, de vieilles femmes déguenillées, accroupies sur les talons, égrenaient leur chapelet. Des hommes entraient, posaient leur mouchoir sur la dalle pour s'agenouiller dessus, disaient leur prière, et se retiraient, très révérencieux. Arrivent deux gamines à moitié nues. La plus grande se hausse jusqu'au bénitier et prend si abondamment de l'eau sainte, que son signe de croix sert à la débarbouiller, puis elle se met à genoux; sa petite sœur l'imite, mais en tournant le dos à l'autel. L'aîné serre dans sa main une bouteille dont l'odeur révèle qu'elle contient du pétrole imparfaitement raffiné; en venant de la remplir chez l'épicier du coin, elle est entrée faire ses dévotions et chercher quelque aubaine. Pendant qu'elle marmotte des fragments de patenôtres, ses yeux fureteurs fouillent l'église, elle nous aperçoit: attention! Au bout de quelques minutes, elle sort, après un nouveau débarbouillage à l'eau bénite, et quand nous sortons à notre tour, nous les trouvons embusquées derrière la porte. Comme par hasard, la petite se laisse choir sur les degrés; bosse au front, hurlements à ameuter la ville. Le rond de cuivre attendu sort de notre poche, et son aspect magique tarit subitement les larmes. Puis, comme une demi-douzaine de petits voyous crasseux qui flânent aux abords du saint lieu jettent des regards sournois sur cette scène, nos deux morveuses décampent au galop avec leur butin. Au coucher du soleil, elles auront gagné une aussi bonne journée que leur père.

(and they are legion in prolific Ireland) devote themselves to the quest of the penny till they are old enough to get their living in some other way. We paused for a while in the Catholic church of Saints Peter and Paul, one of these rich neo-Gothic edifices designed by the architect Pugin and for which Erin always finds money. In the corners, old women in rags, leaning back on their heels, were praying, their rosary beads in their hands. Men would enter, place their handkerchief on the tiled floor, kneel down on it, say a prayer and leave, full of reverence. Then two half-naked little girls appeared. The bigger of the two reached up to the font and scooped out so much holy water that, in blessing herself, she managed to clean herself up. Then she knelt down. Her little sister imitated her, but with her back turned to the altar. The older one clasped in her hand a bottle smelling of badly refined paraffin. On her way from the grocer's cornershop where she had filled it, in she had come to pray and to hunt for some godsend. While she was muttering fragments of the 'Our Father', her weasel eyes scoured the church and then she spotted us: watch out! A few minutes later, out with her, having again cleaned herself up with holy water. When we too left, we found them lying in ambush behind the door. As if by chance, the smaller of the two let herself sink down onto the steps, bruising her forehead. Her screams would send the city into a panic. Out with our purses which, as if by magic, suddenly dried up her tears. Then, as half a dozen filthy little brats hanging around the holy place were casting sly glances over at this scene, our two snotty-nosed little girls sped off with their booty. By sunset, they will have earned as much in the day as their father.

English translation in: Madame de Bovet, Three Months' Tour in Ireland. *Translated and condensed by Arthur Walter. London: Chapman and Hall, 1891, pp. 127-30; last paragraph translated by Grace Neville.*

Jiří Guth

(1895)

Czech original in: *Na zeleném Erinu. Kresby z irských cest.*
Kostelec nad Orlicí: Kunc a Hamerský, 1895, pp. 130-33

[...] PŘIJEL JSEM večer srpnového dne přímo z Youghalu do třetího města irského, Corku, které leží docela na protivném konci než Belfast, opět docela sám, což celkem netrápilo mě mnoho, an místo geologických přednášek německého professora měl jsem příležitost poznati hned noční život bývalé kapitály Corkského království, který venkoncem je právě takový jako noční životy všude jinde.

Bývaly časy, kdy kronikář anglický Camden vypravoval o tomto městě a jeho kraji, že je plno všelikterakých banditů, tak že občané jsou nuceni míti neustále stráž přede dveřmi, jež zavírají nejenom na celou noc, ale také při jídle a při modlení. Nestrpěli tenkrát, aby cizinec přišel do města se zbraní, a sami chodili na procházku a vůbec ven jen v průvodu stráže. Svým sousedům že nedůvěřovali vstupujíce ve sňatky jen mezi sebou, kteréžto poslední okolnost i teď, po 300 letech byla by nás trápila nejmíň, neboť, nemůžeme si pomoci – upřímně řečeno – tamnější děvčata nestojí za groš. Jinak pro svoji bezpečnost nepotřebovali jsme ani šavlí ani houfnic, neřku-li děl, v čemž lišili jsme se podstatně od Oliviera Cromwella, který, když se města zmocnil, všecky zvony dal přelíti na děla. A když purkmistr a snad i zástupcové kléru bázlivě mu to vytýkali, odpověděl docela vážně: 'A proč ne? vždyť prach vynalezl také mnich.' Kronika nepovídá, co na to páni odpověděli.

Cromwell ulil tam děl asi velmi mnoho, uvážíme-li, že už od VII. věku místo to bylo proslulé zbožným obyvatelstvem: žiloť tam tehdy na sedm set kněží a mnichů. Teď jich tam je mnohem méně, neboť kraj

Jirí Guth
(1895)

(Cromwell – Cork compared to Dublin and Belfast – lack of sights)

[...] ON AN evening in autumn I arrived, straight from Youghal, in Cork, the third city in Ireland. It is located directly at the opposite end of the island from Belfast. Again, I was completely alone; however, this did not really worry me too much, as instead of the geological lecturing of a German professor I had the opportunity to immediately acquaint myself with the night life of the former capital of the kingdom of Cork, it being the same throughout as night life anywhere else.

There were times when the English chronicler Camden claimed about this city and the surrounding region that it swarmed with all kinds of brigands, so as the citizens were forced to keep a guard constantly positioned at their door, which door they shut not only during the night but also at mealtimes and while at prayer. In those times the people would not allow a stranger to come into the city while carrying a weapon, and would venture out for a walk solely in the company of a guard. Apparently they distrusted their neighbours, which is why they entered into marriage only amongst themselves. The latter circumstance would in fact worry us very little even now, after 300 years, as – it cannot be helped, and to tell the truth – the local girls are not worth a penny. This notwithstanding, we did not need for our security either sabres or mortars, not to mention cannons, significantly unlike Oliver Cromwell who on capturing the city ordered all bells to be recast as guns. And when the burgomaster, possibly together with representatives of the clergy, timidly objected, Cromwell replied entirely in earnest: 'And why not? Wasn't gunpowder invented by monks, too?' The chronicle does not mention the gentleman's response.

Cromwell must have cast a great number of guns there, considering that already since the seventh century the place had been renowned for the piety of its inhabitants: up to 700 priests and monks used to live there

valně schudl. Krev, která teče další historií Corku právě tak, jako dějinami jiných měst irských a celého Erinu vůbec, odnesl kromě jiných také král Jiří II., jehož socha zmizela před několika lety z promenády Grand Parade: našli ji po dlouhém hledání v bahně řeky Lee.

V Corku nezdržíme se dlouho, nic tam není, leda pěkný kontrast tohoto staroirského města proti anglosaskému Belfastu. Je to podivuhodná směs ulic nových a širokých a starých a křivých, vesměs však špinavých. V Belfastu ruch a moderní honba po penězích, tady život líný, jako bezstarostný, irský. V Dublině to obé jaksi je sloučeno. Tváře jsou tady smavé a živé, inteligentní, a mimoděk vzpomínáš na všecko, co jsi slyšel a četl o původu tohoto plemene a o přistěhovalcích z jižních břehův. Upomínají na ně zejména černé oči a černé vlasy, valně se lišící od zrzavých vousův a našedivělých zřítelnic anglosaských. Irčan je také kontemplativní a má málo energie, tak jako jeho praotcové tam na jihu, a je také nepřítelem práce. I v tom má Cork ráz města jižního (a s ním nejedno město irské v těchhle končinách a také na západě, jako Limerick a Galway), že obyvatelé zdají se žíti více na ulici než doma. Cork, třeba že má nějakých 80.000 obyvatelů, je město jako bez ducha, bez obchodu. A přece má polohu jako stvořenou pro obchod světový: podivuhodně krásný přístav Queenstown, do něhož by se vešlo všecko loďstvo britské, a v němž zastavují všecky transatlantické lodi anglické, a přes to je tam jako po vymření a je-li vůbec ještě nějaký obchod, pak klesá rok od roku. I číslice máme po ruce na toto tvrzení.

Jedni svádějí tu nečinnosť irskou na temperament, neschopnosť raçy, která ani nejpříznivějších podmínek nedovede využíti, druzí zase tvrdí, že to klesání Irska má důvody docela jiné, a že kdyby Irčané mohli vlásti sami sobě, ukázali by vytrvalosť a energii docela jinačí. První mají pro

then. These days, the number is considerably lower, as the area has grown substantially impoverished. The spilled blood, which streams through the successive history of Cork in a manner similar to the rest of the entire Erin, has been paid for – among others – by King George II whose statue disappeared several years ago from the Grand Parade: after a long search, it was found in the mud of the River Lee.

We shall not dwell long in Cork: it has nothing to offer, excepting perhaps a nice contrast which this old Irish town makes with Anglo-Saxon Belfast. The city is a peculiar mélange of new, wide streets with streets old and crooked, nonetheless all largely dirty. In Belfast, a general stir and the modern quest for money, here a life lazy, apparently careless, Irish. In Dublin, both of these aspects seem to be combined somehow. Faces here are smiling and lively, intelligent, and you are unwittingly reminded of what you had heard and read about the origin of this people and about the immigration from the southern shores. The immigrants are recalled mainly by the black eyes and black hair, notably different from the red beards and greyish eyes of the Anglo-Saxons. Moreover, the Irishman is contemplative and has little energy, same as his ancestors in the distant south, and appears to be similarly inimical to work. Cork has a flavour of a southern town (and together with it a great number of Irish towns in this region and also in the west, for instance Limerick or Galway) in regard to an additional fact that the inhabitants seem to live more in the street than at home. Despite Cork having some 80,000 inhabitants, the city looks as if lifeless and without any commerce. However, its location is simply ideal for international trade: a remarkably beautiful port of Queenstown which would accommodate the entire British fleet and which all English transatlantic ships stop at, and yet not a soul in sight; and if any commerce still happens, it diminishes from year to year. We can document this assertion also by figures at hand.

Some attribute the Irish idleness to temperament, the fecklessness of a race incapable to make advantage even of the most favourable conditions, others on the other hand claim that completely different reasons are to blame for the fall of Ireland into decrepitude and that if the Irish could govern themselves, they would show an entirely different kind of endurance and energy. Some arguments can be supplied for the former

svoje výroky i důvody, druzí na ně teprve čekají, až Gladstone a jeho stoupenci prorazí se svojí home-rule. Ale Belfastu daří se znamenitě, a přece podmínky jeho vzrůstu jsou tak podobny těmto zde! Leč začínáme se opět motati v pavučinách politiky, honem z nich ven!

Cork-life is chiefly concerned about two ideas: eating and joking*) — charakterisoval r. 1748 Arthur Murphy veselou mysl Corkských, čímž asi je pověděno, že tyto dvě ideje, jídlo a bezstarostí, celkem přece jen vůdčí ideje všeho lidstva, v Corku dovedly silně vytrysknouti nad obyčejnou úroveň. Idea sladkého 'nicnedělání' udržuje se doposud hodně vysoko, ale s jídlem podle zdání je tam hůř. Není na ně, čehož důkazem, že co chvíli irská bída tahá nás tam za šos. Žebráctví i tady je řemeslem pěkně vyvinutým, a snad kdybychom déle tady byli, poznali bychom — nejednu chudou vdovu, podobnou oné dublínské, u které, když pro žebrotu byla zatčena, bylo nalezeno v tajnostech spodničky 120 liber šterlinků ve zlatě a stříbře, pak ostatních peněz papírových a měděných celkem asi za 7000 zl. a vedle toho pár vařených brambor, něco hrachu a podobné žebrácké drobotiny. Zajímavo je, že protestanté uvalují zodpovědnosť za tento vzácný vývoj, jemuž se v Irsku těší žebrota, na katolíky. Tomu tak je rozuměti, že katolíci neprovádějí dobročinnosť systematicky dávajíce jen, bez ohledu na skutečnou potřebu, kdežto v protestantské Anglii, kde žebrota je zapovězena, dobročinnosť, velikou měrou soukromá, je náležitě zregulována. Tak se stává, že irský žebrák, který rozumí svému obchodu, má slušné příjmy středních tříd a k tomu žádnou práci a žádné starosti. Irčané jakoby žebrotu měli v krvi: natahují ruku z dlouhé chvíle, zvláště když vidí cizince; z deseti jistě aspoň jeden ustrne se nad jejich hadry a jejich špínou.

Vedle těchto a podobných úvah zabíjíme čas prohlížením památností, jichž Cork nemá, třeba že je městem tak starým; delší by byl seznam

---

*) Život v Corku má největší starosť o dvě věci: jídlo a žert.

claim, while the latter is still waiting to be proven after Gladstone and his supporters have managed to break through with their Home Rule. Apart from that, however, Belfast prospers, in spite of the conditions of its growth being so much like the conditions here. But we are once more becoming entangled in the spider-webs of politics: let us leave these tenets promptly!

'Cork-life is chiefly concerned about two ideas: eating and joking,' to quote a description of the merry mind of the Corkonians provided by Arthur Murphy in 1748; which is roughly to say that these two notions – food and lightheartedness – which, all in all, represent leading ideas of the entire humanity – managed to powerfully spurt out above the usual level in Cork. The idea of sweet idleness is still highly valued; nonetheless, it appears that the situation is much worse with regard to food. People have no money to obtain it, and this is proven by the Irish poverty every so often pulling at the tail of our coat. Beggary is a well-developed occupation in this town as well, and it may be that if we stayed here longer we would get to know about a few of those poor widows akin to the one in Dublin who, when arrested for begging, was discovered to harbour in the secrecy of her shift 120 pounds Sterling in gold and silver, together with approximately 7,000 guldens' worth of other kinds of money in paper and copper, and next to that a couple of boiled potatoes, a handful of peas and similar trifles of a beggar. What is interesting is that Protestants put the blame for the extraordinary development concerning beggary in Ireland on the Catholics. This is to be understood as a claim that Catholics do not pursue charity in a systematic manner and merely give without considering whether the need is real, while in Protestant England – where begging has been outlawed – charity, to a large extent run by private hands, is properly regulated. Hence it happens that an Irish beggar, knowledgeable about his trade, has a decent income equivalent to the middle classes, and on top of that no work and no concerns. It is as if the Irish had begging in their blood: they extend their hand as time lies heavy on it, especially when they see a stranger; at least one out of ten will be bound to take pity on their rags and their dirt.

Apart from these and similar reflections, we kill time by inspecting the sights – which Cork lacks, although a town so ancient: the list of

toho, co tam už není, než toho, co tam je. I z těch nejpůvodnějších starých ulic zůstaly jen dvě: Bridewell-Lane, úzká jen 4 stopy, kde se konával trh obilní, a jiná, která slula Velká Alej, proto že byla 12 stop široká. Ani v Corku neubráníme se dojmu schátralosti, která Irskem čiší všude, kde je člověk. S velikým interesem prohlížíme budovy moderní, v nichž vyniká Cathedral of St. Finbarre, v tudorskogothickém slohu, dokončená roku 1870, pak různé *public-houses* atd.

what is not there any more would be longer than that of what there is. Even of the earliest old streets only two have remained: Bridewell Lane, a narrow street of no more than four feet which used to hold corn markets, and one originally called the Great Alley, as it used to be twelve feet wide. In Cork neither can we keep from acquiring the impression of general ruin which permeates Ireland in all places of human presence. With great interest we examine modern buildings, of which particularly the Cathedral of St Finbar stands out; it was built in the style of Tudor Gothic and completed in 1870. Then various public houses, etc.

English translation by Ondrej Pilny.

Charles Legras
(1898)

French original in: *Terre d'Irlande.* Paris: Ollendorff, 1898, pp. 78-82, 87-88.

JOLIE VILLE QUI se déroule comme un ruban sur des collines et sure les rives du fleure Lee, au bord d'une rade merveilleuse. La couleur locale est fortement marquée dans le peuple. Les femmes portent sur la tête, les unes des capelines noires, plissées, ornées par devant de deux larges rubans qui pourraient servir à faire un boucle, mais qui pendent sur la poitrine; les autres, des larges châles bruns, bordés d'une rayure de couleur éclatante, sous lesquels ou voit à peine leurs yeux, comme ceux des Mauresques. En Afrique, cette coiffure protège contre le soleil; en Irlande, contre la pluie. Excepté le chapeau à larges bords, le costume des hommes est simple, mais leur langage est rehaussé d'accent gaélique, aussi extraordinaire en anglais que l'accent de Saint-Flour à Paris. Et jusqu'ici on m'appelait souvent 'gentleman' ou 'sir'; je deviens: 'Votre Honneur!'

Aucun monument intéressant à Cork; mais j'ai-visité les hommes: des propriétaires, des marchands et fort peu de journalistes. 'Monsieur,' m'ont-ils dit, 'les Irlandais font fortune dans tous les pays du monde, excepté en Irlande! En Amérique, nous comptons 8 à 10 millions de compatriotes, et vous savez combien d'argent ils ont envoyé à Parnell et à la National League, lors de la campagne agraire; en Australie, la colonie irlandaise devient chaque jour plus riche et plus prospère, et même en Angleterre, chose étrange, environ 2 millions d'entre nous réussissent à vivre et parfois à faire fortune [...] Voyez-vous, Monsieur, si nous faisons faillite dans notre pays, il faut en accuser les Anglais!' [...]

Hier, j'ai lu dans un journal de la ville: 'Emigrants partis de Cork la semaine passée, 423. Nombre correspondant pour la semaine de l'année dernière, 252.' Le mouvement est donc loin de se ralentir, et, si le paysan irlandais n'était pas le plus prolifique du monde, l'île d'Emeraude, la perle de l'Océan, se transformerait promptement en désert [...]

La baie de Cork. – Un inextricable et gigantesque fouillis de golfes, de promontoires et d'îles. Une flotte peut y disparaître comme une aiguille

Charles Legras
(1898)

(Irish abroad – emigration – Cork harbour)

CORK IS a pretty town that unfurls like a ribbon over hills and along the banks of the River Lee, on the shores of a marvellous harbour. Local colour is clearly to be seen in its inhabitants. Some women wear black headdresses, pleated, and decorated in front with two wide ribbons that could form a bow but that hang down; others wear wide, brown, brightly bordered shawls under which their eyes can hardly be seen, just like Moorish women. In Africa, this protects against the sun; in Ireland, against the rain. Apart from their wide-brimmed hats, the men are dressed simply, but their manner of speaking is heightened by a Gaelic accent as extraordinary in English as the Saint-Flour accent in Paris. Up to now, I have often been called 'gentleman' or 'sir'; now I have become 'Your Honour!'

There are no interesting monuments in Cork; but I made various visits to proprietors, merchants and very few journalists. 'Sir', they said to me, 'the Irish strike it rich in every country in the world, except Ireland! In America, we have 8,000,000 or 10,000,000 compatriots, and do you realise how much money they sent to Parnell and to the National League during the land campaign; in Australia, the Irish colony is becoming richer and more prosperous day by day, and even in England, it's odd to think that about 2 million of us manage to live and even sometimes to make a fortune there [...] Sir, if we fail here in our own country, the English should be blamed for that!' [...]

Yesterday, I read in a Cork newspaper: 'Number of emigrants leaving Cork last week: 423. Number for the corresponding week last year: 252.' The rate of emigration is thus far from slowing down, and, if Irish peasants were not the most prolific in the world, the Emerald Isle, pearl of the Ocean, would quickly become a desert [...]

Cork harbour is a gigantic, inextricable jumble of bays, headlands and islands. A whole fleet could disappear in there like a needle in a haystack. When Francis Drake's fleet was being pursued by the *Invincible*

se cacha si bien dans l'estuaire de l'Owenboy, derrière la grande île, que dans du foin, et celle de Francis Drake, poursuivi par l'*Invincible Armada,* les Espagnols fouillèrent vainement la rade pendant plusieurs jours et se retirèrent, persuadés qu'un mirage magique leur avait dérobé la fuite de l'ennemi.

Un service de bateaux à vapeur parcourt la baie, peu animée; de rares bâtiments de commerce, quelques yachts el des yoles de course, et, deux fois par semaine, la grande agitation d'un steamer transatlantique qui fait escale entre Liverpool et New-York. Aujourd'hui, le ciel et l'horizon n'ont que des nuances tendres et fondues, rien de heurté, et l'on se plaît à croire qu'il y a 'de la joie de vivre' dans les petites villes blanches et les coquettes villas qui s'étagent sur les rives vertes.

Armada, it hid so well in the Owenboy estuary behind the great island that the Spanish searched the harbour in vain for several days before leaving, convinced that some magic mirage had hidden the enemy's flight from them.

A steamboat service crosses the rather lifeless bay; a few merchant ships, a handful of yachts and racing skiffs with, twice weekly, great fuss surrounding the arrival of a transatlantic steamer crossing from Liverpool to New York. Today, the sky and the horizon are swathed in delicate, melted hues, nothing dramatic, and it would be good to believe that there is some *joie de vivre* to be found in the little white towns and the pretty villas built in terraced rows along the green banks.

English translation by Grace Neville.

Charles Schindler
(1903)

French original in: *En Irlande*. Paris: Juven, 1903, pp. 105-112.

CORK, 18 AOÛT. – Cork est la plus grande des villes purement irlandaises. Elle compte un peu plus de soixante quinze mille habitants. A part les fenêtres à guillotine, on dirait une cité normande, mêmes murs gris, mêmes hôtelleries sans apparence et, hélas! même mendicité éhontée jusque de la part des plus petits enfants. Un bébé à peine capable de courir m'a poursuivi, pieds nus, pendant deux cents mètres, en me réclamant 'un petit sou, s'il vous plaît!'

La ville est bâtie sur une île, à l'embouchure de la Lee, jolie rivière bordée de coteaux boisés qui se couvrent peu à peu de villas à l'anglaise. Il faut avoir les deux spécimens sous les yeux pour estimer toute la supériorité des Anglo-Saxons lorsqu'il s'agit d'architecture domestique. Leurs maisons sont sans aucun doute ce que les Anglais ont de mieux, la fantaisie et la commodité s'y associent sans se nuire; leurs larges vitres d'une seule pièce les emplissent de lumière et leurs jardinets les environnent de fraîcheur.

Cork possède un opéra et trois grands journaux; Cork a en outre une exposition.

L'EXPOSITION

Cette exposition se qualifie d'Internationale: l'exotisme n'y est représenté que par la rue du Caire, dont toute exhibition qui se respecte ne peut s'affranchir, et par un pavillon canadien: le reste est presque exclusivement occupé par le 'département de l'agriculture et de l'instruction technique en Irlande'. Le gouvernement, sur l'initiative de M. Plunkett, a dépensé cinq cent mille francs pour donner cette leçon de choses aux Irlandais; M. Hannon, qui représente à l'exposition la 'Société pour l'organisation agricole de l'Irlande' veut bien me guider de section en section.

On a groupé ici des spécimens de toutes les industries que M. Plunkett et ses amis veulent acclimater en Irlande: chapellerie, tissage, tapisserie, verrerie et le reste. Non seulement on y peut voir leurs produits et les instruments

Charles Schindler
(1903)

(Cork exhibition – France and Ireland)

C ORK *18 AUGUST*. Cork is the largest of the purely Irish towns, with a population of just over 75,000 inhabitants. Apart from its sash windows, it looks just like some town in Normandy with the same grey walls, same kinds of unremarkable hostelries and, alas! the same shameless begging even on the part of the smallest children. A barefoot baby hardly able to run followed me for 200 metres looking for 'a ha'penny, please'.

The town is built on an island at the mouth of the Lee. The Lee is a pretty river bordered with wooded slopes which English-style villas are covering little by little. You would need to have these two examples in front of you in order to realise just how much better the Anglo-Saxons are when it comes to domestic architecture. Their houses undoubtedly represent the best of what the English own, a safe alliance of imagination and practicality. Their wide windows of just one pane of glass fill them with light, and their little gardens surround them with freshness.

Cork has an opera house and three major newspapers; in addition Cork has an exhibition.

THE EXHIBITION
This exhibition describes itself as international, although the only example of exoticism in it is Cairo street (which no self-respecting exhibition would do without) and a Canadian pavilion: the rest is almost entirely occupied by the Irish Department of Agriculture and Technical Instruction. On Mr Plunkett's initiative, the Government spent 500,000 francs in order to provide this practical lesson for the Irish; Mr Hannon, who represents the Society for the Organisation of Irish Agriculture at the exhibition, agreed to guide me from section to section.

Examples of all the industries with which Mr Plunkett and his friends want to familiarise Ireland are grouped here: hat-making, weaving, carpet-making, glass-making and so forth. Not only can these products and the

qui servent à les fabriquer, mais des ouvriers exécutent l'ouvrage sous les yeux des visiteurs. Les rénovateurs de l'Irlande économique espèrent triompher de l'objection que chacun leur oppose. Parlent-ils de créer une nouvelle industrie: 'Nous n'y connaissons rien', répond la foule, peu disposée à s'aventurer dans des sentiers nouveaux. Ces routiniers indécrottables verront que ce qu'on leur conseille de faire n'est pas difficile à apprendre.

La Société pour l'organisation agricole de l'Irlande a imaginé des excursions à prix réduits au profit des paysans qui viennent s'instruire ici de tous les coins de l'île. M. Hannon est chargé de les piloter dans le labyrinthe.

UNE CARAVANE DE CAMPAGNARDS
Justement, toute une paroisse du Tipperary vient d'arriver sous la conduite de son curé. Ils sont là six cents paysans endimanchés, qui dépensent chacun près de dix francs pour cette visite. M. Hannon les reçoit. Beaucoup ressemblent à nos paysans bretons; d'autres à de matois normands; quelque-uns sont vêtus avec la correction des gros fermiers d'Angleterre. Certaines femmes ont une physionomie très fine.

Le directeur de l'Exposition leur souhaite la bienvenue. Ils écoutent avec attention. Leur curé, le père Scanlon, un visage franc et sympathique, se charge de répondre pour eux; puis, comme on lui dit que je représente un journal français, il me, serre vigoureusement la main: 'Vive la belle France! ... chrétienne', crie-t-il d'une voix forte.

PRÊTRE ET PAYSANS
[...] A voir le père Scanlon guider ses ouailles, je comprends l'influence du clergé sur les Irlandais, il va de l'un à l'autre, use de la maïeutique chère à Socrate, interroge chacun avec une rare habilité pour le forcer à réfléchir sur ce qu'il a vu, lui demande en même temps son avis sur ses propres conclusions.

Nous entrons dans une baraque de zinc ou un savant écossais discourt sur l'élevage des bestiaux; je suis plutôt surpris en l'entendant discuter des doctrines de Darwin devant ces paysans celtes. Mon curé est enthousiaste. Nous sortons, il ne rencontre pas une de ses ouailles sans

tools used to make them be seen here, but workers actually make them right in front of the visitors. The people involved in revitalising Ireland's economy are hoping to overcome all the objections that everyone is making. When they talk of creating a new industry: 'we know nothing about it', the crowd replies, unenthusiastic about venturing out on new paths. Although they are inveterate creatures of habit, they will realise that what they are being advised to do is not difficult to learn.

The Society for the Organisation of Irish Agriculture thought up reduced-rate excursions for Irish peasants from all corners of the island who are coming here to learn. Mr Hannon is responsible for guiding them around the maze.

A CONVOY OF COUNTRY FOLK

In that context, a whole parish from Tipperary has just arrived under the stewardship of its parish priest: 600 peasants in their Sunday best spending almost ten francs each on this visit. Mr Hannon welcomes them. Many of them look like our Breton peasants, others like crafty Normans. Some are dressed formally like prosperous English farmers. Some of the women's faces are quite beautiful.

The Director of the Exhibition welcomes them. They listen attentively. Their priest, Fr Scanlon, looking honest and likeable, takes it upon himself to answer for them. Then, as he was told that I represent a French newspaper, he shakes my hand vigorously: 'Long live beautiful France – a Christian country,' he shouts loudly.

PRIEST AND PEASANTS

[…] Seeing Fr Scanlon guiding his flock, I understand the clergy's influence on the Irish people. He goes from one to the other, drawing each of them out, as Socrates would have done, questioning them with rare skill to force them to reflect on what they have seen, at the same time asking them for their opinions on his own conclusions.

We go in to a zinc stall where a Scottish expert is talking about raising cattle. I am rather surprised to hear him expounding on Darwin's theories in front of these Celtic peasants. My parish priest is enthusiastic. Out we go, and he does not meet a single member of his flock without

lui montrer la baraque d'un geste: 'Allez voir! c'est très intéressant et très utile, ce qu'on explique là-dedans'!

L'ÉDIT DE NANTES ET L'IRLANDE
Un employé du département de l'agriculture m'explique comment son ministère va chercher dans tous les pays du monde les meilleures méthodes de développer les pécheries irlandaises. A l'Allemagne il emprunte la pisciculture scientifique; à la France, l'ostréiculture. Il ne dédaigne pas les détails les plus infimes et s'occupe de vérifier si les filets bleus ont vraiment pour la pêche aux sardines les avantages que leur attribue les pêcheurs de Concarneau. L'Irlande est un pays maritime et lacustre. La pêche peut lui fournir des ressources presque sans limites.

'Mais,' dis-je à mon professeur, en remarquant les traits méridionaux de son visage, 'auriez-vous des Français dans votre famille?'

'Non, pas du tout.'

'Même pas de lointains ancêtres?'

'Oh! il y a quelque deux cents ans, notre famille est venue d'Auvergne en Irlande après la révocation de l'Edit de Nantes.'

J'avais déjà entendu que les 'religionnaires' avaient beaucoup contribué à la prospérité de Belfast. Leçons que les fauteurs d'intolérance feraient bien de méditer: ce sont des Français pérsécutés qui ont créé la ville la plus prospère de l'Irlande, et, par contre, mainte famille de ce pays-ci a fourni plus d'un brillant officier à l'armée française.

pointing to the stall: 'Go on and see! What they're explaining in there is really interesting and very useful!'

THE EDICT OF NANTES AND IRELAND

A Department of Agriculture employee explains to me how his ministry travels the world in search of the best methods for developing Irish fisheries. From Germany, he borrows expertise on scientific fish breeding and, from France, on oyster farming. Nothing is discounted, not even the smallest details, and care is taken to check if blue netting really is as beneficial for sardine fishing as the fishermen in Concarneau claim. Ireland is a country of seas and lakes. Fishing could bring it almost limitless resources. 'But', say I to my teacher, noticing his Mediterranean features, 'do you have French blood somewhere in your family?' 'No, not at all'. 'Not even distant ancestors?' 'Oh, about 200 years ago, our family came from the Auvergne to Ireland after the Revocation of the Edict of Nantes'.

I had already heard that these religious refugees had made a major contribution to Belfast's prosperity. These are lessons that the critics of intolerance should reflect on: it was persecuted French people who created the wealthiest city in Ireland and, on the other hand, many a family in this country provided a brilliant officer for the French army.

English translation by Grace Neville.

Hachette Guides-Joanne
(1912)

French original in: *Angleterre, Ecosse-Irlande*. Paris: Hachette, 1912 (series: Guides-Joanne), pp. 290-92.

1 65 MIL. CORK, V. DE 78,000 hab., capitale de la province de Munster, est admirablement située sur la Lee, dont les deux bras naviguables, l'un et l'autre, presque jusqu'à leur point de bifurcation, et bordés de quais longs et commodes, enserrent une partie considerable de la vieille ville. Cork est un admirable centre d'excursions dans toute la partie S.-O. de l'Irlande, dont elle est à tous points de vue la ville la plus intéressante.

Gares: *Great Southern and Western Station*, Lower Glanmire Road, lignes de Dublin, Queenstown, Killarney (via Mallow), Waterford et Rosslare (id.) [...] – *Albert Quay Station*, ligne du Cork, Bandon et South Coast Railway, pour Killarney via Glengariff et la 'Route du Prince de Galles'; – *Albert Street Station*, pour Monkstown, Queenstown, Crosshaven, etc.; – *Capwell Station*, pour Macroom et Killarney par la 'Tourist Route' pour Glengariff et Killarney; – *Western Road Station*, sur une petite ile près de l'endroit où la Lee bifurque, trains légers pour Coachford, Blarney, etc.

Hôtels: – *Imperial*, de 1er ordre, St Patrick's Str.; – *Victoria*, St Patrick's Str. (lunch 2 sh. 6, thé 1 sh.6, din. 3 sh., ch. dép. 4 sh., pens. 9 sh); - *Windsor* (lunch 2 sh., thé 1 sh., din. 3 sh., ch. dép. 2 sh. 6); *Lloyd's* George's Str.; – *Grosvenor, Leech's, Hibernian* (prix modérés); – etc.

Trams électriques: – d'une gare à l'autre (1 d.) et pour: –- (2 mil. S.) *Douglas*; – ($^{1}/_{2}$ mil. S.) *Ballintemple*; – *Blackrock*, à l'E.; – *Sunday's Well* à l'O.

Voitures de place (*Cars*): – aux gares et aux nombreuses stations dans les principales rues de la ville; *à la course*, 1 pers. 1 sh., 2 pers., 1 sh. 6; – *à l'heure*: 1 sh. 6 la première h., 9 d. par ? h. en plus. – Prix doubles de 10h. s. à 9 h. mat.

Hachette Guides-Joanne
(1912)

(Cork in a tourist guidebook)

1 65 MILES [FROM Dublin]. CORK, town of 78,000 inhabitants, the capital of the province of Munster, has an admirable setting on the banks of the River Lee. A large part of the old town is encircled by the two channels of the river: flanked by long and commodious quays, both of these are navigable, almost up as far as the point where they diverge. Cork is an ideal base for excursions throughout the south-western part of Ireland, being the most interesting town in the region from every point of view.

Stations: *Great Southern and Western Station*, Lower Glanmire Road, routes to Dublin, Queenstown, Killarney (via Mallow), Waterford and Rosslare (ditto). – *Albert Quay Station*, routes from Cork, Bandon and South Coast Railway, to Killarney via Glengariff and the 'Prince of Wales' route [...] – *Albert Street Station*, for Monkstown, Queenstown, Crosshaven etc.; – *Capwell Station*, for Macroom and Killarney via the 'Tourist Route' for Glengariff and Killarney; – *Western Road Station*, on a small island near the point where the River Lee forks in two, with local trains for Coachford, Blarney etc.

Hotels: – *Imperial*, first-class hotel, St Patrick's Street; *Victoria*, St Patrick's Street (lunch 2 shillings and sixpence, tea 1 shilling and sixpence; dinner 3 shillings and sixpence; half-board 4 shillings, board and lodging 9 shillings); – *Windsor* (lunch 2 shillings, tea 1 shilling, dinner 3 shillings, half-board 2 shillings and sixpence); – *Lloyd's*, Georges Street; – *Grosvenor, Leech's, Hibernian* (reasonably priced); – etc.

Electric Trams: – from one station to the next (1 penny) and for: – (2 miles. S.) *Douglas*; – (¹/₂ mile. S.) *Ballintemple*; – *Blackrock*, to the East; – *Sunday's Well* to the West.

Carriages (*Coaches*): to train stations and to the many stops in the main streets of the city; *single journey*, 1 person. 1 shilling, 2 persons. 1 shilling and sixpence; – *hourly*: 1 shilling and sixpence for the first hour, 9 pence for each subsequent half hour. – Prices are doubled between 10 pm and 9 am.

Postes et telegraphe: – bureau principal dans *George's Str.*, au S. de St Patrick Str.

Théatre: – *Opera House*, Emmet's Place, sur les bords de la Lee.

Services fluviaux: – pour *Queenstown, Aghada* et *Crosshaven* (all. et ret. 1re cl. 2 sh. 2, 3e cl. 1 sh. 6 ; billets d' excursions, les mardi, jeudi et dim. all. et ret. 1 sh. 6, 1 sh.; mêmes prix t. l. j. après 5 h. s.)

[...] La large rue en face du pont [de St Patrick], et la plus belle de la ville, s'appelle St Patrick's Street; elle est bordée de beaux magasins et d'hotels et construite sur des arches sous lesquelles passait autrefois un bras de la Lee, par quoi s'explique sa forme en arc de cercle. – à g. Winthrop Street mènerait à George's Street, où se trouve le bureau de poste. – Continuant à suivre par St Patrick's Street, on passe devant le Victoria Hotel, l'Imperial et les Comercial Buildings, pour arriver à son point de jonction avec la Grand Parade. – A dr. une courte ruelle conduit à la cathédrale catholique de St Peter and St Paul, dont les belles proportions sont malheureusement très à l'étroit au milieu des maisons environnantes.

La Grand Parade est la rue la plus large de Cork; son emplacement était occupé autrefois par un grand dock, recouvert en 1780. Elle contient les Halles (poisson, viande, légumes et fruits). En face des halles, Great George's Street conduirait à Western Road et à la gare du Cork and Muskerry Railway. On voit dans cette rue (à dr.) la Court House, dont le portique d'ordre corinthien 'ferait honneur', d'après Macaulay, à Palladio lui-même [...]

Un bac, un peu en aval de la pointe de l'île [en centre ville], permet de traverser la Lee et d'arriver au Victoria Quay, au S. duquel s'étend une sorte de terrain vague auquel l'imagination irlandaise a décerné le nom de City Park. – A l'E. de Victoria Quay et au-delà du champ de courses, on arrive à la Marina, délicieuse promenade bordée d'arbres, d'où l'on a de ravissantes échappées sur la rivière, et que l'on pourrait suivre jusqu'à Blackrock Castle (1604) sur un promontoire s'avançant dans l'estuaire élargi de la Lee, qui prend ici le nom de Lough Mahon.

Post and Telegraph Offices: – central office on *George's Street*, south of St Patrick's Street.

Theatre: – Opera House, Emmet Place, on the banks of the Lee.

River Transport: for Queenstown, Aghada and Crosshaven (return journey 1st class. 2 shillings and sixpence, 2nd and 3rd class 1 shilling and sixpence; excursion tickets Tuesdays, Thursdays and Sundays return 1 shilling and sixpence; same prices every day after 5 o' clock in the evening).

[…] The wide street facing the bridge [St Patrick's Bridge], the finest street in the city – is called St Patrick's Street; it is lined with beautiful shops and hotels, and is built on the arches under which a branch of the Lee used to flow, which explains its circular form. – On the left, Winthrop Street leads to George's Street where the post office can be found. – Continuing along St Patrick's Street, the traveller passes in front of the Victoria Hotel, the Imperial and the Commercial Buildings, to arrive at the junction with the Grand Parade. – On the right, a short lane leads to the Catholic cathedral of St Peter and Paul, whose fine proportions are unfortunately very compressed in the midst of the surrounding houses.

The Grand Parade is Cork's widest street; a large dock, covered over in 1780, used to be situated there. The Grand Parade contains the Market (fish, meat, vegetables and fruit), opposite which Great George's Street leads to the Western Road and to the Cork and Muskerry Railway station. In this street on the right is the Court House whose Corinthian portico would be a credit to Palladio himself, according to Macaulay […]

A barge, a little downstream from the point of the island [in the city centre], allows one to cross the Lee and arrive on Victoria Quay, south of which stretches a sort of no-man's-land on which the Irish imagination has bestowed the name of City Park. – To the east of Victoria Quay and beyond the race course, one reaches the Marina, a charming tree-lined promenade affording ravishing vistas on the river, and which leads to Blackrock Castle (1604) situated on a headland jutting out into the Lee estuary which, at this point, is quite wide and is called Lough Mahon.

English translation by Gearóid Cronin and Grace Neville.

Richard Bermann
(1914)

German original in: *Irland*. Berlin: Hyperion 1914, pp. 24-30.

DANN WAR es ein trüber nebliger Morgen. Wir stehen auf dem Bootsdeck, an der Stelle, die von der Dampfmaschine angenehm gewärmt ist. Vor uns, auf dem unsympathischen Deck dritter Klasse stehen (jetzt muß es wohl wieder erlaubt sein) zwanzig irische Boyscouts in Uniform, mit aufreizend irisch-grünen Halstüchern und mit gelb gestickten Harfen auf den Rockärmeln, von grünen Shamrock-Kleeblättern ganz zu schweigen. Geputzt mit nationalen Symbolen, und vor allem hochwichtig durch diese Symbole, stehen die langen Burschen da, machen irische Nasenlöcher weit auf und wittern ihr Land. Dort hinten beginnt es. Ein grüner Küstenstreifen; er öffnet sich liebenswürdig und läßt den Dampfer ein.

Und nun kommt ein Labyrinth von Kanälen und Buchten, von Inseln und Vorgebirgen. Es ist wie ein norwegischer Fjord, nur nicht so resolut, weicher, gemütlicher. Das Meer stattet dem Land einen freundschaftlichen Besuch ab und rinnt tief hinein. Kleine Städte mit großen Kathedralen stehen am Ufer und jeder Ort hat seine netten Villenvororte mit gepflegten Gärten. Dann wird die Bucht enger; ein Kanal, schließlich eine Flußmündung. Zwischen grünen Höhen (man versteht sofort, warum Irland die 'Smaragdinsel' genannt wird) liegt eine Stadt. Reizend. Der Dampfer hält. Die Stadt liegt noch immer da. Schon etwas zu lange. Gut, wir steigen aus. Man bemerkt, daß es eine Hauptstraße gibt; nur ist das Hotel, das sie verziert, etwas mäßig. Immerhin, man säubert sich und geht aus. Also das ist die Stadt Cork in Südirland! Es gibt eine Hauptstraße und ferner noch eine Hauptstraße. Letztere heißt *the Grand Parade*; mein Reisehandbuch erzählt, es sei eine sehr schöne Straße und ihr Hauptschmuck sei eigentlich eine Reiterstatue des Königs Georg II., aber die Statue sei nicht mehr da, weil sie loyale irische Untertanen eines Tages in den Fluß geschmissen haben. Es war nicht schön von ihnen, denn wenn sie auch schon rebellisch gesonnen waren, hätten sie einem armen Reisenden das bißchen Sehenswürdigkeit stehen lassen dürfen.

Richard Bermann
(1914)

(Approach to Cork by boat – lack of attractions in Cork – horse show)

IT WAS a dull foggy morning. We are standing on the boat deck, at a spot which is pleasantly warmed by the steam engine. In front of us, on the unpleasant third-class deck (it must be permitted again) stand twenty Irish boy scouts in uniform, with provocatively Irish-green neck scarves and yellow embroidered harps on their jacket sleeves, not to mention the green shamrock leaves. Embellished with these national symbols, and above all feeling very important because of them, the tall boys stand there and open their Irish nostrils wide to draw in the scent of their country. Over there it begins. A green strip of coastline; it kindly opens up and lets the steamer in.

We are entering a labyrinth of canals and bays, of islands and foothills. It is like a Norwegian fjord, just not as resolute, softer, cosier. The sea pays the land a friendly visit and runs deeply into it. Small towns with big cathedrals stand on the banks and every place has its pleasant suburbs with big houses and neat gardens. Then the bay becomes narrower, turns into a canal, finally into an estuary. Between green hills (one understands immediately why Ireland is called the emerald isle) lies a city. Charming. The steamer stops. The city is still there. Perhaps for too long. Fine, we'll get out. One notices that there is a main street; the hotel that adorns it is just somewhat mediocre. Nevertheless, one gets cleaned up and goes out. So this is the city of Cork in the south of Ireland! There is a main street and then another main street. The latter is called the Grand Parade; my tourist guidebook says it is a very beautiful street and its main ornament is the statue of King George II; but the statue is not there any more, since the loyal Irish subjects chucked it in the river one day. It was not very nice of them, for even if they were of a rebellious disposition, they should have left the poor tourist this little bit of attraction.

Indessen, wozu besitzt der Mensch ein Reisehandbuch, als auf daß es ihm die nötigen Sehenswürdigkeiten beschaffe? Also was sagt mein grüngebundenes Reisehandbuch mit den vielen Illustrationen? Es meint, daß Sankt Finn Barr im siebenten Jahrhundert eine Abtei gegründet hat. Hm, aufregend! Ferner hat sich Desmond Macarthy, König von Munster, im Jahre 1172 dem englischen König Heinrich II. ergeben. Natürlich; sobald man Irland betreten hat, fangen die alten irischen Könige an; es ist ein Stichwort gefallen. Nichtsdestoweniger kann ich mir den König Desmond Macarthy nicht besehen; er ist nämlich allerhöchst tot.

Das Reisehandbuch schlägt mir vor, ich könnte mir ja das Gebäude der Bank von Irland ansehen. Oder auch das Haus des Grafschaftsklubs. Mir wird die Wahl schwer; schließlich gehe ich zur katholischen Kathedrale und erlebe eine angenehme Überraschung. Die Kirche ist erst 1879 (von W. Burgess) erbaut worden und ist dennoch ein bedeutendes Kunstwerk. Es gibt in Irland – außer malerischen Ruinen – nicht sehr viele alte katholische Kirchen; die meisten Kathedralen sind seit der Emanzipation der Katholiken neu erbaut worden und, wie es scheint, nicht immer mit Glück. Diese Kirche hier, eine funkelnagelneue und dennoch romanische und – welches Wunder – dennoch schöne Kirche will etwas ausdrücken und sagt es mit starkem Laut: 'Ich bin die alte Kirche der irischen Apostel – ich die neue Kirche, die nicht gestorben ist, die über Cork regiert und über die ganze Insel!'

Der Sakristan sagt, die Kirche sei eins der schönsten Werke der alt-französischen Gotik. Er irrt sich, aber ich gebe ihm dennoch drei Pence. Da bringt er mir ein Buch und meint, ich müsse mich unbedingt eintragen. Solch ein Gentleman wie ich komme nicht alle Tage in seine Kirche.

(Ein düsterer Verdacht betrübt mich: sollte, ja sollte der Mann an meiner Aussprache des Englischen bemerkt haben, daß ich ein Fremder bin? Ich hatte so stark auf Irland gerechnet! Hier sprechen die Leute ein schlechtes Englisch – ich spreche auch ein schlechtes Englisch, also könnte man mich freundlichst für einen echten Iren halten.)

Nach dem Besuch der Kirche entsteht in der Folge der Corker Sehenswürdigkeiten und Vergnügungen wieder eine peinliche Pause. Diese überaus angeregte und anregende Provinzstadt liegt fortgesetzt an den Ufern des Flusses Lee und rührt sich nicht. Folglich muß der

However, what does one possess a guidebook for, but to provide one with the necessary sights? So what does my green-covered guidebook with the many illustrations say?

It maintains that St Finbar founded an abbey in the seventh century. Hm, exciting! Furthermore, Desmond McCarthy, King of Munster, submitted to the English King Henry II in 1172. Of course, as soon as one sets foot in Ireland, the old Irish kings are at their tricks again; we have come across a key concept here. Nonetheless, I cannot view King Desmond McCarthy; he is well and truly dead in all his glory.

The guidebook suggests that I could look at the Bank of Ireland building. Or the house of the 'County Club'. It is a difficult choice; finally I decide to go to the Catholic cathedral and am rewarded with a pleasant surprise. The church was only built in 1879 and is nevertheless an important work of art. In Ireland there are – apart from picturesque ruins – not very many old Catholic churches; most cathedrals were rebuilt after the Catholic Emancipation, and it appears not always with very great success. This church here, a brand new although Romanesque one and – oh wonder! – in spite of it all a beautiful church, wants to say something and says it loudly: 'I am the old church of the Irish apostles – I am the new church, which has not died, and rules over Cork and over the whole island!'

The sacristan says the church is one of the most beautiful specimens of the Old French Gothic style. He is wrong but I still give him his three pence. He brings me a book and says I must write my name in it. A gentleman like me would not come to his church every day.

(A dark suspicion bothers me: should the man have noticed from my pronunciation of English that I am a foreigner? I had banked so much on Ireland! The people here speak poor English – I also speak poor English, so they could have had the grace to take me for a real Irishman.)

After the visit to the church another embarrassing break occurs in the sequence of sights and pleasures in Cork. This excited and exciting provincial city continues to lie on the banks of the River Lee and does not stir. What can a man do but go for lunch? The pubs are terribly

Mensch Mittag essen geben. Die Lokale, die es gibt, sind erschrecklich verlockend. Am Ende einer Wanderung durch die Hauptstraße, oder nein, durch beide Hauptstraßen, sitzen wir an einem leidlich gedeckten Tisch und nun können die irischen Nationalspeisen beginnen. Aber nein, die Speisekarte ist genau so, wie bei Lyons in London, wo ich mir den Magen so sehr verdorben habe. Ich kann ein Roastbeef haben, ein zu wenig oder ein zu stark gebratenes Beefsteak, eine große Auswahl von Erdäpfeln, eine Tasse Tee. Es kostet nicht mehr, als ein nettes Luxus-Frühstück in einem guten deutschen Weinrestaurant ersten Ranges. Immerhin, wenn man ein englisches Mittagessen der Reihe nach mit scharfer Worcestershiresauce begießt, mit Senf bestreicht, mit Pfeffer bestreut, mit Fruchtgelee beträufelt, kommt schließlich doch ein Geschmack in das harmlos biedere Zeug.

Ich sehe manchmal auf die Uhr, aber es ist noch immer nicht morgen früh. Ich bummele durch die Straßen und entdecke zwei Kategorien: schmutzige und langweilige. Die Läden werden mir vor der Nase geschlossen, denn es ist einer der unzähligen irischen Feiertage.

Auf einmal lese ich ein Plakat: irgendwo da draußen wird eine Pferdeschau abgehalten. Ha, ich stürme geradezu auf das Verdeck der elektrischen Straßenbahn. Und nun geht es wieder durch ganz reizende Villenviertel, deren Gärten unter trübem Himmel eine italienische Vegetation umfassen. Ein umzäunter Platz. Bettler. Gedränge. Tickets, please.

Ich gehe durch die Drehtür und weiß plötzlich, daß ich unrecht habe. Ich komme direkt aus London nach Cork und verlange – weil gerade kein geeigneter Zug geht – daß Cork, Südirland, so belebt und interessant sein soll, wie dieses brausende, brüllende London. Hingegen bin ich in einem Lande, wo treffliche Schweine gemästet, edle Pferde gezüchtet werden. So ein Land braucht Marktstädte und sie müssen genau so aussehen wie Cork.

Auf dem großen Platz wirbeln unzählige landwirtschaftliche Maschinen, Dampfmotoren stampfen. Rechen, Dreschflegel, Sensen werden rhythmisch bewegt. Es ist ein buntes Bild. Gutgenährte Farmer mit Sportkappen stehen sachlich vor den Maschinen, bilden kleine Gruppen und sehen zu.

In großen Holzbaracken stehen Pferde; sie werden gleich im Ring vorgeführt werden. Aus einem Schuppen tönt lautes Krähen – und wahrhaftig, klein sind irische Preishühner nicht.

tempting. After a walk through the main street, or rather both main streets, we sit down at a passably laid table: the Irish national dishes may begin. But no, the menu is exactly like the one at Lyons in London, where I got an upset stomach. I can have roast beef, a steak, either under-or over-cooked, a large choice of potatoes, a cup of tea. It doesn't cost any more than a luxury breakfast in a decent first-rate German wine restaurant. Anyway, if you pour spicy Worcester sauce on an English lunch, then spread mustard on it, then sprinkle it with pepper, and top it with fruit jelly, you will finally get a bit of taste into this innocuous, plain stuff.

Every now and again I look at my watch, but it is still not tomorrow morning. I stroll through the streets and discover two categories: dirty and boring. The shops are being shut in front of my nose because it is one of those countless Irish holidays.

Suddenly, I see a poster: somewhere out there a horse show is being held. Ha, I almost storm onto the deck of an electric tram. Once again we travel through very charming suburbs where the gardens enclose Italian vegetation but under a dull sky. A fenced-in area. Beggars. Crowds. Tickets, please.

I go through the revolving door and realise suddenly that I am wrong. I come straight from London to Cork and demand – because there is no suitable train out of it – that Cork, the south of Ireland should be as lively and interesting as this bustling, roaring London. Whereas, I am in a country where proper pigs are fattened and pedigree horses bred. Such a country needs market towns and they have to look just like Cork.

In the big open square, countless agricultural machines swirl around, steam engines pound. Rakes, flails, scythes move rhythmically. It is a colourful picture. Well-fed farmers with sports caps stand matter of factly in front of the machines, form small groups and watch.

The horses are standing in the big wooden sheds; they will be presented in the ring shortly. From another shed we hear loud crowing – Irish prize poultry are certainly not small.

Mein Begleiter ist unzufrieden. Er hat sich Sensationen versprochen, mindestens etwas Jahrmarktstreiben. Nein, das gibt es nicht. An einem einzigen Stand werden künstliche Blumen verkauft, und einige Provinzdamen kaufen diese Blumen, und ihre Urenkel werden sie noch in den ererbten Vasen stehen haben. Sonst – Sämereien, Dungmittel. Eine Bar, in der breitbeinige Männer ohne Leidenschaft, aber mit Hingabe irischen Whisky trinken. Ein bescheidenes Teezelt für die Damen. Das ist alles. Und doch ist ganz Cork hier draußen.

Ich sehe es meinem Begleiter an: er bezweifelt, ob er deswegen extra nach Irland gekommen ist. Ich sage ihm, daß ich deswegen gekommen bin. Heute früh die Buchten und Inseln – morgen die Berge und Seen, ja, das ist die angenehme Zugabe. Was dazwischen liegt, das ist langweilig – und ist der Kern der Sache, ist das Leben. Unselig das Land, das nur dem Touristen etwas bietet; auf dieser Erde sind fast alle malerischen Gegenden unfruchtbar und alle interessanten Bevölkerungen verlumpt. An beiden fehlt es in Irland nicht; aber es gibt auf dieser armen Insel auch Mastschweine und Kartoffeln. Das ist minder interessant und ist die Zukunft und die Hoffnung des Landes. Irland liegt wenige Stunden von London, und London bezieht sein Fleisch aus Australien, und Irland hungert, und beide könnten sie vom irischen Speck satt werden, wenn Irland noch etwas langweiliger würde. Die Engländer haben solche Angst, daß ihnen im Falle eines europäischen Krieges die Zufuhr von Lebensmitteln für ihre Industriestädte abgeschnitten werden könnte. Dennoch dulden sie, daß in ihrem eigenen Lande immer mehr vom fruchtbaren Ackerboden in Lustgärten und Jagdgründe für die Gentry verwandelt wird, und auf der irischen Nachbarinsel haben sie es durch eine beispiellos unsinnige junkerliche Agrarpolitik dahin gebracht, daß die Ackerbauer aus Not zu Hunderttausenden auswanderten, daß heute der beste Teil des irischen Bodens brach liegt, der Rest unrationell bewirtschaftet wird. Jetzt, wo eine antijunkerliche Majorität regiert, sieht England ein, daß jedes neue Kornfeld in Irland, jede neue Kuh auf den luxuriösen irischen Weiden die Position ihres Weltreiches festigt. Ein gesunder Ackerbau in Irland schützt London und Birmingham vor der Kriegsgefahr besser als hundert *Dreadnoughts*, die hungrigen Bürgermägen nichts zu essen geben können.

My companion is unhappy. He had expected something sensational, at least some of the hustle and bustle of a funfair. No, it just isn't there. One single stand sells artificial flowers, and a few country ladies are buying these flowers. Their great-grandsons will still have them in their inherited vases. Apart from that, seed stores, fertilisers. A bar, in which men legs apart drink Irish whiskey without passion but with dedication. A small tea tent for the ladies. That's it. And yet all Cork is out here.

I see it in my companion: he wonders if he came to Ireland especially to see this. I tell him that this is why I came. The bays and islands this morning – tomorrow the mountains and lakes, well, these are the pleasant extras. What lies in between is boring – and is the core of the matter, it is life. Unfortunate is the country that only offers tourists something; nearly all picturesque areas on this earth are barren and all interesting peoples wear rags. There is no shortage of either in Ireland; but this poor island also has porkers and potatoes. They are less interesting but are the future and hope of the country. Ireland is a few hours from London, and London procures its meat from Australia while Ireland goes hungry; both could be fed on Irish bacon, if Ireland were to become even more boring. The English are so afraid that in the event of a European war the food supply to their industrial cities could be cut off. Yet they tolerate the fact that in their own country more and more fertile land is turned into pleasure gardens and hunting grounds for the gentry, and on the neighbouring island of Ireland they have managed, by means of an unequalled, senseless landlord-driven agrarian policy to force hundreds of thousands of farmers to emigrate out of sheer want; today the best part of the Irish soil is lying fallow, with the rest being farmed inefficiently. Now that an anti-landlord majority is in power, England realises that every new cornfield in Ireland, every new cow grazing in the luscious Irish meadows is actually strengthening the position of their empire. Healthy agriculture in Ireland protects London and Birmingham from the danger of war better than a hundred dreadnoughts, which cannot feed the hungry bellies of British citizens. Every

Mit jeder Kartoffel aber, die ein irischer Bauer einem englischen Importeur verkauft, wird zugleich das rebellische Irland fester an das Reich gefesselt. Wenn es dem irischen Bauern gut geht – wem soll er seine Produkte verkaufen, als dem englischen Konsumenten? So etwas verbindet zwei Länder stärker als zehn Foliobände voll politischer Phrasen. Es gibt zurzeit nichts Wichtigeres und Interessanteres in Irland, als die Kartoffelfelder.

Von diesem Standpunkt aus müßten alle guten Iren und noch mehr alle guten Engländer dafür sein, daß man die berühmten Seen von Killarney zuschüttet und auf dem gewonnenen Land Kartoffeln baut. Man möge dieses Löbliche tun, aber bitte, noch nicht in dieser Woche. Ich fahre jetzt bald nach Killarney und ich will dort immergrüne, wild duftende Wälder haben und dunkle Wasserflächen. Ich werde davon träumen. Ich bin nämlich, nachdem ich die Pferdeschau gesehen habe, durchaus dafür, daß es solche Ackerbauzentren gibt wie Cork – aber ich denke, nach einem Corker Tag muß man angeregt schlafen und von etwas anderem träumen. Daß ich von Kartoffeln träumen soll, kann kein glühender irischer Patriot von mir verlangen.

potato the Irish farmer sells to an English importer binds rebellious Ireland tighter to the Empire. When things are good for the Irish farmer – whom should he sell his products to, but to the English consumer? This ties two countries more closely together than ten volumes full of political slogans. There is nothing more important and interesting in Ireland at the moment than potato fields.

Looking at it from this point of view, all good Irish men and women and even more all good English people should be in favour of filling in the famous lakes of Killarney and of planting potatoes in the reclaimed land. This laudable plan should be executed, but please, not this week. For I am about to go to Killarney and want to have evergreen, wildly fragrant woods and dark waters. I will dream of them. After seeing the horse show I am thoroughly in favour of having agricultural centres such as Cork – but I think that after a day in Cork one has to have a decent animated sleep and dream about something else. No fervent Irish patriot can expect me to dream of potatoes.

English translation by Veronica O'Regan.

Henri Béraud
(1920)

French original in: 'Les Vêpres Irlandaises'. In: *Mercure de France*,
15 November 1920.

JE ME mélais, un soir de septembre, aux fidèles qui priaient devant la
prison de Cork, où douze Sinn féiners, refusant toute nourriture,
attendaient la mort. Spectacle médiéval: la multitude, agenouillée sous la
pluie, dans la boue; les mères, par milliers, portant leurs nourrissons sur
les pans de leurs chales noirs; et tout cela, dans une ombre touffue, sous
un bas plafond de feuillages, chantait, sur des airs doux et poignants, des
cantiques. Au premier rang, au pied même des colonnes de la prison, six
ou sept pères franciscains, couverts de la bure, ceints de la cordelière, tous
grands et forts, des géants tonsurés, battaient la mesure avec leurs cruci-
fix noirs. Derrière les barreaux, douze agonisants entendaient chaque soir
ces chants douloureux qui les aidaient à mourir.

Puis les moines partaient et la foule se pressait sur leurs pas. Toucher
l'un de ces religieux eut été, pour un soldat anglais, courir à la mort. Une
seule fois, paraît-il, un homme de la police osa poser la main sur l'épaule
d'un *Irish priest*. Il fut à l'instant immolé.

Henri Béraud
(1920)

*(A hunger strike in Cork at the same time as
MacSwiney's hunger strike in London)*

O N A September evening, I mingled with the crowds of the faithful
who were praying in front of Cork Prison, where twelve Sinn
Féiners, refusing all food, were waiting for death. It was a medieval sight:
the crowd were kneeling in the rain, in the mud; thousands of mothers
carried their infants in the folds of their black shawls; the entire crowd,
shrouded in thick shadow beneath the low canopy of trees, were singing
hymns gently and poignantly. In the first row, at the very foot of the
prison walls, were six or seven cowled Franciscan monks, girt with rope
belts; tall and strong-looking, these tonsured giants were beating time
with their black crucifixes. Every evening, behind the barred windows,
twelve dying men heard the melancholy songs which were helping them
to die.

Then the monks left and the crowd hurried after them. If an English
soldier were to touch one of these clerics, it would have meant instant
death. Once, apparently, a policeman dared place his hand on the shoulder of an 'Irish priest'. He was immediately killed.

English translation by Gearóid Cronin.

Antón Losada Diégues
(1921)

Galician original in: 'Terencio MacSwiney'. In: *Nós*, vol. II, no. 8, 1921, pp. 2-3.

TERENCIO MAC SWINEY

NINGUÉN DUBIDA xa do preto trunfo dos irlandeses na loita de séculos, pol-a súa libertade.

Y-antre todal-as loitas da Grande guerra, y-antre todol-os movimentos de ideas y-os concertos e desconcertos dos pobos despois da desfeita, somentes se presenta limpa, xenerosa, pingando sentimento e xenerosidade en cada fala y-en cada movimento a feiticeira Irlanda. Pr'os irlandeses ricos e probes, iñorantes e cultos os probremas e intereses comerciás, industrials, toda a vida económica pasa ó derradeiro. O vento que move a todol-os curazós irlandeses é o amor á Terra y-unha infinida arela de libertade.

Grande exempro y-escarmento dos homes que non se decatan de qu'a saúde do mundo está na sua espirtualización.

Y-eiquí amóstrase o espello de toda a enerxía y-a espiritualidade do pobo irlandés: Terence Mac Swiney o inmorrente Mayor de Cork, o alcalde de Cork.

O alcalde de Cork foi o protagonista d'unha moi sinxela hestorea. Un home preso, que se deixa morrer de fame, levado d'un ideal. E morreu.

Todo feito por moi pequeno que pareza, ten un sinificado outo, ollado con humanidade. Eisí n-este feito d'un home que se deixa morrer de fame, hai un grande insiño pra todol-os homes, ainda pr'os que se cren na dianteira de toda cultura. O mesmo Mac Swiney deixou a tradución do seu feito: 'Esta é unha loita de resistenza e non han sel-os trunfadores os que mais poidan facer sofrir, senon os que poidan sofrir mais.'

A doutrina do renunciamento, pra salvar á humanidade e pra abranguer o trunfo do ideal é a gran forza do pobo irlandés y-é a grande obra de Mac Swiney cando morría no cárcele de Brixton, y-o seu nome servía de risa ós mais dos homes, embestecidos pol-as preocupaciós

Antón Losada Diégues
(1921)

(Terence MacSwiney as hero for a Galician nationalist)

TERENCE MACSWINEY

NO ONE now doubts that the Irish will soon taste victory in their centuries-long fight for their freedom.

During all the great battles of the Great War, and amidst all the flux of ideas and agreements and discord among nations after the conflict, only enchanting Ireland seems clean, generous, pouring forth feeling and generosity in every word and deed. For Irishmen, whether rich or poor, educated or unschooled, problems and concerns of commerce and industry, all economic life indeed, are of least importance. The spirit that moves all Irish hearts is the love of their Land and a great longing for Liberty.

Wonderful example and warning to men who forget that the health of the world is bound to its spiritual welfare.

And in this man was made manifest the mirror of all the energy and spirituality of the Irish people: in Terence MacSwiney, the immortal Mayor of Cork.

The Mayor of Cork was the protagonist of a very simple tale. An imprisoned man who allows himself to starve to death for an ideal. And he died.

Each action, however insignificant it may appear, has a great meaning when seen from the point of view of humanity. Thus, in this story of the man who allows himself to die of hunger, there is a great lesson for all mankind, even for those who believe themselves in the very vanguard of culture. MacSwiney himself left us with an interpretation of his action: 'This contest of ours is one of endurance – it is not those who can inflict the most, but those that can suffer the most who will conquer.'

The doctrine of renunciation, for the salvation of Mankind, and to achieve the triumph of ideals, is the great virtue of the Irish people and the great work of MacSwiney when he died in Brixton Prison, and his name provoked ridicule in the majority, brutalised by economic problems,

económicas, e pol-as loitas de comercio e pol-os podres ideás de patronos y-obreiros.

Mac Swiney é un nome feito de lús, ante todal-as brétemas do noso tempo. As súas verbas foron tan sinceiras como os seus feitos, e cando estábamos acostumeados a ver na lama as mais sinificativas verbas: Verdade, Xusticia, Libertade, Pátrea, e xa todos no segredo de que eran valeiras, veu Mac Swiney a enchelas, e cando dicía: 'Mañán a tua Terra espertará. ¡E doce morrer por ti Verdade, é por ti Libertade!' craba este falar con toda a forza dos mais sinceiros movimentos do curazón.

Homes haberá que digan qu'o valore de Mac Swiney foi unha virtude pasiva, sin a fecundidade das grandes auciós. ¡Que cegueira! Lonxe dos grandes berros, das bandeiras, músecas, condecoraciós, zoar dos cañós, borracheiras das multitudes ... co espirto ben sereo, na soedade mais fonda, Mac Swiney daba a súa vida, en cada istante pensando que cada paso escara a morte abría un camiño de vida á súa terra.

Non hai enerxía comparabel á que se percisa pra un morrer de cada momento, cando se pode salval-a vida con toda facilidade si se quere. O poder de sofrir supón unha potenza de inhibición que somentes se da nas mais outas representaciós dos homes, y-il é unha verdadeira superación da animalidade, de que tan necesitados están todol-os direutores de pobos, y-os xefes dos sistemas políticos e sociás do mundo.

Mac Swiney o Mayor de Cork é unha manifestación heróica de potenza de inhibición de que é capaz un pobo ó servizo d'un ideal. Y-este ideal nacionalista irlandés é amor y-é pace. O querer desenrolar co'a posibel libertade o amor a unha Terra, é ser nacionalista y-o querer d'iste xeito a unha pátrea, é comprendel-o amor a outras terras y-é comprender con fonda cordialidade a outros homes.

O nacionalismo d'Irlanda e de Mac Swiney ten un fundamento d'amore, de comprensión, e d'idealidade. É un nacionalismo de calidade máisima, eisí como hai nacionalismos de moita cuantidade, de moitos kilómetros cadrados e de moitos millós d'homes, que non teñen calidade, porque están feitos sobre do intrés, e da forza.

O probema antimilitarista, a desfeita dos armamentos e das guerras non pode ser resolto, senon c'un deixamento de considerare como probremas fundamentás do progreso humán, o desenvolvemento material y-

the struggles of commerce and the rancid ideas of bosses and workers.

MacSwiney is a name swathed in light among all the smog and mist of our age. His words were as sincere as his actions, and just as we were used to seeing the most important words besmirched: Truth, Justice, Liberty, Country, and all now convinced that they were empty of meaning, along came MacSwiney to fill them again, and when he said, 'Tomorrow your Land will awake. It is sweet to die for you, Truth, and for you, Liberty!' he endows this speech with all the power of the sincerest emotions of the heart.

There will be those who say that MacSwiney's courage was passive, wanting the productive virtue of great actions. Purblind would they be! Far from the loud cries, the flags, music, decorations, the roar of the cannon, drunken crowds … MacSwiney, in peace of mind, and deepest solitude, gave his life, always conscious that each step towards death opened a path to life for his country.

There is no force or energy to compare with that necessary for a man to die slowly, minute by minute, when he can save himself in a moment if he wishes. This power of suffering implies that capacity for self-sacrifice which is found only in the best examples of humankind, and it constitutes a resounding victory over man's animal nature, so necessary for all leaders of peoples, and heads of political and social systems throughout the world.

MacSwiney, Mayor of Cork, is a heroic example of the capacity for self-sacrifice to a people in the persecution of an ideal. And this Irish nationalist ideal is love and is peace. The wish to develop love for one's country alongside its possible freedom, is the essence of nationalism, and to love one's country in this way is to understand the love of others for their lands and understand other men in a spirit of deep cordiality.

Irish nationalism and that of MacSwiney is based on love, understanding and idealism. It is nationalism of the highest quality, just as there are nationalisms of great quantity, many square kilometres, and many millions of inhabitants, which do not have quality, being constructed on influence and by force.

The anti-militarist problem, the disasters of weapons and wars, are not susceptible of resolution except by abandoning the assumption that

os fins económicos. Somentes espirtualizando as aspiraciós y-as doores da vida pódese chegar á comprensión, y-a perfeución nas concencias e nas vontades. Y-eisí veu o seu camiño o grande Mac Swiney.

Mac Swiney, nome santo de mártir e de héroe espello de patriotas, mestre dos amadores da sua Terra os galegos bos e xenerosos non esquecen o teu eisempro, e como te seguiron nos teus sofrimentos, síguente nos desexos de Verdade, Xusticia e Libertade, e pregan a Deus s'estenda a Galiza a fecundidade do teu esforzo.

material progress and economic motives are fundamental problems of the advancement of humanity. Only by spiritualising the hopes and the pain of life may one arrive at a true understanding, and the purification of conscience and will. That was the vision and the path of the great MacSwiney.

MacSwiney, sainted name of martyr and of exemplary patriotic hero, teacher of the lovers of his land: the good and generous men of Galicia do not forget your example, and, as they followed you in your suffering, so also do they follow you in desiring Truth, Justice and Liberty, and pray that God may extend to Galicia the fruit of your sacrifice.

English translation by Martín Veiga and David MacKenzie.

Simone Téry
(1923)

French original in: *En Irlande: de la Guerre d'indépendence à la guerre civile (1914-1923)*. Paris: Flammarion, 1923, p. 54.

IL N'Y eut pas que des martyrs humains, il y eut aussi des villes martyres. Cork est restée la plus célèbre, et j'ai vu, quelques mois après, une grande partie de la ville encore en ruines, tout un quartier transformé en un amas de décombres, au milieu desquelles de petites baraques en bois s'étaient installées, comme chez nous, dans les villes dévastées du Nord. Des bombes ayant été jetées sur un camion de la police auxiliaire, le soir du 11 decembre 1920, des incendies pendant la nuit s'allument à tous les coins de la ville; l'hôtel de ville, la bibliothèque Carnegie, 18 des plus grands magasins de Cork, la plus belle rue de la ville, Patrick Street, s'écroulent dans les flammes. Malgré les mensonges officielles – sir Hamar Greenwood soutint gravement à la chambre des Communes que le feu avait de Patrick Street gagné l'hôtel de ville, alors qu'il en est éloigné de plusieurs centaines de mètres, de l'autre côté de la rivière! – les enquêtes démontrèrent péremptoirement que les incendies avaient été allumés par des membres des forces de la Couronne, en arrosant les maisons de pétrole et en lançant des bombes incendiaires; bien plus, ils coupèrent les tuyaux des pompes à incendie, et s'amusèrent à tirer sur les sauveteurs et les pompiers, dont plusieurs furent blessés.

Simone Téry
(1923)

(Anglo-Irish war in Cork)

P EOPLE WERE not the only martyrs: towns and cities were martyrs too. Cork has remained the most famous of these, and I witnessed, a few months after the events in question, a considerable part of the city still in ruins, a whole area transformed into a heap of rubble in the middle of which small wooden shacks had been erected, as in the devastated towns and cities back home in the north of France. After bombs were thrown at a lorry of the auxiliary police on the evening of 11 December 1920, every corner of the town was set ablaze during the night; the City Hall, the Carnegie library, eighteen of Cork's largest shops, St Patrick's Street, the town's finest street: all crumbled in the flames. Despite officials and their lies – Sir Hamar Greenwood gravely assured the House of Commons that the fire had spread from St Patrick's Street to the City Hall, although it is several hundred metres away on the other side of the river! – enquiries proved conclusively that the fires had been lit by members of the Crown forces who had doused the houses with petrol and thrown petrol bombs. Not only that but they cut the fire hoses and shot at the rescuers and firemen for a lark, injuring several of them.

English translation by Grace Neville.

J. Gust. Richert
(1925)

Swedish original in: *Irland och Irländerna*. Stockholm: Åhlen & Åkerlunds
Förlag, 1925, p. 188-89.

CORK, HUVUDSTADEN i provinsen Munster, med omkring 100,000 invånare, har ett utomordentligt vackert läge i en rik vegetation och med en hamn som räknas bland världens bästa. Gatorna skulle vara vackra örn de ej vanpryddes av så otroligt fula hus och så många ruiner, minnesmärken från *black-and-tans* och irregulars operationer. Invånarna i Cork, liksom i denna landsända i allmänhet, äro kända för älskvärdhet och vänlighet – men icke för pålitlighet, påstår man i norra Irland. Thackeray skildrar entusiastiskt kvinnornas *ladyhood*, varpå vi sågo ett par vackra exempel på Hotel Imperial: städerskan var en drottning, uppasserskan en prinsessa.

J. Gust. Richert
(1925)

(Cork after the war – Cork women)

CORK, THE capital of the province of Munster, with about 100,000 inhabitants, is situated in astoundingly beautiful surroundings with rich vegetation and with a harbour reckoned to be among the best in the world. The streets would be beautiful if they had not been spoiled by so unbelievably ugly houses and so many ruins, monuments from the Black and Tans and the Irregulars' operations. The people of Cork, as in this part of the country in general, are renowned for their charm and kindness – but not for reliability, as it is claimed in Northern Ireland. Thackeray paints an enthusiastic image of the women's ladyhood, and we certainly did see some beautiful examples at the Imperial Hotel: the cleaner was like a queen, the attendant a princess.

English translation by Carl Gilsenan Nordin.

Joseph Kessel
(1925)

French original in: Mary de Cork. Paris: Gallimard, 1925
This version from *Mary de Cork*. Paris: Emile Hazan, 1929, pp. 16-18.

Dans la rue, il bruinait. Les gouttes animaient de courtes vibrations la rivière dont Art et Mary suivaient la berge. Le crépuscule traînait sa brume presque au ras des matures dépouillées et les bateaux semblaient des épaves luisantes.

Beckett tenait sa femme par la taille. Qu'elle était fragile et faible, et légère! Et comme invinciblement elle prenait vigueur, comme elle appelait à son unique service la force dont il se sentait empli. Ils marchaient sans parler, heureux tous deux et craignant obscurément qu'un mot ne vint rompre cette félicité qui les protégeait contre le froid, la bruine et leurs aspirations ennemis.

La ville était d'une tristesse hargneuse. De rares passants longeaient les quais. Les maisons vieilles et pauvres portaient les blessures de la guerre civile: des planches mal jointes rapièçaient les devantures fracassées à coups de crosses, les balles avaient laissé leurs traces sur les murs écaillés. Partout des mendiants pétrissaient la boue de leurs pieds nus. La rivière roulait un flot lent et morne et la pluie enduisait les rues, les demeures et les gens d'un terne éclat, d'une patine sans beauté.

Mais ni Beckett, ni Mary ne s'apercevaient de cette laideur, de cet ennui. Leur vie entière avait été enveloppée et ils n'imaginaient pas qu'il put y avoir cité plus noble que celle de Cork, citadelle de la liberté irlandaise, asile du recueillement, de la lutte et de la prière.

Comme ils passaient devant le pont qui donne sur l'hôtel de ville, une troupe glapissante d'enfants les arrêta. Ils couraient comme poursuivis par un péril mortel. Les haillons qui les couvraient à peine laissaient voir dans la pénombre des plaques mates de peau. Leurs pieds nus insensibles martelaient le pavé raboteux. Ils agitaient tous les feuilles fraîchement imprimées, leurs voix stridentes clamaient les titres des journaux. Lorsqu'ils aperçurent le couple, leur meute turbulente l'assaillit.

Joseph Kessel
(1925)

(Extract from a novel)

OUT IN the street, it was drizzling. The river was quivering under the raindrops as Art and Mary walked along its bank. Twilight was dragging its mist down as low as the bare masts, and the boats looked like glistening wrecks.

Beckett had his arm around his wife's waist. How slight and delicate she was, and how light! And how irresistibly she was gaining strength, how she garnered to herself alone the energy that he felt filled him. They walked along together in contented silence, vaguely fearful lest some word should rupture this happiness that protected them against the cold, the drizzle and their differing hopes.

The city was aggressively miserable. A handful of passers-by walked along close by the quays. The wounds of the civil war could be seen on the poor, old houses: windows smashed in by rifle-butts mended with badly joined planks; bullets had left their mark on the flaking walls. Everywhere beggars pounded the mud with their bare feet. The river flowed, slow and dismal, and the rain coated the streets, houses and people with a dull glean, a sheen bereft of beauty.

But neither Beckett nor Mary noticed this ugliness, this dreariness. Their entire lives had been enveloped, and they could not possibly imagine any city as noble as Cork, bastion of Irish freedom, haven of peace, of struggle and prayer.

As they passed the bridge opposite the City Hall, a squealing crowd of children stopped them. They were running as if fleeing from some deadly danger. In the gloom, the rags that barely covered them revealed dull blotches on their skin. Their bare feet hammered the uneven pavements without hurting them. They were all waving the latest newspapers, their shrill voices yelling out the newspaper titles. On seeing the couple, the unruly pack fell upon them.

Beckett, en riant, se frayait un passage à travers ce petit peuple bruyant et joyeux malgré la bise qui lui bleuissait les doigts. Mais les enfants étaient tenaces et leur tourbillon se reformait sans cesse, audacieux, suppliant.

Art, pourtant, était décidé à ne pas se laisser fléchir. Son instinct de bonheur le lui interdisait, car dans chaque journal l'attendaient des listes de morts et parmi eux les noms de ses camarades ou ceux de Mary. Elle comprenait sa répugnance et de son côté tâchait de se défaire des petits vendeurs obstinés. Mais l'un d'eux, distinguant l'uniforme de Beckett, s'accrocha aux pans de sa vareuse et cria d'une voix impudente et fraîche:

'Prenez-moi un journal, capitaine. Mon père a été tué par ces damnés rebelles.'

'Donnez-lui trois bobs,' murmura Mary.

Beckett sentit qu'elle avait en même temps que lui songé à leur enfant.

Beckett laughingly cleared a passage for himself through this happy, noisy little gang, despite the north wind that was turning his fingers blue. But the children were single-minded and they kept on regrouping, swirling around him, daring, pleading.

Art, however, was determined not to allow himself to give in. His sense of happiness would not permit him to do so, because in every newspaper lists of the dead were waiting for him, including names of his friends, or of Mary's. She understood his reluctance, and was also trying to get away from the dogged little newspaper sellers. But one of them, recognising Beckett's uniform, caught hold of the tails of his tunic, and shouted in a clear, cheeky voice:

'Buy one of my papers, Captain. My father was killed by them bloody rebels'.

'Give him three bob [shillings],' Mary murmured.

Beckett felt that, at the same time as himself, she had thought of their child.

English translation by Grace Neville.

Luís Amado Carballo
(1927)

Galician original in: *Proel. Pontevedra: Alborada, 1927. This text in Obra completa*, Vigo: Galaxia, 1995, p. 45.

TABERNA

Chove fóra. Nas pozas
aboia a luz do gas.
Na lameira da rúa
enterráse un cantar.

Mariñeiros de Amberes,
de Cork e Rotterdam…
O acordeón borracho
fala inglés, alemán…

…………………………

Na folla do coitelo
foxe a luz cal no mar.

Luís Amado Carballo
(1927)

(A poem)

TAVERN

Outside it is raining.
Gaslight floats on puddles.
A song lies buried
in the muddy street.

Sailors from Antwerp,
Cork and Rotterdam…
The drunk accordion
speaks English, German…

…………………………..

On the blade of the knife,
light flashes as on the sea.

English translation by David Mackenzie and Martín Veiga.

Pierre Frédérix
(1931)

French original in: *Irlande: Extrême-Occident.* Paris: Gallimard, 1931, pp. 93-95

U N BRAS de mer, enfoncé dans la campagne, me donne quelques moments d'espoir. Mais la ville, malgré tous ses ponts, ses quais, malgré les bateaux, est vilaine. Ce qui reste d'elle dans les yeux et répond le plus vite à l'effort de la mémoire, ce sont ses clochers gothiques en pâtisserie blanche. Ornés de clochetons, étayés d'arcs-boutants, il n'est pour rivaliser avec eux de laideur que les fontaines. Un marché aux puces où des femmes en châle hésitent entre les bénitiers, les statuettes et les savates, une ou deux promenades publiques plantées d'arbres, le long de la rivière, mettent un peu de couleur dans le gris. Et si la rue principale flambe neuf, on sait pourquoi.

En mars 1920, le Lord-Maire de Cork, Sinn-Feiner notoire, fut tué dans sa maison, en présence de sa femme, par des hommes à face noircie. Pour le venger, les Volontaires firent sauter la caserne. Le coroner rendit ce verdict: 'Nous accusons de meurtre volontaire Lloyd George, Lord French, etc ...' Le Lord-Maire suivant fut ce Mac Swiney qui, déporté en Angleterre, se laissa mourir de faim. Vers la même époque, dix-sept auxiliaires anglais furent massacrés, dans un faubourg de Cork par des Volontaires irlandais. D'où la riposte le 11 décembre, après le couvre-feu, des 'Black and Tans' en uniforme, le pillage et l'incendie systématique de Patrick Street, la grande rue commerçante de l'endroit. Le général Macready admet lui-même que ce furent des Auxiliaires anglais qui brulèrent le centre de la ville. 'Colonnes volantes', expliquait le Secrétaire pour l'Irlande à Londres.

Cork, aujourd'hui, fête le centenaire de l'émancipation catholique. Un air de jubilation règne sur la rue. Ce peuple irlandais, si proche ici des Gaulois, gai, simple, irascible, aimant comme un jouet son clocher de Shandon, aux horloges détraquées, rouges sur deux faces, blanches sur les deux autres, oublie ses chantiers navals, ses fabriques d'engrais, sa nouvelle usine Ford, immense laboratoire de verre, et accroche aux fils de

Pierre Frédérix
(1931)

(Anglo-Irish war – centenary of Catholic emancipation)

A N INLET, set deep in the countryside, fleetingly gives me hope. However, the town, despite all its bridges, quays and boats, is ugly. The most vivid and lingering impression that it leaves in the memory is of its Gothic steeples which seem to be made of white confectionery. Adorned with pinnacles and shored up by buttresses, only the fountains can match them in ugliness. A flea market where the shawled women wander from stall to stall, hesitating between holy water fonts, holy statues and slippers, and a couple of tree-lined promenades along the river, inject some colour into the grey. And if the main street looks brand new, well, we know why.

In March 1920, the Lord Mayor of Cork, a well-known Sinn Féiner, was murdered in his house, in front of his wife, by men with blackened faces. To avenge his death, Volunteers blew up the barracks. The coroner returned this verdict: 'We accuse Lloyd George, Lord French, etc ... of voluntary manslaughter.' The next Lord Mayor was the famous MacSwiney who, after being deported to England, died on hunger strike. At around the same time, seventeen English auxiliary soldiers were murdered by Irish Volunteers in a Cork suburb. Hence the reprisals, carried out on 11 December, after the curfew, by uniformed 'Black and Tans': the pillage and deliberate arson of St Patrick's Street, the town's main commercial street. General Macready himself admits that it was English auxiliary soldiers who set fire to the city centre. 'Flying columns' was the explanation proffered by the Secretary for Ireland in London.

Today, Cork is celebrating the centenary of Catholic emancipation. An atmosphere of jubilation reigns in the streets. These Irish, so close in this regard to the Gauls, light-hearted, down-to-earth and short-tempered, as fond of Shandon steeple as if it were a toy, with its broken clocks, red on two sides, white on the other two sides, forget their shipyards, their fertiliser factories, their new Ford factory which looks like a

241

téléphone des fleurs en papier. La procession vient de finir: deux kilomètres de prêtres, de moines, de civils, d'enfants de chœur, le Saint Sacrement adoré par les fidèles à genoux sur le trottoir. *Ego sum panis vitae* flamboie près des réclames de whisky, au milieu d'un pavoisement commercial, parmi les écussons aux armes des cités irlandaises, sur les réverbères dédiés à Notre Roi le Christ. Et toutes des boutiques m'offrent O'Connell en carte postale, un vrai lascar celui-là – pas comme ce conciliateur de Grattan, statufié à Dublin – un catholique du cru, sans coupage; si le parlement avait osé lui refuser son siège, le pays prenait feu.

huge glass laboratory, and hang paper flowers on telegraph wires. The procession has just finished: a line of priests, monks, civilians and altar boys over a mile long, with the Blessed Sacrament venerated by the faithful who kneel on the pavements. On the lamp-posts dedicated to Christ Our King, the motto *Ego sum panis vitae* hangs shining alongside the whiskey advertisements, in the midst of the commercial hub, among the banners bearing the arms of Irish cities. In all the shops postcards of Daniel O'Connell are on sale, a bit of a rogue by the look of him – unlike the conciliatory Grattan, commemorated by a statue in Dublin – he was of pure, unadulterated Catholic stock. Had Parliament dared to refuse him the right to take his seat, the entire country would have risen up in arms.

English translation by Gearóid Cronin.

Mario Borsa
(1934)

Italian original in: *La tragica impresa di Sir Roger Casement*.
Verona: Mondadori, 1934.

Q UANDO UN irregolare o un regolare cadeva in una imboscata, la rappresaglia era feroce. I *Black and Tans* arrivavano sul luogo di notte con autocarri, senza ufficiali, con tutto il materiale necessario, esplosivi, petrolio, bombe incendiarie. I contadini fuggivano in comitiva inseguiti dalle fulcilate. Alcuni cadevano. Case, cascinali, fienili, granai, tutto andava in fiamme.

Un *Auxi* essendo stato ucciso ed undici feriti un una imboscata presso Cork, la sera stessa i *Black and Tans* e gli *Auxis* prendevano d'assalto la parte più bella della città, tiravano sulla popolazione, appiccavano il fuoco alla Biblioteca Carnegie, al City Hall, ad altri edifici municipali e a una cinquantina di case private. Si è calcolato che i danni salirono a parecchi milioni. 'Cork – scrive un prete – pareva Lovanio.'

Tutto ciò si capisce, non era 'ufficiale'. In alto si pretendeva di 'ignorare'. Ma nemmeno il terrore dei *Black and Tans* e degli *Auxis* induceva all'obbedienza la popolazione né stroncava la guerriglia piena di sorprese, di trovate, di agguati, di insidie – la guerriglia anonima, torva, sinistra, che non dava tregua, che appariva, colpiva e spariva come un fulmine – *hit and run!* (colpisci e scappa!) – che insanguinava le strade di campagna e le vie di città e lasciava dove arrivava morti e feriti. [...]

Quando nel marzo 1920 il Sindaco di Cork fu ucciso in casa sua, sotto gli occhi della moglie, da alcuni uomini mascherati, ne prese il posto un giovane poeta, Terence Mac Swiney. Arrestato il 12 agosto, condannato il 16 a due anni di lavori forzati, poi deportato il 17 in Inghilterra, egli cominciò tosto lo sciopero della fame e morì il 25 ottobre, dopo settantaquattro giorni di martirio e di lenta agonia, durante i quali gli Inglesi fecero di tutto per nutrirlo, riuscendovi solo una volta mentre il prigioniero, fuori di sé, cantava nel delirio la canzone patriottica: 'Avvolgetemi nella bandiera verde ...' [...]

Mario Borsa
(1934)

(Black and Tans – Terence MacSwiney)

WHEN A regular or irregular [soldier] fell in an ambush, the revenge was fierce. The Black and Tans would arrive in the area at night in armoured cars, without officers and armed with all the necessary material: explosives, petrol, incendiary bombs. The farmers would flee in groups followed by bullet shots. Some would fall. Homes, farm houses, hay-barns, grain-houses, all went up in flames.

After an Auxi had been killed and eleven injured in an ambush near Cork, that same evening the Black and Tans and the Auxis attacked the most beautiful part of the city, shooting at the population and setting fire to the Carnegie Library, the City Hall and other municipal buildings along with about 50 private houses. It has been calculated that the damages reached many millions. 'Cork,' wrote a priest, 'resembled Louvain.'

All this, one must understand, was 'unofficial' and in higher places, people pretended to 'ignore' events. But not even the terror of the Black and Tans and the Auxis induced obedience in the population, nor did it stop the guerrillas who were full of surprises, tricks, ambushes and traps – the anonymous guerrilla, dark and sinister, who left not a trace, who appeared, struck and disappeared in a flash – hit and run! Who bloodied the country roads and the city streets leaving behind death and injury. [...]

When the Lord Mayor of Cork was killed, under the eyes of his wife, in his house in March 1920 by some masked men, his place was taken by a young poet, Terence MacSwiney. He was arrested on the 12th August, condemned on the 16th to two years of forced labour and deported to England on the 17th. He commenced a hunger strike and died on the 25th October after 74 days of martyrdom and slow agony, during which time the English did all possible to feed him, succeeding only once when the prisoner, beside himself, deliriously sang the patriotic song 'Wrap the green flag round me ...' [...]

La Guerra civile (1922-23) fu un episodio dei più penosi della storia irlandese. [...] Verso la metà di agosto morí improvvisamente Arthur Griffith, affranto dalla fatica e logorato dalla lotta. Il Primo Presidente della Dail Eireann fu sostituito da W.T. Cosgrave, un uomo di lettere e di nobile fede [...] Quasi contemporaneamente Collins, l'eroico Mick, cadde in una imboscata presso Cork, colpito da una palla alla testa. La follia sanguinaria e fratricida finí a mezzo il 1923. [...]

L'Inghilterra ha avuto l'accortezza ed il buon gusto di nominare come suo primo rappresentante della Corona a Dublino non un Inglese, ma un Irlandese, anzi un nazionalista provato, e provato anche dal carcere, come M. Timothy Healy. Ho conosciuto 'l'ineffabile Tim' a Londra negli anni in cui con la sua *verve*, il suo umorismo, le sue sarcastiche interruzioni era il godimento quotidiano dei Comuni.

The Civil War (1922-23) was one of the most painful episodes of Irish history. Towards the middle of August Arthur Griffith died suddenly, shattered by exhaustion and worn down by fighting. The first president of Dáil Éireann was replaced by W.T. Cosgrave, a learned man of noble faith [...] Almost at the same time, Collins, heroic Mick, fell in an ambush near Cork, hit by a bullet in the head. The bloody, divisive madness finished mid-way through 1923. [...]

England had the good sense and taste to nominate as their first royal representative in Dublin not an Englishman but instead an Irishman, in fact a proven nationalist (proven even in prison), Timothy Healy. I met the 'irrepressible Tim' in London in the years in which his *verve*, humour and sarcastic interruptions were the daily entertainment of the Commons.

English translation by Anne O'Connor.

Alfonso Daniel Rodríguez Castelao
(1938/39)

Spanish original in: *Cadernos (1938-1948). Escolma.* Ed. by Iris Cochón, Francisco Dubert, Alfonso Mato and Henrique Monteagudo. Vigo: Galaxia / Penzol, 1993, p. 65.

Todas las previsiones del enemigo fracasaron. Fracasó la política de aislamiento del pueblo. Fracasaron las ayudas fascistas y nazis. Fracasó la indiferencia ante los asesinatos de la aviación extranjera. Fracasó incluso ese juego de abrir y cerrar la frontera para prolongar la guerra y causar la debilitación de los dos bandos. Fracasó todo cuanto se hizo para que nos entregáramos. Y ahora se intenta vencernos por hambre ...

Bien. España será el Alcalde de Cork. Pueden llorar ante la agonía de los niños y mujeres como lloraba el pueblo irlandés alrededor de la cárcel en donde agonizaba el Alcalde de Cork; pero el Ejército comerá y luchará hasta vencer.

Alfonso Daniel Rodríguez Castelao
(1938/39)

*(Terence MacSwiney in a speech written between 1938 and 1939
in defence of the Spanish Republic)*

ALL THE enemy's plans failed. The policy of isolating the people failed. Fascist and Nazi assistance failed. Indifference to the murderous air-raids by the foreign air force failed. Even that game of opening and closing the border to prolong the war and bring about the weakening of both sides failed. Everything that was done to make us surrender failed. And now they try to defeat us by starvation ...

Very well. Spain will be as the Mayor of Cork. They can weep at the suffering of women and children like the Irish people cried outside the prison where the Mayor of Cork lay dying; but the Army will eat, and will fight to victory.

English translation by David Mackenzie and Martín Veiga.

Kees van Hoek
(1945)

Dutch back-translation of: *Country of my Choice. An Irish Panorama.*
Tralee: *The Kerryman*, 1945, pp. 68-73.

O<small>P WEG</small> naar Cork wordt een kleine omweg naar Cobh beloond met een groot genoegen, want de rivier de Lee opent vergezichten als Rijnpanorama's. Al het welig groen, de volle bladertooi van de bomen glansde in een nieuwe frisheid. Vanuit Rushbrook keken we uit over de wijde baai. Achter ons hoge muren, helemaal overgroeid met struiken en rood gekelkte fuchsia's, verscholen fraaie huizen; voor ons schitterde de zon, diepblauw en groen op het drukke water, bezaaid met allerlei jachten en zeilschepen.

Ik wandelde naar boven door de steil oplopende stad, waar de straten zelf brede platte trappen zijn, bedaard haarspeldbochten draaiend om hoekhuizen die zich aan beide zijden als scheepsboegen uitstrekten. Boven de toppen van de winkels aan de zeezijde rijzen bomen op, boven de kronen van die bomen beginnen halvemaanvormige straten met huizen, en daar weer bovenuit torent het grote terras waarop op zijn beurt de grote kathedraal is gebouwd. Terwijl ik in de hitte van de midzomermiddag straten met witgekalkte huisjes beklom, straten zo steil dat ze wel rechtop leken te staan, jengelden de versleten grammofoonplaten van het amusementspark hun melancholieke herinneringen de Mariablauwe lucht in.

Eens verlieten zo'n dertigduizend emigranten per jaar Ierland door deze Atlantische toegangspoort op zoek naar de belofte van een Nieuwe Wereld – net zo als duizenden hier weer teruggekeerd zijn naar hun geboorteland. Waarlijk, geen welkom-thuis kon inspirerender zijn dan dat van de grandioze kathedraal die de wijde boog van groene heuvels en kleine huisjes bekroont, van weidse promenades waar het blauwgroene water tegenaan klotst, van bloemen overal, en van wolken in de lucht zoals alleen Ierland ze heeft, als een krans om de hemelkoepel.

Kees van Hoek
(1945)

(Streets – Sunbeam Wolsey factory – walk along the Lee)

O N THE way to Cork, a little detour to Cobh proves pure delight, for the River Lee here opens vistas like Rhine panoramas. All the lush green, the heavy foliage of the trees shone in a new freshness. From Rushbrooke we looked over the wide bay. Behind us tall walls, overhung heavily by shrubs and red chaliced fuchsias, sheltered beautiful houses; before us the sun dazzled, deep blue and green on the animated water studded with yachts and sails of every description.

I strolled up the climbing town, where the very streets are broad flat staircases, making leisured hairpin bends round corner houses straddled like ships' bows. Over the top of the sea-front shops trees rise; above the crowns of these trees crescents of houses begin; above them again towers the terrace on which, in its turn, the great Cathedral is built. As in the noonday midsummer heat I climbed streets of whitewashed houses, streets so steep that they looked almost perpendicular, the worn gramophone records of the amusement park whined their melancholy memories into the Marian blue sky.

Once upon a time some 30,000 emigrants left Ireland every year through this Atlantic gateway for the promise of a New World – as thousands have returned here to the country of their birth. Truly no welcome back could be more inspiring than that of the grandiose cathedral crowning the wide crescent of green hills and small houses, of spacious promenades lapped by blue-green water, of flowers everywhere, and of clouds in the sky as only Ireland has them, with which to garland the dome of heaven.

METROPOOL AAN DE LEE

De toegangsweg naar Cork, vooral vanaf de kant van Cobh, is er een van grandeur – de trotse rivier, de golvende heuvels, de weidse luchten, de uitgestrekte avenues – zelfs tot het hart van de stad zelf, waar Patrick Street, de South Mall en de Parade monumentale hoofdstraten zijn. Geïmponeerd door deze indrukwekkende toegangsweg na al de nauwe straatjes van de landelijke steden waar ik doorgekomen was, liep ik op de late avond van mijn aankomst de South Mall af. Haar uitgestrektheid wordt zelfs niet beperkt door straatlantaarns want de lichten zijn opgehangen aan kabels, helemaal langs het midden van de avenue tot aan de schitterende Romeinse fontein, die de Grand Parade verfraait.

Vanuit mijn hoge hotelraam is de schilderachtige vierkante Shandon Tower die uitsteekt boven de Griekse zuilenrij van de Dominican Church, mjin wekker. Op een avond liep ik terug van het mooie 'Lacaduv', uitstijgend boven een bocht van de Lee waar deze op zijn landelijkst is; in de stilte na 't middernachtelijk uur ziet de stad eruit als een fee met lichtjes helemaal over de talrijke plooien van haar gewaad, totdat je bij de brede bocht van Patrick's Street komt, 's nachts is het net de Melkweg. Onder de dubbele lijn van hoge lantaarnpalen in het midden van de brede straat glimt de lange rij taxi's alsof ze zo uit de showroom komen. Ik ben er nooit langsgekomen zonder tenminste één chauffeur naarstig bezig te zien het politoer op te poetsen. Over het gladde asfalt – zo'n verschil met Dublin's O'Connell Street die kriskras met tramrails doorsneden is – glijden soepel rode dubbeldekkers.

Patrick Strect is vol cafés; één heeft een grote biljartruimte en ziet er van buitenaf gezellig uit, zo met de lampen laag boven de groene tafels. Op de hoek van de kade verrijst, verblindend wit, een 'pub' die wel een moderne karavanserai in Casablanca lijkt, met een reusachtige bloembak over de hele lengte van de voorgevel. Onder de klassieke brug glijden witte zwanen stil over de zwarte spiegel van de Lee, vanwaar straatlantaarns op de steilste heuvelstraat van Ierland een slinger naar de sterren vormen.

MODERNE INDUSTRIE

In de ogen van de Britse pers is Ierland nog steeds het land van de veenpoel,

Lee Metropolis

The approach to Cork, especially from the Cobh side, is one of grandeur – the proud river, the rolling hills, the wide skies, the spacious tree-lined avenues – even to the heart of the city proper, where St Patrick's Street, the South Mall and the Parade are monumental thoroughfares. Impressed by this imposing approach, after the narrow streets of the country towns through which I had passed, I walked on the late evening of my arrival down the South Mall, its spaciousness not even narrowed by street lanterns, since the lights are suspended on cables all along the centre of the avenue, to that magnificent Roman fountain which ennobles the Grand Parade.

From my high hotel window the picturesque square Shandon Tower is my alarm clock, peeping out above the Grecian colonnade of the Dominican Church. I walked back one night from beautiful 'Lacaduv', rising over a bend of the Lee at its most sylvan; in the stillness long past the midnight hour, the city looks like a fairy with lights all over the many folds of her gown, until one comes to the broad bend of St Patrick's Street, at night like a milky way. Underneath the double line of the wide street's tall, centred lampposts, the long rank of taxis shines as if fresh from the showroom. I have never passed it without seeing at least one driver intently engaged in polishing the polish. Over the smooth asphalt – such a change from Dublin's crisscross, tram-line-littered O'Connell Street – slide smooth red double-decker buses.

St Patrick's Street is full of first-floor cafés; one has a vast billiard room, cosy-looking from outside, what with lamps low over green tables. At the quay corner rises, dazzlingly white, a public house like a modern caravanserai in Casablanca, with a huge flower box all along the façade. Underneath the classic bridge white swans glide silently over the dark mirror of the Lee, from which the string of street-lamps up the steepest hill street in Ireland, spins a garland to the stars.

Modern Industry

To the cross-Channel Press, Ireland is still the land of the bog, the

de bouwvallige hut en de geduldige ezel. Ik zou deze schrijvers willen meenemen, in een van de in Cork geassembleerde auto's – en ze rammelen niet! – naar de Sunbeam-Wolsey fabriek om voor zichzelf te zien wat modern Ierland vermag.

Ik ben rondgeleid door fabriek en opslagruimten door de vriendelijke onderdirecteur William Dwyer. Het erkerraam van zijn kantoor ziet uit over de bedrijfsweg, het vijf verdiepingen hoge gemetselde hoofdgebouw en al de andere gebouwen die eromheen ontstaan zijn vanaf het moment dat deze grootindustrieel aan de slag ging. Het is werkelijk een opmerkelijke prestatie. Nog geen twintig jaar geleden begon Sunbeam Knitwear, de recessie trotserend, in de oude Corkse Butter Market; vijf jaar later breidden zij zichzelf uit met de produktie van zijden kousen en werd de fabriek verplaatst naar een leegstaande vlasmolen in Blackpool, een noordelijke voorstad van Cork. Vandaag de dag is Sunbeam-Wolsey, met duizend werknemers, na Guiness en Jacobs, de op twee na grootste fabriek in Ierland.

In Cork wordt zelfs de wol zelf gesponnen – de grondstof wordt aangevoerd uit Australië, terwijl de ruwe zijde uit Japan komt. Deze onderneming groeit snel; een honderd meter lange vleugel herbergt hun eigen kamgareninrichting, waarvoor de fabriek de wol van Ierse schapen gebruikt.

Er is iets fascinerends aan moderne machines. In een reusachtige hal worden de spinmachines gecommandeerd als een eersteklas regiment. Hun gonzen klinkt alsof er een eskader vliegtuigen boven hangt, met een geklik erin gemixed omwille van de harmonie neem ik aan. Slechts een paar meisjes zijn er nodig om een oogje te houden op deze eindeloze rijen gecultiveerde, bijna menselijke machines, waarop de duizenden wolspoelen, wel tweehonderd per machine, eruit zien als melkflessen in een hypermoderne etalage, zo snel en heftig draaiend dat ze, paradoxaal genoeg, leken stil te staan. Deze paradox overtrof zichzelf in de zijdespinafdeling; een werveling van hoog gierend geluid met achttienduizend toeren per minuut. Een pond pure zijde, zoals de Japanse zijderupsen die vlijtig ontwikkelen in hun poppen, levert honderdduizend meter op. Zijde is een zeer grillige grondstof. Als de temperatuur en vochtigheid niet precies goed zijn kunnen er onmogelijke afwijkingen in de lengte

tumbledown cabin, and the patient donkey. I would like to take these writers – in one of the Cork-assembled cars, and they do not jolt! – to the Sunbeam-Wolsey factory to see for themselves what modern Ireland is able to do.

I had been round the factory and store rooms with affable Deputy William Dwyer. The bay window of his office overlooks the factory highway, the five storeys tall brick main building, and all the others which have sprung up around it the moment this captain of industry got going. It is really a conspicuous achievement. Less than twenty years ago Sunbeam Knitwear – braving the slump – started in the old Cork Butter Market; five years later they branched out with the man-ufacture of silk stockings and the factory was moved out to a disused flax mill in Blackpool, a northern suburb of Cork. Today, with 1,000 employees, Sunbeam-Wolsey is, after Guinness and Jacobs, the third largest factory in Ireland. In Cork they even spin the wool themselves – the raw material is brought from Australia, just as the raw silk comes from Japan. That development is growing apace; a vast 400-yard wing holds their own wool-combing plant, as the factory utilises the wool of Irish sheep.

There is something fascinating in modern machinery. In a giant hall the spinning machines are marshalled like a crack regiment. Their zoom-ing sounds as if an air squadron hovers overhead, with a click-clack-click thrown in for harmony's sake, I presume. It takes only a few girls to keep an eye on these endless rows of well-disciplined, almost human machines, on which the thousands of wool-gathering spools (200 per machine) look like milk bottles in an ultra-modern show window display, rotating so fast and furiously that they appeared, paradoxically, to be motionless. That paradox excelled itself in the silk spinning department; 18,000 revolu-tions a minute with a whirl of high screeching sound. One pound of pure silk, as the Japanese silk worms diligently cuddle them in their cocoons, produces 300,000 yards. Silk is a most temperamental material. Unless the temperature and humidity are dead right one would experience

van kousen optreden. In een vleugel waar honderden aluminium, met kousen overtrokken benen, op hun kop zogezegd, langs bezige handen ronddraaiden – het zag eruit als een scene in een realistische revue – werd de zijde daarom bewaard in kleine glazen kubussen, gekoesterd met warmte en aandacht.

Zo gaat het toe in de moderne industrie.

WANDELING LANGS DE RIVIER

Elke reisgids voor Cork vermeldt een wandeling die iedere toerist aanbevolen kan worden, die van Blackrock terug naar de stad langs de kronkelende Lee. Nergens maakt de rivier zulke fascinerende bochten, en vooral op een midzomeravond is het net een Rijnpanorama, het zou ergens bij Bacharach kunnen zijn. Op de achtergrond ligt halfverscholen het pittoreske Blackrock Castle. Je komt voorbij de huizen van prominente inwoners van Cork; in de velden achter hun tuinen staat het koren bijeengebonden in gouden schoven. Verder gaat het langs Marino, die boulevard van een mijl lang, waar de dubbele rij linden en iepen elkaars kronen raken en zo de rijweg overspannen.

Van de rivier komt het regelmatige ritme van roeiploegen in training – geplons, geknars en een bons, terwijl de boten over het water vliegen onder de zwaaiende lichamen van hun roeiers. Op de dicht begroeide overkant verschijnen lichtpuntjes bij de riante villas van Montenotte, en als je dichter bij de stad zelf komt, maken de lantaarns aan de rivier met hun sterke licht een spoor, een bevende lijn over de stilte van de zich in't duister hullende rivier.

Snobistische zwanen glijden langs in de waterplas, onder de belommerde oude bomen zien ze er erg wit uit. Verderop doemt de geheimzinnige massa van enorme malterijen op, de lichtjes verschijnen in de hooggelegen rij bungalows rond Sunday's Well; van verre komen flarden muziek van een kermis over het water. En de koele spitsen van de Saint Finbar staan strak tegen de nachthemel.

Translated by Wim van Schie.

impossible variations in the length of stockings. Hence, in a wing where hundreds of aluminium stocking-clad legs, standing on their heads, so to say, were revolving past busy hands – it looked like a scene from a realistic revue – the silk was kept in small glass-plated cubicles, pampered with heat and attention.

Such is the pattern of modern industry.

RIVER PROMENADE

Every Cork guidebook lists a walk which can be recommended to any tourist, that from Blackrock back to the city along the winding Lee. Nowhere does the river bend look so fascinating like a Rhine panorama, as it could be somewhere near Bacharach, and never so much as on a midsummer evening. Behind nestles picturesque Blackrock Castle. One passes the houses of prominent Corkonians; in the fields beyond their gardens the oats are gathered in golden sheaves. Along Marino, that mile-long boulevard, the double row of tall lindens and elms, which touch their crowns, spans the driveway.

From the river comes the regular rhythm of rowing crews at practice – a splash, a creak and a throb as the boats fly over the water under the swaying bodies of their oarsmen. On the thickly wooded opposite bank, dots of light appear with the spacious villas of Montenotte, and as one comes nearer the town proper, the lamps close to the quays trace their strong light in a quivering line over the silence of the darkening river.

Snobbish swans glide by in the pool of water, very white they look beneath the shaded old trees. Beyond looms the mysterious bulk of huge malting houses; the lights are appearing in the ridge of bungalows round Sunday's Well; from the distance, the flaring music of a Fair travels over the water. And the cool spires of St Finbarr's stand stark against the night sky.

For source see page 250.

Henrik Tikkanen
(1957)

Swedish original in: *Paddy's land. Irländska skisser.* Stockholm: Natur och
Kultur 1957, p. 61-74.

I CORK hade jag ständigt känslan av att ha tagit ett glas tor mycket.
Redan på morgonen när jag steg upp, likaväl som på kvällen när jag
gick och lade mig. Vi bodde på Victoria hotel, det bästa i stan. Det var
hotellets fel att jag alltid raglade en smula. Ändå hade de inte bytt ut vatt-
net i karaffen mot whisky. Men det fanns inte ett plant golv eller en rak
linje i det hotellet. Lutningen på golvet i vårt rum var så stor att Pau
knappast hann fatt en Dinky-toys-bil som rullade över det. Vi gick alla
och svajade, gäster och betjäning, och det gav en angenämt lättfärdig
samhörighetskänsla. Jag trodde länge att de hade byggt hotellet på fri
hand, men Marshall sa att huset hade satt sig. Det var byggt på gyttjig
grund. Lia och jag var väldigt rädda för att hotellet skulle tröttna på att
sitta och lägga sig i stället.

Det var lite synd om Marshall. Han undervisade i konstskolan och
arbetade på en relief som om fyra veckor skulle avtäckas av statsminister
de Valera. När vi kom Försummade han sin undervisning och leran i
reliefen torkade och sprack. Gastfriheten gick framom allt annat.

'Cead mile failte', hundratusen tusen gånger välkommen, blir man
hälsad i Irland. Vi hade känslan av att det inte prutades en enda gång på
det i Cork och därför älskar vi staden.

Grand Parade är ett ståtligt namn på en gata. På denna gata står de
irländska pat600ernas nationalmonument. Att vara irländsk patriot har
aldrig varit att deltaga i stora parader och därför är det kanske, riktigt att
monumentet liknar en kyrka, en bön om frihet, ett tack för befrielsen.

På samma gata, alldeles nära frihetsmonumentet, finner man Labour
Party's hus. Det är smalt som en mager yngling och inklämt mellan prydliga

Henrik Tikkanen
(1957)

(Victoria Hotel – Grand Parade – on the streets of Cork)

IN CORK I had the constant feeling of having had a little too much to drink, from waking up in the early morning to going to bed at night. We were staying at the Victoria Hotel, the best place in town. My constant staggering was the hotel's fault. Yet they had not changed the water in the decanter into whiskey. There was, however, not one even floor nor straight line in the entire hotel. The slope of the floor in our room was so steep that Pau was hardly able to catch a Dinky-toy-car rolling across the floor. Everybody was swaying, guests as well as servants, and the effect was an agreeably daring feeling of togetherness. I long thought that the house was built by free hand, but Marshall told me that the clay foundation had caused the house to sag. Lia and I were very afraid that the hotel would get tired of sagging and instead lie down to take an eternal rest.

Marshal was a heart-rending figure. He was teaching at the School of Art and was working on a relief, which in four weeks' time would be unveiled by Prime Minister de Valera. When we came he neglected his teaching and the clay in the relief dried and cracked. Hospitality was Marshal's main concern.

Céad míle fáilte, 100,000 thousands times welcome, is the Irish way of greeting. We had the feeling that this was not compromised even once during our time in Cork, and that is why we love the city.

Grand Parade is a proud name for a street. On this street the national monuments of the Irish patriots can be found. Being an Irish patriot has never included taking part in great parades and that is probably why the monument looks like a church, a prayer of freedom, a thanks for being set free.

On the same street, close to the monument of freedom, you find the house of the Labour Party. It is as thin as a meagre youth and squeezed

affärsbyggnader. Huset är ljusrött och färgen flagar som från ett nordiskt socialistparti, men anspråkslösheten är exemplarisk. Dearbets lösa som står församlade utanför W. Dillon's möbelaffär i nedre våningen litar inte på att de skall få Shea's bröd dagligen utan att göra någonting åt saken.

Marshall sa att han bodde i ett lustigt hus. Han bjöd oss hem till sig och vi kunde själva konstatera att han bodde i ett lustigt hus. Ytterdörren stod alltid öppen och låset i dörren var bara en prydnad. Ändå skulle en tjuv ha kunnat komma över ett rikligt byte. Varje rum var översållat med saker. Tavlor, skulpturer, gitarrer, gamla glas, båtmodeller, sköldar och åldriga klockor låg spridda överallt, och mitt i denna f örnarna röra satte sig Marshall vid sin harpa och sjöng några irländska sånger för oss.

Huset hade en cirka tjugo kvadratmeter stor gård som vette mot floden Lee och mot stadens centrum. På denna lilla gård växte en otrolig mängd av olika träd och växter och där fanns massor med små skulpturer utplacerade i vegetationen. Dessutom hade Marshall byggt ett utsiktshus för regniga dagar. Utsikten var magnifik. Vita svanar simmade i floden som, makligt flöt mot havet mellan mju-kt rundade gröna stränder och det lätta soldiset förskönade staden som en skicklig make-up.

När vi skulle gå skänkte Marshall impulsivt ett gammalt Waterfordglas åt Lia. Vi sa adjö, for vi skulle resa tidigt följande morgon. Det var inget lätt farväl, Marshall hade blivit en del av vårt Irland, en kär del.

– 'Se till att ni åker ner till Kinsale,' sa han. 'Det är en fin stad.'

Vi lovade göra det. Marshall gömde sig bakom sitt skägg och vinkade, men jag kunde ändå se att han var rörd.

Vi hade redan somnat när det knackade på dörren och portieren kom upp med ett paket. Han sa att det var från en skäggig herre. Vi öppnade paketet och det innehöll fyra Dinky-toys-bilar åt Pau och Nina ...

Av alla gator i Cork var Ever Green Street den bedrövligaste. Husen är

between polished commercial buildings. The house is red and paint flakes are falling off like from a Nordic Socialist party, but the modesty of the building is exemplary. The unemployed who are gathered outside W. Dillon's furniture shop on the ground floor do not trust that they will get Shea's daily bread without having to do something about it.

Marshal said that he lived in an odd house. He invited us home and we could agree that it indeed was odd. The front door was always open and the lock was only there for decoration. Still the house seemed to be quite a target for thieves. Every room was abundant with various bits and pieces. Paintings, sculptures, guitars, old pieces of glassware, boat models, shields and antique clocks lay scattered everywhere, and in the middle of this exquisite mess Marshall sat down by his harp and sang some Irish songs for us.

The house had a yard of about twenty square meters that opened out towards the river Lee and the city centre. On this little yard an unbelievable number of trees and plants flourished and there was an abundance of small sculptures scattered randomly in the vegetation. Besides this Marshal had erected a conservatory for rainy days. The view was glorious. White swans swam in the slow moving river, which circled its way past rounded green hills on its way towards the sea and the gentle sunshine gave the town an enriching make-up.

When we were about to leave, Marshal, under a moment's impulse, gave Lia an old Waterford glass. We took our leave, for we were due to go early next morning. It was not an easy farewell, Marshall had become a cherished part of our Ireland.

'You will have to go down to Kinsale,' he said. 'It's a nice town.'

We promised to do so. Marshall hid behind his beard and waved, but I could see he was touched.

We had already fallen asleep when there was a knock on the door and the porter came up with a package. He said a bearded gentleman delivered it. We opened the package and it contained four Dinky-toy-cars for Pau and Nina ...

Of all the streets in Cork, Evergreen Street is the worst. The houses are

lika enahanda som hickningar, exakta kopior av varandra. Gatan ligger långt från centrum och den skulle aldrig ha fångat min uppmärksamhet om den inte hade haft detta odödliga namn.

Jag parkerade i hörnet av Ever Green Street och Barrack Street och rätt framför mig hade jag Dorney's juveleraraffär. Juveleraraffär var ett epitet som gick helt i stil med det optimistiska namnet Ever Green Street, för det fanns inte en juvel i butiken. På en ställning som såg ut att vara sammanfogad av två cykelgafflar hängde sex fickur och under ställningen satt ägaren och pillade med innanmätet på en väckarklocka.

Förbi denna affär vandrade på tjugo minuter prototyperna för världens alla misslyckade existenser. Imbecilla, gamla alkoholiserade kvinnor, arbetslösa, halta, lytta, fattiga och hungriga människor. Ingen intresserade sig för juveler. Förbi affären vandrade också präster läsande sin bibel och de lyfte inte blicken från boken för att se på juveler eller elände.

as monotonous as hiccups, exact copies of each other. The street lies far from the centre and it would not have caught my attention if it had not been for the immortal name.

I parked my car at the corner of Evergreen Street and Barrack Street right in front of Dorney's Jeweller's shop. Jewellery was an epithet that suited the optimistic name of Evergreen Street perfectly, because there was not one single jewel in the entire shop. On a stand, which looked like it was constructed from two joined forks of a bicycle, hung six pocket watches, and under the stand the owner sat and fiddled with an alarm clock.

In the space of twenty minutes prototypes of all the unfortunate characters of the world passed by the shop. Retarded, old alcoholic women, unemployed, crippled, deformed, poor and starving people. Not one turned their attention towards the jeweller's. The passing priests saw neither jewels nor misery, their attention turned solely towards the open Bible in their hands.

English translation by Carl Gilsenan Nordin.

Hilding Fagerberg
(1963)

Swedish original in: *Säckpip och herdelur. Intryck från en resa genom Skottland och Irland.* Hässleholm: Svantessons Boktryckeri, 1963, p. 229-233.

DET ÄR en solig och varm eftermiddag, och vi är i moderna och charmfulla staden Cork, där Shannons kyrkklockor tonar ut melodier över den sköna floden Lee varje timme och kvart och för övrigt så ofta som någon turist besöker kyrktornet.

Cork är en blomstrande stad med modern bebyggelse efter en brand 1920. Den är byggd på en ö vid floden Lee och har ursprungligen växt upp kring ett kloster och en klosterskola grundad av S:t Finbar på 500-talet.

Vi tar in på stadens moderna och trevliga vandrarhem, sätter vårt bagage där och finner det skönt att ha vårt nattlogi ordnat utan större kostnad och bekymmer. Där har vi gasspis, om vi vill Itoka oss något, varmt och kallt vatten, en säng att vila i och en plats där vi kan skaka av oss gammalt resdamm. Denna gång får vi gemensamt rum med sex bäddar så vi står oss gott och kan lugnt bege oss ut på *sightseeing*.

Lite bråttom har vi med Cork, då vi absolut måste ha tid för Blarney Stone, som vi hört mycket berättas om.

Vi finner Cork vara en egendomlig kombination av modernt brådskande affärsliv och glad lättjefull bekymmerslöshet. Modernt klädda människor i shoppingcentrum kontrasterar med de svartklädda vältalande affärsmännen vid kolkajerna, och längs de breda gatorna möter vi kvinnor med svarta ochalar på gammaldags vis.

Efter Dublin är Cork den största staden i Eire med 80,000 invånare. Den har stora industrier på båda sidor om floden Lee som utgör Fordfabrik, Dunlop bildäcksfabrik, ylleindustri, bryggeri, garveri m fl.

Irland har ekonomiska problem och är i avsaknad av många råmateriel. Många ger sitt stöd till regeringens verkliga ansträngningar att

Hilding Fagerberg
(1963)

(Economic problems – emigration – Shandon)

IT IS a sunny and warm afternoon and we are in the modern and charming city of Cork, where the church bells of Shandon sound their melodies over the beautiful River Lee every hour and a quarter and as often as a tourist pays a visit to the bell tower.

Cork is a thriving city with modern buildings after a fire in 1920. It is situated on an island by the River Lee and originally sprung up around a convent and a convent school founded by Saint Finbar in the sixth century.

We decide to lodge in the city's pleasant and modern hostel, where we leave our luggage and feel satisfied that our night's accommodation is settled without any major expense or complications. Here we have a gas stove, where we can prepare food, hot and cold water, a bed to rest in and a place to shake off the dust from our travels. This time our room contains six beds, so there is more than enough, and with a calm sense of mind we decide to go sightseeing.

In Cork we are in a slight hurry, we definitely need to have plenty of time for the Blarney Stone, about which we have heard so much.

We find Cork to be a peculiar combination of vibrant, bustling shops and a friendly, relaxed feeling of light-heartedness. Modern clad people in shopping centres contrast sharply with darkly dressed animated businessmen in the coal yards, and along the broad streets we meet women wrapped in old-fashioned black shawls.

Apart from Dublin, Cork, with its 80,000 inhabitants, is the largest city in Eire. It has large industries on both sides of the River Lee with a Ford factory, a Dunlop tyre factory, woollen mills, breweries and tanneries, amongst others.

Ireland has economic problems and lacks many raw materials. Many people give their support to the government's strenuous work to attract

draga till sig utländskt kapital och uppföra nya industrier för att öka arbetsmöjligheterna. Men ändå föredrar många irländare att investera sina tillgångar i utländska företag, då särskilt i England. Men det är inte bara pengar, som dragés ut ur den gröna, älskade ön. Varje år ger sig 40.000 irländska män och kvinnor i ålder upp till 70 bort från sin ö för att söka arbete utomlands. Ända sedan potatisskörden slog fel 1840 och det blev hungersnöd har folkmängden sjunkit från 6¹/₂ mill. till mindre än 3 millioner. Ungefär 6 mill. irländare har emigrerat till de ständiga rikedomarna i Australien och USA.

Och nere vid Corks hamns har emigrantskaran samlats, och mången mor och syskonskara har gråtit och vinkat farväl åt kära, som för sin bärgnings skull lämnat fosterlandet. Corks hamn är stor och en av de äldsta och mest skyddade hamnarna på ön. Den är centrum för seglatserna och kan berömma sig av att ha den äldsta seglarklubben i världen, Kungliga seglarklubben i Cork, grundad 1720.

Vi ser många barn i 4-5 års åldern, och då särskilt många pojkar. Vi kallar dem småknattar dessa livliga irlandssöner som utgör landets hopp och framtida löfte.

Floden Lee delar sig i två stora huvudkanaler och gör Cork rik på broar och trevliga promenadstråk. De backiga gatorna höjer och sänker sig som en musikalisk accent mellan bebyggelsen. Och den förtjusande 3-filade avenyen the Mardyke går till Fitzgerald park, där stadsmuséet ligger med intressanta kollektioner mest av lokalt historiskt intresse.

Flera kyrkor höjer sina tinnar över stan, men den mest kända är som nämnts Shandon Church, som ligger i norra delen av Cork. Två sidor av kyrktornet är byggda av röd sandsten och två av grå kalksten. Man säger också: 'Partly coloured like the people red and white is Shandon Steeple.' Kloekorna, som är gjutna av Rudhall av Gloucester och upphängda 1752 gör nu varje dag hela staden Cork klingande.

foreign capital and to create new industries in order to increase employment possibilities. But still many Irish prefer to invest their money in foreign companies, especially in England.

But it is not only money that is dragged out from the green, beloved island. Every year some 40,000 Irish men and women of all ages up to 70 leave their island in search of work abroad. Since the days of the potato crop failure in 1840 and the resulting famine the population has dropped from 6,000,000 to less than 3,000,000 today. About 6,000,000 Irish have emigrated to the everlasting riches in Australia and the USA.

And down by Cork harbour the emigrants have gathered, and many a mother and family has cried and waved farewell to their loved ones, who for the sake of their survival have left their motherland.

Cork's harbour is large and is one of the oldest and best-protected harbours on the island. It is the centre for sailing and proudly proclaims itself as having the oldest nautical club in the world, The Royal Sailing Club, established in 1720.

We see many children of four to five years old, especially many boys. We call them 'little lads', these spirited sons of Ireland upon whom this country's hopes and future relies.

The River Lee parts into two large channels and as a result Cork's beautiful walkways and bridges are abundant. The hilly streets sink and rise like a musical melody between the houses. And the delightful three-lane avenue called the Mardyke leads to Fitzgerald Park, where the city's museum lies with its interesting collections, mostly of local historical interest.

The spires of several churches tower over the town, but the most famous is Shandon church, which is situated in the northern part of Cork. Two sides of the steeple are built in red sandstone and two sides are in grey limestone. There is a saying: 'Partly coloured like the people, red and white is Shandon Steeple.' The bells, which were cast by Rudhall of Gloucester and erected in 1752, are still today engulfing the entire town of Cork with their sound.

English translation by Carl Gilsenan Nordin.

h.c. artmann
(1965)

German original in: *Atlas. Zusammengestellt von deutschen Autoren.*
Berlin: Wagenbach, 1965, pp. 246-51.

VERFEHLTES UNTERFANGEN SICH EINER GEOGRAFIE ZU ERINNERN

Mein schuß hat die ausgestreckte hand der steinnymphe um einige
Zentimeter verfehlt, ich habe zu wenig geschlafen, tauge nichts, habe
vorbeigeknallt. Eine schar erschrockener krähen scheucht auf, schwärmt
über den riesigen pinien, die vor dem herrenhaus stehen, und fliegt
endlich davon.

 – John, sagt miss C. zu mir, – John, du hast kein recht, dich hier auf
meinem grund und boden derart aufzuführen! – Sie steht vor meinem
halbgesenkten revolver, sieht mich nicht an und stößt einen ihrer hohen
Absätze wütend in die weiche wiesenerde. Dann wendet sie sich mir zu
und sagt mit ungewöhnlich scharfer stimme: – Warum kannst du dich
nie wie ein normaler, gesitteter mensch aufführen? Du benimmst dich
wie ein untier, wie ein monster!

 – Ich bin ein untier, ich bin ein monster ... entgegne ich ihr mit
erzwungener ruhe. Ich stecke meinen revolver zurück; ich würde sie jetzt
am liebsten erwürgen ... Fünfzig hellseherinnen, zweiundzwanzig giftmi-
scher, drei hostienräuber, elf pferdediebe, zehn verräter und ein künstlich-
er mensch regen sich in der unterirdischen höhle über der ich eben stehe,
du liebe zeit! es ist förmlich, als läge zwischen mir und dem da nichts als
eine dicke daunendecke ... Ich laufe mit großen Sprüngen an die chaussée,
werfe mich in den kleinen Citroën und notiere, ehe ich den motor anlasse:
C. county C. Ireland, sommer, enttäuschung, 5 Uhr nachmittags.

Ich kannte diese stadt einmal sehr gut. Heute erinnere ich mich an
ihre straßen und gassen nur hin und wieder im traum. Es ist immer sommer und ich friere nicht. Manchmal ist ein breiter fluß in der nähe, er
liegt im nordosten, manchmal gibt es auch einen stadtwald, sehr aus-
gedehnt, sehr tief, aber von häusern umgeben; seltener gelange ich in

h.c. artmann
(1965)

(A short story set in Cork and elsewhere)

A FAILED ATTEMPT AT MENTAL RECONSTRUCTION OF A GEOGRAPHY

My shot missed the stone nymph's outstretched hand by a few centime-
tres. I didn't get enough sleep; I'm good for nothing: that's why my shot
went wide of the mark. A flock of startled crows shoot upwards, hovering noisily over the giant pine trees standing in front of the mansion
before finally flying away.

– John, says Miss C. to me, – John, you have no right to behave
yourself like that on my property! – She stands in front of my lowered
revolver, not looking at me, and angrily thrusts one of her high heels into
the soft earth of the meadow. Then she turns to me and says in an unusually sharp voice: – Why can't you behave like a normal, civilised human
being? You're behaving like a beast, a monster!

– Me, a beast, a monster ... I respond, forcing myself to speak
calmly. I put my revolver back in its holster. At this moment I would
dearly love to strangle her ... Fifty female clairvoyants, twenty-two poi-
soners, three robbers of Eucharistic hosts, eleven horse thieves, ten trai-
tors and one artificially-created human being stir in the subterranean
cave above which I am standing at this moment. Dear God! It is as if
there was nothing between me and him there except a thick quilt
stuffed with duck feathers ... With great loping strides I reach the
avenue and hurl myself into the little Citroën. Before switching on the
engine I jot down a note: C. county C. Ireland, summer, disappointment, five o'clock in the afternoon.

I once knew this city very well. These days I only remember its
streets and lanes now and again in a dream. It is always summer and I'm
not frozen with the cold. Sometimes there is a river close by to the North
East; sometimes there is also a municipal forest taking up a wide area,

ihm an eine lichtung, auf dieser steht immer ein altes Karussel mit kän-
guruhs und schwänen, für die man tramkarten löst ...

Ich fahre durch diese stadt niemals mit bus oder trambahn, manchmal jedoch mit einem VW, und ich verliere stets seine räder, sie springen
gummig irre irgendwohin in die gegend, der motor streikt, die steuerung
wird frischer teig, ich muß halten und zu fuß weiter gehen. Meistens
gehe ich ja zu fuß, manchmal aber bewege ich mich mittels riesenhafter,
schwebender luftsprünge vorwärts, gleite gemächlich nieder, verspüre
einige meter vor dem wiederberühren des bodens eine art spannung -
und lande frei und sicher. Es kommt auch vor, daß ich die vorsprünge
und fassaden von hohen häusern erklettere; die steilen wände biegen sich
von meiner last wie aufgestellte matratzen.

Vor dem bahnhof stehen die taxis in langen dreierreihen, es ist alles
so einfach und jeder der fahrer hat den stadtplan fix und fertig im kopf.
Ich nehme kein taxi. Ein lift bringt mich auf das schwindelerregende
plateau eines eiffelturms, von welchem ich beobachten kann, wie ver-
schwenderisch die architekten der dächer der stadt mit der anbringung
von laufstegen umgegangen sind: blauuniformierte polizisten
marschieren darauf, ihre maschinenpistolen sind entsichert, sie schnüf-
feln sich über ihre schmalen lebensunterhälte, sie suchen jemanden,
mich wahrscheinlich.

In diesen straßen und gassen befinden sich häufig torturhotels,
verhörszentralen (da schlagen sie dir die zähne in den kragen) und
gewöhnliche gefängnisse. Das wirklich große gefängnis aber steht,
unter vollkommen andersgearteten luftverhältnissen, außerhalb der
Stadt, schon auf dem lande, eine art zitadelle oder falsche tudorburg.
Ich komme verstohlen oder mit mühsam gedämmter hast heraus,
beginne zu laufen, laufe, laufe immer schneller, lasse die wachen weit
hinter mir zurück, und ihre abzeichen werden planeten eines eben ver-
lassenen sonnensystems ...

Ich erreiche wieder die stadt, sie öffnet sich mit gedröhn wie ein
gefälschtes Mailand. Alle trambahnen sind dunkelblau, nicht eine oliv-
grün, wie ich es gerne hätte ... Ich muß mich zusammennehmen: am
liebsten würde ich sie mit meinem revolver durchlöchern.

Neue häuserblocks werden aufgeführt, alte abgetragen; in der nähe

very dense but surrounded by houses. Only very infrequently do I reach a clearing in this forest. In this clearing there is always an old merry-go-round with kangaroos and swans. Tram tickets must be purchased to ride on them ...

I never travel through this city by bus or tram, although I frequently drive a VW. I am constantly losing the wheels; they bounce crazily away in rubbery style, ending up I know not where. The engine dies. The steering turns into fresh dough. I have to stop and continue on foot. Mostly I go on foot in any case. Frequently, it must be said, I proceed by means of gigantic leaps in the air, gliding gently downward. I notice a sort of tension a few metres before touching the ground again – and then I land, safe and sound. It also happens that I scale the ledges and façades of tall houses; their steep walls, like mattresses standing upright, bend under my weight.

In front of the station there are three long rows of taxis. Everything is very simple and every single driver has the street plan perfectly mapped out in his head. I don't take a taxi. A lift brings me onto the vertiginous platform of an Eiffel Tower from where I can see that no expense has been spared by the architects who have provided walkways on the city's roofs. Policemen in blue uniforms, their machine guns cocked, are marching on these walkways. They whinge to each other about their meagre livelihood. They are searching for somebody. Probably me.

Numerous torture hotels, interrogation centres (where they sink their teeth into your neck) and ordinary prisons are to be found in the city's streets and lanes. The really big prison, with its quite different quality of air, is situated in the countryside adjacent to the town. It is a citadel or imitation Tudor fort. Furtively or with scarcely contained speed I make my way out and begin to run, run, run faster and faster, leaving the sentries far behind me, their insignia of rank becoming planets of a solar system that I have left in my wake ...

Once more I reach the city, its throbbing noise reveals it to be a counterfeit Milan. All the trams are navy blue, not the olive green that I would prefer. I must pull myself together. I would dearly love to riddle them with bullets from my revolver.

New blocks of houses are being built, old ones pulled down. A Bronze

einer lieben erinnerung hat man auf solch einem freigelegten grundstück eine schmiede aus der bronzezeit entdeckt: ich sehe mir die fundstelle an, es sind eine menge dinge säuberlich am boden ausgebreitet. Ich denke abermals an meine ruhende waffe.

Oft meide ich die gegenden mit ausgrabungen und lasse sie, obgleich man vor ihnen nie sicher ist, links liegen, und schlage mich in andere stadtviertel, besonders in solche, die an breiten flüssen liegen, dort ist man am ungestörtesten. Zu den breiten flüssen kommt man meistens durch straßenunterführungen oder tunnels, man kommt an schlachthäusern vorbei, aus denen tiere brüllen, passiert vorstadtkinos mit stummfilmerinnerungen, und träumende bedürfnisanstalten, und vermoderte textilienhandlungen – bis man endlich die große brücke erreicht, die über den fluß führt. Hier ist immer die endstelle der trambahn, hier macht sie unter sommerlich versonnten bäumen, platanen, kastanien, was weiß ich, ihre schleife. Kirchen oder tempel sind keine da; möglicherweise eine verfallene alte moschee voller schlangen, grillen und storchen, aber viele wasserhydranten gibt es, die es vergessen haben, wie man den durst löscht ...

Jenseits des flusses wohnen einige mädchen, die ich von früher her kenne, die ich einmal gekannt habe, deren häuser ich aber nie wieder zu finden vermag, alles suchen vergeblich, wohl aber tauchen aus schattigen alleen hin und wieder die mütter der mädchen auf, sehen mich verdächtig an, halten regenschirme, lauern drohend ... Ich muß flüchten.

Ich gelange auf dieser flucht stets in gebietskrankenkassen oder andere bürohäuser, riesenkomplexe mit viel zu raschen paternosteraufzügen, unmöglich wieder auszusteigen, sinnlos, sie rasen förmlich auf und ab, ich stemme mich mit aller gewalt gegen die liftwände, dehne sie, stoppe solcherart den lift. Steige ich aus, bin ich immer in der 24. etage und sehe durch die fenster nach einer grünfläche, die zu einem college gehört, baseballplatz, und nach den schmalen minaretten der St Omarsmoschee, deren grüne und veilchenfarbene smalten am schönsten im frührot sind, und abermals, auf den laufstegen der umliegenden dächer, die blauen polizisten, schnuppernd und schnüffelnd, mit abziehbereiten maschinenpistolen.

Und oft sehe ich mich selbst auf der leinwand eines immens großen kinos in vistavision: ich betrete einen dunklen raum, hotelzimmer oder ähnliches, drehe das licht an und sage: und da dachtest du, in dieser

Age smithy has been discovered on an exposed piece of ground close to a lovely memento, where a house once stood: I look at the site. A multitude of items are neatly laid out on the ground. Once again I think of my dormant weapon.

Often I avoid the areas with archaeological digs and, although one can never be immune to them, I give them the cold shoulder and strike off to other areas of the city, particularly those on wide rivers where there is the least likelihood of being disturbed. One comes to the wide rivers by underpasses or tunnels, passing by abattoirs where animals are bellowing, walking past suburban cinemas with their reminders of the silent film era, past dreaming public conveniences and crumbling textile outlets - until finally the great bridge that spans the river is reached. This is always the terminus for the tram. Here, under trees basking in the summer sun - plane trees, chestnut trees, whatever - the tram executes its loop for the return to the city. Churches or temples there are none, possibly an old mosque that has fallen into ruin, full of snakes, crickets and storks, but there are many water hydrants that have forgotten how to quench thirst ...

Some girls that I know from times past live on the far side of the river; girls that once I knew but whose houses I can never manage to find; all my searching is in vain, although now and then their mothers pop out of shady tree-lined avenues and look at me suspiciously, brandishing their umbrellas at me as they lie in wait... I have to take flight.

My flight always lands me in the offices of the Regional Health Insurance Fund or similar office buildings, gigantic complexes with paternoster lifts that operate much too swiftly, making it impossible to get out again. To no purpose they race up and down. With all my strength I press myself against the walls of the lift, causing them to stretch, thus stopping the lift. When I get out I am always on the 24th floor, looking out the window at the green space of a baseball ground that belongs to a college; then at the slender minarets of the St Omar mosque whose green and violet coloured tips are at their most beautiful in the early sunlight; then once more on the walkways of the surrounding roofs, at the whinging blue-clad policemen nosing about with their machine guns at the ready.

And often I see myself on the screen in vista vision in a vast cinema:

schönen stadt würden dir geschminkte Algerierinnen wie tauben ins bett flattern. . . . Immer, wenn ich enttäuscht bin, kommt mir die lust, gezielte schüsse abzugeben - und ich stehe mit Cléo am rechten ufer des Lee in C. und sehe das theatergebäude, halbzerstört, ausgebrannt, wahrscheinlich schon um 1921 zeitgebombt, der zuschauerraum, glücklicherweise leer, hob sich in zeitlupe himmelhoch und verteilte seine Stukkatur, seine kalk-blumen, gerecht wie aus einem füllhorn der Iustitia ...

– Schau, sagte Cléo, – in diesen sprüngen hat sich der efeu festge setzt.

– Ja, sagte ich, – und in den dachbalken nisten die selben schwalben, die wir gestern im college durch den leseraum fliegen gesehen haben ...

Cléo lehnt sich immer an meine linke brustseite, glücklich über den schönen julitag. Plötzlich fährt sie wie von einem skorpion gestochen zurück, springt einige schritte von mir weg und schreit vollkommen aus der fassung geratend: – John, du hattest mir versprochen, nie wieder diesen revolver anzurühren, und eben habe ich ihn gespürt, leugne es nicht, ich bin ja kein narr, man kann sogar die leichte ausbuchtung an deinem jackett sehen ... Oh, du untier, du monster! – Ja, sage ich, – hat-test du anderes erwartet?

Ich laufe gehetzt durch den wald, erreiche die lichtung, springe auf die riesige, bereits fahrende drehscheibe des karussels, steige ins innere des flitterschwans, er hat einen apfelsinfarbenen schnabel und schwarze augen, seine vielen spiegel reflektieren eben so oft mein bizarres bild, ich bezahle, bekomme mein trambillet und merke, gegenüber in einem baum sitzend, ein mädchen, das aus einer großen tüte pralinen ißt, sie wirft mir welche zu, ich versuche zu fangen, mein karussel läßt mir dazu keine zeit. Ich beginne zu wassertreten und erhebe mich wie ein vogel aus dem nest, ich fliege mit gleichmäßigen beinbewegungen über die morgenfrische, glänzende stadt, ich lande auf einem nach teer und regen riechenden lagerplatz zwischen aluminiumhangars, man schießt sofort auf mich, ich schieße sofort zurück. Es ist ein jammer: meine pro-jektile platzen bereits einige meter nach verlassen der mündung als lächerlich kleine graue staubpilze. Ich höre stimmen, die sich über meine unzulänglichkeit als schütze unterhalten: es sind nicht die stim-men von lagerwächtern oder polizisten, nicht die stimmen von mädchen oder eleganten passantinnen, es sind stimmen, die gar keine stimmen

I enter a dark room – a hotel room or the like – turn on the light and say: and you thought that in this beautiful city Algerian women wearing heavy make-up would flutter dove-like into your bed … Whenever I am disappointed I get the urge to fire a few well-aimed shots – and I'm standing with Cléo on the right bank of the river Lee in C., looking at the half-destroyed burnt-out theatre that was probably time bombed in 1921. The auditorium, fortunately empty, heaved itself to the sky in slow motion, scattering its stucco work and plaster flowers impartially like the goddess Justitia dispensing from a horn of plenty.

Look, said Cléo, – ivy has taken root in these cracks. – Yes, I said, – and the swallows nesting in the rafters are the same ones that we saw flying through the reading room in college yesterday …

Cléo is always leaning on the left side of my chest, happy with the July day. Suddenly, as if stung by a Scorpion, she jerks back, runs a few steps away from me and, completely losing control, screams: – John, you promised me you'd never touch that revolver again, and I've just felt it. Don't deny it, I'm not a fool; you can even see the bulge of it inside your jacket … Oh, you beast, you monster! – Yes, I say, – what else did you expect?

I am running frantically through the forest. I reach the clearing and jump on the moving turntable of the merry-go-round and climb into the interior of the tawdry swan. The swan has an orange-coloured beak and black eyes. Each of its numerous mirrors reflects my bizarre image. I pay, receive my tram ticket and notice a girl sitting in a tree across the way, eating chocolates from a large paper bag. She throws some to me, I try to catch them, but the merry-go-round doesn't give me time to. I begin to tread water and rise up like a bird from its nest. I fly with regular movements of my legs over the city that glitters in the freshness of the morning. I land between two aluminium hangars in a depot that smells of tar and rain. I am immediately shot at and I immediately return fire. It's pathetic: my projectiles explode in little puffs of dust a few metres after leaving the muzzle. I hear voices discussing my inadequacy as a marksman. The voices are not those of security men or policemen; nor are they of girls or elegant ladies passing that way. They are voices that

sind, überhaupt nichts besagen; ich ärgere mich gar nicht, ich weiß, ich kann besser schießen als tausend andere und versuche es: ich treffe ein zwischen zwei äste geklemmtes herz-as durch die mitte ...

... und sehe mich wieder vor dem einfamilienhaus in der viale San Gottardo, einer gegend voller brunnen und alphörnern. Ich gehe am garten vorbei, sehe aber nur die mutter und die jüngere Schwester, sie aber sehe ich nicht. Ich beobachte eine weile mutter und jüngere schwester, sie beschäftigen sich mit farbigen wollknäueln, und mit einem male bin ich viele straßen weiter weg in einer gegend aus semaphoren, zeitungen und abschieden: telefonzellen gehen auf kleinen eisernen löwentatzen umher, sie machen dabei die typischen, knappen drehungen von polizisten, und speien beim mindesten druck auf einem ihrer vielen knöpfe beträchtliche summen münzen, meine taschen fassen diesen reichtum kaum ... Ich verliere alles wieder bis auf den letzten rappen, pfennig, groschen, öre, quäle mich mit unsinnigen gedanken aus reue und heimweh, eine septemberliche nostalgie nähert sich in einem flatternden kleid, klar taucht sie aus dieser irren geografie auf, ich sehe wieder das Annesley Voisey-haus in der dämmerung, es wendet mir wie stets die hinterfront zu, seine gänge und keller sind teils verschüttet, teils unversperrt, gefährlich zu betreten, die besitzerin ist immer ganz nah zur hand, sie hält ein lorgnon, sie darf mich nicht sehen, ich bin unerwünscht, aber ich bringe es dennoch fertig bis zu miss C. vorzudringen. . .

– Was suchst du hier in unserem haus, sagt sie, – ich hasse dich, lasse dich nicht mehr blicken! Da, schau hinaus auf die zerstörte balustrade ... du hast sie gesprengt! 1921, das theater, war es dir nicht genug? Du bist ein anarchist, ein untier, ein monster, mir graut vor dir, dein blut kommt aus der retorte eines Dr. Frankenstein, geh, ich ertrage es nicht länger, dich anzusehen ...

Sie weint. Ich möchte sie in diesem augenblick am liebsten erwürgen ... Im immer dämmriger werdenden garten bewegt die steinnymphe fast unmerklich die hand, sie will mir eine sinnestäuschung einreden, ich weiß schon, ich kenne sie doch von vielen begegnungen her; sie kann mir nichts vormachen, ich weiß genau: sie bewegt sich wirklich, und sie weiß: ich werde keines dieser mädchen mehr finden, obgleich ich sie alle noch immer so nahe vermute – fast so, als wären sie mir wie mein eigener schatten an die schuhe geheftet.

I know that I can shoot better than a thousand others and put it to the test: wedged between two branches is an Ace of Hearts; I hit it in the centre ...

... and again see myself in front of the detached house in the viale San Gottardo, a region full of wells and alpenhorns. I walk past the garden, see the mother and the younger sister, but not her. For a while I observe the mother and the younger sister. They are busy with balls of coloured wool, and all at once I am many streets further away in a region of semaphores, newspapers and leave-takings: telephone boxes walk about on small, iron lion's paws, executing in the process the economic movements of police-men. At the tiniest amount of pressure on one of their many buttons they spit out a considerable number of coins; my pockets can scarcely contain this largesse ... I lose it all again, down to the last Rappen, Pfennig, Groschen, Öre. I torment myself with nonsensical thoughts of remorse and homesickness; a September-like nostalgia approaches in a flapping dress; rising clearly to the surface of this crazy geography. Again I see the Annesley Voisey house in the twilight. As ever it is the rear of the house that is turned towards me. Its corridors and cellars are partly filled in and in part still accessible, but dangerous to enter. The lady of the house is always close at hand. She holds a lorgnon, she must not see me, I am unwelcome. But I manage, nevertheless, to get to see Miss C ...

– What do you want in our house, she says, – I hate you. I never want to see you again. There! Look at the destroyed balustrade ... you blew it up. 1921, the theatre: wasn't that enough for you? You're an anarchist, a beast, a monster; you fill me with revulsion. Your blood comes from the retort of a Doctor Frankenstein. Go, I can't stand looking at you any longer ...

She weeps. At this moment I would dearly love to strangle her. As the twilight encroaches on the garden the stone nymph almost imperceptibly moves her hand; I know well that she wants to persuade me that this was an illusion. I know her well from previous encounters; she cannot fool me. I know perfectly well that she really moves and she knows: I will never find any of these girls again, although I sense that they are all still so near – almost as if they were, like my own shadow, attached to my shoes.

English translation by Kevin Power.

Karl Gustav Gerold
(1972)

German original in: *kennwort: remember.* Dublin: The Dolmen Press, 1972, pp. 30-32.

DEN LEE HINAB

Den Lee hinab, den Lee hinauf!
Es bläst der Nordnordwest.
Sturmwolken für den Ausverkauf.
Der Himmel tut die Schleusen auf.
Halt deine Mütze fest!

Den Lee hinauf, den Lee hinab!
Im Tauwerk reisst es schwer.
Der Regen klopft in flottem Trab.
Balladensänger in dem Pub.
Gib einen Whiskey her!

HIER IST CORK

Hier ist Cork. Die Winde tosen toll,
reissen heftig an den Takelagen.
Wagen, Räder auf dem Kai geparkt.
Menschen in verschlissenen Kledagen.

Licht rinnt milchig über feuchte Strassen.
Liebespaare in den Schatten fliehn.
Alkoholisch gröhlen die Matrosen
in der Bar: 'The Orange and the Green.'

Ein Novembertag wie viele schon.
Vor den Kinos bilden sich die Schlangen.
Frachter, schwarz, mit angeschrammter Haut,
die in Wut das offne Meer verlangen.

Karl Gustav Gerold
(1972)

(Two poems)

DOWN THE LEE

Down the Lee and up the Lee!
The Nor-Nor-West is on the rampage.
A clearance sale of stormclouds.
The sky opens its sluice-gates.
Hold on there tight to your cap!

Up the Lee and down the Lee!
It's hard-going in the rigging.
The cantering rain pounces down.
Ballad-singers take over the pub.
Another ball-of-malt over here!

THIS IS CORK

This is Cork. Winds rage wildly,
fiercely tearing at the rigging.
Cars and bikes parked on the quay.
Men in threadbare clothes.

Light runs milky on wet streets.
Courting couples seek the shadows.
Drunken sailors brawl in a pub:
'The Orange and the Green.'

A November day like all the rest.
Queues form outside cinemas.
Freighters, black, with scarred hulls,
look to the open sea in anger.

Gilles Rosset
(1974)

French original in: *Le Point d'Irlande*. Paris: Denoel, 1974, p. 306.

QUAND J'EUS garé la voiture dans le parking, et que je m'extirpai du siège, mes jambes me soutinrent avec difficulté. La langueur m'engourdissait. Je ne coordonnais plus mes mouvements.

Cet aéroport, en rase campagne, ou plutôt en rase prairie, avec ses hangars et ses bâtiments transparents, me parut extravagant. Les deux ou trois avions posés sur le gazon prenaient l'allure d'oiseaux atteints de gigantisme. Les goélands – des cormorans peut-être – étaient si gros, qu'ils ne pouvaient plus battre des ailes. Ils demeuraient à l'engrais comme d'énormes ruminants. Bientôt, il leur pousserait des cornes et leur gésier se transformerait en une succession d'estomacs-réservoirs.

A l'intérieur du hall désert, la bizarrerie s'accentua. Qui prenait l'avion à Cork? Des voyageurs égarés comme nous, des revenants d'on ne sait quelle randonnée à travers les brouillards? Le style moderne de l'édifice accentuait la désolation du lieu. Je plaçai nos valises dans un chariot que je poussai. Je retombais en enfance. C'était mon landau, cadeau du Père Noël. Mais où était mon ours?

Etions-nous arrivés trop en avance, l'avion avait-il du retard, la pluie rendait-elle la piste impraticable? Le silence planait dans l'immense vestibule.

Gilles Rosset
(1974)

(*Cork airport*)

WHEN I had parked the car in the car park, and having extricated myself from the driver's seat, my legs could hardly hold me up. I felt stiff and lethargic. I could no longer co-ordinate my movements.

This airport, set out in the open countryside or rather in the open plain, with its hangars and transparent buildings, appeared excessive. The two or three aeroplanes resting on the grass looked like grossly over-sized birds. The seagulls – or maybe cormorants – were so big that they could no longer flap their wings. They were being fattened up like giant cows. Soon, they would grow horns and their gizzards would become a series of stomach reservoirs.

Inside the deserted hall, things became even more bizarre. Exactly who boarded planes in Cork? Travellers lost just like us, others returning from some excursion through the fog? The place felt all the more desolate given the modern style of the building. I put our suitcases on a trolley and started pushing. I was sinking back into childhood. This was my pram, a present from Father Christmas. But where was my teddy bear?

Had we arrived too early, was the plane late, was the runway closed due to rain? Silence hovered over the huge hall.

English translation by Grace Neville.

Hans Christian Kirsch
(1979)

German original in: *Irland. Die Freuden der Grünen Insel.*
München: Universitasverlag, 1979, pp. 68-71.

Some say the devil's dead,
Some say he's hardly
Some say the devil's dead
And buried in Killarney.
Some say, he rose again,
Some say, he rose again
And joined the British army.

Irische Folklore

CORK GEFIEL uns. Schwer zu erklären, warum. Es ist keine Großstadt, obwohl es 100000 Einwohner zählt. Es ist keine Kleinstadt und natürlich erst recht kein Dorf. Und doch hat es etwas von alledem.

Es ist weltoffen und urban, und dann scheint es wieder, als liege es vergessen am Ende der Welt.

Die Nähe des Meeres, die Brise Ozeanluft, die in die Stadt hinein-weht, aber auch die ländliche Umgebung, in der das verborgene, das gälische Irland lebendig ist, prägen in gleichem Maße den Charakter dieser Stadt. Da sind die Frauen, die Stachelbeeren verkaufen, in ihren weiten Kapuzenumhängen, und die Bauern mit den Schwarzdorn-stöcken, und da sind andererseits die Kaufleute, schlagfertig, gerissen, eine weiche Sprache sprechend, in der sich die Worte zu kräuseln scheinen, und dann ist da die Lee, die herrliche Lee, mit ihrer zweigeteilten Flur, wie der englische Dichter Spenser geschrieben hat. Und wirklich, überall, wo der Fluß ins Bild kommt, am Lavitt- und Merchants-Quai, und dort, wo sich der andere Arm am Albert- und Union-Quai in die Innenstadt drängt, ist der besondere Reiz von Cork gegenwärtig. Es wäre falsch, von Schönheit zu reden. Ich suche nach einem Vergleich,

Hans Christian Kirsch
(1979)

(Streets and shops – Mercier Press – War of Independence)

Some say the devil's dead,
Some say he's hardly
Some say the devil's dead
And buried in Killarney.
Some say, he rose again,
Some say, he rose again
And joined the British army.

Irish Folklore

WE LIKED Cork. Hard to explain, why. It is no city, although it has 100,000 inhabitants. It is no small town and, of course, in no way a village. And yet it has something of all of these.

It is open to the world and urbane, and then it seems once again as if it lies forgotten at the end of the world.

The proximity of the sea, the breeze of ocean air which blows into the town, but also the rural surroundings where the hidden, the Gaelic Ireland is alive, shape in equal measure the character of this town. On the one hand, there are the women selling gooseberries in their loose hooded shawls and the farmers with the blackthorn staffs, and on the other there are the business people, quick-witted, crafty, speaking a soft language in which the words seem to ripple, and then there's the Lee, the glorious Lee, with its 'divided floode', as the English poet Spenser wrote. And, truly, wherever the river is in sight, at Lavitt's and Merchant's Quays and where the other arm presses its way into the inner city at Albert and Union Quays, the particular attractiveness of Cork is apparent. It would be wrong to talk of beauty. I search for a comparison and

und seltsamerweise fällt mir Berlin ein, das alte Berlin, der dunkle, harte Reiz, den manche Partien an den Kanälen hatten, das Rußig-Städtische. Nor sagt, ich solle erwähnen, daß Cork die einzige Stadt in Irland außer Dublin war, in der wir italienische und chinesische Restaurants entdeckten. Und vergiß nicht, sagt sie, den Bus voller singender Männer. Nun, freilich singen auch anderswo Männer im letzten Bus, das heißt, meist grölen sie halbbetrunken, aber diese Männer, die spät abends von der Arbeit zurückkamen, sangen mit einer swingenden Gelassenheit, nicht laut, und einer spielte auf einer Metallflöte dazu, und der Schaffner klopfte mit den Fingern den Takt.

Ich denke auch an die Hauptstraße, die St Patricks Street, mit ihren hübschen, ordentlichen Geschäften, den vielen Buchhandlungen und den sympathischen Kneipen. Natürlich wird man sagen, in der Hauptstraße jeder größeren Stadt gibt es schöne, große Geschäfte, aber trotzdem ist es hier anders. Diese Läden sind nicht protzig, sie sind gediegen, nicht aufwendig, sondern solid, und was die Buchhandlungen angeht, für die ich natürlich überall eine Schwäche habe ... was hätte ich darum gegeben, einen ganzen Tag in der staubig-dunklen Höhle dieses Antiquariats am Lavitt-Quai zubringen zu dürfen ...! Die Vielzahl der Buchhandlungen, auf die man in Cork stößt, mag vielleicht etwas damit zu tun haben, daß diese Stadt traditionsgemäß Irlands Journalisten und Schulmeister hervorgebracht hat, und daß bekannte zeitgenössische Schriftsteller, wie Daniel Corkery, Frank O'Connor, Sean O'Faolain und Lennox Robinson, aus Cork stammen.

Ich denke an den Spaziergang hinauf zum St. Patricks Hill – eine steile Gasse, von der aus man einen guten Ausblick über die Innenstadt hat. Hier entdeckten wir das Stammhaus der Mercier Press. Die kleinen weißen Taschenbücher dieses Verlages sollte sich jeder merken, der an modernen Interpretationen irischer Literatur, Folklore und Volkskunde interessiert ist. Man kann sich mit ihnen, ohne viel Geld aufzuwenden, eine ganze irische Bibliothek anlegen.

Ich denke an den Fluß, und wie ich staunte, als ich über die Ufermauern in der Innenstadt ins Wasser sah und feststellte: es war durchsichtig, flaschengrün und wimmelte von Fischen. Dies in einer Stadt, in der es viel Industrie gibt!

curiously I come upon Berlin, old Berlin, the dark, hard attractiveness some parts of the canals had, the sooty city style. Nor says, I should mention that Cork was the only city in Ireland apart from Dublin where we discovered Italian and Chinese restaurants. And don't forget, she says, the bus full of men singing. Now, admittedly men also sing in other places on the last bus home, that is to say, mostly they bawl out half-drunk, but these men, coming home late at night from work, sang calmly and with a swing, not loudly, and one of them played along on a tin whistle, while the conductor kept time with his fingers.

I also think of the main street, St Patrick's Street, with its pretty, respectable shops, numerous bookshops and congenial pubs. Of course, it might be said that in the main street of any larger town there are beautiful, big shops, but nonetheless it's different here. These shops are not showy, they are dignified, not lavish but solidly built, and as for the bookshops, for which I, of course, have a weakness everywhere … what would I have given to be able to spend a whole day in the dark and dusty cavern of that second-hand bookshop on Lavitt's Quay …! The multitude of bookshops you come across in Cork may perhaps have something to do with the fact that this city has a tradition of producing Ireland's journalists and schoolteachers and that well-known contemporary writers, such as Daniel Corkery, Frank O'Connor, Sean O'Faoláin and Lennox Robinson, hail from Cork.

I think of the walk up St Patrick's Hill – a steep laneway, from where you get a good view of the city centre. Here we discovered the seat of Mercier Press. Anyone interested in modern interpretations of Irish literature and folklore should take note of the small white paperbacks of this publishing house. Without spending much money, you can build up a whole Irish library with them.

I think of the river, and how amazed I was as I looked over the walls in the city centre into the water and realised it was clear, bottle-green and teeming with fish. This in a city which has lots of industry.

Obwohl Cork eine sehr alte Stadt ist – *Corcaigh* heißt auf gälisch der sumpfige Platz – und 820 n. Chr. von norwegigen Wikingern auf der Insel zwischen den beiden Flußarmen gegründet wurde, findet man heute kaum noch alte Bauten. Der Stadtwall, die Kirchen, die Abteien, von denen in den Chroniken so viel, die Rede ist, sie sind verschwunden.

Im irisch-englischen Krieg der Jahre 1919-1921 brannten große Teile von Cork nieder. Der Bürgermeister MacCrutain wurde von der Polizei erschossen, sein Nachfolger MacSwiney starb nach einem Hungerstreik von 75 Tagen im Brixton-Gefängnis.

Es waren die gefürchteten 'Black and Tans', Hilfstruppen, die die Engländer aus Arbeitslosen und Veteranen des Ersten Weltkrieges gebildet hatten, welche damals beispielsweise eine ganze Straßenseite der Patrick Street niederlegten.

Freilich muß man, wenn man von Cork spricht, den Pfefferbüchsenturm von Shandon erwähnen, der in einem Arme-Leute-Viertel 1772 an der Stelle einer älteren Kirche, halb aus Sandstein, halb aus grauem Kalkstein, errichtet wurde, und dessen Glockenspiel Father Prout mit seiner sentimentalen Heimatpoesie, die zu zitieren ich mir hier versage, weltberühmt machte.

Although Cork is a very old city – *Corcaigh* means 'the marshy place' in Irish – and was founded in 820AD by Norwegian Vikings on the island between the two arms of the river, there are scarcely any old buildings to be found today. The city wall, the churches, the abbeys, mentioned so frequently in the chronicles, have disappeared.

In the War of Independence during the years 1919 to 1921, large sections of Cork were burned to the ground. The Lord Mayor MacCurtain was shot dead by the police, his successor, MacSwiney, died following a 75-day hunger strike in Brixton Prison.

It was the feared Black and Tans, auxiliary units created by the British from the ranks of the unemployed and the veterans of the First World War, who at that time destroyed one complete side of St Patrick's Street.

Of course, if one talks of Cork, one has to mention the pepper-pot tower of Shandon which was built in 1772, half sandstone, half limestone, in a poor quarter of the city, replacing an older church and whose bells were made famous by Father Prout and his sentimental regional poetry which I'll refrain from quoting here.

English translation by Jean E. Conacher.

Olli and Riitta Jalonen
(1980)

Finnish original in: *Matkailijan Irlanti*. Helsinki. Otava Publishers Ltd., 1980, pp. 100-02.

CORK ON Dublinin jälkeen suurin kaupunki koko tasavallassa. Se on Irlannin Tampere – ja Turku. Corkilaiset ovat tunnettuja kotipaikkarakkaudestaan. Joskus oma kehu haisee liikaakin, sanovat irlantilaiset jotka eivät asu Corkissa. Tai jotka eivät ole siellä syntyneet. Corkilaisuus säilyy sen verran vahvana, että vielä Dubliniin muutettuaan corkilainen muistaa kaiholla paikallista herkkuruokaa, mustaa verimakkaraa. Turkulainen matkailija löytää myös kotoisia piirteitä Corkista. Lee-joki virtaa rauhallisesti kaupungin halki, ja suurien laivojen satama tuo kaduille kansainvälistä väriä.

Paitsi laivalla Corkiin pääsee myös lentoteitse, junalla, tai autolla jotain monista pääteistä. Waterfordin ohella Cork on Etelä-Irlannin liikenteen solmukohta. Asukkaita jokilaakson ja kukkuloiden kaupunkiin mahtuu 130,000.

Iirinkielinen nimi Corcaigh merkitsee rämeistä paikkaa. Kaupunki on rakennettu suon saarille, ja pohjavesi on yllättävän lähellä katujen ja talojen alla. Vanhat corkilaiset muistavat vielä ajan, jolloin jalkakäytävät olivat puusta, ja talvisin tulvan noustessa ne saattoivat rikkoutua ja silloin pystyi näkemään joen virtaavan jalkakäytävän alla.

Nykyään Lee-joki kulkee kaupungin halki kahta kanavaa pitkin, ja talvitulvat pystytään välttämään.

Pääkatu on St Patrick's Street, jossa on upea 1800-luvun puolivälissä rakennettu silta. Siitä pääsee Pyhän Patrikin kukkulalle, joka nousee lähes äkkijyrkästi. Kukkulalta näkee kauas kaupungin kattoja, pääasiassa tummanruskeita ja mustia. Punakattoisten talojen aluetta corkilaiset itse kutsuvat 'Kremliksi'.

Corkin historia alkaa 500-luvulta, jolloin Pyhä Finbar perusti kirkon ja koulun Leen etelärannalle. Tämän paikan löytää parhaiten

Olli and Riitta Jalonen
(1980)

(A marshy place – Cork sights)

C ORK IS the second biggest city after Dublin in the Republic. It is the
Tampere and Turku [two Finnish cities] of Ireland. The Corkonians
are known for their love and pride in their city. Sometimes their self
importance is very obvious, say the Irish who are not living in Cork.
Being a Corkonian stays with one so strong that even the ones who have
moved to Dublin are wistfully longing for the local delicacy, black pud-
ding. A traveller from Turku can also find familiar features in Cork. The
River Lee flows peacefully through the town, and the harbour for big
ships brings international colour to the streets.

Besides arriving to Cork by boat, you can also get there by plane,
train or car, using one of the many main roads. Along with Waterford,
Cork is a main traffic junction in southern Ireland. The city, with a river
valley and hills, holds 130,000 inhabitants.

The Irish name *Corcaigh* means 'marshy place'. The town is built on
islands in a bog, and ground water is surprisingly just underneath the
streets and houses. Old Corkonians can still remember the time when
the pavements were made from wood, and during the winter when
waters rose with floods they broke and then one could see the river flowing underneath.

Nowadays the River Lee runs through the town along two canals,
and winter floods can be avoided.

The main street is St Patrick's Street, which has a grand bridge, built
in the middle of the nineteenth century. From there you can get to St
Patrick's Hill, which rises almost precipitiously. From the hill you can see
far; the roofs of the town houses are mainly dark brown or black. The
area with red roofs is called by Corkonians, 'Kremlin'.

Cork's history began in the sixth century, when St Finbar established a church and a school to the south side of the River Lee. This

kysymällä yliopiston, University Collegen, sijaintia. Finbarrin koulu pysyi kaksi vuosisataa merkittävänä, ja kaupunki alkoi kasvaa sen ympärille. Mutta vuonna 820 tulivat viikingit, jotka eivät koulusivistyksestä paljoa välittäneet, vaan polttivat koko kaupungin ja ryöstivät mitä ryöstettävissä oli. Joitain vuosia myöhemmin he purjehtivat rämeiseen lahden perukkaan uudestaan ja asettuivat sinne asumaan. Näin Cork perustettiin kahteen kertaan.

Kuuluisin nähtävyys on Shandon Church Leen pohjoispuolella. Sen torni on puolittain punaista ja puolittain valkoista kiveä ja se kohoaa yli 40 metrin korkeuteen. Jos haluaa osoittaa olevansa turisti, voi pienestä maksusta saada soittaa kirkonkelloja. Muita Corkin kirkkoja ovat protestanttinen Cathedral of St. Finbarre, St Mary's Cathedral, St Mary's Dominican Church ja Father Mathew Memorial Church.

Leen eteläkanaalin rannalla on massiivinen kaupungintalo City Hall, jonka kuvan yövalaistuksessa useimmat matkailijat valitsevat Siksi postikortiksi, joka lähetetään Corkista. Pääposti muuten sijaitsee Oliver Plunkett Streetin varrella.

Kesäaikaan Corkin kulttuuritarjonta on rikasta. Siellä pidetään mm. elokuvajuhlat kesäkuussa ja kuorolaulu-juhlat huhti – toukokuun vaihteessa. Corkin kirjallisuus-ja tiedeseura (*the Cork Literary and Scientific Society*) on Irlannin vanhin; se perustettiin jo vuonna 1820.

place is best found by asking the location of University College. Finbar's school held its importance for two centuries and the town began to grow around it. But in the year 820 the Vikings came, who did not care much about school education – they burned down the whole town and raided all that there was to take. Some years later they sailed again to the end of the boggy bay and settled there. Thus, Cork was founded twice.

The best known sight is Shandon Church on the north side of the Lee. Its steeple is built half in red and half in white stone, and rises over 40 metres in height. If you want to show that you are a tourist you can for a small fee ring the church bells. Other churches in Cork are the Protestant Cathedral of St Finbar's, St Mary's Cathedral, St Mary's Dominican Church and the Father Matthew Memorial Church.

On the bank of the Lee's southern canal stands a massive City Hall, a picture of which in night lighting most tourists choose for *the* postcard to send from Cork. The main post office is situated on Oliver Plunkett Street.

During the summer Cork has rich cultural supply. Among others, a Film Festival is held in June and a Choral Festival in April-May. The Cork Literary and Scientific Society is the oldest in Ireland, it was established already in 1820.

English translation by Mari Moran.

Marc Giannesini
(1984)

French original in: 'Une semaine en Irlande'. In: *Le Monde*, 23 August 1984.

DIMANCHE

CORK – CŒUR de l'Irlande rebelle, elle fit perdre la tête à tous les conquérants qui voulurent se l'approprier. Cork trône sur une petite colline habillée de lourds monuments 'gothiques' ou 'doriques' du dix-neuvième siècle, rivalisant de médiocrité avec d'énormes bâtisses de briques rouge-manoir hitchcockiens.

Sa seule coquetterie est sa plage, non loin d'un centre réduit à deux rues qui tournent en rond. Cette immense ligne de sable couleur café, balisé à espaces regulières de cabanes mauves, affiche de grands airs de dame victoriennes. Ses activités: Cork accueille une semaine par an un festival de cinéma et un autre de jazz.

Ce soir, rien ou presque. Dans l'un de ces petits pubs-salons de velours rouge, douillet, l'une des chaînes de télévision diffuse un documentaire sur les grèves ouvrières de Limerick qui, si l'on en croit les images et les commentaires, est tragique, mais qui manifestement n'émeut personne. Deux jumelles, l'une rousse, l'autre blonde, boivent goulument une pinte de bière et attendent leur *folksinger* en blouson. Là enfin, avec sa guitare et ses éternelles rengaines de costauds, reprise en chœur par des hommes-tonneau. Premier coup de sonnette, deuxième. C'est l'heure. 23h30, on ferme, c'est la loi.

LUNDI

CORK - Vent du nord force 7. Le baromètre exagère. Pluie battante tout de même. Ne mettre le nez dehors qu'à la condition de longer les murs et de sauter de trottoir en trottoir. Les passants s'abritent où ils peuvent, dans les confortables *lounges* ou dans les halls des administrations, où quelques clochards grognent et quelques petites filles rousses 'tapent' dix pennies à un Américain dodu. Quand il pleut, Cork tourne en rond. Dans l'un de ces halls frileux, entre une caisse d'enregistrement et un guichet une dizaine de photos sont accrochées au mur. L'une d'entre elles

Marc Giannesini
(1984)

(Night life – entertainment – rain)

SUNDAY

CORK – THE heart of rebel Ireland, it confounded all its would-be con-querors. Cork sits triumphantly atop a small hill dotted with heavy nine-teenth-century 'Gothic' or 'Doric' buildings, matched in their architectural mediocrity by vast red brick mansions like something straight out of Hitchcock.

The only thing it has going for it is its beach, situated not far from a centre, reduced to just two streets going nowhere. This immense stretch of coffee-coloured sand marked at regular intervals by mauve cab-ins has all the snooty airs of some Victorian lady. As for activities, Cork hosts a week-long film festival and a jazz festival every year.

This evening, there is little or nothing to do. In one of these cosy lit-tle pub-salons decorated in red velvet, a TV channel is showing a docu-mentary on the workers' strikes in Limerick. If the images and commen-tary are to be believed, there is a certain tragedy about all this, but no one seems moved by it. Twins, one redhead, the other blonde, knock back a pint of beer, one red, one pale, and wait for their black-jacketed folksinger. He arrives eventually with his guitar and his endless, tough-guy, clichéd songs while men shaped like barrels join in the chorus. A bell rings once, twice. Time's up: 11.30 pm: closing time. That's the law.

MONDAY

CORK – A gale force 7 wind. The barometer is overstating things. The rain, nevertheless, is torrential. The weather is so bad that if you do dare to ven-ture out you have to slink along the walls and hop from pavement to pave-ment. People take refuge where they can, in cosy lounges or in the halls of the public buildings where tramps grumble to themselves and a few red-haired young girls cadge tenpence off a portly American. When it rains, Cork comes to a standstill. In one of the draughty hallways, between a cash register and a ticket office, ten or so photographs hang on the wall.

représente un petit convoi funèbre qui passe, des hommes portant un cercueil et, derrière, tenant un cierge, une femme serre la main d'une fillette en socquettes blanches; tout cela est étrange à voir, les blouses sombres, les cierges, la lumière éteinte d'un après-midi moyen et le cercueil silencieux qui attend une charrette de bois tirée par un âne impatient. Tout est immobile, figé, la scène a certainement eu lieu au début du siècle. Un grand photographe anonyme a pris en flagrant délit quelques-uns de ses concitoyens tout aussi anonymes. Un instant happé, volé au temps. La vie d'hier et celle d'aujourd'hui n'ont aucun contact, sinon la mélancolie. D'autres clichés montrent le travail des cheminots, ou celui des colossales brasseries. La dernière, fixe, lointainement, un homme robuste haranguant une foule bouche cousue, casquette humblement posée sur les genoux. De simples images où se manifeste l'humanité tout entière, sans aucun arrière-plan politique.

Non loin, un minuscule salon de thé expose fièrement une douzaine de lithographies de Van Gogh, peut-être le seul peintre à avoir si vivement coloré des paysages aussi noirs.

Les vitrines bon marché style années 60 pullulent de reproductions épouvantablement bâclées de Renoir, Degas, Monet. Les impressionnistes font un ravage, ici aussi.

Entre deux averses franches, visite de la School of Art, abusivement appelée Art Gallery, où sont exhibés, à l'entrée, des squelettes, des crânes qui semblent vous convier dare-dare à visiter les nombreuses horreurs picturales régionales. Sentiment de cauchemar, vite dissipé par une surprenante éclaircie et la visite d'un de ces jardins dont les Anglo-Saxons ont le secret. Celui-là est une utopie végétale, une cour des miracles où l'espace calme est à peine troublé par le cliquetis des jets d'eau et des fontaines rigolotes.

20 h 30. – L'Irish National Ballet a terminé sa tournée hier, et ce soir, à l'Ivernian Theatre de Cork, c'est une première. Une dizaine de comédiens jouent une pièce de Mary Elizabeth Burke-Kennedy, célèbre pour ses adaptations des grands textes celtes. *Women in Arms* (*Femmes armées*), satire de la condition féminine à travers les âges, pièce hautement caustique si l'on en croit les éclats de rire, mais que notre connaissance très approximative de la culture gaélique ne nous a pas permis d'apprécier à sa juste valeur.

One depicts a small funeral procession, with men carrying a coffin while, behind, a woman holding a candle shakes the hand of a girl wearing white socks: it all looks very strange, the dark clothes, the candles, the dim light of a drab afternoon and the silent coffin awaiting a wooden cart, drawn by an impatient donkey. Everything in the scene, which must have occurred at the turn of the century, is motionless and frozen. An unknown great photographer has captured some of his equally obscure compatriots unawares. A snatched moment, stolen from time. The world of yesterday and of today have nothing in common, apart from an enduring melancholy. Other photographs show railwaymen at work, or employees working in the huge breweries. The last photograph focuses from afar on a sturdy-looking man haranguing a tight-lipped crowd, their caps humbly placed on their laps. Simple pictures, in which all of humanity are featured, with no political backdrop.

Nearby, a tiny tea room proudly displays a dozen or so lithographs by Van Gogh, perhaps the only painter to have painted such drab landscapes in such vivid colours.

The cheap 1960s-style windows are full of atrocious reproductions of pictures by Renoir, Degas and Monet. The Impressionists are all the rage here too.

In between two downpours, we visit the School of Art, misleadingly called an Art Gallery, where the skeletons and skulls on display in the entrance appear to be inviting us to come in quick and inspect the many daubs in which the region seems to specialise. The sense of nightmare is quickly alleviated by a sudden spell of sunshine and a visit to one of those gardens of which the Anglo-Saxons seem to know the secret. This one is a verdant utopia, an off-beat place where the calm is barely disturbed by the gurgling water of the funny-looking fountains.

8.30pm. – The Irish National Ballet finished its tour yesterday, and this evening, at the Ivernian Theatre in Cork, there is an opening night. About ten actors are performing a play by Mary Elizabeth Burke-Kennedy, famous for her adaptations of great Celtic texts. *Women in Arms* is a satire about the condition of women throughout the ages, a highly caustic play judging from the laughter from the audience, but one which we were unable to appreciate fully due to our very rudimentary knowledge of Gaelic culture. *English translation by Gearóid Cronin and Grace Neville.*

295

Jyrki Jahnukainen
(1985)

Finnish original in: 'Cork: Irlantilaisia lähellä Jumalaa'.
In: *Helsingin Sanomat Kuukausiliite* [monthly supplement], March 1985.

M IKSI NÄMÄ ihmiset tuntuvat niin tutuilta? Missä olen tavannut heidän laisiaan aikaisemmin? Ehkä Frank Capran filmeissä. Tai lap-
suudessani, viisikymmentäluvun Suomessa.

ISÄ MATHEW'N EDESSÄ
'Hey, mister, come and give me a hand!'
Katselen Corkin suojeluspyhimyksen patsasta ja pohdiskelen, mikä tämä
Isä Mathew mahtoi olla miehiään. Köyhien Isä ainakin, mutta sen lisäksi
Kohtuuden Apostoli vaiko peräti Raittiuden? Miten tuon nyt suomentaisi ...
'Hey, mister, tulkaa auttamaan!'
'Ai, minäkö?' Nyt vasta huomaan parikymmenvuotiaan tyttösen,
joka viittilöi kadun toiselta puolelta. Jalkakäytävällä makaa
punatukkainen ukko, jolla on tyhjä pullo kädessään ja pieni
lammikko allaan. Olisihan näitä kotonakin.
'Hänen täytyy päästä kotiin, ei häntä tähän voi jättää lojumaan.
Auttakaa minua nostamaan hänet pystyyn.'
Ajatus ei suuremmin innosta, mutta eipä tässä muu auta kuin tart-
tua vasemmalla ukon tahmeaan kouraan ja viedä oikea käsi kostean
kainalon alle ja ruveta nostamaan.
'Mitäs nyt tehdään? Ööh, tunnettekos te hänet?' yritän udella
hienotunteisesti.
'En tunne, mutta tiedän missäpäin hän asuu. Sinne on sen verran
matkaa, että parasta hakea taksi. Odottakaa te tässä sen aikaa!'
Tyttö kirmaisee kohti Patrick Streetiä ja minä jään pitelemään ukkoa
pystyssä. Ehdin juuri tajuta seisovani vieraassa kaupungissa ja vieraassa
maassa keskellä jalkakäytävää tuntematon puliukko kainalossani, kun-
tyttö jo tulee takaisin.
Kampeamme ukon taksin takapenkille, tyttö istuutuu hänen viereensä,

Jyrki Jahnukainen
(1985)

(Tramps – prayers – travellers – poitín – unmarried mothers)

WHY DO these people feel so familiar? Where have I met their kind before? Maybe in films of Frank Capra. Or in my childhood, in 1950s Finland.

IN FRONT OF FATHER MATTHEW

'Hey, mister, come and give me a hand!'

I look at the statue of the patron saint of Cork and ponder what kind of man this Father Matthew might have been. At least Father to the poor, but also Apostle for Moderation or maybe even for Temperance? How would you translate that into Finnish …

'Hey, mister, come to help!'

'Oh, me?' Only now I notice the girl in her twenties, who gestures on the other side of the street. An old man with red hair lies on the pavement having an empty bottle in his hand and a small puddle underneath him. You would find these at home.

'He has to get home, one can't leave him lying here. Please help me to get him up.'

The thought doesn't really inspire me, but I just have to grab with my left hand the sticky paw and bring the right underneath the damp armpit and start heaving.

'What do we do now? Ehm, do you know him?' I try to pry tactfully.

'I don't know him, but I know the area where he lives. It is so far that I better get a taxi. Please wait here for a while!'

The girl sprints towards St Patrick's Street and I'm left to hold the old man steady. I just realised that I was standing in a strange town, in a foreign country, in the middle of a pavement with an unknown drunkard at my side when the girl already comes back.

We push the old man to the back seat of the taxi, and the girl sits

As Others Saw Us

kiittää ja sanoo selviytyvänsä omin avuin tästä eteenpäin. Taksi on mennyt menojaan, ennen kuin keksin sanoa mitään tilanteeseen sopivaa. Mieleeni tulvahtaa kuva ovelista veijareista ja typerästä turistista – *Puhallus*. Haluaisin koettaa, onko lompakko vielä tallella taskussa, mutta en kehtaa. Isä Mathew saattaisi nähdä.

RUKOILKAA

'Please, pray for Betty, who is recovering after an operation.'

Vihreään tauluun on nastalla kiinnitetty pieni sininen lappu, jossa pyydetään rukoilemaan leikkauksesta toipuvan Bettyn puolesta. Sen vieressä on toisia lappuja:

'Rukoilkaa pohjoisirlantilaisten puolesta, että he pian saisivat rauhan.'

'Rukoilkaa Sylvian ja hänen aviomiehensä puolesta, jotta he voisivat taas elää sovussa.'

'Rukoilkaa kolmannen maailman ihmisten puolesta.'

Saint Finbarren katedraalissa on hämärää ja viileätä, vaikka ulkona paistaa keskipäivän aurinko. Kirkko on satavuotias, kalkkikivestä rakennettu, Corkin komein vaikka onkin protestanttinen.

Ulkopuolella on vaikuttavia korkokuvia, sisällä kaiverruksia ja mosaiikkia. Ja pieni taulu, jossa on pieniä sinisiä lappuja ja kehotus: 'Sinua pyydetään rukoilemaan.' Seison taulun edessä kymmenen minuuttia tai puoli tuntia ja ajattelen omaa sinistä lappuani ja sitä minkä puolesta pyydän heitä rukoilemaan.

Enkä saa sitä lappua koskaan kirjoitetuksi, sillä vaikka heidän surunsa pysäyttää minut miettimään, en osaa jakaa omaani heidän kanssaan.

MATKALAISET

'Jumala teitä siunatkoon, nuori mies', sanoo viidenkymmenen ikäinen nainen Oliver Plunkett Streetillä, kun annan hänelle taskuni pohjalta löytyvät kolikot.

'Nyt saan lapsilleni ruokaa täksi illaksi.'

Vai oliko se lapsenlapsille? En tahdo millään saada selvää hänenpuheestaan, eikä se johdu hänen rikkinäisistä hampaistaan eikä liikenteen melustakaan. Hänen murteensa on vain niin toivottoman paksua. Ja puhe vuolasta, keskeytymätöntä.

298

beside him, she thanks me and says that she'll manage on her own from here. The taxi is well gone by the time I find anything appropriate to say.

An image of sly rascals and a stupid tourist comes to my mind – *Sting*. I would like to try if my wallet was still safely in my pocket, but I don't dare, Father Matthew might see.

PLEASE PRAY

'Please, pray for Betty, who is recovering after an operation.'

A small blue note asking to pray for Betty recovering after an operation has been fixed with a thumbtack to the green board. There are other notes beside it:

'Please, pray for the Northern Irish, so that they may soon get peace.'

'Please, pray for Sylvia and her husband, so that they can live in harmony again.'

'Please, pray for the people in the Third World.'

It's dark and cool in St Finbar's Cathedral, although the noon sun shines outside. The church is 100 years old, built in limestone, and is the most magnificent in Cork, despite being Protestant.

Outside it has impressive reliefs, inside carvings and mosaics. And a small board with small blue notes and encouragement, 'You are asked to pray'. I stand in front of the board ten minutes or half an hour and think about my own blue note and about what I would ask them to pray for.

I don't ever get that note written, because although their grief makes me think, I can't share mine with them.

TRAVELLERS

'God bless you, young man,' says a woman in her fifties on Oliver Plunkett Street, when I give her the coins found in the bottom of my pocket.

'Now I can get food for my children tonight.'

Or was it grandchildren? I hardly can understand her speech, and it isn't only because of her broken teeth, or the noise of the traffic. Her accent is just so hopelessly thick. And her speech is fast flowing, endless.

Hän on traveller, matkalainen; heitä on Irlannissa ehkä 30,000. He elävät tänään kuin mustalaiset ennen muinoin, kerjäävät, kaupustelevat, asuvat hevosvankkureissa tai asuntovaunuissa.

Mutta he eivät ole romaaneja eivätkä kuulu mihinkään muuhunkaan toisista irlantilaisista poikkeavaan rotuun tai heimoon. Pikemminkin päinvastoin, he ovat punatukkaisempia ja pisamaisempia ja itsepäisempiä – siis irlantilaisempia kuin muut irlantilaiset. Heissä ei ole vierasta verta.

Heitä on kevään mittaan kerääntynyt kaupungin liepeille parisataa perhettä. Corkin sanomalehdet puhuvat traveller-kriisista: pitääkö heitä sietää, pitäisikö heitä auttaa, miksi he eivät suostu sopeutumaan yhteiskuntaan.

Vanhat travellerit ovat lukutaidottomia, siksi ne puhuvat ja tarinoivat mielellään ja pitkään. Kun vihdoin pääsen irrottautumaan ja jatkamaan matkaa, nainen on juuri alkanut kertoa, mitä hän ajattelee tekopyhistä papeista – luullakseni.

LUOPIO-TED

'Oletko koskaan maistanut pot-stilliä?'

Ensin en ymmärrä kysymystä, mutta sitten valkenee: 'Ai, *moonshinea,* pontikkaa. Katsos kun minä olen Suomesta ja meillähän sitä vasta ...'

'Mutta oletko maistanut viisi vuotta vanhaa?' Ted täsmentää, 'Minä tarjoan sitä sinulle — todella tehokasta ainetta. Viime kesänä meillä kävi eräs hollantilainen pariskunta, joka pahaa aavistamatta ...'

Mutta Ted itse ei ota pisaraakaan, vaikka on irlantilainen mies.

Eikä hän käy kirkossa, vaikka on katolinen.

'Ei minulla ole mitään Jumalaa vastaan, mutta vihaan uskontoa, sitä miten se kahlitsee täällä kaikkia ihmisiä, varsinkin naisia.'

'Haluatko kuulla, miten kieroja ihmisiä tosiuskovaiset irlantilaiset voivat olla?'

'Tässä lähellä, kaupungin laidalla on aidattu puisto, jossa sijaitsee *Sacred Heart Home.* Se on nunnien ylläpitämä sairaala nuoria, aviottomia äiteja varten. Todella kaunis paikka ...'

'Mutta kaikki potilaat tulevat maaseudulta tai sitten Dublinista. Dublinissa taas on samanlainen sairaala, sinne corkilaiset tytöt menevät.'

'Jos haluat kirjoittaa kotiin vanhemmillesi, että olet äkkiä muuttanut

She is a Traveller; there are about 30,000 of them in Ireland. They are living today as the gypsies used to – begging, selling, living in horse-drawn wagons or trailers.

But they are not Romanies, nor do they belong to any race or tribe differing from the other Irish. Rather, on the contrary, they are more often with red hair and freckles and more stubborn – so more Irish than the rest of the Irish. They don't have foreign blood.

Around 200 Traveller families have gathered on the outskirts of the town during spring. Cork newspapers talk about a Traveller crisis: do they need to be tolerated, should they be helped, why don't they agree to adjust to the society?

The old Travellers are illiterate, therefore, they like to talk and tell stories a lot. When I eventually free myself and get to continue my journey, the woman has just started to tell what she thinks about the hypocritical priests – I suppose.

RENEGADE TED

'Have you ever tasted pot-still?'

First I don't understand the question, but then it dawns on me. 'Oh, *moonshine*. You see, I am from Finland and we just …'

'But have you tasted five year old?' Ted specifies. 'I'll offer it to you – it's very effective stuff. Last summer we were visited by a Dutch couple, who suspecting no evil …'

But Ted himself doesn't take a drop, although he is an Irish man.

Nor does he go to mass, though he is a Catholic.

'I don't have anything against God, but I hate religion, the way it confines everybody here, particularly women.

'Do you want to hear how crooked the true religious Irish can be?

'Near here, on the outskirts of the town, is a fenced park, where the Sacred Heart Home is located. It is a hospital, kept by the nuns, for young, unmarried mothers. Very beautiful place …

'But all the patients come from the countryside or from Dublin. In Dublin there is another similar hospital, it's there where the Cork girls go.

'If you want to write home to your parents to tell that you have suddenly

Australiaan, niin nunnat huolehtivat siitä, että kirjeesi postitetaan Australiasta. Ja jos vanhempasi vastaavat, kirje tulee Australian kautta sinulle. Arvaapa, millaiseksi naiseksi siinä itsensä tuntee!'

'Yleensä tyttö uskoo, ettei hänestä ole äidiksi, ja jättää lapsensa nunnien huostaan ja adoptoitavaksi. Toinen mahdollisuus on käydä Englannissa ja tulla takaisin lapsen ja vihkisormuksen kanssa – aviomies valitettavasti kuoli liikenneonnettomuudessa ...'

Ehkä Tedillä on muitakin syitä olla käymättä kirkossa. Vaikka onkin irlantilainen. Eihän hän myöskään ole punatukkainen eikä merimies eikä nimeltään Patrick.

TURISTIN CORK

[...] Vuosisatainen köyhyys ja englantilainen esivalta näkyvät valitettavasti yhä irlantilaisessa keittiössä. Kansallisruoka lammasmuhennos on oikeastaan muunnelma vanhemmasta kansallisruoasta perunasopasta. Muu onkin sitten tuontitavaraa, ja brittiläiseen tapaan ruoka yleensä, valmistustavasta riippumatta, maistuu höyryssä keitetyltä. Hinta takaa laadun mutta ei makua. Onneksi aamiainenkin on englantilaista perua: tukeva ja maukas.

Janoiselle Cork tarjoaa hyvää ja huonoa. Tee on vahvaa ja hyvää, kahvi laihaa ja surkeata. Irish coffee – kahvia, viskiä, ruskeata sokeria ja paksua kermaa – on oikeastaan Shannonin lentokentän baarissa turistien iloksi syntynyt juoma, mutta sitä voi silti tilata kapakassa joutumatta naurunalaiseksi. Irlantilaista viskiä sopii kehua paikkakuntalaisille, kun taas olutta kannattaa suositella ystävilleenkin. Corkissa on kaksi panimoa: Murphy's on tummaa *stout*ia, Beamish & Crawford vaaleata *lager*ia.

Unohtumattomia nähtävyyksiä Corkissa ei oikeastaan ole – kaupunki kun on hävitetty ja poltettu moneen kertaan, eikä siellä ole asunut kuninkaallisia eikä upporikasta ylimystöä. Parasta on pikkukaupunkilainen, menneen ajan tunnelma, jonka tavoittaa kävelemällä kaupungin kaduilla. Hyviä kävelyreittejä löytää opaskirjasesta 'Tourist Trail', jonka saa matkailutoimistosta.

moved to Australia, the nuns will make sure that your letter will be posted from Australia. And if your parents reply, the letter will arrive via Australia to you. Can you guess what kind of a woman you feel yourself be!

'Normally, the girl believes that she is not fit to be a mother and leaves her child in care with the nuns to be adopted. Another possibility is to visit England and come back with a child and wedding ring – a husband unfortunately dead in a traffic accident.'

Maybe, Ted has also other reasons not to go to church. Even though he is Irish. He doesn't have red hair either, and he is not a sailor nor is his name Patrick.

THE TOURIST'S CORK

[…] Centuries-long poverty and English rule is still unfortunately evident in the Irish kitchen. The national dish, Irish Stew, is actually just a variation of an earlier national dish, potato soup. Everything else is imported, and in the British manner food normally, regardless of method of cooking, tastes boiled. The price guarantees quality, but not taste. Fortunately also, the breakfast is of English inheritance: substantial and tasty.

For a thirsty person, Cork offers good and bad. Tea is strong and good; coffee weak and poor. Irish coffee – coffee, whiskey, brown sugar and thick cream – was actually invented in the bar at Shannon airport for the tourists' delight, but one can still order it in a pub without being laughed at. You can praise Irish whiskey to the locals, whereas beer you can recommend to your friends as well. There are two breweries in Cork: Murphy's is dark *stout* and Beamish & Crawford is *lager*.

There aren't actually any unforgettable sights in Cork – the town has been plundered and burned so many times, and no royalty or rich nobility have lived there. The best thing is the small town, old-time feel that one can sense while walking around the streets.

English translation by Mari Moran.

Robert Mallet
(1985)

French original in: *Ellynn*. Paris: Gallimard, 1985, pp. 196-97.

'QU'EST-CE QUE C'EST?'

Il essaie de lui expliquer, à l'aide de mots aussi simples que possible, ce qu'est une usine et à quoi sert le gigantesque tuyau de briques qui en sort. Ce n'est pas facile. Ellynn, très attentive:

'Pourquoi on l'a mise là, l'usine, avec la cheminée?'

Aubry trouve une réponse toute simple:

'Parce qu'on est à côté de Cork. On met les usines près des grandes villes.'

De fait, la capitale du comté est toute proche. En arrivant au sommet d'une colline, on découvre l'immense quadrillage des maisons d'où émergent, piqués çà et là, des clochers effilés et des immeubles-tours. Par chance, le beau temps est de la partie. A travers une brume légère, mêlée de fumées translucides, les toits en vagues rectilignes luisent, et les vitres que frappe le soleil étincellent. On dirait une mer étale qu'animeraient les jeux de la lumière. Ellynn pousse un cri de surprise et d'admiration. Elle n'a encore jamais vu que des bourgades rurales [...] Au fur et à mesure du trajet, les maisons deviennent plus hautes, il y en a qui sont si élevées, si droites, si rectangulaires avec leurs parois de verre qu'elle dit :

'C'est comme des grosses boîtes d'allumettes!'

Puis elle demande:

'Qu'est-ce qu'on fait dans ces maisons?'

'On y vit, on y travaille.'

'Il y a des petits enfants dans ces maisons?'

'Bien sûr.'

'Mais ils ne peuvent pas jouer.'

'Ils vont dans de grands jardins qu'on appelle parcs publics. Tiens, en voilà un. Nous allons justement descendre.'

Robert Mallet
(1985)

(Extract from a novel: a Frenchman accompanies a neighbour's little girl, on her first visit to Cork city)

'HAT'S THAT?'

Using the simplest words possible, he tries to explain to her what a factory is and what the gigantic brick tube rising from it is for. It's not easy. Paying special attention, Ellynn asks:

'Why did they put the factory there, with the chimney?'

Aubry finds a very simple answer:

'Because it's near Cork. They put factories near cities'.

In fact, the county's capital is close by. From the top of a hill, the immense criss-cross of houses comes into view, with slender steeples and blocks of flats rising up over them here and there. The weather is fine, fortunately. Roofs in straight waves glisten through the light mist mixed with translucent fumes. Windows sparkle in the sunlight. The whole scene looks like some becalmed sea brought to life by the dancing light. Ellynn lets out a cry of surprise and admiration. Up to now, she had never seen anything apart from rural towns and villages […] As they go along, the houses become taller. Some are so lofty, so straight, so rectangular with their glass sides that she says:

'They're like giant matchboxes!'

Then she asks him:

'What do people do in those houses?'

'They live, they work'.

'Are there small children in those houses?'

'Of course'.

'But they have no place to play'.

'They go and play in big gardens called public parks. Look, there's one. We're just getting out of the car, in any case.'

La circulation est dense, la foule remplit les trottoirs. Ellynn prend la main d'Aubry. A Mount Auburn, elle est dans son élément, elle ne craint rien. Elle marche à côté d'Aubry, va et vient selon son rythme, comme un chien. Ici, elle a besoin de se sentir protégée. C'est elle qui a eu l'initiative du geste qu'Aubry aurait eu sûrement, mais il préfère qu'elle l'ait devancé. Ils traversent le parc public où s'offre un grand espace libre, sans massif. Des enfants y lancent en l'air des ailes d'étoffe colorée qui planent ou virevoltent en obéissant autant aux ordres de leurs maîtres qu'à ceux du vent. Ellynn, fascinée, observe leur carrousel et les gestes des joueurs.

'Ce sont des cerfs-volants,' dit Aubry.

'Ça ne vole que dans les villes?'

'Non, partout où il y a du vent!'

'Alors, ça peut voler à Kilcrohane?'

'Bien sûr. Nous en reverrons d'autres. Maintenant il faut aller faire les courses.'

Cette fois-ci, c'est lui qui prend sa main et l'entraîne vers la rue principale où se trouvent les commerces de Cork. Elle se retourne pour regarder une fois encore les cerfs-volants, puis elle est accaparée par les vitrines. Elle voudrait s'arrêter devant chacune. Aubry pense qu'en l'emmenant dans un grand magasin il satisfera d'un seul coup ses multiples curiosités. Il en profitera pour faire les achats qu'il a prévus. Elle ouvre tout grands les yeux sur cette accumulation de richesses variées. Il la conduit au rayon de l'habillement sans qu'elle se doute de ses intentions. Ils regardent ensemble les robes pour petites filles. Elle tombe en arrêt sur l'une d'elles, une robe en cottonade à fleurs de couleurs vives.

'Oh, qu'elle est belle!'

'Tu aimerais avoir une robe comme celle-là?

Traffic is heavy. People crowd onto the footpaths. Ellynn takes Aubry's hand. In Mount Auburn [in west Cork], she is in her element, she is fearless. She walks alongside Aubry, coming and going according to her rhythm, like a dog. Here, she needs to feel protected. It is she who takes the initiative to hold his hand, although he would certainly have done so, but he is happy that it was she who made the first move. They cross the public park with its free and open space, wide and clear. Wings of coloured cloth are being flung by children up into the air. They hover or swirl, obeying their masters' orders as much as the wind. Ellynn, fascinated, looks at their weaving patterns and at the players' movements.

'Those are kites,' says Aubry.

'Can they fly only in towns?'

'No, they can fly wherever there is wind.'

'So could they fly in Kilcrohane?'

'Of course. We'll see others. Now we must go and do the messages.'

This time, it is he who takes her hand and leads her towards Cork's shopping area on the main street. She turns around to see the kites once more, before being mesmerised by the shop windows. She would love to stop in front of every one of them. Aubry thinks that by bringing her into a big store, he will satisfy her many curiosities all at once. He will use the opportunity to do all the shopping he had planned. Her eyes open wide at this accumulation of varied riches. He leads her to the clothing section although she does not suspect why. Together they look at the dresses for little girls. She stops short in front of one of them, a cotton dress with brightly coloured flowers.

'Oh, it's just so beautiful!'

'Would you like to have a dress like that?'

English translation by Grace Neville.

Manfred Schewe
(1987)

German original in: 'Szenische Eindrücke aus dem Inselalltag'. In: H.-C. Oeser (ed.), *Irland. Ein politisches Reisebuch.* Hamburg: VSA, 1987, pp. 11-13.

D ER DEUTSCHE Keltologe Julius Pokorny schrieb in den 20er Jahren in einem Vorwort zu einer Anthologie irischer Gedichte: 'Der Ire ist der typische Sanguiniker.' Bei allem Respekt vor der antiken Temperamentenlehre: Einem aus rund 5 Millionen unterschiedlichen Individuen bestehenden Volk (Nord- und Südirland zusammengenommen) kann man keinen ‚typischen' Charakter andichten. Was ist mit dem Melancholiker in der dämmerigen Ecke des Pubs, dem Phlegmatiker, den nichts vor ein Uhr mittags aus dem Bett bringt, und dem cholerischen Unionisten Ian Paisley? Solche Typen gibt es in jedem Volk, sie machen überall die bunte menschliche Vielfalt aus. Was folgt, sind also nicht Aussagen über den irischen 'Nationalcharakter', sondern persönliche Wahrnehmungen und Überlegungen eines Deutschen, der schon seit mehr als vier Jahren irischen Alltag (er)lebt.

Sonntagmorgen. Die Straßen sind wie leergefegt. Als ich in die Nähe der Church of the Immaculate Conception komme, kostet es mich einiges Geschick, mein Auto auf der engen Straße durch die endlose Reihe geparkter Vehikel zu manövrieren, die meisten davon unter allem TÜV (den es in Irland nicht gibt). Ganz Cork scheint in der Kirche zu sein — wenn nicht im Pub. Es fällt mir immer wieder auf, wie tief der Katholizismus in den Menschen verankert ist, ihre politischen und Moralvorstellungen beeinflußt. Der Busfahrer, der sich bekreuzigt, wenn er die St. Vincent Church passiert; die vielen ulkigen Devotionalienläden, in denen sich der 'heilige Kitsch' türmt; die Vehemenz, mit der eine 20jährige Studentin in einer Diskussion über eine neue Scheidungsgesetzgebung ihre Argumente vorbringt – wörtlich übernommen aus dem Hirtenbrief der irischen Bischöfe. Und die vielen Marienstatuen in den Schulen und die vielen Nonnen, die an der Universität studieren, und die Priester in der Fernsehtalkshow und ...

Manfred Schewe
(1987)

(Impressions of Cork people and Cork life)

IN A foreword to an anthology of Irish poems in the 1920s, Julius Pokorny, a German authority on the Celts, wrote: 'The Irishman is the typical sanguine individual.' With all due respect to the ancient theory of the four temperaments, one can't consider a race of 5,000,000 different individuals (taking Northern and Southern Ireland as a whole) as having a 'typical' character. What about the melancholy person sitting in the shadowed corner of the pub, or the phlegmatic one who can't be persuaded to get out of bed before one in the afternoon? And what of the choleric Unionist Ian Paisley? Every race of people has such types; they all contribute to the colourful variety of humankind. The following is therefore not a pronouncement on the Irish 'national character' but the observations and reflections of a German who has been living and therefore experiencing everyday Irish life for more than four years.

Sunday morning. The streets are deserted. As I near the Church of the Immaculate Conception I require more than a little skill to manoeuvre my car between the seemingly endless rows of parked cars on the narrow road. Most of them would never get through TÜV [the German MOT test, which doesn't exist in Ireland]. All Cork seems to be in church – if not in the pub. Again and again I notice how deeply rooted Catholicism is in the people here, and how it influences their political and moral attitudes: the bus driver who blesses himself passing St Vincent's church; the numerous quaint shops piled high with pious bric-a-brac and devotional objects for sale to the faithful. Then there is the vehemence with which a twenty-year-old student presents her argument in a discussion on the new divorce legislation, quoting verbatim from the Irish Bishops' pastoral letter. In the schools there is a plethora of statues of the Blessed Virgin; a large number of nuns study at the university and priests take part in TV chat shows, and …

Gerne erzählt man sich im Pub, dem Treffpunkt für so viele Iren. Je verqualmter und voller, desto heimischer scheinen sie sich darin zu fühlen. Nicht nur das Glas Guinness lockt sie herbei (das ist ohnehin zu teuer!), sondern ihr Sinn fürs Soziale. Im Pub erzählt man sich humorvoll seine neueste Geschichte, scherzt herum, schmiedet Pläne, sorgt sich um das Befinden eines gemeinsamen Freundes. Interessant, daß man sich hier erkundigt: Wie steht's mit deinem *social life*? – ein Ausdruck, der sich nicht leicht ins Deutsche übersetzen läßt. Der Fragende interessiert sich dafür, mit wem man Umgang hat; mit wem man sich wo, wie oft trifft; was man zusammen unternimmt. Der Pub kann auch leer sein; bis auf zwei Männer, die in einer Ecke einander ins Ohr flüstern. Geheimhaltung: ein Relikt aus konspirativen Tagen?

Es fällt mir oft auf, wie besorgt und selbstverständlich hilfsbereit viele Menschen in Irland sind. Sich um den bedürftigen Nächsten kümmern ist noch immer geltender Leitsatz. Beweis hierfür ist die Existenz ungezählter kirchlicher und karitativer Organisationen, die in selbstlosen Sammelaktionen besonders zur Weihnachtszeit dem Staat viele seiner Wohlfahrts- und Fürsorgepflichten abnehmen. Wenn Wohltätigkeit Sozialpolitik ersetzt, ist es allerdings auch kein Wunder, daß selbst Parteien, die für die Scheidung eintreten, damit kein Bürgerrecht erstreiten, sondern 'Mitgefühl in die Verfassung' (Slogan der Labour Party) einschreiben wollen. Muß man nicht den Hut abnehmen (oder das Kopftuch) vor der immens hohen Geldsumme (IR£ 7 Mio.), die in diesem relativ kleinen Land als Beitrag zur Kampagne des Iren Bob Geldof gesammelt wurde, um zu helfen, weitere Hungerkatastrophen in Äthiopien zu vermeiden? Zu dieser Form unmittelbarer Mitmenschlichkeit gehört auch eine andere Form der Großzügigkeit: Toleranz. Jemandem in abgetragenen, gar zerrissenen Kleidern wird selbst im vornehmen Hotel der Drink nicht verweigert. Beurteilt man jemanden, dann nicht vorschnell nach seinem Äußeren.

In solch weitherziger Umwelt gedeiht wohl ein irischer *character* (Unikum). Ausgefallenen Typen begegnet man öfter als in der geebneteren BRD: dem Stotterkauz auf dem Barhocker, der deutsche Marschlieder summt; in der Fußgängerzone dem monomanen Sandwichboard-Träger, den man in den Stadtrat wählte, um den eigenen

People here enjoy swapping stories in pubs, which are the meeting place for so many Irish men. The smokier the atmosphere and the fuller it is, the more at home they seem to feel there. It's not just the pint of Guinness (which is too expensive anyway!) that lures them; rather it is their instinct for socialising. In the pub a man tells his latest story amusingly, jokes with people, makes plans and inquires after the welfare of a mutual friend. It is interesting that people in the pub ask: How's your social life? – an expression that is not easy to translate into German. The question demonstrates an interest in your circle of friends, whom you meet, where and how often, and what you get up to together. The pub can also be empty save for two men sitting in a corner whispering to each other. Secrecy: perhaps a relic of more conspiratorial days?

I often notice how many Irish people are genuinely and instinctively helpful. Caring for those in need is a principle that is still very much alive. The proof of this is to be found in the existence of countless church and charitable organisations with unpaid volunteers whose fundraising efforts, particularly in the Christmas period, relieves the government of its duties in the area of public welfare. When charity takes the place of social policy it is little wonder that even parties favouring the introduction of divorce don't see it as a Civil Rights issue but seek to have compassion written into the Constitution (The Labour Party slogan is: 'Compassion in the Constitution'). Shouldn't one take one's hat off in acknowledgement of the enormous amount of money (IR£ 7,000,000) raised in this relatively small country by Irishman Bob Geldof in the campaign to prevent a recurrence of the Ethiopian famine catastrophes? Allied to this direct humanitarian aid is another form of generosity: tolerance. Even in a high-class hotel a person in shabby or torn clothes will not be refused a drink. If people are judged then not immediately by their external appearances.

An Irish 'character' flourishes in such a broad-minded environment. Eccentrics are to be found more often in Ireland than in the more socially conformist Federal Republic of Germany. There is the man with a stammer on the bar stool who hums German marching songs. There is the monomaniac sandwich-board man who is elected to the City Council

Stadthonoratioren eins auszuwischen; dem Gedichtehändler, der seine Verse schreibt und sie im berufsmäßigen Straßenverkauf unter die Leute bringt; der Predigerin, die seit Jahren mit weit geöffneten Armen in hohem Singsang ein persönliches Evangelium verkündet. Sollte etwas dran sein, an den Psychiatrie-Studien, die davon ausgehen, daß in Irland abweichendes Verhalten verbreiteter ist als anderswo?

Unvermutet kommunikativ sind viele Iren. In ein Gespräch zu geraten ist die einfachste Sache der Welt; besonders als Ausländer ist man Objekt insularer Neugier und bleibt es, solange man sich eine Kritik an Irland verkneift. Auffallend, daß Selbstkritik oft in der unverbindlichen 3. Person Plural erfolgt, unter Ausschluß der eigenen Person. Das ewig rätselhafte Wetter ist naheliegender Anlaß, die Politik nicht selten Ventilthema des Gesprächs. Es gibt wohl nur wenige, die die Politik nicht als Riesenschwindel ansehen.

Die Wörter 'offiziell' und 'lästig' sind für viele Iren Synonyme, Vorschriften in der Regel ein Greuel, mannigfaltig die Wege, sie zu umgehen. Nach vier Jahren Irland tritt sogar mein deutscher Fuß bei Rot nicht gleich aufs Bremspedal. Die Ordnungshüter sind im allgemeinen nachsichtig, verteilen eher leichte Tadel als Bußen, lassen mit sich reden. Als verstünden sie den Landsmann oder die Landsmännin, die im Verkehr zur Sünde neigen. Eine angenehme Haltung, der ich im irischen Alltag immer wieder begegne: Die Sympathie gilt dem unerfreulich oder nachteilig Betroffenen.

Sich-Zeit-Nehmen für jemanden, ihm geduldig zuhören: ein Verhalten, das den Menschen in Irland noch nicht abhanden gekommen ist. Bölls schöner, auf Irland gemünzter Satz 'Als Gott die Zeit schuf, hat er genug davon gemacht' scheint in den Köpfen der Iren weiterzuhallen; Verspätungen bei Verabredungen und dementsprechend lange Wartezeiten sind nichts Außergewöhnliches. Interessant, daß der *mañnana*-Gedanke im Irischen sprachlichen Ausdruck gefunden hat: 'Amárach, déanfaidh mé é amárach' (morgen, morgen werd ich's tun). Doch ist absehbar, daß der irische Zeittakt – der auf agrargesellschaftliche Tage zurückgehende Luxus – sich dem kontinentalen immer mehr angleichen wird. Mir kommt die Patrick Street in den Sinn, Corks Hauptstraße; die Eile, mit der die Fußgänger sie überqueren, die

in order to put one over on the local dignitaries. The trader in poetry writes his own verses and runs a small business selling them to passers-by on the street. Nearby, her arms wide open, is a woman preacher with a sing-song voice who has for years been proclaiming her personal gospel. Is there something to be said for the claim made in psychiatric studies that deviational behaviour is more widespread in Ireland than elsewhere?

Irish people are unexpectedly communicative. Getting into conversation is the easiest thing in the world. A foreigner in particular is an object of insular curiosity and remains so as long as he avoids making any criticism of Ireland. It is noticeable that self-criticism is exercised in the non-binding third person plural, thus excluding the speaker's own opinion. The eternally mystifying weather is an obvious starting point of a conversation, politics often a safety valve. There are very few who do not consider politics to be a gigantic fraud.

The words 'official' and 'annoying' are synonyms for many Irish people; as a rule they consider regulations an outrage and many are the means employed to get round them. After four years in Ireland even my German foot doesn't automatically hit the brake pedal when the traffic light is red. The guardians of public order are generally lenient, more inclined to issue a word of warning than a fine, and ready to listen to reason, as if they understood their fellow-countryman or woman who inclines towards sin while in the driving seat. A pleasant aspect that I regularly encounter in Irish everyday life: the victimised or the disadvantaged are on the receiving end of sympathy.

Taking the time to listen to somebody patiently: this is an attitude of Irish people that has not yet disappeared. Böll's lovely phrase inspired by Ireland: 'When God made time, he made enough of it' seems to find a resonance in the minds of Irish people. Being late for appointments and the resultant long delays are nothing extraordinary. It's interesting that the concept of *mañana* has found linguistic expression in the Irish language: *Amárach, déanfaidh mé é amárach* (tomorrow, I'll do it tomorrow). However, it is conceivable that the rhythm of Irish life – a luxury that goes back to the days of an agrarian society – will adapt more and more to the continental one. I'm thinking of St Patrick's Street, Cork's main thoroughfare, and the speed with which pedestrians cross it;

Hetze und Hektik, mit der Einkäufe in der Mittagspause oder spätnach-
mittags erledigt werden, das Branden des Verkehrs.

Ein sonniger Samstagnachmittag. Welche Gelegenheit zu einem
Ausflug! Auf in den Fitzgerald's Park! Ganze Großfamilien auf den
Rasenflächen, sonnenbadend in kniehoch aufgekrempelten
Hosenbeinen und leicht geöffneten Blusen. Jungen waten durch das
seichte Teichwasser, Eltern umstehen die Rutsche oder geben ihrem
schaukelnden Sprößling einen Schubs, an allen Ecken und Park-Enden
Kindergeschrei. Vor dem Parktor – denn auch der *Ice-Cream-Man* hat
gemerkt, daß ausnahmsweise die Sonne scheint – ein Verkaufsstand mit
unwiderstehlichen Verlockungen: Cadbury Schokolade, Lollipops, Soft
Drinks, Chips ... Der Stand ist umschwärmt von kaufenden Daddies,
Mummies, Grannies; im Arm oder an der Hand ihre leckenden,
lutschenden Lieblinge.

Sonntagabend. Der Park ist ein einziges Papier- und Plastikmeer;
und wird es bleiben, bis der Wind den Abfall in alle Himmelsrichtungen
davonbläst. Irgendwo bleibt er dann liegen. Meine deutsche Vorprägung
– ich kann nicht anders – läßt mich Nachlässigkeit assoziieren. Ihr
begegne ich öfters, z.B. im Umgang mit Handwerkern.

Daß wir ein halbes Jahr gefährlich lebten, weil mit der Umstellung
auf Naturgas an unserem Umlauferhitzer im Bad nicht die nötigen
Veränderungen vorgenommen wurden – das entlockte dem Mann von
der Gasgesellschaft nur einen Halbsatz: 'Could have been very dangerous, you know.' Daß die Reparatur dann 3 Monate dauerte, kostete mich
manchen Geduldsfaden. Daß danach immer noch der Einschaltknopf
fehlte und wir uns einen weiteren Monat mit einer Rohrzange behelfen
mußten, um heiß duschen zu können – an solche alltäglichen Erlebnisse
gewöhnt man sich, lernt damit zu leben.

Wo findet man Erklärungsansätze für die Verhaltensweisen und
Einstellungen, die einem im irischen Alltag auffallen? Daß der Pub
sozialer Treffpunkt für so viele durstige Iren ist, läßt sich aus der
Geschichte des 19. Jahrhunderts erklären. Damals wurden breitangelegte
Kampagnen gegen den hohen Alkoholismus in der irischen Bevölkerung
durchgeführt, deren Ziel u.a. die Verbannung jeglichen Alkohols aus
denWohnhäusern war. (Einem Anführer dieser Anti-Alkoholkampagnen,

of the hectic speed with which the shopping is done during lunch break or in the late afternoon; of the surging traffic.

A sunny Saturday afternoon. What an opportunity for a day out! Off to Fitzgerald's Park! Extended families on the grassy areas, sunbathing with trousers rolled up to the knee and modestly unbuttoned blouses. Boys wading through the stagnant water in the pond; parents standing by the slides or giving their offspring a push on the swings. The sound of children's voices in every corner echoing from end to end of the park. In front of the park gate – because the ice-cream seller has also noticed that the sun is shining – a stand with irresistible temptations: Cadbury's chocolate, lollipops, soft drinks, crisps ... The stand is besieged by Daddies, Mummies and Grannies buying suckables and lickables for the little darlings held in their arms or holding their hands.

Sunday evening. The park is a veritable sea of plastic and paper, and will remain so until the wind blows the litter in all directions. It will then lie somewhere else. My inherited German characteristics – I can't help them – make me associate such a scene with sloppiness. Sloppiness I encounter often. When dealing with tradesmen, for example.

That we lived dangerously for six months because the necessary adjustments hadn't been made on our water heater in the bathroom when changing to Natural Gas was dismissed in half a sentence by the man from the gas company: 'Could have been very dangerous, you know.' That on top of this the repairs took another three months severely tested my patience. The starting button was still missing after all that and we had to make use of pliers for another month in order to be able to have a hot shower: one gets accustomed to such everyday experiences and learns to live with them.

How can one begin to find an explanation for the conduct and attitudes to be found in Irish everyday life? That the pub is the meeting place for the social life of so many thirsty Irish people can be explained by reference to the history of the nineteenth-century. Wide-ranging campaigns were carried out in that period against the high incidence of alcoholism in the Irish population. Among their aims was the banning of any form of alcohol from private houses (a monument to Father Mathew, the leader of this anti-alcohol campaign, was erected in a prominent position

Father Matthew, wurde in Corks Patrick Street an prominenter Stelle ein Denkmal gesetzt.) Darüber hinaus muß man berücksichtigen, daß die relativ große irische Durchschnittsfamilie in verhältnismäßig kleinen Häusern oder Wohnungen lebt. Der Gefahr, daß man sich gegenseitig auf die Füße tritt, entziehen sich insbesondere viele Männer. Im Pub sind sie gerne unter sich. Die Sprüche, die unter ihnen geklopft werden, deuten auf Männerhaltungen hin, in denen Patriarchalisches durchscheint. Die Pubs auf dem Lande sind nicht selten voll von Junggesellen. Kommen sie von ihrer Trinktour zurück, so wartet die 'Mum' in der Regel mit dem Essen auf sie. Die Verhätschelung durch die Mütter mag Mitursache sein für die hohe Zahl der Unverheirateten auf dem Land und für Probleme beim Freien. Geheiratet wird in der Regel erst, wenn der Hof übernommen wird. Gibt's die Richtige nicht im Dorf, so besteht immer noch die Möglichkeit Lisdoonvarna. In diesem Ort in Co. Clare treffen sich Heiratslustige aus allen Himmelsrichtungen zum *matchmaking*; Heiraten werden hier arrangiert.

Traumatisch die Erfahrung der Großen Hungersnot (1845-48), in deren Verlauf ca. 1 Mio. Iren starben und 1,5 Mio. auswanderten. Der hohe Sensibilitätsgrad in der irischen Bevölkerung für hungerleidende Menschen in anderen Teilen der Welt muß sicherlich, wenn auch nicht ausschließlich, vor diesem Hintergrund gesehen werden. Das Mißtrauen gegen Autorität, den Staat und seine Vertreter, Ignoranz gegenüber Vorschriften und innerliche Abwehr von (Ver-)Ordnung – nehmen diese Haltungen nach jahrhundertelanger Unterdrückung durch eine fremde Macht Wunder?

Freilich neigen viele Iren zu der bequemen Haltung, Probleme von heute mit dem traurigen Verlauf der nationalen Geschichte zu entschuldigen. Ein wenig widersprüchlich bleiben die starken Vorbehalte gegenüber der ehemaligen Kolonialmacht einerseits und die starke Orientierung am englischen Modell andererseits, z.B. in Bereichen wie Erziehung, Architektur, Sozialwesen. Das irische Selbstbild ist zu großen Teilen von den Briten geprägt; sie sind die Folie, gegen die sich die Iren abheben.

Die weitverbreitete Allergie gegen einengende Ordnung erklärt noch nicht hinreichend, warum Plastik- und sonstiger Abfall unbedacht in die Landschaft geworfen wird. Man muß in Betracht ziehen, daß in diesem

in Cork's St Patrick's Street.) As well as that, it must be taken into account that the relatively large average Irish family lives in comparatively small houses or flats. The danger that family members will get in each other's hair is avoided by men in particular, who withdraw from the family home. In the pub they enjoy being men amongst men. The notions they express point to a one-dimensional masculinity coloured by patriarchal attitidues. On returning from their alcoholic outing, 'Mum' will, as a rule, be waiting for them with a meal. Pampering by the mother may be a contributory reason for the high number of unmarried people and the problems of courtship in the rural areas. As a rule, a man doesn't get married until he has taken over the farm. If the right woman is not to be found in the village, there is always Lisdoonvarna. Those eager to marry descend from all quarters on this Co. Clare town for matchmaking: marriages are arranged here.

The experience of the Great Famine (1845-48), in which 1,000,000 Irish people died, and as a result of which 1,500,000 emigrated, was traumatic. This background would certainly, if not completely, explain the high degree of sensibility of the people of Ireland towards those suffering from famine in other parts of the world. Mistrust of authority, the State and its representatives, ignorance of regulations and inner resistance to the forces of order and ordinance – is it any wonder that these exist after centuries-long oppression by a foreign power?

It is true to say that many Irish people are inclined to go for the soft option by blaming the problems of today on the sad course of the country's history. A little contradictory is the tendency, on the one hand to have strong reservations towards the former colonial power, while on the other there is a strong sense of orientation towards the English model in the areas of education, architecture and social organisation. The Irish self-image is to a great degree influenced by the British; they are the standard against which the Irish measure themselves.

The widespread allergic attitiude towards restrictive order still doesn't adequately explain why plastic and other rubbish are thrown away- with no care for the landscape. One must consider the fact that serious

relativ dünnbesiedelten, weiträumigen Land eine verstärkte Industrialisierung, mit Begleiterscheinungen wie Disziplinierung und Reglementierung, erst seit den 50er Jahren eingesetzt hat. Eine Haltung wie Respekt vor der Umwelt – so zeigt die kontinentale Erfahrung – scheint sich erst dann herauszubilden, wenn eine Industriegesellschaft an ihre Grenzen gestoßen ist.

Noch haben wir es in Irland mit keiner ausgesprochenen Industriegesellschaft zu tun. Die soziale, mitmenschliche Haltung, von der weiter oben die Rede ist, erklärt sich wohl aus einer noch weitgehend agrargesellschaftlich bestimmten Mentalität. So viele kleine Alltagsbegebenheiten erinnern mich stark an mein unjüngst noch bäuerliches norddeutsches Heimatdorf im Emsland, einer 'benachteiligten' Region in Niedersachsen. Auch dort erfolgte eine systematische Industrieansiedlung erst seit den 50er Jahren.

Trotz aller Probleme, die der Wandel mit sich bringen mag: Die Iren – so das Ergebnis einer Umfrage – betrachten sich als glücklich (74%); glücklicher als die Menschen in den meisten anderen europäischen Ländern. Wer die Iren im Alltag erlebt, glaubt es ihnen.

industrialisation, with its concomitants of discipline and regimentation, has only taken place in this relatively thinly populated, spacious country since the 1950s. An attitude of respect for the environment – and the continental experience demonstrates this – only seems to come about when an industrial society has reached its limits.

In Ireland we still cannot speak of a completely industrialised society. The socially-conscious, neighbourly attitude mentioned above can be explained in terms of a society that is still broadly agrarian in its mentality. So many small everyday situations remind me of my north German home village in Emsland, an 'economically disadvantaged region', that was until quite recently a farming community. There, too, a systematic programme of establishing industry has been in train since the 1950s.

In spite of all the problems that change may bring with it, the Irish – according to the results of a survey – consider themselves happy (74%); happier than the people in most other European countries. Anybody who has to deal with Irish people in daily life will believe them.

English translation by Kevin Power.

Reinhard Ulbrich
(1988)

German original in: *Irland: Inseltraum und Erwachen*. Leipzig: Edition Leipzig, 1988, pp. 197-201.

WEITER GEHT'S nach Cork. Das ist die zweitgrößte Stadt der Republik und das Zentrum des Südens. Fast gibt sich der Ort selbst ein wenig südländisch mit seinen weißen Brücken und den engen Straßen, die beiderseits des Flusses Lee terrassenförmig ansteigen, immer wieder durchschnitten von einem wirren System steiler Treppen. Wenn man das Auto irgendwo abstellen könnte, gäbe es hier mindestens zwanzig Kirchen, ein gutes Dutzend öffentlicher Gebäude, etliche Brücken und zwei Denkmäler zu besichtigen. Wie gesagt, wenn man könnte. Um parken zu dürfen, muß man nämlich eine spezielle Plakette haben, um die kaufen zu können, muß man parken, was wiederum nicht geht, weil man ja keine Plakette besitzt. Der Hauptmann von Köpenick hätte an Cork vermutlich seine Freude gehabt. Was soll's, es muß auch mal ohne das amtliche Abzeichen gehen, denn die verrückteste Sehenswürdigkeit wollen wir uns doch wenigstens ansehen. Das ist ein Glockenspiel in der Sankt-Annen-Kirche, gebaut von einem Mann namens Shandon, der wohl nicht ahnte, was er der Nachwelt mit seiner Konstruktion antun würde. Speckige Bindfäden baumeln von der Decke, und wenn man daran zieht, läutet's hoch droben. Alte Pappkartons liegen auch noch herum, auf denen steht 'Waltzing Mathilda 31168451' oder 'Oh, Susanna 44343434321'. Damit werden nicht etwa die Telefonanschlüsse bestimmter Damen bekanntgegeben, die das Nachtleben von Cork bereichern, sondern es handelt sich schlicht um die Reihenfolge, in welcher die numerierten Strippen betätigt werden müssen, um so etwas Ähnliches wie eine Melodie aus den Glocken herauszuquälen. Ganz richtig aber trifft es keiner, und zustande kommt meist nur ein heilloses Gedröhne. Überraschungen hält eine Kiste bereit, in der die gesammelte musikalische Drangsal deutscher Herkunft ver-

Reinhard Ulbrich
(1988)

(Parking in Cork – visit to Shandon)

O NWARDS TO Cork. It's the second largest city in the Republic and the capital of the south. The place almost exudes a Mediterranean air, with its white bridges and narrow streets rising up in terraces on both sides of the River Lee, time and again criss-crossed by a chaotic system of steep steps. If you were able to park your car somewhere, there would be at least twenty churches here, a good dozen public buildings, any number of bridges and two monuments to visit. As I say, *if.* But to be allowed to park, you need a special disc, in order to buy one, you have to park, which in turn isn't possible because, of course, you don't have a disc. Quite a conundrum.* What the hell, we'll just have to do without the official badge because, if nothing else, we want at least to see the craziest of sights, the bells at St Anne's Church, built by a man named Shandon, who clearly had no sense of what he would be inflicting upon posterity with his handi-work. Greasy strings dangle from the ceiling and when you pull at them, you hear the bells up high. Also lying around are old cardboard boxes upon which are written 'Waltzing Matilda 31168451' or 'Oh, Susanna 44343434321'. These are not the contact numbers of certain women who enrich the night life of Cork, but simply the order in which the numbered strings must be pulled in order to entice some-thing like a tune from the bells. No one gets it quite right and the most you achieve is a helpless drone. One box contains surprises in the form of the complete collection of German musical suffering. Because love

---

* *Translator's note*: the German original refers to the Captain of Köpenick, the protagonist of a play of the same title by Cark Zuckmayer exposing the absurd-ities of German officialdom.

wahrt wird. Weil die Heimatliebe mit dem ebenfalls anwesenden Herrn Müller-Lüdenscheidt aus Dortmund durchgeht, kommen wir in den unvergeßlichen Genuß der 'Ode an die Freude', sehr frei nach Beethoven gebimmelt. 'Wärst du doch in Düsseldorf geblieben' ist leider nicht am Lager, dafür aber ein Opus mit dem Titel 'Wooden Heart', Herz aus Holz. Dazu wird verblüffenderweise die Melodie von 'Muß i denn zum Städtele hinaus' geboten, was wir gleich als Wink mit dem Zaunpfahl nehmen wollen, das Weite zu suchen.

for his country gets the better of our companion, Mr Müller-Lüdenscheidt from Dortmund, we indulge in the unforgettable pleasure of 'Ode to Joy', very freely adapted from Beethoven. '*Wärst du doch in Düsseldorf geblieben*' ['If only you had stayed in Düsseldorf!', a well-known German folksong] is sadly not amongst the collection, but instead there is a work bearing the English title 'Wooden Heart'. Astonishingly the melody suggested is that of the well-known German folksong '*Muß i denn zum Städele hinaus*' ['So I must leave this little town', a Swabian folk song], which we take as a clear signal to venture further afield.

English translation by Jean E. Conacher.

Christoph Potting / Annette Weweler
(1990)

German original in: *Irland. Ein Reisebuch in den Alltag.* Reinbek: rororo 1990
(Anders Reisen), pp. 217-20.

WO SICH der River Lee zum Lough Mahon weitet, wo ein tiefer
Meeresfjord einem aufgeplusterten Hafen Platz gibt, dort liegt
Cork, mit 130000 Einwohnern drittgrößte Stadt der Insel.

Cork: eine hügelige Stadt, kulturelles Zentrum des größten – gleich-
namigen – Countys: Irlands 'heimliche' Hauptstadt. Die vermögenden
Farmer Irlands sitzen nicht in Dublin, sondern im Agrarzentrum der
Provinz Munster. Den höchsten 'Wolkenkratzer' Irlands bestaunen
zweifelnd zwei Farmer in Bronze; die Markthallen in der Innenstadt
bieten die Schätze des landwirtschaftlich reichen Umlandes feil und sind
beispielhaft für eine gelungene Stadtarchitektur, die ansonsten in Cork
nicht gerade üppig gesät ist. Die vor wenigen Jahren abgebrannten vik-
torianischen Hallen sind mittlerweile neu aufgebaut und mit modernen
Baumaterialien ergänzt worden.

Eine Ansammlung von Hängen und Stufen, Kirchtürmen und
Brücken geht schnell über in graue Vorstädte. Mit Dublin scheint die
Stadt den unerbittlichen Zugriff von Häuserspekulanten und
Schreibtischtätern gemein zu haben. Die lieblichen Fassaden des
O'Sullivan Quay mußten bereits einem abwaschbaren Büromonstrum
weichen. In symbolischer Nachbarschaft, nur in Rufweite entfernt, hat
die 'Quay Coop' ihr Zuhause, Irlands einziges 'richtiges' Alterna-
tivzentrum mit Buchladen, vegetarischer Küche, Kleiderladen, Schwulen
– und Frauengruppen und einer Lebensmittel-Coop, die die wenigen
biologisch-dynamischen Lebensmittel vertreibt, die auf den ansonsten
eher chemisierten Farmen West-Corks produziert werden.

Cork City, von der 'Industrial Development Authority' zum stra-
tegischen Platz für Industrieansiedlung auserkoren, steht vor der Aus-
zehrung. In den achtziger Jahren haben zahlreiche multinationale
Fertigungsstätten wie Ford und Dunlop ihre Werkstore geschlossen, und

Christoph Potting / Annette Weweler
(1990)

(Alternative Cork – solar energy in Fota – oil boom – environmental pollution)

A T THE point where the River Lee broadens out into Lough Mahon, where a deep sea fjord makes way to a puffed-up harbour, there lies Cork, with its 130,000, inhabitants the third largest city on the island.

Cork: a hilly city, cultural centre of the largest county of the same name: Ireland's 'secret' capital. The prosperous farmers of Ireland don't sit in Dublin but in the agricultural capital of the province of Munster. Two bronze farmers gaze in wonder and doubt at the highest 'skyscraper' in Ireland; the Market Halls in the city centre offer for sale the jewels of the agriculturally rich land around Cork and are a fine example of a successful city architecture, which there isn't exactly an abundance of in the city. The Victorian halls, burned down a few years ago, have been rebuilt in the meantime and finished off with modern building materials.

A collection of slopes and steps, church towers and bridges, give way quickly to the grey suburbs. The city seems to share with Dublin the unrelenting attack from property speculators and behind-the-scenes movers. The pretty façades of Sullivan's Quay have just made room for a monster of sterile offices. In symbolic neighbourhood, just a stone's throw away, the 'Quay Co-op' has its home, Ireland's only 'real' centre of alternative living, with a bookshop, a vegetarian restaurant, a clothes shop, gay and women's groups and a food co-op which sells the few organic foods which are produced in the otherwise chemical-ridden farms of west Cork.

Cork city, selected by the Industrial Development Agency to take up a strategic position for industrial development, is suffering from consumption. In the 1980s, numerous multinational production plants like Ford and Dunlop closed their factory gates and the electronics industry

die verbliebene Elektronikindustrie kann die Arbeitslosen nicht beschäftigen. Die Frage ist, wie lange North Star Computers, Western Digital, Hanimex und Motorola noch bleiben werden.

In Cork liegen die Widersprüche oft dicht beieinander. Auf Fota Island, einer hübschen Insel am Osthafen, haben sich gleich dreierlei irische Unvereinbarkeiten angesiedelt: in trauter Nachbarschaft ein ungewöhnliches Freiwildreservat, weder Zoo noch Safaripark, eher ein Stück Land, auf dem sich Tiere fast wie in freier Wildbahn bewegen können; gleich nebenan die nukleare Müllkippe des hauseigenen Testreaktors der Universität Cork; und schließlich das erste kommerzielle Sonnenenergieprojekt. 55000 Siliziumzellen speisen die Aggregate zur Bewirtschaftung von 250 Milchkühen. Die mit deutscher Hilfe betriebene 50000 Watt-Anlage soll zeigen, daß sich die Nutzung des Sonnenlichts gerade für die Milchproduktion und -verarbeitung besonders gut eignet. Im Sommer nämlich, wenn die Wiesen grün und die Euter prall sind, stellt die Sonne genügend Energie zum Betreiben von Melk- und Kühlmaschinen zur Verfügung. Und da im Winter für die Milchproduktion weniger Energie benötigt wird, reicht auch dann noch der bescheidenere Output der Kollektoren.

ÖLFLUTEN

[...] Die Küste Cork-Waterford im Jahre 2001: Neue Satellitenstädte und petrochemische Industrien schießen aus dem Boden, die Region ist überschwemmt mit ausländischem Kapital und fremden Arbeitskräften. Farmer verkaufen Bauland zu astronomischen Preisen, der Ölboom sucht den Süden der irischen Republik heim. Als zu Beginn der achtziger Jahre die Ölmultis Gulf und Esso die Ölfunde vor der irischen Küste für profitabel erklärten, machte sich in Irland eine wahre Öl-Euphorie breit. Das schwarze Gold vor der Küste soll alle wirtschaftlichen Schwierigkeiten Irlands auf einen Schlag lösen, die enorme Staatsverschuldung für Öl- und andere Energieimporte der Vergangenheit angehören, Irlands Währung an den Börsen begehrt sein wie keine andere. In wenigen Jahren soll sich eine pittoreske Küste und eine landwirtschaftliche Region in einen 'synthetischen' Wirtschaftsraum verwandeln. Was internationale Unternehmen bisher in Irland nicht

which remains cannot employ those on the dole. The question is how long North Star Computers, Western Digital, Hanimexand Motorola will remain.

In Cork, the contradictions often lie side by side. On Fota Island, a beautiful island off the East Harbour, three Irish unreconcilables have settled in close proximity: an unusual wildlife reserve, neither zoo nor safari park, but rather a piece of land on which animals can move around almost freely; right beside it, the nuclear dump of the University of Cork's own test reactor; and, finally, the first commercial solar energy project. 55,000 silicon cells feed the generators needed to farm 250 milking cows. The 50,000 watt plant, operated with German assistance, is intended to show that the use of sunlight is particularly suitable for milk production and processing. In the summer, for example, when the meadows are green and the udders swollen, the sun produces enough energy to drive the milking and cooling machines. And as in winter less energy is needed for milk production, the more modest output of the collectors still suffices.

OIL FLOODS

[...] The Cork-Waterford coast in the year 2001: new satellite towns and petrochemical industries shoot up out of the ground, the region is flooded with foreign capital and foreign workers. Farmers sell building land for astronomical prices, the oil boom strikes the south of the Irish Republic. When, at the beginning of the 1980s, the oil multinationals Gulf and Esso declared the oil reserves off the Irish coast profitable, widespread oil euphoria broke out in Ireland. The black gold off the coast was to solve all Ireland's economic problems in one fell swoop, the enormous national debt caused by oil and other energy imports would be consigned to the past. Ireland's currency would be sought after at the stock exchanges like no other. In a few years a picturesque coastline and an agricultural region was to be transformed into a 'synthetic' economic space. What until then international companies had not achieved in Ireland would be realised by Irish oil.

schaffen konnten, das irische Öl soll es endgültig bringen.

Alles spricht dafür, daß es der irischen Südküste so ergehen könnte wie den Shetland-Inseln. Nur 150 Meilen von den größten Ölfeldern der Nordsee entfernt, hat sich die Inselgruppe vom Ölschock nie erholen können. Ausländische Konzerne überrollten eine kleine landwirtschaftliche Lebensgemeinschaft. Der 'spin-off'-Effekt des unvermittelten Reichtums: Geisterstädte, Kriminalität. Zerstörung lokaler, gewachsener Industrien, Inflation. Der Reichtum fließt in die Taschen derer, die das Öl aus der See holen: BP, Gulf und andere Ölkonzerne, die nach wenigen Jahren ihre Bohrinseln dorthin schaffen, wo hauseigene Geologen neue profitable Funde versprechen. Zurück bleibt eine verwundete Region, der die Preise zum Überleben längst davongelaufen sind.

Everything points to the Irish south coast suffering the same fate as the Shetland Islands. Only 150 miles from the largest oilfields of the North Sea, this group of islands has never managed to recover from the oil shock. Foreign concerns steamrollered a small agricultural community. The spin-off effect of sudden riches: ghost towns, crime, destruction of homegrown industries, inflation. The riches flow into the pockets of those who take the oil from the sea, BP, Gulf, and other oil companies, who, after a few years, move their drilling platforms where in-house geologists promise new profitable reserves. All that remains is a wounded region that can no longer pay the escalating costs of survival.

English translation by Jean E. Conacher.

Sabine Boebé
(1991)

German original in: *Eines Fürsten Irland. Auf Pücklers Spuren.* Berlin: Reiher
Verlag, 1991, pp. 227-30.

V ON DEN beiden Gefängnissen gibt es erstaunlicherweise noch immer
Überbleibsel. Aber ach, wieviele Meilen muß man suchend die Stadt
durchstreifen, bevor man nach dürftigen, mehr vermuteten als wirklich
gewußten Hinweisen vom Stab im Tourismusbüro das findet, was Pückler
so hoch gelobt hat. Der gewaltige griechische Portikus des einen schließt
ein Stück Universitätsgelände zum River Lee hin ab, eine leere Fassade,
ohne Gebäude dahinter. Klage noch, und auch Anklage. Das im 'gotischen' Stil erbaute Gefängnis wurde in Königin Victorias Zeiten
passenderweise erst als Kaserne genutzt, später dann als Frauengefängnis.
Jetzt liegt es wüst in Trümmern. Nur die festungsartige Südmauer, hoch
über River Lee, mit dem Eingangsportal, das aussieht, wie zu einer Burg
gehörig, trotzt den Zeiten, manifestiert Dauerhaftigkeit. Häftlinge gibt es
dem Vernehmen nach nicht mehr in Cork. Das Hauptstaatsgefängnis
Irlands ist in Portlaoise. – Cork ist keine 'Rebel City' mehr.

Schmuddelige kleine Steppkes kommen heran, sehen meine
Kamera, bieten sich an, mich vor dem zugemauerten Gefängnisportal zu
fotografieren. Sind sie nun eigentlich zutraulich oder doch schon
zudringlich? Oder wollen sie nur ein paar 'bobs' verdienen? Ich gebe
ihnen lieber meine beiden Äpfel und ein paar deutsche Hustenbonbons,
die ich bei mir habe. Ein heller Blick, ganz rasch. Nicht so helle Zähne
werden beim breiten Dankgrinsen sichtbar; und schon sind sie fort.

Von hier oben kann ich die Stadt ganz gut überblicken. Sie wuchert
und wuchert pilzartig in die Breite, landeinwärts mit endlosen Vorstädten,
seeseitig mit Raffinerien, Öltanklagern, Industrieanlagen, Stahlwerken
und anderen, die alle von wirtschaftlicher Prosperität sprechen.

Und die Militärbaracken? Weg sind sie! In den Himmel ragt heute da,
wo sie wohl waren, Irlands höchstes Hochhaus: mit siebzehn Stockwerken
die Verwaltung von Irlands größter Grafschaft, Cork County.

Sabine Boebé
(1991)

(Prison ruins – greyhound races)

A MAZINGLY, THE remains of the two prisons can still be found. But alas, how many miles does one have to roam through the city searching, before one finds what Pückler [see his text on page 56 ff] praised so highly, for the meagre directions from the staff in the tourist office were more guesswork than based on factual knowledge. The massive Greek portico of one of them shuts off a part of the University campus that goes down to the River Lee, an empty façade, with no building behind it. A symbol of lament still, but also of indictment. The prison built in 'Gothic' style was fittingly used as a barracks in Queen Victoria's time and later as a women's prison. Now it lies in wild ruins. Only the fortress-like south wall, high above the River Lee, with the entrance gate that looks like it belongs to a castle, defies time and displays endurance. There are apparently no more prisoners in Cork. The main state prison is in Portlaoise. – Cork is no longer a 'rebel city'.

Grubby little lads come up to me and look at my camera. They offer to take my photograph in front of the prison gate. Are they actually trusting or a bit pushy? Or do they just want to earn a few bob? I prefer to give them my two apples and a few German throat lozenges that I have on me. A bright, fleeting glance. Not so bright teeth are visible when they thank me with broad grins; then they are gone.

From up here I can get a good view of the whole city. It mushrooms out in all directions, inland with endless suburbs, towards the sea with refineries, oil-tank depots, industrial estates, steel works and the like which all tell a tale of economic prosperity.

And the military barracks? They are gone! Today Ireland's highest skyscraper reaches into the sky where they once stood: seventeen storeys high, the administration of Ireland's biggest county, County Cork.

Was kann man abends machen? 'The Dubliners' gastieren gerade in der Stadt. Karten? Ausverkauft seit Wochen! Also auf zum greyhound track in der Western Road! Dreimal wöchentlich geht's in Cork rund. Wieviele tausend Menschen sind wohl hier? Auf der Tribüne ist jeder Platz besetzt. Die Wettschalter sind umlagert. Acht Rennen gibt es heute. Flutlicht. Elektronische Anzeigetafel.

Kurzgeschorenes Grün im Oval. Eßbares, vornehmlich Frittiertes, ist an vielen Stellen erhältlich. Bier, viel Bier. 'Murphy's', nicht so sehr das aus Dublin.

Die Windhunde des ersten Rennens werden vorgeführt. Ihre Besitzer oder die Trainer haben sie eng angeleint. Sehnige Renner sind das; braune, graue, weiße, schwarze, gefleckte, gestromte. Sie zittern vor Rennfieber, sind eingezurrt in ulkige Westchen, auf denen ihre Startnummern stehen. Das Publikum schätzt sie ab mit kundigen Blicken. Wettende – und das sind hier fast alle – plazieren ihre Voraussage am Totalisator oder beim Buchmacher. All diese Sachverständigen wechseln Geld gegen kleine bunte Zettelchen. Manche kaufen ganze Blöckchen davon.

Jetzt werden die sechs whippets von ihren Herren in die Startboxen manövriert. Manche der Vierbeiner mögen das nicht, machen Schwierigkeiten. Es wird nun ganz still auf der Tribüne; erstaunlich still. Dann, ein Ruf, die Klappen der Boxen fliegen auf, die elektronisch regulierte Hasen-Attrappe saust los. Die Hunde preschen hervor und jagen – wie immer vergeblich – wie besessen dem Flederwisch nach. Gleichzeitig mit alledem bricht ein ohrenbetäubendes Anfeuerungsgeschrei los, hört nicht auf, bis der ganze Kurs durchrast ist. Geschmeidige, kraftvolle, weit-ausgreifende Bewegungen. Für die Normaldistanz von 525 yards brauchen die Tiere etwa dreißig Sekunden: Stundengeschwindigkeit fast sechzig Kilometer!

Es tritt eine Pause ein. Die nächsten sechs Renner werden vorgeführt. Nach der Besichtigung neuer Run auf die Wettschalter. Schließlich ist alles bereit für den zweiten Adrenalin-Ausstoß, sowohl bei den sporttreibenden Hunden, als auch bei den zuschauenden Menschen. – Nach acht mal dreißig Sekunden, mit den Pausen nach insgesamt etwa zwei Stunden, ist alles vorbei. Die Gewinner machen Kasse. Das dauert! Alle

What can one do in the evenings? 'The Dubliners' are giving a guest performance in the city at the moment. Tickets? Sold out for weeks! So, off to the greyhound track on the Western Road! The greyhounds race three times a week in Cork. How many thousands of people might be here? Every place on the stand is occupied. The betting stalls are thronged with people. There are eight races today. Flood lights. Electronic score boards.

In the oval – a neatly-cropped lawn. Food, primarily deep-fried, can be got in many places. Beer, lots of beer. 'Murphy's', less so its competitor from Dublin.

The greyhounds for the first race are being presented. Their owners or trainers keep them on a tight leash. They are sinewy runners; brown, grey, white, black, mottled, striped. They are trembling with excitement in anticipation of the race, lashed into funny jackets with their starting numbers on them. The crowd sizes them up with expert eyes. Gamblers – here that is almost everyone – place their bets at the tally or at the bookmakers. All these experts exchange their money for small colourful slips of paper. Some buy whole books of them.

Now the six whippets are manoeuvred by their masters into the starting boxes. Some of the animals don't like it and cause problems. Now silence descends onto the stand; it becomes amazingly quiet. Then, a shout, the doors of the boxes fly open and the electronically controlled dummy hare bolts away. The dogs dash forward and obsessively chase the colourful bundle – however vainly it may be. At the same time a deafening roar of encouragement breaks out and doesn't stop until the race is over. Lithe, powerful, striding movements. For the normal distance of 525 yards the animals need about 30 seconds: almost 60 kilometres per hour!

Then there is a break. The next six runners are presented. After the viewing, a new run on the betting kiosk. Finally, everything is ready for the second burst of adrenaline, both for the dogs and the spectators. – After eight times 30 seconds, plus breaks, i.e. after about two hours overall, everything is over. The winners cash in their betting slips. This takes

anderen wandern ... ja, wohin? Vielleicht nach Hause; wahrscheinlicher in ein Pub. Man muß die Rennen ja besprechen, egal, wie heiser man sich geschrien hat.

Wo eben noch die vielen Rennbegeisterten waren, sieht's nun aus wie beschneit: Abertausende von Wettzettelchen bedecken den Boden. Die Hoffnungen des Abends sind bei vielen zerstoben, zerflattert, zertreten. – Hunderennen, das sind die Pferderennen des einfachen Mannes. Sie werden wichtig genommen. Manche Hunde sind bekannt wie Stars. Ein solcher Star war 'Master McGrath'. Ihm ist in Dungarvan sogar ein großes Steindenkmal gesetzt; ihm, dem Sieger vieler Rennen.

a while! All the others head off – where to? Maybe home, but more likely to a pub. The race has to be discussed, no matter how hoarse one's voice is from shouting.

It now looks as if snow has fallen on the ground where the racing fans stood: thousands of betting slips cover the ground. For many, the hopes of the evening are shattered, strewn in the wind, stamped into the ground. – Dog racing, that is the poor man's horse racing. It is taken seriously. Some dogs are famous like film stars. Such a star was 'Master McGrath'. In Dungarvan they erected a large monument to him, the winner of many races.

English translation by Veronica O'Regan.

Alessandro Baricco
(1994)

Italian original in: *Novecento*. Milan: Feltrinelli, 1994, p. 44.

L IVERPOOL NEW YORK Liverpool Rio de Janeiro Boston Cork Lisbona Santiago del Cile Rio de Janeiro Antille New York Liverpool Boston Liverpool Amburgo New York Amburgo New York Genova Florida Rio de Janeiro Florida New York Genova Lisbona Rio de Janeiro Liverpool Rio de Janeiro Liverpool New York Cork Cherbourg Vancouver Cherbourg Cork Boston Liverpool Rio de Janeiro New York Liverpool Santiago del Cile New York Liverpool, Oceano, proprio in mezzo. E li, a quel punto, cadde il quadro.

Alessandro Baricco
(1994)

(Extract from a novel – ocean crossings)

L IVERPOOL NEW YORK Liverpool Rio de Janeiro Boston Cork Lisbona Santiago del Cile Rio de Janeiro Antille New York Liverpool Boston Liverpool Amburgo New York Amburgo New York Genova Florida Rio de Janeiro Florida New York Genova Lisbona Rio de Janeiro Liverpool Rio de Janeiro Liverpool New York Cork Cherbourg Vancouver Cherbourg Cork Boston Liverpool Rio de Janeiro New York Liverpool Santiago del Cile New York Liverpool, the Ocean, the very middle of it. And there, at that point, the painting fell.

English translation by Louise Sheehan.

Ralph Giordano
(1996)

German original in: *Mein irisches Tagebuch*. Köln: Kiepenheuer und Witsch, 1996, pp. 66-77.

V ON MACROOM auf der vielbefahrenen N 22 kommend, verfranze ich mich auch diesmal bereits am Stadtrand hoffnungslos. Nachdem ich eine volle Stunde brauchte, um bis zur Innenstadt vorzudringen, bleibe ich dort endgültig stecken. Gerade als ich resigniert aufgeben und mit dem Koffer weitergehen will, klopft ein älterer Herr ans Wagenfenster: 'Sie sehen so ratlos aus – kann ich Ihnen helfen?' Bedrückt nenne ich mein Ziel. Er geht um den Wagen herum, steigt ein, lotst mich mit freundlichen, aber energischen Hinweisen durch den Verkehrswirrwarr der City von Cork und findet mühelos das Hotel Metropol. Dann verschwindet er lächelnd, kaum daß ich ihm meinen Dank abstatten konnte. Eine gute Lehre – der Wagen kommt sofort in die Garage und wird dort bis zur Abreise bleiben. Auch in Cork ist man heute per pedes am schnellsten.

Sein Zentrum liegt zwischen dem North Channel und dem South Channel des River Lee, und die St Patrick's-Brücke, wenige Schritte vom 'Metropol' entfernt, führt direkt in die Stadtmitte.

Ich beuge mich über das Geländer – träge fließt das Wasser seewärts und mit ihm allerlei Treibgut, Papier, leere Flaschen, große Schmutzplacken. Möwen lassen sich auf dem Wasser nieder, fliegen aber gleich wieder auf, als fürchteten sie sich, vergiftet zu werden. Eine Plakette verkündet einem uninteressierten Publikum, wer den Grundstein für die Brücke legen ließ und wann: der Earl of Carlisle, Lieutenant Sir John Arnott, Mitglied des Londoner Parlaments und Bürgermeister am 10. November 1859. Also noch zu Zeiten der briti-schen Herrschaft über Irland, an die mit guten Gedanken zu erinnern gerade die Corker wenig Grund hatten. Während der Höllenlärm der *rush hour über Patrick's Bridge* liegt, rekapituliere ich meine historischen Kenntnisse der Stadtgeschichte.

Der Name Cork stammt von Corcaight, was auf gälisch 'sumpfiger Ort'

338

Ralph Giordano
(1996)

(*Metropole Hotel – monuments – English market – Dan Lowrey's pub – Shandon – Father Matthew Memorial Church*)

D RIVING FROM Macroom on the very busy N22 I get hopelessly lost on the outskirts of the city. Having expended an hour getting to the city centre I end up completely stuck. Just as I am about to give up in resignation, take my suitcase and go the rest of the way on foot, an elderly man taps on the car window: 'You look very lost – can I help you?' Despondently I tell him my destination. He walks around the car, gets in and pilots me through the chaotic turbulence of Cork city traffic with clipped but friendly directions, resulting in a quick and smooth arrival at the Metropole Hotel. Then he disappears smiling before I have the chance to express my gratitude. A good lesson: the car goes into the hotel garage and stays there until I leave. These days, in Cork, like everywhere else, the pedestrian reaches places faster.

The city centre lies between the North and South Channels of the River Lee, and St Patrick's Bridge, a few steps from the 'Metropole', leads directly to the city centre.

I lean over the parapet – the river flows sluggishly towards the sea, bearing with it all sorts of flotsam and jetsam; paper, empty bottles, big blobs of coagulated dirt. Seagulls glide down on the water only to fly up again immediately, as if they were afraid of getting poisoned. An inset plaque on the bridge informs an uninterested public of the personage and date involved in the laying of the foundation stone: the Earl of Carlisle, Lieutenant Sir John Arnott, Member of Parliament and Lord Mayor of Cork, on the 10th of November 1859. In other words, during the days of British power in Ireland, a period which Corkonians in particular have no reason to look back on with any great fondness. During the hellishly noisy rush hour on St Patrick's Bridge I run a recap on my knowledge of the city's history.

The name Cork comes from *Corcaigh*, the Irish (Gaelic) word for 'a

heißt und eine Gründung des heiligen Finbar aus dem 7. Jahrhundert war. Nachdem die Wikinger den Ort 820 und später noch mehrere Male überfallen und gebrandschatzt hatten, betritt mit den Anglonormannen 1172 der übermächtige Nachbar England unter Heinrich II. die irische Szene – und dabei wird es auch hier bis in unser Jahrhundert bleiben. Dazwischen wechselte eine bunte Reihe von Eroberern einander ab, nimmt 1495 der britische Kronprätendent die Stadt ein, werden die Einwohner 1644 vertrieben, wenige Jahre später die Zurückgekehrten von Cromwells Truppen massakriert und 1690 die Befestigungen geschleift. Im irischen Unabhängigkeitskampf gegen die britische Militärmacht verlieren 1920 zwei Bürgermeister ihr Leben und brennen große Teile der Stadt nieder. Wahrlich, Cork hat seinen Teil abbekommen.

Die Gegenwart hat allerdings auch ihre Härten.

Auf der Brücke sitzt ein Bettler, eingemummt, und hält den Passanten einen roten Becher hin. Zehn Schritte weiter spricht mich ein junges Mädchen, nein, ein Kind von zwölf, dreizehn Jahren an und will Geld. 'Wofür? Hasch, drugs?' – 'Nein', sagt sie ganz ernsthaft, 'für Essen'. Zwei Minuten später hat sie auf der Brücke einen jungen Mann angesprochen, verhandelt offenbar mit ihm, sieht zu mir hin und winkt mir freundlich zu.

Am Eingang des großen Kaufhauses am Merchant's Quay hockt ein junger Mensch, neben sich einen schottischen Schäferhund und ein Pappschild, auf dem steht: 'Würden Sie bitte einem Mann und einem Hund helfen, die hier gestrandet sind? Danke und Gott segne Sie.'

Bilder, wie ich sie in der Provinz nicht gesehen habe.

St Patrick's Street, der große Korso, birst vor Energie – Massen von Menschen, als wäre die ganze Einwohnerschaft der Insel in dieser buntscheckigen Verkaufsallee zusammengekommen. Blauweiß gestrichene Gebäude mit römischen Rundbögen, Fassaden von tristestem Schwarz, dann wieder anheimelnde Giebelhäuser, grün-weiß, entzückende Balkons, und auf dem Dach von Tracey's Shoes schlägt ein großer Busch aus.

Weiter – Marks & Spencer, unvermeidlich; *Men's wear* und *Boy's wear*, mit Hemden bis oben vollgestopfte Schaufenster; Optiker neben Pubs; rot-grüne Fahnen in der Eingangstür eines indischen Restaurants; 'Castelli Romani', Leuchtzeichen schon am hellichten Tage; etwas weiter

marshy place' and the city was founded by St Finnbar in the seventh century. After the Vikings invaded, first in 820 and frequently thereafter, burning the city to the ground, the Anglo-Normans from the much mightier neighbour, England, came on the scene in 1172 – and stayed there until the twentieth century. In between there was a series of conquerors; in 1495 a pretender to the English throne took the city. In 1644 the citizens were driven out and, having returned were massacred a few years later by Cromwell's troops. The city's defences were razed in 1690. In the Irish struggle for independence against British military power, two Lord Mayors lost their lives and large tracts of the city were burnt down in the struggle. Truly, Cork has suffered its share.

The present also has its hardships.

A muffled-up beggar sits on the bridge holding out a red beaker to passers-by. Ten steps further on I am stopped by a young girl – no, a child of twelve or thirteen – who asks me for money. 'What for? Hash? Drugs?' 'No,' she says, earnestly; 'for food.' Two minutes later she stops a young man on the bridge, apparently bargains with him and waves to me amiably.

A young man squats on the ground at the entrance to the big shopping centre on Merchants Quay. Beside him a Scottish sheepdog and a cardboard sign with the words: 'Would you please help the man and his dog stranded here? Thank you and God bless you.'

Images that I have never seen in the rural provinces.

St Patrick's Street, the great corso, is bursting with energy – crowds of people, as if the whole population of the island had come together in this colourful commercial thoroughfare. Buildings painted blue and white with Roman arches, façades of mournful black, then again cosy, green and white gabled houses with charming balconies; a large bush has sprouted on the roof of Tracey's Shoes.

Further on, the inevitable Marks and Spencer, Men's Wear and Boys' Wear, the shop windows choc-a-bloc with shirts; opticians next door to pubs; red and green flags in the entrance to an Indian restaurant; Castelli Romani, its sign lit up in broad daylight; a little further on the name of

der Name einer Gaststätte in chinesischen Schriftzeichen. Und Werbung, Werbung, Werbung, wohin das Auge fällt – für Beauty Saloons, für Aer Lingus, die nationale Luftlinie, für Clancy's Food and Drink und, wolkenkratzerhaft, für Toyota.

Die kühl verglaste Oper, auf deren Spielplan derzeit *The Plough and the Stars* steht; davor ein Brunnen, auf seinem Rand Plaketten mit den Entfernungen zu europäischen Metropolen: Athen 2,875, Paris 841, Madrid 1,320, Lissabon 1,460 Kilometer. Geschäfte nur für Glückwunschkarten, vor allem mit knackigen Babies in knalligen Farben; andere Läden, die nichts verkaufen als pinkfarbene Schleifchen, Barbiepuppen, Kinderspielzeug, Taschenmesser, Pralinen. Woanders fußballfeldgroße Verkaufsflächen, einzig dekoriert mit dem grellbunten Universum internationaler Zeitungen und Zeitschriften.

Dann von der St Patrick's Street nach links eingebogen in die Grand Parade und, vorbei am City Market, Corks 'Hallen', weiter bis ans Ende der Allee.

Dort, am Schnittpunkt der Grand Parade und der South Mall, stoße ich auf ein Denkmal, das im Stadtplan stolz als 'National Monument' bezeichnet wird, in mir aber, wie andere Beispiele dieser Art, einen seltsamen Zwiespalt erzeugt.

Es ist errichtet worden für die irischen Freiheitskämpfer gegen die britische Herrschaft, für die McCarthys und Mahoneys, die O'Connells, Kellys und Duffys, und zeigt die Fieberkurven aufständischer Unruhe – 1789, 1803, 1848, 1867, 1916 – die äußerst beeindruckende Liste eines unbeugsamen Drangs nach Unabhängigkeit.

Aber was sich da dem Auge bietet, ist nicht zum Anschauen. Der metallene Zuckerbäckerturm, die vollbrüstige Jungfrau Eire, überdacht und gestützt auf ein schräg stehendes Hochkreuz, die Lyra, *das* irische Symbol neben dem Kleeblatt – und das alles schief und spitz und irgendwie mickrig-verfehlt.

Was da staketumstanden aufsteigt, zeugt ebenso wie zahlreiche andere über die Republik verstreute Denkmale von großer Kunstferne und anzweifelbarer Ästhetik. Das schafft peinliche Gefühle in Betrachtern, die sich mit der irischen Geschichte verbunden fühlen und Anteil daran nehmen, produziert etwas, das ich gern in mir niederschlagen würde und das doch da ist. Ich habe hundert Male erlebt, wie wohlwol lende Bertrachter

a restaurant in Chinese script. And advertisements, advertisements, advertisements as far as the eye can see – for beauty salons, for Aer Lingus, the national airline, for Clancy's food and drink, and, in huge, sky-scraping letters, for Toyota.

The austere glass-fronted Opera House where *The Plough and the Stars* is playing at present; in front of it a fountain with inset plaques on its side showing the distance between Cork and European cities. Athens 2,875, Paris 841, Madrid 1,320, Lisbon 1,460 kilometres. Shops that sell only greeting cards especially of bonny babies in garish colours; other shops selling nothing except pink hair bows, Barbie dolls, children's toys, pocket knives, chocolates. Elsewhere, sales floors the size of football pitches dressed only with the brightly-coloured universe of international newspapers and magazines.

Then, turning left from St Patrick's Street into the Grand Parade and past the English Market – Cork's *Les Halles* – and on to the end of the street.

There, at the junction of the Grand Parade and the South Mall, I come upon a memorial which the city map proudly describes as a 'National Monument'. Like other examples of its genre it evokes conflicting emotions in me.

It was erected for the Irish freedom fighters who took on the might of Britain: the McCarthys, the Mahoneys, the O'Connells, the Kellys and the Duffys, and demonstrates the temperature curve of rebellion: 1789, 1803, 1848, 1867, 1916: a most impressive list marking the indomitable drive towards independence.

But what meets the eye is not worth looking at. The metallic tower in wedding-cake style; under a roof, the full-bosomed maiden Éire supported by a slanting High Cross, a harp, the symbol of Ireland apart from the Shamrock – and the whole thing is skewed and angular and somehow a miserable failure.

Just like many other monuments scattered over the Republic, this one, standing tall inside its palisade, is mute testimony to a great remoteness from real art and a questionable aesthetic sense. An observer empathising with and interested in Irish history finds that the monument creates a feeling of embarrassment. It produces a reaction in me that I would like to banish, but it is there nonetheless. A hundred times I have seen well-disposed

Liebhaber des Landes, davor den Kopf schüttelten oder ihn einzogen. Ausländer, gewiß, doch assistiert von den Stimmen kritischer Iren. Aber seltsam – auch diesmal, wie schon früher an dieser Stelle, vollzieht sich bald ein innerer Umschwung, der einer anderen Bewertung Platz macht. Denn gerade, weil sie so hilflos bemüht sind, das historische Drama, dem sie entwuchsen, adäquat widerzuspiegeln, gerade weil die Kluft zwischen der unermeßlichen Leistung des irischen Kampfes um Freiheit und den Versuchen seiner äußeren Manifestation so erkennbar ist, gerade deshalb haben diese Monumente auch etwas Rührendes an sich. Um den Spagat zu begreifen, der sich da auftut, muß man wohl wirklich länger im Land gewesen sein, muß man lokale Mentalitäten erschnüffelt, kollektive Haltungen begriffen haben, oder sie wenigstens erahnen. Es hat einer großen Strecke meiner 25 Jahre Bekanntschaft mit Irland und den Iren bedurft, um davon eine Vorstellung zu bekommen.

Gleichzeitig frage ich mich hier, am Ende der Grand Parade: Müssen das Ehrenmal und seine Pendants der irischen Jugend an der Wende vom 20. zum 21. Jahrhundert nicht vorzeitlich erscheinen? Haben sie irgendeinen Bezug zu einer Daseinswirklichkeit, in der die EU-Mitgliedschaft der Republik Irland und Großbritanniens selbstverständlich geworden ist und Spannungen zwischen beiden Staaten höchstens im Rahmen solcher Gemeinsamkeit entstehen können (in diesem Zusammenhang einmal abgesehen von der Nordirlandfrage)? In der Tat haben sich gegenüber der Geschichtssituation, der die Denkmale entwuchsen, die europäischen Verhältnisse inzwischen so grundlegend verändert, daß sich Fragen wie diese ganz von allein aufdrängen. Ich werde versuchen, darauf Antworten zu bekommen.

Jetzt aber auf die Grand Parade zurück und, wie gewohnt, zum Tee in den ersten Stock der 'Hallen', Cork's City Market, das geräumige, weitverzweigte und mehrgeschossige Labyrinth eines Freß- und Warentempels, an dem unmißverständlich abgelesen werden kann, daß Irlands Anschluß an die Sitten und Gebräuche des Kontinents Von der Bazarstimmung der siebziger, noch der achtziger Jahre ist hier nichts mehr zu spüren, auch nicht von dem damals vergleichsweise bescheidenen Angebot, abgesehen von den Fischhallen, deren Auslagen seinerzeit genauso aussahen wie heute. Die Wandlungen haben nicht im

observers, lovers of Ireland shake or pull in their heads at the sight of it: foreigners, of course, yet supported by the voices of critical Irish people.

Yet strangely – on this, as well as on previous occasions – as I look at the monument a mood swing gradually causes a revision of my initial judgement. It is exactly because these monuments try so hopelessly to reflect adequately the historical drama that brought them into being, precisely because there is such a great chasm between the infinite achievement of the Irish battle for freedom and its external manifestation, that there is something moving about them. In order to understand the divide that is opening here one needs to have been in the country for a longer period of time; to have mentally eased one's way into the local mentality, to have comprehended collectively held attitudes, or to have at least sensed them. It has taken me most of my 25 years of acquaintance with Ireland and the Irish to get some idea of them.

At the same time, here, at the end of the Grand Parade, I ask myself whether young Irish people on the cusp of the twentieth and twenty-first centuries may not consider the monument and its counterparts prehistoric. Does it have any relation to the reality of today, in which equal membership of the Republic of Ireland and the United Kingdom in the European Union is taken for granted, and any tensions between the two States are contained by this common European framework (with the exception, it must be said, of the Northern Ireland question)? Questions like these arise automatically, because the historical circumstances that gave rise to the erection of these monuments have fundamentally changed in Europe. I must try to get answers to the questions.

Now, however, back to the Grand Parade and, as ever, a cup of tea on the first floor of the English Market, that spacious labyrinth of many pathways and storeys; a temple devoted to the human appetite and to consumerism, from which one can unerringly deduce that Ireland's association with continental habits and customs is, at least in this area, permanent.

The bazaar-like atmosphere of the 1970s and 1980s has long since gone, as has the comparatively modest range of goods. Only the displays in the fish stalls look the same today as they did then. The changes did not take place in the sea; they took place in Ireland's sociology. Awakened needs must be satisfied.

Meer, sie haben in der Soziologie Irlands stattgefunden. Geweckte endgültig ist, jedenfalls auf diesem Gebiet.

Bedürfnisse wollen befriedigt werden.

Dagegen wäre nichts einzuwenden, nur spüre ich dennoch in mir einen leisen Stich, den Verlust einer mir noch bekannten Originalität, wie ich da vom Rande des offenen Cafés auf Stände und Auslagen hinunterschaue. Das alles ist, finde ich von hier oben, ein wenig zu sauber, zu ordentlich, zu abgepackt, zu – europäisch. Wenn man das sieht, in seiner Uniformität, dann könnte man sich auch woanders wähnen, in Antwerpen, in Stockholm oder irgendwo in Deutschland. Da nivelliert sich etwas, und das in erdteilhafter Dimension.

Völlig originell geblieben dagegen, aus der Gründerzeit stammend, Mittelpunkt einer lichten Rotunde im Parterre und ausgestattet mit der magischen Fähigkeit, die Betrachter erst gehörig zu erschrecken, dann aber herzhaft zu bestricken, ist hier allein der alte Springbrunnen!

Das tropft und leckt da unten nur so vor sich hin, rauscht hoch, fällt wieder zurück, begießt plätschernd metallene Wassertiere und Lotusblüten und läßt aus einem schweren Becken eiserne Pflanzen- und Blütenstelen hervorwachsen. Neben drei reiherähnlichen Vogelgeschöpfen am Rande strebt ein mächtiger Kelch aufwärts, aus dem noch ein zweiter wächst. Diesem wiederum entspringt etwas, das mit seinem Bukett schwingender Antennen ausschaut wie das Knollenhaupt eines extraterrestrischen Wesens, das abheben möchte, aber nicht kann. Ein antizipierter und aufs unschuldigste pervertierter Dali ist das, ein Kitsch längst jenseits von Gut und Böse, eine Mißgeburt von solcher Eindruckskraft, daß keine andere Wahl bleibt als die der sofortigen Kapitulation vor ihrer Scheußlichkeit.

Erwachsene bleiben davor wie angewurzelt stehen, Kinder werden von Eltern hochgehoben, patschen ins Wasser, jubeln und kreischen. Ich starre, wie vor zwanzig Jahren zum erstenmal, von hier oben wieder fasziniert auf das in seiner dumpfen Ehrlichkeit umwerfende Scheusal herab, und schmeiße, wie damals schon und wie es alle tun, ein paar Münzen in das Becken.

Das blinkt darin, meist kupferbraune Ein- und Zweipencestücke, aber auch helle Zehner, die glitzern wie silbrige Fischbäuche.

Die ganze Zeit über sind angenehme Klaviertöne zu vernehmen hier oben, etwas separiert, spielt ein weißhaariger Pianist all die weichen,

There is nothing wrong with that, except that I feel a little stab at the loss of the originality I used to know as I look down from the balcony on the stalls and goods displayed below. From up here I find everything a little too clean, too well organised, too well-packaged – too European. Looking at this uniformity one can easily imagine oneself somewhere else; in Antwerp, in Stockholm, or somewhere in Germany. One senses a levelling-off on a continental scale.

One eccentric original has remained: the Art Nouveau fountain in the middle of a bright rotunda in the parterre. It possesses a dual magical capacity: it gives observers a nasty fright and then it charmingly beguiles them.

It trickles and murmurs to itself down below, then sends up a jet of spray that falls back again, sprinkling and splashing metal aquatic animals and lotus blossoms, and causing iron plants and flowers to blossom in the heavy basin. Next to three heron-like figures, a calyx thrusts upward, a second one issuing forth from it. From this, in turn, springs something which, with its nosegay of waving antennae, resembles the bulbous head of an extra-terrestrial being that is attempting, unsuccessfully, to levitate. The fountain anticipates and by its utter innocence perverts Dalí; it is trash far beyond good and evil, a monstrosity so powerfully impressive that, when confronted with its hideousness, all one can do is capitulate immediately.

Adults are rooted to the spot at the sight of it. Children lifted up by their parents splash in the water, giggling and screaming. I stare down at the eyesore, so overwhelming in its dull honesty, fascinated just as I was the first time, twenty years ago. And just as I did then, and just as everybody does, I throw a few coins into the basin.

Coins gleam in the basin, mostly brown copper pennies or two penny picces, but there are also bright ten-penny pieces glittering like the silver bellies of fish.

The pleasant sounds of a piano are audible the whole time up here. At a remove from the tables, a white-haired pianist is playing all the soft, gentle melodies that contrast so gratifyingly with the violent sound of

sanften Melodien, die sich wohltuend abheben von dem gewalttätigen Sound der Rockbands. Es ist Musik, wie ich sie, hoffnungslos altmodisch, so gern höre, von Tommy Dorsey bis Glenn Miller, 'Tea for Two', 'Begin the Beguin', 'Some of These Days', 'Once in a While' oder 'Two Sleepy People'. Auch 'The Best of Frank Sinatra and Carlos Jobim' dringt zu mir: 'Wave', 'This Happy Madness', 'Close to You'. Der Klavierspieler bedient die Tasten ohne Unterbrechung und ganz hingegeben, das Gegenteil von jenen Musikern, deren Spiel eigentlich nur der ersehnten Pause zustrebt. Er macht ein erstauntes Gesicht, als ich ihm applaudiere, freut sich und kommt später an meinen Tisch.

Am Abend dann im Dan Lowrey's, Corks berühmtestem Pub, gleich neben dem Hotel 'Metropol'.

Erste Eindrücke.

Dunkle Holztäfelung; Bänke an der Wand, mit Blumenmustern überzogen, gobelinhaft; hinter der Theke eine ausladende Phalanx auf dem Kopf stehender Flaschen; alte Petroleumlampen mit elektrischen Kerzen, nostalgische Werbeplakate, damals 'Reklame' genannt – 'Player's navy cut cigarettes, mild and medium' auf einem Riesenspiegel. Vergilbte Guinness-Plakate, Postkarten längst vergangener Zeiten – 'Good luck in your new job'. Daneben, zentral postiert, Blickfang für die Gäste, Trophäen von Pub-Wettbewerben, 1991, 1992 und 1993 – 'First prize Dan Lowrey's Tavern, 13 MacCurtain Street, Cork'.

Nach hinten, 'Welcome' über dem Eingang, ein zweiter, kleinerer Raum. Flackernder Kamin; eine Wanduhr mit römischen Ziffern und rasch hin- und herschlagendem Pendel; auch hier Nostalgie – 'Guinness Extra Stout, brewed in Dublin and London', Reklame von einst, unaggressiv.

An der Theke sind alle Hocker besetzt, ich sehe nichts als Bier, helles und dunkles.

Zwei junge Frauen neben mir – die eine vor sich Cola, die andere Mineralwasser mit Zitrone – geben mir den Mut, nach einem Softdrink zu fragen. Zu meiner Beruhigung löst die Bestellung bei der Wirtin keine sichtbare Reaktion aus.

Es ist der erste Pub, den ich berüchtigter Nichtalkoholtrinker aufsuche. Während der Fernsehaufenthalte in Irland haben die Teammitglieder

rock bands. It is music which I, hopelessly old-fashioned, love to listen to: from Tommy Dorsey to Glenn Miller; 'Tea for Two', 'Begin the Beguine', 'Some of these Days', 'Once in a While' or 'Two Sleepy People'. 'The Best of Frank Sinatra and Carlos Jobim' waft across to me: 'Wave', 'This Happy Madness', 'Close to You'. The pianist, completely engrossed in the music, manipulates the keys without interruption; the opposite of those musicians whose playing expresses only the desire to get to the hotly-awaited interval break as quickly as possible. His face expresses surprise when I applaud him. He is pleased and later joins me at my table.

Then, in the evening in Dan Lowrey's, Cork's most famous pub just next to the 'Metropole'.

First impressions.

Dark wainscoting. Benches along the wall covered in floral patterns like gobelin tapestry; behind the bar a jutting phalanx of upturned bottles; old kerosene lamps with electric candles; nostalgia-evoking advertisements, one on a giant-size mirror for Player's 'navy-cut cigarettes, mild and medium'. Faded Guinness posters, postcards from times long past: 'Good luck in your new job.' Close by, centrally positioned to catch the patron's attention, trophies for interpub competitions: 1991, 1992 and 1993 – 'First prize, Dan Lowrey's Tavern, 13 MacCurtain Street, Cork.'

Towards the back, 'Welcome' above the entrance to a second, smaller room. A fire flickers in the grate; a wall clock with Roman numerals and a pendulum swinging rapidly back and forth; here, too, nostalgia – 'Guinness Stout, brewed in Dublin and London', non-aggressive advertising in days of yore.

All the bar stools at the counter are taken; I see nothing but dark and light-coloured beer.

Two young women near me – one with Coke, the other with mineral water and a slice of lemon – give me the courage to order a soft drink. To my relief the landlady doesn't react visibly to my request.

It's the first pub that I, notorious non-drinker of alcohol, have ever been in. When filming in Ireland, the members of the television crew

immer ohne mich gehen müssen. Diesmal, für das Buch, spüre ich, daß ich um diese urirische Institution nicht herumkommen werde, hier nicht und anderswo ebensowenig.

Immerhin, der Bann ist gebrochen, und nach der freundlichen Annahme meines Bekenntnisses zu Limonade scheint eine innere Hemmschwelle überwunden.

'Mind step' – 'Vorsicht, Stufe' – mahnt ein Schild vor Verlassen des Pubs. Draußen, in Höhe des ersten Stocks, zwei Kandelaber, dazwischen 'Dan Lowrey's. Established 1897'.

Ich gehe die Straße hinunter zur St Patrick's Bridge. Es ist nach 20 Uhr, viele Geschäfte sind noch geöffnet – die Pathologie deutscher Ladenschlußzeiten ist hier unbekannt.

Von der Brücke, am rechten Ufer des North Channel, die erleuchtete Front von Dunnes Stores am Merchant's Quay, während sich die angestrahlte Hinterfront des Hotels 'Metropol' im ruhigen Wasser wie ein dauerbelichtetes Foto ausmacht.

Cork liegt nicht an der See, aber über Cork Harbour und Lough Mahon im Strömungsgebiet ihrer Gezeiten. Der Wasserspiegel unter der Brücke liegt deutlich höher als vorhin.

Der Aufstieg zu St Ann's Shandon ist beschwerlich und führt vorbei an ausgeschlachteten Gebäuden und leeren Fensterhöhlen. Aber mein schlechtes Gewissen drängt mich aufwärts zu diesem bisher ausgesparten Wahrzeichen von Cork – bei den Dreharbeiten war immer zuwenig Zeit dafür.

Verblüffend der pepperpot genannte 36 Meter hohe Turm der Kirche. Wie ein dreifach ausgefahrenes Teleskop sieht er aus und ist berühmt wegen des Spiels seiner acht Glocken. Es heißt, gegen ein geringes Entgelt können auch Besucher sie zum Klingen bringen.

Aber nicht heute, wie sich herausstellt. Das eine Pfund, das zu zahlen ist, wird für den Eintritt erhoben, die Kirche ist auch ein Museum. Bänke mit Samtkissen, an den Marmorwänden Namen Verstorbener, darunter häufig die Floskel 'who departed this life'. Was wohl nichts anderes besagen soll, als daß der Tod kein Ende, sondern ein Anfang sei.

Alte Bücher, darunter *Opera omnia, printed 1647*, und vergilbte Handschriften, eine walisische Bibel von 1718 – alles sicher unter Glas.

always had to go without me. This time, for the book, I sense that I won't be able to get around such a quintessential Irish institution, either here- or anywhere else.

Anyway, the long-standing spell is broken, and after the friendly acceptance of my predilection for lemonade, my inner threshold of inhibition seems to have been crossed.

'Mind the step' warns a sign as one leaves this smaller room. Outside, two candelabra hang from the ceiling, between them a sign proclaiming: 'Dan Lowrey's. Established 1897.'

I go down the street to St Patrick's Bridge. It's after eight o'clock. Many shops are still open. The pathology of German closing time for shops is unknown here.

From the bridge, on the right bank of the North Channel I see the illuminated front of Dunnes Stores on Merchant's Quay, while the flood-lit rear entrance of the 'Metropole' is mirrored in the calm river water like a permanently illuminated photo.

Cork is not on the sea but lies above Cork harbour and Lough Mahon on a stretch of water affected by its currents and tides. The water level under the bridge is visibly higher than before.

The walk up to St Ann's Shandon is hard going. It leads past vandalised buildings and empty window frames. However, my bad conscience drives me onward and upward to this hitherto unvisited Cork landmark: when filming here there had never been enough time for it.

The 36-metre high church tower – called the pepper pot – is amazing. It looks like a telescope with its three barrels extended and is famous for the melodiousness of its eight bells. A notice informs me that visitors may play the bells on payment of a small fee.

But, as it turns out, not today. The entrance fee of one pound covers only the visit to the church, which is also a museum. Long pews with silk cushions; on the marble walls the names of the dead. Recurring between the names the flowery phrase: 'Departed this life ...' Which is to say that Death is not an end but a beginning.

Old books, among them *Opera omnia* printed in 1647 and faded manuscripts; a Welsh Bible from 1718 – all securely under glass. A

Ein Gedenkstein, 'In loving memory' für den 1934 verstorbenen Dr
Philipp George Lee, weil er über vierzig Jahre treuer Besucher von St Ann's
Shandon war. Er muß mit seinen Besuchen also 1894 begonnen haben.

Ich dagegen breche den meinen ab, weil er untergeht in dem Lärm,
den nahe dem Eingang ein einsamer Staubsauger macht, der zwar unbe-
dient herumsteht, aber nicht abgestellt worden ist. Noch lauter ist das
Geschnatter des weiblichen Personals, zwei Frauen, deren durchdrin-
gende Stimmen ohne Unterlaß durch den Kirchenraum hallen.

So rette ich mich – Pflicht hin, Pflicht her – die Roman Street herunter
und über die St-Patrick's-Brücke in Richtung Anderson's Quay auf das
Custom House zu, das Zollhaus am Zusammenfluß des Nordkanals mit
dem Südkanal. Dort liegt er vor mir, der Hafen von Cork – Silos, häßliche
Gebäude, Grauklötze, hohe Schornsteine. Doch da eine himmelblaue
Brigg, weithin leuchtend mit ihren Groß-, Heck- und Bugsegeln, und der
von Hamburg her vertraute Anblick an der Pier vertäuter Seeschiffe.

Über den Union Quay zum George's Quay am Südkanal. Alte Holzstege,
verfaulte Balken, an denen abzulesen ist, daß die Flut noch drei Meter höher
steigen kann; Boote, kieloben, Zeugen längst vergangener Hafentätigkeit.

Auf der anderen Straßenseite reges Leben, die irre Front von
Fitzpatrick's *second-hand shop*. Vor dem Schaufenster, draußen, alte
Wagenräder, gammelige Pumpen, Transportfahrräder mit einem
großen Korb über dem kleineren Vorderrad; Kochtöpfe, Kessel, Pflüge,
Sämaschinen, Riesensägen, gewaltige Schöpflöffel – zu nichts mehr
nütze, als angestaunt zu werden oder die Phantasie anzuregen, wie
die Welt dieser Utensilien einst ausgesehen haben mag. Und hinter
lebensgroßen Madonnenstatuen die modernsten Kühlschränke, Herde
und Waschmaschinen unserer Zeit.

Dazu irische Volksmusik aus einem unsichtbaren Lautsprecher.

Über die Parlament-Bridge hinüber zu Father Matthew's Memorial
Church, Wirkungsstätte des 'Apostels der Mäßigung' (1790-1856), der
einen von vornherein aussichtslosen Kreuzzug gegen den irischen
Alkoholismus führte. Dennoch wurde dem streitbaren Theobald Matthew
am 10. Oktober 1861 von der Stadt ein Denkmal errichtet. Das hat sei-
ther zwar an der Ecke St Patrick's Bridge und Lavitt's Quay erfolgreich
allen Wettern getrotzt, ist aber trotzdem nicht verschont geblieben vom

memorial tablet – 'in loving memory of the late Dr Philip George Lee, died 1934, a loyal visitor to Shandon for over 40 years'. He must have begun his visits there in 1894.

I, however, break off my visit because it is ruined by the noise of a vacuum cleaner near the entrance. The machine is unattended but not switched off. Louder still is the chatter of the staff: two women whose penetrating voices resound unceasingly through the body of the church.

So, duty or not, I escape down Roman Street, crossing St Patrick's Bridge, then head in the direction of Anderson's Quay, arriving finally at the Custom House that stands at the confluence of the North and South Channels. There it lies before me: Cork harbour – silos, ugly buildings, grey blocks, tall chimneys. Suddenly a sky blue brig with huge, gleaming white sails fore and aft and the sight of ships tied up at the pier, which I know so well from Hamburg.

Along Union Quay to George's Quay on the South Channel. Old timber paths and rotten beams from which it can be deduced that the tide can rise three metres higher than at present; boats, keels up, are evidence of long-gone activity in the harbour.

The other side of the street is a hive of activity; the fantastic front of Fitzgerald's Second-hand Shop. In front of the window old cart wheels, rusty pumps, messenger boys' bicycles with huge baskets over the smaller front wheel; saucepans, kettles, ploughs, sowing machines, huge saws, enormous ladles – all useless now except as objects of curiosity or a means of stimulating a fantasy of what the world of these utensils might have looked like. And, behind life-size statues of the Madonna, the most up to the minute refrigerators, cookers and washing machines of our own day.

And Irish folk music from an invisible loudspeaker into the bargain.

Across Parliament Bridge and down to Father Mathew's Memorial Church, the base for the activities of this 'Apostle of Temperance' who waged a war against Irish alcoholism that was doomed from the beginning. Nevertheless, the city erected a memorial to the combative Theobald Mathew on the 10th of October 1861. Standing on the corner of St Patrick's Bridge and Lavitt's Quay ever since, it has successfully weathered all storms but is not immune to the fate of most monuments,

Schicksal der meisten Denkmale, nämlich notorisch unbeachtet zu bleiben.

In der Kirche glüht es elektrisch – Wachskerzen sind ausrangiert, und der technische Ersatz funktioniert sogar. Man muß ein Geldstück in einen Schlitz werfen und auf einen Knopf drücken, dann leuchtet es rot oder blau auf. Nach einiger Zeit erlöscht das Licht wieder.

Davor kniet jetzt eine alte Frau, wirft eine Münze ein, bewegt die Lippen und schweigt dann mit geschlossenen Augen. So bleibt sie, lange nachdem das blaue Licht vor ihr ausgegangen ist. Blau ist auch die Statue der Muttergottes. In der einen Hand hält sie einen Goldstab, an den das Jesuskind faßt, das sie im anderen Arm trägt und das seinerseits eine Kugel mit Kreuz stützt, den Globus, obschon der bekanntlich weder völlig christianisiert war noch ist.

Davor Blumen.

Hier, in diesem Kirchentempel, ist Mäßigung gepriesen worden, irgendwie paradoxerweise, denn die sozialen Zustände im damaligen Irland hatten ohnehin den Charakter einer unfreiwilligen Kollektivaskese. Das Elend war einer der großen Gründe für jene Sucht, die Father Matthew so nachhaltig bekämpfte und so ergebnislos, weil seine Ursachen andauerten.

Weithin zu sehen ist die Kirchturmspitze von Father Matthew's Memorial Church auch von der Cook Street aus. Aber in diesem alten Viertel ist von Mäßigung oder Enthaltsamkeit keine Rede. Es liegen Uhren, Gold und Juwelen aus, und ein ungeheurer Lastwagen lädt in bauchigen Fässern Bier ab, Murphy's Irish Stout. Das dauert lange, wobei das Fahrzeug noch den Zugang zu einer anderen belebten und vielbefahrenen Straße versperrt. Aber keiner regt sich auf, keiner hupt, alle warten geduldig, bis der Weg wieder frei wird.

Eine junge Frau in einem langen Mantel und mit Haaren, die ihr Gesicht fast verdecken, holt eine Geige aus dem Kasten, schließt einen Verstärker an und beginnt talentiert zu spielen, irische Weisen, wobei sie sich in abgezirkelten Drehungen bewegt. Eine Mutter mit zwei Kindern ist die erste, die eine Münze in den Kasten wirft.

In einem Wettbüro geht es akut um Pferderennen, die auf dem Monitor verfolgt werden können. Jemand schreibt ununterbrochen

that is to say: nobody gives it so much as a passing glance.

The interior of the church is electrically aglow. Wax votive candles have been scrapped and they have been replaced by an efficiently functioning technology. One throws a coin in a slot, presses a button, and one of the blue or red lights on the stand comes on. After some time it goes out again.

An old woman kneels before the stand and puts in a coin. Her lips move in silent prayer, her eyes closed. She remains thus long after the light has gone out. The statue of Our Lady is also blue. In one hand she holds a golden rod grasped on the other end by the little baby Jesus, whom she is holding in the other arm. He, for his part, is holding a sphere topped by a cross: the globe, although it a well-known fact that the world neither is nor ever was completely Christianised.

Flowers in front of the statue.

Temperance was preached here in this Christian temple. This is something of a paradox for the social situation in the Ireland of that time was characterised by an involuntary collective asceticism. Poverty was one of the main reasons for the addiction which Father Mathew battled against so vigorously; a campaign that was ultimately unsuccessful, because its causes persisted.

The tip of the spire of Father Mathew's Memorial Church can be seen from afar. And also from Cook Street. In this venerable quarter, however, there is no sign of moderation or abstinence. There are displays of watches, gold and jewels. Bulbous barrels of beer – Murphy's Irish Stout – are being unloaded from a large delivery lorry. It takes a long time and the lorry blocks vehicular access to another busy street. But nobody gets excited. Nobody sounds their horn; everybody waits patiently until the way is clear again.

A young woman in a long coat, with hair that almost covers her face, takes a violin out of its case, attaches an amplifier and begins a talented rendition of Irish tunes, her body gyrating with precise, clearly defined movements as she plays. A mother with two children is the first to throw a coin into the violin case.

Horseracing, which can be followed on a monitor, is the burning interest in a betting office. One of the employees spends all his time

Zahlen auf eine Tafel und macht hinter Pferdenamen die Zeichen des neuesten Standes. Die Luft ist dick, in des Wortes buchstäblicher und übertragener Bedeutung. Alle gucken abwechselnd gebannt auf den Bildschirm und auf die Tafel. Wetterfeste Gestalten, etliche am Stock, aber auch sie von großer Ausdauer. Anwesend sind nur Männer. Einer läuft wie ein hungriger Tiger im Käfig auf und ab, schiebt sich zwischen die anderen, den Kopf eingezogen, und starrt auf den Fußboden, als fürchte er von Bild und Tafel eine Katastrophe. Dann *finish*, Endspurt, Peitsche, Auslauf hinter der Ziellinie, die schmalen Hinterteile der Jockeys – Walsh Man heißt der Sieger. Im Wettbüro heisere Schreie des Triumphes und der Enttäuschung. Und schon geht's weiter.

Das genügt – raus.

Die Verkehrsampeln von Cork sind blindenfreundlich. Sie geben einen Ton von sich, solange auf Grün geschaltet ist, und verstummen bei Rot. Die Passanten, die sehen können, warten allerdings meist nicht auf Grün, und das nicht nur in Cork.

Im Foyer des Hotels 'Metropol', abends.

An einem Nebentisch sitzen drei wohlondulierte Damen unter einem Gemälde von Venedig. Ich schätze alle drei in gleichem Alter, so um die sechzig. Sie haben meine Neugierde erregt, und deshalb beobachte ich sie seit einigen Tagen, dezent, hoffe ich, und so, daß sie davon nichts bemerkt haben. Was ich inzwischen herausbekam, ist, daß sie keine Gäste des Hotels sind, sondern Einwohnerinnen von Cork, die hier zweimal die Woche ihren Plausch halten.

Sie tragen die frischen Farben eines unverwüstlichen Frauentypus, einer Gattung, die das kontinentale Europa nicht kennt. Da ist Englisches, ist Britisches im Spiel, nicht von der Abstammung, es sind Irinnen, aber vom Habitus her.

Es ist ein Vergnügen, den dreien zuzuschauen.

Sie sind auf die diszipliniertete Weise lebenslustig, stecken in adretten, ihrem Alter durchaus angepaßten Textilien, aber ohne auf einen distinguierten Schick zu verzichten.

Und natürlich trinken sie Tee.

Wach achten sie auf jede Bewegung und alle Personen in ihrer

writing numbers on a board and the latest odds after the horses' names. Both literally and metaphorically the air is thick. Everyone is tensely switching their attention from the screen to the board and back. Weather-beaten figures, some leaning on walking sticks, but showing great stamina. Only men are present. One of them paces up and down like a caged tiger, pushing in between the others, his head pulled in, staring at the ground as if fearing a catastrophe from the screen or the board. Then finish; a final spurt, the whip, slowing down after passing the winning post, the small buttocks of the jockeys. The winner is a horse called Walsh Man. In the betting office there are hoarse cries of triumph and disappointment. And then it starts all over again.

That's enough. Out I go.

The traffic lights in Cork are kind to the blind. They emit a sound when the pedestrian light is green and fall silent when they turn red. The sighted pedestrians, however, hardly ever wait for green, a phenomenon not confined to Cork.

Evening: in the foyer of the hotel 'Metropole'.

At a table next to me under a painting of Venice sit three ladies with impeccably waved hair. I reckon that all three are the same age, around 60. They aroused my curiosity and so I have been observing them for some days; unobtrusively, I hope, so they won't have noticed. By now I have gathered they are not guests at the hotel but citizens of Cork who meet here twice a week for a chat.

They boast the fresh complexions of an indestructible type of femininity; a kind that is unknown in continental Europe. There is something English, something British about them, not by birth – they are Irish – but in their deportment.

It is a pleasure to observe them.

They are high-spirited in a most disciplined way. Snappily dressed in outfits perfectly appropriate to their age, they display a distinguished chic.

And, of course, they drink tea.

They take note of every movement and person around them and I was also the focus of their attention but they quickly lost interest when

Umgebung, wobei sie auch mich im Auge hatten, wenngleich mit rasch schwindendem Interesse, da ich es sichtbar nicht erwiderte.

Das stimmte selbstverständlich nicht, sondern entsprang einer Zurückhaltung, die mir geboten schien, um meine Beobachtungen ungestört fortsetzen zu können. Ganz im Gegensatz zu meiner sonstigen Kontaktfreudigkeit spüre ich, vielleicht zu Unrecht, eine deutliche innere Hemmung, ihnen meine geheimen Sympathien zu offenbaren, obwohl sie mir aus allen Nähten platzen. Ich fürchte, und das wahrscheinlich wieder gänzlich unbegründet, die Ablösung ihrer natürlichen 'Primärhaltung' durch eine sekundäre, wenn ihr innerer Kreis aufgebrochen würde. Dabei hätte ich ihnen gern Fragen gestellt, befürchte aber, sie könnten sich von mir als Studienobjekte mißbraucht fühlen. Und daran stimmte ja auch einiges, denn ich bin ganz wild auf irische Sonderheiten und spezifische Charaktereigenschaften, und da hinein passen mir die drei nur zu gut. So blieb es also bei der heimlichen Liebe, die ihnen scheinbar unbeteiligt zusah und zuhörte, wie sie da am gleichen Platz unter dem Gemälde saßen, plauschten, Tee tranken und redeten, unbefangen, nicht laut, aber so, daß jeder hätte mithören können. Von ihren Männern und ihren Berufen, den Ehen ihrer Söhne und Töchter, der Gesundheit und Krankheit ihrer Enkelinnen und Enkel. Von der Präsidentin Mary Robinson (in den höchsten Tönen), von Taoiseach John Bruton, dem Ministerpräsidenten (weniger enthusiastisch), sowie von Kulturveranstaltungen in Cork, allerdings ausschließlich solchen, denen sie lieber fernbleiben wollten.

Ich habe sie hartnäckig observiert, die drei wohlondulierten Damen im Foyer des Hotels Metropol, middle class, lebender Beweis, daß England nach wie vor nahe ist, und doch durch und durch irisch. Ich kenne ihre Namen nicht, aber die – wenn auch einseitige – Begegnung mit ihnen hat mich ermutigt, mich endlich an einen kleinen Katalog irischer Charakteristika zu wagen, ganz ohne Anspruch auf Vollständigkeit, auf Richtigkeit der Beurteilung und ohne absichtsvolle Auslese. Auch da, wo Kritik auftaucht, ist sie bestimmt von jenen Sympathien, die das subjektive Destillat meiner Verbindung zu diesem Land und seinen Menschen sind.

I visibly did not return it.

Which, of course, was not the case at all. I was employing the discretion I considered necessary in order to be able to continue my observation without being disturbed. Very much in contrast with my wonted sociability I sensed, maybe wrongly, a definite inhibition about revealing my secret sympathies towards them although they were dying to be let free. I feared – and again, probably quite without reason, – the replacement of their 'primary behaviour' by a 'secondary' one if their inner circle were to be broken. For all that, I would have liked to ask them questions, yet fear that they might have felt misused as objects of study. And there was something to that, as I am crazy about Irish peculiarities and specific, characteristic qualities, and the three displayed these all too clearly. And so it remained a secret love that, apparently disinterested, watched and listened to them as they sat in the same place under the same painting, chatting, drinking tea, and speaking quite uninhibitedly; not loudly but loud enough that anybody could have overheard what they were saying. About their husbands and their jobs, their sons' and daughters' marriages, the health and illness of their granddaughters and grandsons. About President Mary Robinson (in most approving tones), about the Taoiseach John Bruton (less enthusiastically), as well as about cultural events in Cork, but only those that they wished to steer clear of.

I observed them persistently in the foyer of the hotel Metropole: the three ladies with their impeccably waved hair; middle class: living proof that England is as close as ever, and yet they were Irish through and through. I don't know their names but my encounter with them, although one-sided, finally encouraged me to be daring enough to draw up a little catalogue of Irish characteristics. It makes no claim to be comprehensive or accurate in its pronouncements and has not been subject to a deliberate selection process. Where criticism surfaces it is tempered by those sympathies that are the subjective distillate of my connection with this country and its people.

English translation by Kevin N. Power.

Martín Veiga
(2000)

Galician original in: *Southword* (Cork) 2, no. 3, 2000, p. 12.

Escuro Lugar

Habito o fondal dunha lagoa
(ou pode ser pantano, visguenta braña acaso)
con cortizas de piñeiro, pétalos murchos de amarelle.

Contemplo, tendido na lama,
a superficie ateigada de ponlas,
cisco, follas mortas aboiando na corrente,
revelando o lento fluír das augas,
dos despoxos.

Xace no profundo a vida vexetal,
raíces sustentan pontes, edificios,
terman de min, dan alicerce
aos cansos membros de meu.

Examino coidadosamente a vida darredor:
larvas, insectos delicados, vermes
a se nutrir da corrupción
de corpos minúsculos
(mesmo pode ser pardal ou rato)
que apodrecen na ribeira, entre ramaxes,
orixinando vida nova, humus esencial que vivifica.

Observo tamén as aves da xunqueira
– garza esvelta, ávida gaivota
preto das augas entoldadas.

Martín Veiga
(2000)

(A poem)

DARK PLACE

I dwell at the bottom of a lake
(or maybe a marsh, or even a sticky swamp)
with bark of pine tree and withered petals of daffodil.

Lying on the mud, I gaze
at the surface covered with branches,
pine needles, dead leaves floating in the stream,
revealing the slow flow of the waters,
of the waste.

Vegetal life lurks in the depths,
roots hold up bridges, buildings,
they bear me up, laying the framework
of my weary limbs.

I carefully examine the life around me:
larvae, delicate insects, worms
living off decay:
small bodies
(perhaps of sparrow or of mouse)
that rot on the shore, among branches,
creating new life, essential, revivifying humus.

I also observe the birds in the reedbeds
– slender heron, scavenger seagull
by cloudy waters.

Olla máis alá como o estorniño
escorrenta grallas e corvos,
como se oculta baixo tellas de lousa.
Olla os muros de pedra, a sebe de toxos
onde só pousan grises lavandeiras, destemidas,
– tal vez a pega, en días de chuvia,
mais nunca o tímido merlo.

Fronte aos pasais cubertos polo lique
reparo nos detritos, cousa nosa:
unha fibela rota, un petador ferruxento
que xa non baterá porta ningunha
– (el pode ser un anzol, quizais a rella dun arado),
ou un penique vello.

Volvo finalmente a mirada cara á beira,
ao pole que impregna os terróns, os calados restos.

Procuro tépedo abeiro nesta friaxe,
toda a calor que albergan os teus ollos,
o tacto da túa man, o teu alento lene,
unha cálida luz para o estraño,
escuro lugar no que habito:

                              raíz, semente,
avolto sedimento dun corazón desgastado.

Look beyond at the starling
as it chases off rooks and ravens,
hides under roof-slates.
Look at the stone walls, the gorse hedge
on which only the bold grey wagtail lands,
– maybe a magpie too, on rainy days-
but never the shy blackbird.

Facing the mossy stepping stones
I notice our debris:
a broken buckle, a rusty knocker
that will never sound on a door again
– maybe a hook or even a ploughshare-
or an old penny.

Finally I turn my gaze towards the shore,
towards pollen that impregnates the sod, the silent waste.

I seek a cosy nook in this coldness,
all the warmth that your eyes enclose,
the touch of your hand, your soft breath,
a warming light for the strange
dark place in which I dwell:

                              root, seed,
stirred sediment of an exhausted heart.

Translated by David Mackenzie and Martín Veiga.

María do Cebreiro
(2001)

Galician original in: perfida erín (digital edition), 2001. Also in: In *Amastra-n-gallar*, no. 2, 2002, pp. 66-67.

A Venecia Irlandesa

Colle unha coliflor, pártea pola metade.
Aí tés un hemisferio,
o lado máis austral,
as circunvolucións do teu pasado.

Seguramente andades
coa punta dos maimiños sobre o lee,
e os pregos da materia sumerxidos
nun río de pegadas.
Bed-rock, lino nalgures, é o nome que lle deron os xeólogos
a un estraño accidente que transcorre
nas correntes estremas. Co uso do guión,
pretendían reducir a cualidade insólita
do máis fondo dos ríos.

Un leito de dureza que fai da auga corrente saba mol
e dos pés vosos, auga. Tamén ós venecianos lles aprenden
a cantar de xeonllos sobre as dornas.
É un xeito de afacerse á decadencia móbil
na que toda cidade se resolve.
Perdereime, se vou,
na banda máis azul da camiseta.

(sempre que a miña nai me daba de mamar,
vestíase con roupa de liño transparente.

María Do Cebreiro
(2001

(A poem)

THE IRISH VENICE

Take a cauliflower, cut it in half.
Behold! A hemisphere,
the more southerly side,
the circumvolutions of your past.

You are probably walking
on your little toes on the lee,
and the sunk stone folds
under the footsteps of the river.
Bed-rock, I read somewhere, is the name geologists
give to the strange features that
shape the river-bed.
By using the hyphen,
they attempt to attenuate the unusual
mysteries of the depths of rivers.

A bed of hardness that turns running water into a soft sheet
and your feet into water. They also teach Venetians
to sing kneeling down in their boats.
It is a way of getting used to the stages of decay
which shapes every city.
I will get lost, if I go,
in the bluest stripe of my T-shirt.

(when my mother suckled me,
she would always wear transparent linen clothes.

Aínda lle son alérxica a tódolos tecidos,
incluído o seu pelo).

En qué burato negro perdín o meu carné de identidade,
requisito do tránsito.
O meu fanado punto de chegada:
unha cidade ergueita sobre as augas dun río.
Se de pronto espertase do seu profundo sono,
veriamos sorrir ó triste heráclito

(a eternidade é un órgano de feira
que Deus desafinou
antes do seu sonado suicidio.
O tempo é un maragato
que o pulsa no teclado e pón a cabra
enriba da banqueta.
Despois da súa función
deixa quedar os pesos
e colle as perras chicas)

A non ser que tamén na doce erín
teña lugar o mal das augas altas
e a perla do feinismo se vexa, cal padrón,
sometida a un periódico naufraxio.

I am still allergic to all fabric,
including her hair).

In what black hole did I lose my identity card,
without which travel is denied.
My putative destination:
a city rising from the waters of a river.
If he were to wake suddenly from his deep sleep,
we would see sad heraclitus smile.

(eternity is a fairground organ
put out of tune by God
before his famous suicide.
Time is a gypsy
who presses the keys and puts the goat
on the stool.
After his performance
he leaves the silver
and takes the coppers)

Unless they are also troubled
in sweet erin by high waters
and the fenian pearl is subject, just as padrón town
to regular shipwreck.

English translated by David Mackenzie and Martín Veiga.

Parlement Européen
(2001)

French original in: *Document de Séance 1999-2004.*
Final A5-0428/2001, 27 November 2001.

PROPOSITION DE RÉSOLUTION

RÉSOLUTION DU Parlement européen sur la 'Capitale européenne de la culture 2005' (2001/2221(INI))
Le Parlement européen,
- vu le Traité instituant la Communauté européenne et notamment son article 151,
- vu la décision 1419/1999 du Parlement européen et du Conseil du 25 mai 1999 instituant une action communautaire en faveur de la manifestation 'Capitale européenne de la culture' pour les années 2005 à 2019
- vu le Rapport du jury du 28septembre 2001 sur la proposition irlandaise de la 'Capitale européenne de la culture' pour 2005,
- vu le rapport de la commission de la culture, de la jeunesse, de l'éducation, des médias et des sports (A5-0428/2001),

A. considérant que la 'Capitale européenne de la culture' est un événement important pour le développement de la dimension culturelle au sein de l'Union, et notamment dans le cadre de l'élargissement,
B. considérant que, conformément à l'article 2 paragraphe 3 de la décision 1419/1999 du Parlement européen et du Conseil du 25 mai 1999, le Parlement européen peut exprimer son avis, dans un délai de trois mois, sur la proposition présentée par le jury,
C. considérant que, conformément à l'article 4 de la décision 1419/1999 du Parlement européen et du Conseil du 25 mai 1999, 'une période de préparation serait souhaitable' afin de permettre le bon déroulement des événements,
1. demande à la Commission et au Conseil de soutenir la proposition de la ville de Cork, en tant que 'Capitale européenne de la culture' pour 2005;

European Parliament
(2001)

(Report on Cork's application to become European Capital of Culture submitted to the European Parliament)

RESOLUTION OF the European Parliament on the 'European Capital of Culture 2005' (2001/2221 (INI))

The European Parliament,

- having regard to the Treaty establishing the European Community, and in particular Article 151 thereof,

- having regard to Decision 1419/1999 of the European Parliament and of the Council of 25 May 1999 establishing a Community action for the European Capital of Culture event for the years 2005 to 2019,

- having regard to the report of the selection panel of 28 September 2001 on the Irish nomination for the 'European Capital of Culture' for the year 2005,

- having regard to the report of the Committee on Culture, Youth, Education, the Media and Sport (A5-0428/2001),

A. whereas the European Capital of Culture is an important event for the development of the cultural dimension within the Union, particularly within the context of enlargement,

B. whereas, pursuant to Article 2(3) of Decision 1419/1999 of the European Parliament and of the Council of 25 May 1999, the European Parliament may, within a period of three months, give its opinion on the nomination put forward by the selection panel,

C. whereas, pursuant to Article 4 of Decision 1419/1999 of the European Parliament and of the Council of 25 May 1999, 'the desirability of preparation time' should be borne in mind to ensure that the events run smoothly,

1. Calls on the Commission and the Council to support the nomination of the city of Cork as the 'European Capital of Culture' for the year 2005;

2. prend note du rapport du jury et notamment de ses remarques quant à la dimension européenne que la ville choisie devra dûment développer en vue de cet évènement et propose d'établir un dialogue avec les responsables de cette manifestation afin qu'une réelle valeur ajoutée européenne soit mise en oeuvre;

3. demande à la Commission d'établir un rapport d'évaluation sur les résultats de cette manifestation, selon l'article 6 de la décision 1419/1999/CE du Parlement européen et du Conseil du 25 mai 1999, et notamment sur les aspects liés à la procédure établie à l'article 2 afin d'établir une éventuelle révision notamment pour tenir compte des prochaines adhésions des pays candidats;

4. charge sa Présidente de transmettre la présente résolution au Conseil et à la Commission.

2. Notes the selection panel's report, particularly its remarks on the need for the city selected to take appropriate steps to enhance its European dimension in preparation for the event; proposes that a dialogue be initiated with the officials in charge of the event to ensure that real added European value is achieved;

3. Calls on the Commission to draw up a report evaluating the results of that event pursuant to Article 6 of Decision 1419/1999/EC of the European Parliament and of the Council of 25 May 1999, and in particular the aspects connected with the procedure laid down in Article 2 thereof, in order to make any adjustments necessary, particularly with a view to the forthcoming accessions of the applicant countries;

4. Instructs its President to forward this resolution to the Council and Commission.

For source, see page 374.

Christophe Boltanski
(2002)

French original in: 'Cork hospitalière, sauf pour "eux"'. In *Libération*, 17 May 2002

JOE O'CALLAGHAN ne parle pas du sujet qui lui brûle les lèvres. Son tract n'en fait pas non plus mention. C'est inutile. Dans la ville, tout le monde sait pourquoi l'ancien maire travailliste se présente comme candidat indépendant aux élections législatives irlandaises qui se tiennent aujourd'hui. Sur le pas de leur porte, les habitants lui jettent des regards entendus. 'C'est bien ce que vous avez dit sur ... nos amis.' […] La peur est trop récente pour être formulée. Dans un pays fier de son hospitalité, chacun s'exprime par demi-mots ou antiphrases. 'Ah! Voilà monsieur réfugié', s'exclame une femme. Devant le journaliste, un retraité précise qu'il n'a 'rien contre eux'. Mais 'les laisser venir chez nous et les payer à ne rien faire', ça le 'rend malade'. A chaque fois, le candidat O'Callaghan opine de la tête et prend sa suite à témoin: 'Vous voyez! Ils sont d'accord avec moi.'

Expulsé du Labour. En octobre, il a provoqué un tollé avec ses propos sur l'immigration. L'Irlande est 'submergée', avait-il déclaré, ajoutant: 'Ces gens exploitent un droit de résidence qui a été aboli partout ailleurs en Europe'. Il avait réclamé une refonte de la Constitution afin de ne plus accorder la nationalité à tout enfant né sur le sol irlandais, et exigé le renvoi des demandeurs d'asile coupables d'actes 'criminels'. A ce jour, seuls huit réfugiés ont été déférés devant le tribunal de Cork, pour ivresse ou tapage nocturne […]

La deuxième ville du pays, forte de 150 000 habitants, abrite environ 2 500 demandeurs d'asile. Nigérians, Rwandais, Roumains ou Kurdes. Tous arrivés de fraîche date. Ils s'entassent à quatre par chambre dans d'anciens hôtels reconvertis en centres d'accueil. Ils n'ont pas le droit de travailler tant que leur dossier n'a pas été accepté. Dans l'attente d'une réponse qui peut mettre cinq ans à arriver, l'Etat les loge, les nourrit et leur verse 19 euro par semaine. Ces visages, jusque-là inconnus, nourrissent toutes sortes

Christophe Boltanski
(2002)

(Xenophobia in Cork)

JOE O'CALLAGHAN does not discuss this hot topic, nor does his flier mention it. It doesn't have to. Everyone in Cork knows why the former Labour Party mayor is going forward as an Independent candidate in the Irish general election that is taking place today. On their doorsteps, people look at him knowingly. 'What you said about … our friends was spot on', they say […] This is a fear too recent to be put into words. In a country proud of its hospitality record, half-words and irony say it all. 'Ah, there's yer man, the refugee', says one woman. With the journalist present, a retired man explains that he has 'nothing against them'. But 'allowing them to come here and paying them to do nothing' makes him 'sick'. The candidate, O'Callaghan, nods in agreement each time, and calls on his followers as witnesses. 'You see, they agree with me.'

In October, he provoked outrage with his comments on immigration and was expelled from the Labour Party. He had declared that Ireland was being 'flooded', adding, 'these people are exploiting a right of residence that has been abolished everywhere else in Europe.' He had called for the reform of the Constitution so that Irish nationality would no longer be given to all children born on Irish soil, and had demanded that asylum seekers found guilty of 'criminal' acts would be sent home. To date, only eight refugees have been brought before the court in Cork, for drunkenness and disturbing the peace at night […]

Cork, Ireland's second city with its 150,000-strong population accommodates about 2,500 asylum seekers, including Nigerians, Rwandans, Romanians and Kurds – all recent arrivals. They are crowded four to a room in former hotels converted into reception centres. They do not have the right to work until their dossier has been accepted. Waiting for a reply can take five years. In the meantime, the State offers them board and lodgings and gives them 19 euro a week. Their

de rumeurs. 'On n'est pas raciste, mais quand on voit que ces demandeurs d'asile sont mieux traités que nous, ça ne va plus. Au rythme où ils arrivent, ils seront majoritaires dans dix ans', explique un troisième.

Associations d'aide. Un soir dans un pub, Latif Serhildan, un Kurde de Turquie, a été assommé à coup de bouteille. 'Bâtard', 'retourne dans ton pays', lui a-t-on lancé. Depuis son arrivée en 1993, 'les gens sont devenus plus agressifs'. Il préfère parler d'ignorance que de racisme. 'Une radio FM racontait que les réfugiés s'achetaient des voitures ou des maisons avec leurs allocs. L'animateur croyait vraiment à tous ces mythes. Nous lui avons expliqué la situation. Depuis il est plus correct.' De nombreux Irlandais se mobilisent contre la xénophobie. 'Les demandeurs d'asile reçoivent beaucoup de soutien. Dans les petites localités, ils sont souvent très bien accueillis', souligne Piaras MacÉinrí, directeur du Centre irlandais d'étude sur l'immigration. Partout naissent des associations d'aide aux réfugiés. A Cork, le NASC offre un service juridique, des cours d'anglais et d'informatique et peut compter sur une centaine de volontaires.

A la veille de la campagne, les partis se sont tous engagés par écrit à ne pas exploiter la peur de l'immigration. La classe politique commence à prendre la mesure du danger. En février, un étudiant chinois a été tué dans les rues de Dublin avec une barre de fer. Selon une enquête réalisée par Amnesty auprès de 600 membres de minorités ethniques, cinq personnes sur six déclarent avoir été victimes de racisme.

faces, unknown in Cork up to now, give rise to all kinds of rumours [...] 'We're not racist, but it's ridiculous that these asylum seekers should be treated better than ourselves. At the rate at which they're arriving, they'll be in the majority in ten years time', explains an O'Callaghan supporter.

Help groups have sprung up. In a pub one evening, Latif Serhildan, a Turkish Kurd, was hit by a bottle. 'Bastard', 'go back to where you came from', people shouted at him. Since he arrived here in 1993, 'people have become more aggressive', he says. He prefers to put this down to ignorance rather than racism. 'An FM radio was saying that refugees were buying cars and houses with their allowances. The presenter really believed all these myths. We went and explained the situation to him. Since then, his reports are more balanced'. Many Irish people have got involved in combating xenophobia. 'Asylum seekers get lots of support. They are often well received in small localities', stresses Piaras MacEinri, Director of the Irish Centre for Migration Studies. Associations to help refugees are being set up everywhere. In Cork, NASC offers legal aid along with English and computer classes, and can count on 100 volunteers.

On the eve of the election campaign, all the political parties gave a written undertaking not to exploit people's fear of immigration. The political class is beginning to recognise the potential danger of the situation. Last February, a Chinese student was killed on the streets of Dublin with an iron bar. An Amnesty investigation into 600 members of ethnic minorities revealed that five people in every six declared that they had been victims of racism.

English translation by Grace Neville.

Fabienne Darge
(2003)

French original in: 'Fiona Shaw, drôle de tragédienne'. In: *Le Monde*, 18 March 2003.

Fiona Shaw, l'interprète de Médée, Electre et autres rôles pas franche-ment comiques, passe son temps à faire rire son entourage, qui adore sa santé de bonne vivante, son *Irish humour* et sa générosité.

Ce samedi soir glacial de début février à New York, Fiona, qui a joué deux fois Médée, rôle épuisant, dans la même journée, est en pleine forme: dans sa loge du Brooks Atkinson Theatre, au cœur de Broadway, c'est elle qui débouche les bouteilles de vin et met tout le monde à l'aise avec sa gentillesse un peu rude d'Irlandaise. Quand on lui demande d'où vient cette énergie, elle répond qu'elle l'a dans les gênes, que sa mère, à 79 ans, joue encore au tennis tous les jours.

Fiona est née à Cork, deuxième ville d'Irlande 'pas franchement fun', en 1955, dans une famille de scientifiques cultivés. 'A la maison, on jouait de la musique, on disait des poèmes ... Cork n'était pas très bien pourvue sur le plan théâtral, mais la vie chez nous était un théâtre per-manent! Sans doute est-ce cela qui m'a donné le goût des textes, l'amour des mots'.

Pour rassurer son père, pas enthousiaste à l'idée qu'elle rejoigne la planète des saltimbanques, elle fait des études de philosophie. Et déboule enfin, au début des années 1980, à la Royal Academy of Dramatic Art de Londres: étudiante plus âgée que les autres, plus passionnée, elle est débauchée, dès 1982, par le National Théâtre, puis rejoint la Royal Shakespeare Company en 1985, où elle restera quatre ans. Son territoire, alors, est celui de la comédie.

Elle croise une première fois Deborah Warner, la grande rencontre personnelle et professionnelle de sa vie, en 1982, alors que celle-ci vient de fonder sa compagnie, le Kick Theatre, et travaille sur un Woyzeck. Les deux femmes n'accrochent pas. Le déclic aura lieu en 1988: Deborah Warner est metteur en scène invité par la Royal Shakespeare Company

Fabienne Darge
(2003)

(A *Cork actress*)

F IONA SHAW who plays Medea, Electra and other roles that are frankly not funny, spends her time making those around her laugh: they adore her healthy joie de vivre, her 'Irish humour' and her generosity.

Here in New York on this freezing cold Saturday evening early in February, Fiona, who has played the exhausting role of Medea twice in one day, is in great form: in her dressing room at the Brooks Atkinson Theatre, in the heart of Broadway, it's Fiona who is opening the wine and putting everyone at ease with her fairly energetic Irish affability. When asked where this energy comes from, she replies that it is in her genes, and that her mother, at 79, still plays tennis every day.

Fiona was born in Cork, Ireland's second city ('not really a fun place') in 1955 in a family deeply involved in science and the arts. 'At home, we played music, we recited poems ... Cork was not very well provided for where theatre was concerned, but life in our house was like non-stop theatre! That's probably what's given me my taste for texts, my love of words.'

She studied philosophy in order to reassure her father who was not keen on her joining the world of the strolling players. And so she ended up in the early 1980s at the Royal Academy of Dramatic Art in London. Older and more passionate than the other students, she was enticed away in 1982 by the National Theatre. Then in 1985 she joined the Royal Shakespeare Company where she stayed for four years. Her area at that point was comedy.

It was in 1982 that she first came across Deborah Warner, the great professional and personal encounter of her life, just after Warner had set up her company, Kick Theatre, and was working on a Woyzeck play. The two women did not get on. That changed in 1988: Deborah Warner was

377

et propose à Fiona Shaw l' Electre de Sophocle. Et puis, l'Irlandaise vol-
canique et la jeune Anglaise rigoureuse issue d'une famille quaker de
Burford ne se quitteront quasiment plus, donnant lieu à l'une des aven-
tures théâtrales les plus passionnantes de ces dernières années.

guest producer at the Royal Shakespeare Company and offered the role of Sophocles' Electra to Fiona Shaw. Since then, the volcanic Irishwoman and the severe young Englishwoman from a Quaker family in Burford have rarely been apart, resulting in one of the most passionate theatre adventures of these last few years.

English translation by Grace Neville.

Piero Calì
(2004)

(Italian text written for this volume)

RICORDI DELLA CITTÀ SUL FIUME LEE

ARRIVAI A Cork una sera nebbiosa all'inizio dell'autunno del 1956. Avevo trascorso due anni a Dublino dove avevo lavorato come assistente d'italiano a UCD e dove avevo insegnato all'Italian Institute. Ero venuto a Cork ad incontrare la Professoressa Byrne-Costigan, Direttore del Dipartimento di Lingue Romanze, per ultimare gli accordi riguardo ad un posto di lavoro dello stesso tipo a UCC. La signora Byrne-Costigan viveva da qualche parte lungo la Western Road dove mi accompagnò l'amico che mi aveva dato un passaggio. Non fu facile trovare l'indirizzo: si potevano a malapena scorgere i pali della luce, così spessa era la nebbia che li avvolgeva. Dove ero arrivato? Cork sembrava così umida, molto più umida di Dublino, ma non faceva freddo. L'aria era umida ma allo stesso tempo leggera – o 'shoft' come avrei sentito poi pronunciare dalla gente quando parlava del tempo. In ogni caso la foschia gradualmente scomparve e presto fui in grado di esplorare la città e i suoi dintorni. Dopo pochi giorni gradualmente individuai le strade più trafficate come pure le stradine strette ai loro lati, le chiese, i monumenti, gli edifici pubblici e mi colpiva spesso il loro calcare bianco e l'arenaria rossa. Era una realtà urbana unica che avevo spesso l'opportunità di contemplare dalla collina di Sunday's Well.

E poi i ponti, eh, ce n'erano così tanti! 'Sai, Cork è la Venezia del Nord', qualcuno mi disse. Bhe, con un po' di immaginazione, quella considerazione poteva essere ritenuta valida considerando che grandi strade trafficate come Patrick Street, Grand Parade e South Mall fino a qualche secolo fa erano vie d'acqua utilizzate dalle navi ogni qual volta venivano a caricare e a scaricare le merci. Certo la connessione con Venezia era ideale, ma a Cork c'erano anche altri punti di riferimento che riecheggiavano una presenza italiana ancor più concreta. Nomi quali Montenotte e Tivoli erano stati dati a aree residenziali in cima alle colline

Piero Calì
(2004)

(Italian connections)

Reminiscences of the city by the Lee

I ARRIVED in Cork on a foggy evening in the early autumn of 1956. I had spent two years in Dublin as a junior assistant in Italian at UCD and had taught at the Italian Institute, I had come to meet Professor Byrne-Costigan, Head of the Romance Languages Department, to finalise plans for a similar position at UCC. The lady lived somewhere along the Western Road and I was taken there by the friend who had given me a lift. It wasn't easy to find the place: one could hardly distinguish the street-lamps, so thick was the fog enwrapping them. Where had I come to? Cork seemed so damp, much damper than Dublin. But it wasn't cold. The air felt moist yet soft – 'shoft' as I would often hear people referring to the weather later on. But naturally the mist would clear and soon I would be able to explore the city and its environs. After a few days the wide thoroughfares as well as the narrow lanes behind them, the churches, the monuments, the public buildings gradually came into my view and I was often struck by the white limestone and the red sandstone of their structure: a unique urban reality that I was often able to contemplate with a bird's eye view from the heights of Sunday's Well.

And the bridges, well, there were so many of them! 'You know, Cork is the Venice of the North', somebody said to me. Well, with a bit of imagination, you could appreciate that claim considering that modern thoroughfares like St Patrick's Street, Grand Parade and South Mall up to a couple of centuries ago were waterways used by ships whenever they came to load and unload their cargoes. The Venice connection was an ideal one, but in Cork there were other landmarks that echoed a more concrete Italian presence. Montenotte and Tivoli were the names given to residential areas on top of sloping hills overlooking the harbour, the former so called by a merchant prince who first built his villa there to

che digradano sopra al porto. La prima era stato chiamata così da un principe mercante che per primo costruì la sua villa lì in ricordo del luogo della vittoria di Napoleone nel nord Italia mentre la seconda inevitabilmente ricorda uno dei famosi giardini di Tivoli vicino a Roma. Venni a conoscenza del fatto che Riverstown House, magnifica residenza a Glanmire, un tempo appartenuta ad un vescovo di Cork, era stata decorata dai famosi fratelli Fancini nel diciottesimo secolo, ma quando vidi il mosaico di stile bizantino rappresentante un Cristo in trono nell' abside della chiesa di San Francesco, anch'esso opera di artisti italiani, non potei fare a meno di pensare al maestoso Cristo Pancreatore nella Cattedrale di Monreale fuori della città di Palermo nella mia natia Sicilia. Durante la mia visita all'Imperial Hotel a South Mall notai una fotografia appesa ad un muro vicino all'entrata, intitolata *La Conversazione* ritraente una scena di ritrovo sociale con un'atmosfera distinta, ricorrente in tutta l'Europa del diciannovesimo secolo. Ma fuori, vicino all'entrata, mi vennero mostrati dei cerchi di ferro appesi ai muri che venivano un tempo usati per legare i cavalli che tiravano le 'Macchine Lunghe', ossia le carrozze della grande rete di trasporti che Bianconi, il ragazzo di Treviso nel nord Italia, aveva dato all'Irlanda nello stesso periodo. E poi, come molti altri luoghi di mare intorno all'Europa, anche Cork aveva la sua 'Marina', il bel viale alberato su uno dei moli al porto. In generale per un italiano appena approdato alla seconda città più grande d'Irlanda era l'atmosfera più congeniale.

Tuttavia, più che le pietre e lo scenario, furono le persone che mi fecero apprezzare e piacere il posto. Il loro carattere amichevole, l'assenza di distacco, il loro spirito e vivacità mi fecero sentire a mio agio. Non dimenticherò mai la volta in cui conobbi il sindaco di Cork ad un ricevimento in occasione del primo festival cinematografico di Cork al quale, fra l'altro, partecipò come ospite d'onore Vittorio De Sica, il famoso attore e regista. Dopo lo spettacolo, mentre si beveva qualche bicchiere di vino, mi venne presentato Alderman Seán Casey, il sindaco, che era vestito con tutte le insegne rappresentanti il suo ruolo. Chiacchierammo amabilmente e di tanto in tanto rispondevo nel tipico modo italiano: 'Sì, signore' oppure 'certo signore'. Ad un certo momento mi interruppe e mi disse: 'Il mio nome è Seán …' Io rimasi stupito ma sorpreso e piacevolmente colpito dall'informalità della sua osservazione. [...]

record the place of a Napoleonic victory in northern Italy, the latter inevitably reminding one of the famous Tivoli gardens near Rome. I learned that Riverstown House, a magnificent residence in Glanmire, which once belonged to a former Archbishop of Cork, was decorated by the famous Francini brothers in the eighteenth century, but when I saw the Byzantine-style mosaic representing an enthroned Christ in the apse of St Francis Church, this also the work of Italian craftsmen, I couldn't help but think of the majestic Christ Pantocreator in Monreale Cathedral outside Palermo in my native Sicily. Visiting the Imperial Hotel on the South Mall I noticed a picture hanging on a wall near the entrance entitled *La Conversazione*, a scene of social gathering in a genteel atmosphere, customary in the whole of nineteenth-century Europe. But on the outside, near the entrance, I was shown some iron rings hanging on the walls: these were once used to tie up the horses driving the 'Long Cars', the coaches of the great road transport network that Bianconi, the boy from Treviso in northern Italy, had given to Ireland in the same period. And like many other seaside places all over Europe, Cork too had its 'Marina', the lovely tree-flanked avenue by one of the quays in the harbour. On the whole it was a most congenial atmosphere for an Italian just landed in the second largest city in Ireland.

But more than the stones and the setting it was the people who made me appreciate and like the place. Their friendly attitude, lack of aloofness, wit and liveliness made me feel at ease. I will never forget the time when I met the Lord Mayor of Cork at a reception on the occasion of the first Cork Film Festival at which, incidentally, Vittorio De Sica, the great actor and film director, was guest of honour. After the show, over drinks in a hotel, I was introduced to Alderman Seán Casey, the Lord Mayor, dressed in the full regalia of his office. We were chatting amiably and every now and then I would reply as an Italian would: 'Yes, my Lord' or 'Of course, my Lord'. At a certain point he interrupted and said: 'My name is Seán ...' I was amazed but surprised and delighted at the informality of his intervention. [...]

La vita a Cork era piacevole, varia e spesso eccitante come quando il giovane e emergente Luciano Pavarotti cantò un assolo come membro di un coro italiano che prese parte al festival corale internazionale nel municipio. All'Opera House ricostruita vedemmo più spettacoli di opera italiana di quanti ne avevamo visti in Italia e ascoltammo tanti dei concerti spesso tenuti al municipio. Dopo due anni in una casa in affitto, con l'aiuto di alcuni amici, comprammo un piccolo bungalow a due miglia dalla città su una collina sovrastante il Lee. Per usare un'espressione del posto la comprammo 'per una canzone'. Si trovava in cima ad un pendio coperto di ginestra spinosa e da lì la vista era mozzafiato. Pian piano la facemmo diventare casa nostra, praticamente ricostruendola. Renata, con il suo pollice verde, creò un bellissimo giardino di fiori e verdure: avevamo addirittura carciofi perchè una signora italiana, un'amica che viveva a Tivoli, ci aveva dato qualche pianta per farci incominciare. Ovviamente non c'era bisogno di dare da bere al giardino: ci pensava la buona pioggia irlandese. Ma per bere e per le necessità domestiche avevamo la nostra fonte che ci dava acqua della miglior qualità. Avremmo potuto iniziare un commercio imbottigliandola quando la moda dell'acqua minerale arrivò in Irlanda! Nel giardino c'era un grande albero di mele qualità Bramley che permetteva un gran raccolto ogni anno e una quantità esagerata di torte di mela che i bambini coprivano con la ricca crema irlandese. Come altre famiglie avevamo il nostro fornaio, fruttivendolo e macellaio per le nostre spese: fornivano articoli per la miglior combinazione di ingredienti italiani e cucina italiana. Poi arrivarono i supermercati con il loro rifornimento più ricco di cibi continentali ma non dimenticherò mai la pescivendola che, dietro al suo bancone all'English Market, ti chiamava sempre 'my love' nel più gioviale dei toni!

Life in Cork was pleasant, varied and often exciting as when the then young and upcoming Luciano Pavarotti sang a solo piece as a member of an Italian choir taking part in the International Choral Festival in the City Hall. In the reconstructed Opera House we enjoyed more performances of Italian Grand Opera than we had ever done in Italy and listened to so many more concerts like those often held in the City Hall. After two years in rented accommodation and with the help of some friends we bought a little bungalow two miles from the city on a hill overlooking the Lee. To use a local expression we bought it 'for a song'. It was situated on top of a gorse-covered slope and the view from there was breathtaking. Gradually we made it our home, practically re-building the place. Renata, with her green fingers, created a wonderful flower and vegetable garden: we even grew artichokes as an Italian lady, a friend who lived in Tivoli, had given us some plants to start us off. Of course, there was no need to water the garden: the good Irish rain did the job. But for drinking and domestic needs we had our own spring which gave us top quality water. We could have gone into business bottling it when the mineral water fashion hit Ireland! In the garden there was a big Bramley apple tree that gave an abundant crop each year and an indecent quantity of apple tarts that the kids would top with rich Irish cream. Like other families we had our own baker, grocer and butcher for the shopping: they supplied the goods for the best combination of Irish ingredients and Italian cuisine. Then came the supermarkets with their richer supply of continental foodstuffs but I will never forget the lady fishmonger who, behind her counter in the English Market, in the most jovial tone would always call you 'my love'!

English translation by Anne O'Connor.

Allessandro Gentili
(2004)

(Italian text written for this volume)

STATIO BENE FIDA CARINIS

*Once you've decided to go to Tipperary
you'll realise you no longer belong to yourself*
Desmond O'Grady

IL MIO arrivo a Cork, quel tardo settembre 1981, fu vero approdo della mia barca a un'isola, una delle molteplici dell'arcipelago Europa, e altra dalla terraferma della mia Toscana. Ero così venuto ad avviare il confronto con l'altro-da-sé, nella condizione di chi è chiamato a trasmettere il sé del suo rapporto con la sua lingua e la sua cultura a questo altro-da-sé, altro già per altra lingua e civiltà. Ero a Cork per dare. Ma dare è, in sé, anche ricevere.

Mi sistemai in una *guest-house*, la Redclyffe House, sulla Western Road. Una guest-house, o pensione che sia, può forse apparire anonima, impersonale, come dimora. Una stanza occasionale. Ma una stanza di tante occasioni, porto o stazione di continui arrivi e partenze, teatro di volti e figure molteplici, stanza di mobile immaginazione. Mrs O'Brien, proprietaria della Redclyffe e originaria di Limerick, era donna di squisite arti di ospitalità, e di senso dell'umorismo. L'altro ospite permanente era un anziano scozzese, 'Mr Mac', che lavorava nel glass blowing centre del Science Building di UCC. Ho ancora una campanella di vetro che egli fece e mi diede in dono. *A very bitter man*, Mr Mac sognava di isole nel sole del Mediterraneo. A Malta, o a Cipro, o alle Canarie, trascorreva ogni anno un paio di settimane. Gli riusciva difficile spiegarsi perché io, che da un paese mediterraneo provenivo, fossi finito in questo *filthy weather* irlandese. Una volta mi provai a lanciare il termine *European integration*. Ma Mr Mac non afferrò. [...]

In quei giorni una fastidiosa uveite, contratta durante il servizio militare, mi affliggeva l'occhio destro. Fu così che venni a richiedere una

Alessandro Gentili
(2004)

(UCC – Cork poets)

STATIO BENE FIDA CARINIS

Once you've decided to go to Tipperary
you'll realise you no longer belong to yourself

Desmond O'Grady

MY ARRIVAL in Cork in late September 1981, was a true landing of my boat on an island, one of the many of the European archipelago, a change from my firm ground in Tuscany. I had come to confront the 'other' from myself. And besides, I had come to transmit the self of my relationship with my language and culture to the other, to another language and civilisation. I was in Cork to give. But giving, in itself, is to receive.

I found lodgings in a guest house: Redclyffe House on the Western Road. A guest house or 'pensione', whatever you like to call it, might seem an anonymous, impersonal abode. An occasional room. But a room for many occasions: a port or station for continual arrivals and departures, a theatre of various people and faces, a room of mobile imagination. Mrs O'Brien, the owner of the Redclyffe, a Limerick woman, had exquisite hospitality skills and a sense of humour. The other permanent guest was an elderly Scotsman, 'Mr Mac', who worked in the glass blowing centre in the Science Building in UCC I still have a glass bell which he made and gave as a present to me. 'A very bitter man', Mr Mac dreamed of sunny islands in the Mediterranean. Every year he spent a few weeks in Malta, or Cyprus or in the Canaries. He found it hard to understand how I, who came from a Mediterranean country, had ended up in this filthy Irish weather. Once I tried to propose the notion of European integration but Mr Mac was having none of it. [...]

In those days, an annoying eye infection contracted during military service was troubling my right eye. I therefore booked in for a visit to the

visita medica nel reparto di oculistica dell'Eye, Ear and Throat Hospital sulla Western Road. I mattoni rossi di quel vecchio edificio e i legni scuri dei suoi interni piuttosto cupi mi affascinavano, e intimorivano. E l'occhio destro cominciava a far davvero male. Venni visitato da un cortese gentiluomo di oculista. Alto, slanciato, affilati i lineamenti del volto e il naso. Mi colpirono i suoi occhi, luminosi, e il suo sguardo, intenso e intelligente. La luce di quegli occhi nella cupezza di quell'ospedale, nel reparto di oculistica in specie, rassicurava e incoraggiava, da sé riusciva positiva allegoria, quasi dantesca, del dal buio alla luce. L'iniezione di cortisone nell'occhio destro a malapena la avvertii. Il tocco di quella mano e di quelle dita, lunghe e anch'esse affilate, era leggero e morbido. L'oculista era Denis Wilson. Il padre dell'attrice Fiona Shaw. Dopo la visita e l'iniezione, parlammo, Denis ed io. Dell'Italia, naturalmente. Denis lo avrei dopo rivisto molte volte, alle conferenze e alle festicciole della Dante Alighieri Society di Cork. Infatti, erano diversi i medici che frequentavano la Dante. Lì li accomunava la loro passione per l'Italia. Ricordo bene Dick Barry, pediatra, che durante la seconda guerra mondiale si era fatto Cassino, dove aveva assistito una partoriente italiana. Ricordo bene anche Donald Buckley, dermatologo, e naturalmente Eoin Callaghan, neurologo, e Ted Buckley, neurochirurgo, mariti rispettivamente delle mie colleghe Anne e Maeve. Devo dire che il frequentare tutti questi medici in momenti di allegra convivialità mi aiutò a superare una certa avversione che verso i medici avevo fino ad allora provato. Questi di Cork, così alla mano, mi parevano tanto diversi, per certo in meglio, da molti medici italiani, irraggiungibili, in specie in quegli anni, perfino da se stessi, distanti e perduti nella loro ragnatela di potere, potere di vita e di morte.

E la città di Cork? Città di colline, ponti, chiese e campanili. Venivo piano piano a camminarla, questa nuova isola. Il centro della città esso stesso un'isola circondata dalle acque del North River e del South River. Il sabato 'Pana', St Patrick's Street, il Canal Grande di Cork, brulicava di gente. Alta, il pomeriggio, si levava la voce di Geronimo, lo strillone: '*Evening Echoooo!*' Una bramosia di acquisti sembrava possedere quelle folle. Anche quella irlandese si rivelava un società di consumi. Di negozi. Di prodotti. Di automobili. Intenso il traffico nel centro. Cork dava a eye

specialist in the Eye, Ear and Throat Hospital on the Western Road. The red bricks of that old building and the dark, somewhat gloomy interior woods both fascinated and intimidated me. And my right eye began to really hurt. I was seen by a gracious gentleman of an oculist: tall, slim with thin features on his face and nose. His bright eyes struck me and his intense and intelligent look. In the gloom of that hospital, especially in the eye section, the light in those eyes reassured and encouraged, causing positive almost 'dantesque' happiness, of moving from darkness to light. I barely felt the injection of cortisone into my right eye. The touch from that hand, from those long and slim fingers, was light and soft. The oculist was Denis Wilson, the father of the actress Fiona Shaw. After the visit and the injection, Denis and I talked. About Italy, naturally. I would later see a lot more of Denis at the meetings and parties of the Cork Dante Alighieri Society. In fact, a variety of doctors attended the 'Dante' where they were united in their passion for Italy. I remember well Dick Barry, a pediatrician who had experienced Cassino during the war and had helped an Italian woman give birth. I also remember Donald Buckley, dermatologist and naturally Noel Callaghan, neurologist and Ted Buckley, surgeon, husbands respectively of my colleagues Ann and Maeve. I have to say that meeting all of these doctors in happy, convivial situations helped me overcome a certain aversion I had felt towards doctors until then. These affable doctors from Cork seemed so different, in a good sense, to many Italian doctors who, especially in those years, were unreachable, cut off even from themselves, distant and lost in their web of power, power over life and death.

And what about Cork city? A city of hills, bridges, churches and bells. I slowly walked this new 'island'. The centre of the city was itself an island surrounded by the waters of the North River and the South River. On Saturdays, 'Pana', St Patrick's Street, the Grand Canal of Cork, was heaving with people. In the afternoon, the pitched voice of Geronimo would raise the cry of '*Evening Echoooo!*' A shopping mania seemed to possess the crowds. Even Irish society was demonstrably consumerist. Shops, products, cars. Congested traffic in the centre. Cork

vedere che la *téchne* stava definitivamente conquistando anche la cattolica Irlanda e quel che era rimasto dell'Irlanda di Yeats. Il processo di secolarizzazione stava ormai giungendo a compimento. Spinto anche dalle relazioni speciali con gli Stati Uniti d'America e dalla lingua inglese, il nuovo latino del nuovo impero. La vittoria del no al referendum sul divorzio nel 1986 sarebbe stata solo una vittoria di Pirro. Certo che la disoccupazione in quei primi anni ottanta era ancora alta in Irlanda. La crisi economica si faceva sentire. Ricordo la crisi alla Ford, a Cork. Però, a ripensarci ora, il paese si avviava allora a passare da un passato e una tradizione di civiltà rurale a un futuro prossimo che diremmo di tecnologia avanzata e servizi, saltando quella fase di industrializzazione che aveva caratterizzato la storia di altri paesi europei. Le folle del sabato in St Patrick's Street erano peraltro anche folte di bambini e giovani. Nuova energia. Nuove generazioni. A differenza dell'Italia che già in quegli anni stava diventando un paese di vecchi. Fra le cinque e le sei del pomeriggio *Pana* si svuotava. Correvano tutti al loro tea. Per ritrovarsi la sera accalcati nei *pub*, in quelle celle, accaldate coinvolgenti, di legni scuri, vetri, acre odore di birra, di fumo (ora non più) e altro. Non vi erano distinzioni di classi sociali nella generale partecipazione a questo rito, quasi pagano, del bere, a questo raggiungimento di puri stati bacchici. Anch'io vi partecipavo, vi indulgevo. In certe serate di pioggia, vento o nebbia, il rito si spiegava da solo. Al *pub* ti sentivi al sicuro, protetto, al caldo di una buona compagnia. Un *fond embrace*, che forse neppure lo stesso Fr. Matthew, *The Apostle of Temperance*, avrebbe disdegnato.

Di Italiani, residenti a Cork in quei primi anni ottanta, a parte Piero Calì e due o tre dirigenti della Ferrero, non ve ne erano molti. Di quelli che vi erano i più gestivano locali del tipo *Fish & Chips* o *Take Away*. In Washington Street vi era un ristorante italiano che frequentavo spesso. Il proprietario, Tony, persona di squisita generosità, era originario di Mazara del Vallo, in Sicilia. Tante sere, o meglio tante notti, dopo che gli ultimi avventori avevano lasciato il ristorante, Tony ed io restavamo a fare quattro chiacchiere davanti a un buon bicchiere di vino. O davanti a un piatto di pesce dell'Atlantico cucinato secondo una buona ricetta siciliana. [...]

Appena arrivato a Cork mi misi a leggere Frank O'Connor. Anche Daniel Corkery. Era una lettura quasi doverosa. Ma della poesia irlandese

showed that technology was irretrievably conquering both Catholic Ireland and that which was left of Yeats' Ireland. The secularisation process was by now nearing completion, propelled in part by the special relationship with the United States and with the English language, the new Latin of the new Empire. The victory of the no vote in the divorce referendum in 1986 was to be a mere Pyrrhic victory. Unemployment in those early 1980s was, without doubt still high in Ireland. The economic crisis made its presence known. I remember the Ford crisis in Cork. However, looking back, the country was already moving from a past and a tradition of rural life to a near future of advanced technology and services, skipping the industrial phase which had characterised the history of other European countries. The Saturday crowds on St Patrick's Street were full of children and youngsters. New energy, new generations. A contrast to Italy which in those years was already becoming an elderly nation. Between five and six in the afternoon Pana emptied. They all ran home to their tea before regrouping in the evenings in the pubs, in those warm, inviting cells of dark woods and glasses, bitters smells of beer and smoke (now a thing of the past) and more. There were no class distinctions in the general participation in this almost pagan rite of drinking, in this pure bacchanal gathering. I too participated and indulged. On certain wet, windy or foggy evenings, the rite was self-explanatory. You felt secure, protected in the warmth of good company in the pub. A fond embrace which maybe not even Fr Mathew, the Apostle of Temperance would have scorned.

In those early 1980s, apart from Piero Calì and two or three directors of Ferrero, there were not many Italians living in Cork. Most of those living there ran fish and chip shops or takeaways. I regularly went to an Italian restaurant in Washington Street. Tony, the owner and a man of exceptional generosity, was originally from Mazara del Vallo in Sicily. Many evenings, or rather, many nights when the last customers had left the restaurant, Tony and I would stay on for a chat over a glass of good wine or over an Atlantic fish dish cooked to a good Sicilian recipe. [...]

As soon as I got to Cork, I set about reading Frank O'Connor and Daniel Corkery. It was an almost dutiful task. However, I knew little,

moderna, del dopo-Yeats per intenderci, sapevo poco, quasi niente. E dire che già allora la poesia risiedeva al centro dei miei studi accademici, dei miei interessi. Nella *coffee room* di UCC, mi pare nell'ottobre del 1981, venni a fare la conoscenza di Seán Lucy, *Professor of Modern English*. Rimasi subito affascinato dalla finezza delle sue maniere, dall'eleganza del suo Inglese caratterizzato da un leggero naturale accento britannico. Pochi giorni dopo Seán mi fece dono della sua raccolta *Unfinished Sequence and Other Poems*. Su quei testi poetici avviai subito un'opera di traduzione dall'Inglese in Italiano. La traduzione! Questo demone che ancora mi possiede. Questo atto di disperazione e di follia nel tentativo, appunto disperato, di reduplicatio di quanto non è reduplicabile. Però un traghettamento, il tradurre, porta e ponte fra due isole. Passavamo molte ore insieme, Seán ed io, a verificare l'accuratezza linguistica delle mie versioni, i loro suoni. La mia copia di *Unfinished Sequence* serba ancora su alcuni testi i segni a matita vergati dalla mano di Seán che leggeva i suoi versi e ne scandiva la metrica. In quei giorni egli stava lavorando ad una nuova raccolta: *Other Business*. Quel dattiloscritto ce l'ho ancora. Grazie allo stimolo e ai suggerimenti di Seán iniziai a leggere Austin Clarke, Patrick Kavanagh, Tom Kinsella, Seamus Heaney, John Montague. Venni così a scoprire la poesia più vera, nella lingua inglese, di quegli ultimi decenni del Novecento.

Fu proprio nell'ufficio di Seán che conobbi *The* Montague, come Seán stesso diceva. Gli occhi strinti, grin disarmante, quello straordinario senso dell'umorismo, dell'ironia, le palme delle mani all'insù, quello *stammer*, che qualcuno, credo Derek Mahon, ha definito *mythical*: questi i tratti e i gesti che di John subito notai. Divenimmo presto amici, the Montague ed io. E questa amicizia dura ancora, salda. Conobbi Evelyn. Frequentavo la casa di John ed Evelyn a Grattan Hill. Quegli splendidi volumi della Dolmen Press. Gli splendidi lavori di patchwork di Evelyn. Una e Sibylle erano deliziose. John era fonte inesauribile di aneddoti, racconti, commenti, su autori, sulla poesia, la letteratura in genere, sulla musica e sull'arte. Ultimate che ebbi le mie versioni da *Unfinished Sequence*, iniziai alcuni tentativi di traduzione da *The Rough Field* di John. Seán Lucy era ancora lì ad incoraggiarmi. Un pomeriggio, a un tavolo del mitico Long Valley Bar, su una copia di *The Rough Field* John

almost nothing about modern Irish poetry, post Yeats, I mean. And to think that even then poetry was at the centre of my academic studies, and my interests. In the coffee room of UCC in October 1981, I think, I first got to know Seán Lucy, Professor of Modern English. I was immediately struck by the refinement of his manners and the elegance of his English which was characterised by a slight, natural, British accent. A few days later, Seán gave me a present of his collection, *Unfinished Sequence and Other Poems.* I immediately started to translate these poems from English into Italian. Translating! That demon which still possesses me. This act of desperation and madness in the desperate attempt to duplicate that which cannot be duplicated. It is, however, a ferry journey, this translating, a door and a bridge between two islands. Seán and I spent many hours together, checking the linguistic accuracy of my versions and their sounds. My copy of *Unfinished Sequence* still has the pencil marks on some of the texts written by Seán who read the texts and marked out the metre. In those days, he was working on a new collection: *Other Business.* I still have that manuscript. Thanks to Seán's encouragement and suggestions I started to read Austin Clarke, Patrick Kavanagh, Tom Kinsella, Seamus Heaney, John Montague. In this way, I discovered the most genuine poetry in English of the final decades of the twentieth century.

It was actually in Seán's office that I met 'The Montague' as Seán himself used to say. The piercing eyes, the disarming grin, the extraordinary sense of humour, of irony, the upheld palms of his hands, that stammer which someone, I think Derek Mahon, defined as mythical; these are the traits and the gestures belonging to John which struck me immediately. The Montague and I soon became friends. A continuing, sturdy friendship. I met Evelyn. I used to go to John and Evelyn's house on Grattan Hill. Those splendid volumes from the Dolmen Press. The splendid patchwork creations by Evelyn. Una and Sibylle were wonderful. John was an inexhaustible source of anecdotes, stories, comments on authors, poetry, literature in general and on music and art. When I had finished my translations from *Unfinished Sequence,* I attempted some translations from John's *The Rough Field.* Seán Lucy was still there encouraging me. One afternoon, at a table in the mythical Long Valley

scrisse questa dedica: 'For Alessandro, from his friend, Giovanni Montecchi, marvelling at his courage in translating this monster'. E di coraggio, a tradurre *The Rough Field*, ce ne voleva tanto. Coraggio, o forse meglio incoscienza. In quei primi anni ottanta *the* Montague stava anche lavorando a *The Lost Notebook*, la *nouvelle* o *novella* ambientata a Firenze. Così capitava spesso che le conversazioni fra John e me, a Cork, volgessero verso Firenze, i suoi musei, le strade, le trattorie, i casamenti. Alla fine di giugno del 1986 John sarebbe rimasto una settimana da noi, a Firenze, dove partecipammo al Nono Congresso Mondiale dei Poeti nell'occasione di Firenze Capitale Europea della Cultura. John aveva con sé il *Notebook* nella sua versione pressoché finale e tanta voglia di rivedere e riscontrare Firenze.

Attraverso Montague venni a frequentare *the* Triskel Arts Centre. Conobbi Tom McCarthy, del quale ammiravo *The Sorrow Garden*. Frequentavo anche il Cafe Lorca in Washington Street. Lì a volte leggeva le sue poesie Ciaran O'Driscoll. Ciaran lo rividi alcuni anni fa a Perugia, insieme con Seán Dunne, a un convegno sulla letteratura irlandese. Parlammo di Cork nei primi anni ottanta, e sulla copia della sua raccolta *Listening to Different Drummers* Ciaran scrisse: 'To Alessandro, in memory of nights at the Café Lorca'. Attraverso Montague conobbi Desmond O'Grady, a Kinsale, allo Spaniard. Da lassù, da quella collina, in una giornata luminosa, l'Atlantico ricorda il Mediterraneo. Desmond, Desmondo, come Montague ed io lo chiamiamo, e la sua opera poetica: personificazione e modello letterario in uno della filosofia dell'arcipelago come *sight of others*, dell'esplorazione, del viaggio come ritorno a sé, alla verità in interiore. Quel che io a Cork andavo allora cercando, Desmond lo aveva già estesamente cercato, in Europa, in Medio Oriente, in America. Allo Spaniard erano lunghe conversazioni, su paesi lontani, sulla poesia italiana e sui maestri italiani del Novecento, sul senso della disciplina della traduzione che Desmond aveva appreso da Pound. I miei rapporti di amicizia con Desmond sono ancora stretti, e frequentemente ci scambiamo prove di traduzioni poetiche dall'Italiano in Inglese e dall'Inglese in Italiano.

Nell'anno accademico 1983-84, a UCC, la classe di Italiano di terzo anno era particolarmente brillante, e simpatica. [...] Faceva parte di quella classe di terzo anno una ragazza tedesca, Christine, allora studentessa

Bar John wrote the following dedication on a copy of *The Rough Field*: 'For Alessandro, from his friend, Giovanni Montecchi, marvelling at his courage in translating this monster!' And certainly, much courage was needed to translate *The Rough Field*. Courage or maybe ignorance. In those early 1980s, *The* Montague was also working on *The Lost Notebook*, his novella set in Florence. It was thus common that our Cork conversations would often turn to Florence, its museums, the streets, the 'trattorie', the buildings. At the end of June 1986, John stayed with us for a week and we participated in the Ninth World Congress of Poets during Florence's year as the European City of Culture. John had his almost complete version of the *Notebook* with him and a great desire to revisit and encounter Florence.

Through Montague I started to frequent the Triskel Arts Centre. I met Tom McCarthy, whose *The Sorrow Garden* I admired. I also frequented Café Lorca in Washington Street. Ciaran O'Driscoll sometimes read his poetry there. I met Ciaran again some years ago in Perugia with Seán Dunne at a conference on Irish literature. We spoke of Cork in the early 1980s and on a copy of his collection *Listening to Different Drummers,* Ciaran wrote: '*To Alessandro, in memory of nights at the Cafe Lorca.*' Through Montague I also met Desmond O'Grady in Kinsale at the Spaniard. From up there, from that hill, on a bright day, the Atlantic reminds of the Mediterranean. Desmond, Desmondo (as Montague and I call him), and his poetic work: both the personification and literary model of the philosophy of the archipelago as sight of others, of exploration, of the voyage as a return to the self, to the interior truth. That which I searched for in Cork, Desmond had extensively searched for in Europe, in the Far East, in America. At the Spaniard, we had long conversations about distant lands, Italian poetry, the Italian greats of the twentieth century, and the sense of the discipline of translation which Desmond had learnt from Pound. My friendship with Desmond is still strong and we frequently exchange drafts of poetic translations from Italian into English and from English into Italian.

In the academic year 1983-84, the third year Italian class was particularly brilliant and friendly. [...] There was a German girl in that third year class, Christine, a student at the time in the *Übersetzer- und*

presso la *Übersetzer- und Dolmetscherschule*, scuola per interpreti e traduttori, di Zurigo, e per il primo e il secondo trimestre dell'anno accademico 1983-84 a UCC. [...] Conosceva bene, lei, l'Irlanda, e la amava. L'Irlanda rurale, forse quella più vera. I suoi genitori già dai primi anni settanta avevano una casa a Castlecove, nella contea di Kerry. Iniziammo a uscire insieme, Christine ed io. Memorabile quell'autunno del 1983. Il dono di questo amore nella città di Cork. La sera si andava per *pub*, spesso al *HIB* in *Oliver Plunkett Street*, al *Cork International Film Festival*, al *Guinness Jazz Festival*. Montague, incuriosito, mi chiedeva spesso degli sviluppi di questo *romance*, il suo *grin* un sorriso di compiacimento. Già a novembre Christine non frequentava più le mie lezioni di traduzione. Per evitare imbarazzi. Insieme prendemmo poi in affitto una vecchia casa, *Coronella*, in *Glasheen Road*. Al momento del contratto la proprietaria, una signora di Cork che per molti anni aveva fatto l'infermiera a Londra, ci chiese se eravamo sposati. Diplomaticamente risposi che eravamo *una coppia*. La signora sorrise, e firmammo il contratto. Quanto a sposarci, ci saremmo poi sposati nell'agosto del 1985. Nel settembre di quello stesso anno ci trasferimmo a Firenze.

Questo, in breve, il resoconto dei miei anni a Cork. La 'perdita' del mio mondo e la vista-conoscenza di un *altro*. Il frutto, *natîja* in arabo, così direbbe Desmondo, del viaggio. Il farsi straniero per meglio comprenderlo, e in qualche modo riaverlo, il proprio mondo. Ogni estate, prima di raggiungere Castlecove, Christine ed io ci fermiamo sempre qualche giorno a Cork. Un ritorno, quasi un pellegrinaggio, alla sorgente. Al nostro *inizio*.

Dolmetscherschule, a school for interpreters and translators in Zurich, who was in UCC for the first and second terms of 1983-84. [...] She knew Ireland well and loved rural Ireland, maybe the truer part. From the early 1970s her parents had a house in Castlecove in County Kerry. We started going out, Christine and I. A memorable autumn in 1983. The gift of this love in the city of Cork. In the evening we would go to the pubs, often to the Hi B in Oliver Plunkett Street, or to the Cork International Film Festival, or to the Guinness Jazz Festival. Montague, curious, would often ask me about the developments in this romance, his grin one of contentment. Already by November, Christine had stopped attending my translation lectures, in order to avoid embarrassment. We rented an old house together, Coronella on the Glasheen Road. When signing the contract, the owner, a Cork woman who had worked for many years as a nurse in London, asked us if we were married. I diplomatically replied that we were a couple. She smiled and we signed the contract. As for getting married, we tied the knot in August 1985. In September of that year we moved to Florence.

In brief that is the story of my years in Cork. The 'loss' of my world and the viewing and knowledge of another. The fruit, *natîja* in Arabic, as Desmondo would say of the journey. To become a stranger in order to know oneself better and in a manner, to regain one's world. Every year, before going to Castlecove, Christine and I stay for a few days in Cork. A return, almost a pilgrimage, to the source. To our start.

English translation by Anne O'Connor.

Thomas Kabdebo
(2004)

(Hungarian poem written for this volume)

CORK

1972 augusztus 15-én
Az Oranje Nassau óceánjártam én
Az Azori Szigetek mentén akkora vihar támadt
Hogy a luxushajó a mozgásba belefáradt.

Ingott, reszketett s rajta minden turista
Söt, a kapitány, a pursar, János és Pista
Végigrókázta a 20.000 tonnás fedélzetét
Elengedtem volna az utazás eme élvezetét.

Amikor, ahogy jött, megállt az orkán
S a távirdász rámkiáltott, ahogy kifért a torkán:
'Uram, számára rádióüzenet érkezett'
S egy papírszelettel nyújtott nekem jobbkezet.

A Corki Egyetem registrárja üzente:
A könyvtárigazgatói állás nincs még betöltve
'Interjúra várjuk, e hó, augusztus 16-án
Pontosan négy óra harminckor délután.'

Hipp hopp, ahol akar az ember, ott terem
Én tán Corkban, ha lett volna helikopterem.
S habár a könyvtár úgy Corkban fontos dolog
Most az Atlanti Óceán közepén rostokolok.

Thomas Kabdebo
(2004)

(A poem)

CORK

On August 15th 1972
I was crossing the ocean on Oranje Nassau
Then a tempest broke out by the Azores.
So huge, that the liner stopped moving.

It pitched and shook and with it the travellers
Moreover, the captain, the pursar, and Tom-Dick-and Harry
They all covered the deck with their vomit
I hardly think we were on a pleasure cruise.

Then, as it came, the tempest has stopped
The telegrapher shouted at me:
'Sir, you have a radiotelegram'
And handed a piece of paper with his right hand.

The registrar of Cork University sent a message
'The directorship of the library is still open
We are asking you for an interview
At 4.30 pm on August 16th.'

One can be wherever one wants to be
Had I a chopper I could have reached Cork
Where the library is of great importance
But as for now, I am stuck on the Ocean.

English translation by Barbara Simon.

Juan Casas Rigall
(2004)

(Spanish text written for this volume)

Rory Gallagher visto desde España

EN EL *Irish Examiner* del 10 de junio de 2004, Dan MacCarthy escribe sobre el noveno aniversario de la muerte de Rory Gallagher. El artículo discurre como entrevista a un buen conocedor de la música de Rory, Marcus Connaughton, quien al comienzo de la conversación afirma: 'It would be interesting to put a figure on the numbers of people who will come to Cork purely to follow in Rory Gallagher's footsteps'.

Pues bien, yo soy una de esas personas. Viajo a menudo a Irlanda por afinidad familiar – aunque vivimos en España, mi mujer es natural de Rathcoole, Co. Cork. Todos los años, Cork es visita obligada; y, durante cada estancia en la ciudad, caminar por los rincones que Rory frecuentó es siempre un placer melancólico.

El recorrido comienza en la parte alta de Cork, en MacCurtain Street. A la altura del número 29, una placa nos recuerda: 'Rory Gallagher (1948-1995), musician and composer. He lived on this street'. La dedicatoria está enmarcada por dos imágenes: un busto de Rory y una Fender Stratocaster, la más emblemática de sus guitarras. No es casualidad: la placa se halla junto al Crowley's Music Center, la tienda de instrumentos musicales en donde, en el año 1963, Rory compró una Stratocaster de segunda mano, la misma guitarra con que tocaría durante toda su vida. La memoria de Rory, cómo no, pervive en Crowley's, en donde, además de recordarlo con algunas viejas fotos, nos informarán amablemente sobre su casa familiar, apenas a unos números de allí: se nota de inmediato que están acostumbrados a atender preguntas sobre él. Pero, en MacCurtain Street, las huellas de Rory afloran a cada paso, como en el pub The Corner House, de paredes cubiertas por imágenes de músicos y un rincón dedicado a Rory, con la portada de algún LP y fotografías de actuaciones en directo, una de ellas con Phil Lynott.

En el centro de Cork, una bonita plaza lleva el nombre de Rory Gallagher,

Juan Casas Rigall
(2004)

(A Cork musical hero)

RORY GALLAGHER THROUGH SPANISH EYES

IN THE *Irish Examiner* on July 10th 2004, Dan MacCarthy writes about the ninth anniversary of Rory Gallagher's death. The article was based on an interview with a connoisseur of Rory's music, Marcus Connaughton, who at the beginning of the conversation affirms: 'It would be interesting to put a figure on the numbers of people who will come to Cork, purely to follow in Rory Gallagher's footsteps.'

And, well, I'm one of those people. I often travel to Ireland because of family connections – although we live in Spain, my wife is a native of Rathcoole, Co. Cork. Every year, visiting Cork is a must; and during every stay in the city, walking through the nooks and crannies which Rory frequented, is always a melancholic pleasure.

The tour begins in the high part of Cork, in MacCurtain Street. At number 29, there is a plaque that reminds us: 'Rory Gallagher (1948-1995), musician and composer. He lived on this street'. The remembrance plaque is surrounded by two images: a bust of Rory and a Fender Stratocaster, the most emblematic of his guitars. It is no accident that the plaque finds itself next to Crowley's Music Centre, the musical instruments shop, in which in 1963 Rory bought a second-hand Stratocaster, the same guitar he would go on to play all his life. The memory of Rory is alive and well in Crowley's, where apart from remembering him with some old photographs, they will happily tell you about his family house, just some metres down the road; it's immediately evident that they're used to answering questions about Rory. But, on MacCurtain Street, the footprints of Rory flower with every step. In 'The Corner House' pub, the walls are covered with images of musicians and a corner is dedicated to Rory. There are also some covers of LPs and photographs of live sessions, one of them with Phil Lynott.

In the centre of Cork, a beautiful square is named after Rory Gallagher

con una escultura de bronce dedicada a su memoria. Si no justamente la librería de viejo de esa misma plaza, seguro que el propio Rory frecuentó otras de las muchas librerías de Cork en busca de novelas de Dashiell Hammett, el escritor americano a quien dedicaría la canción 'Continental Op'.

Rory está enterrado en las afueras de Cork, en el cementerio de St. Oliver de Ballincollig. En su tumba, la sencilla inscripción contiene únicamente su nombre; en la cabecera está representado el sol en su ocaso, pero, si se contempla con atención, uno de los rayos se convierte en el diapasón de una guitarra. Y siempre hay algo más, que hace difícil contener la emoción: deben de contarse por cientos las personas que, al cabo del año, tributan a Rory un sencillo homenaje al depositar en su túmulo una púa, un bottleneck, una cuerda de guitarra ...

La influencia de la música de Rory Gallagher ha sido fundamental en España, en donde, entre quienes nacimos durante la dictadura de Franco y conocimos la democracia siendo adolescentes, es considerado como el músico irlandés por excelencia, por encima incluso de Van Morrison. El rock y, sobre todo, el blues y el jazz, fuera de las grandes ciudades, eran géneros inhabituales hasta en las emisoras de radio ¡en la de mi pueblo, no había ni un solo disco ... de los Beatles¡ Muerto el dictador, desde 1975 el panorama musical experimentó un notable desarrollo. No era necesario viajar a una capital para conseguir discos de los Animals, Muddy Waters o Charlie Parker. Y, en los expositores de las nuevas tiendas musicales, nos llamaba poderosamente la atención un joven de pelo largo y patillas afiladas, vestido con vaqueros y camisa de cuadros, y una guitarra que, con cada nueva grabación, tenía los barnices más y más rayados. Se llamaba Rory Gallagher y, después de lanzar excelentes discos con el grupo Taste, firmaba ya en solitario. Pero, más allá de su imagen, escuchar su música fue todo un descubrimiento: su voz sincera y enérgica, la guitarra punzante y la armónica llorona, el sencillo formato de trío o cuarteto desgranando blues-rock con elementos jazzísticos y de música tradicional. Rory amalgamaba lo mejor de los bluesmen del Mississippi y el zydeco de Clifton Chenier con el rock de Chuck Berry, el skiffle de Lonnie Donegan y la hondura de John Coltrane. Una enciclopedia musical compendiada en un estilo único, justamente lo que

with a bronze sculpture dedicated to his memory. Rory would have frequented antique bookshops in Cork, like the one found in this square (if not this very one!), searching for novels by Dashiell Hammet, a US writer to whom he dedicated the song 'Continental Op'.

Rory is buried on the outskirts of Cork, in St Oliver's cemetery in Ballincollig. On his tomb, the simple inscription only mentions his name. On the headstone the setting sun is represented, but if you look closely, you will notice that the rays of the sun turn into the tuning fork of a guitar. And there's something more, which makes it hard to not get excited about: hundreds of people, every year, pay tribute to Rory with a simple homage by placing a pick, a bottleneck, a guitar string, etc. on his grave.

Rory Gallagher's music has been a fundamental influence in Spain. Those of us who were born during Franco's dictatorship and got to know democracy as adolescents know Rory to be the Irish musician who was second to none, even above Van Morrison. Rock, and above all, blues and jazz, were rarely heard even on radio stations, outside of the big cities – in my town, there was only one record ... from The Beatles! Since the death of the dictator, the musical panorama experienced a notable development. It was no longer necessary to travel to a large city to get records like The Animals, Muddy Waters or Charlie Parker. In the posters of the new music shops a young man with long hair and his trademark sideburns dressed in jeans and a checked shirt along with his guitar caught our eye – with each new recording its scratch plate was more and more worn. His name was Rory Gallagher, and after launching excellent records with his band Taste, he was now recording solo. But beyond his image, to listen to his music was a powerful discovery: his voice was sincere and energetic; his guitar was pounding, his harmonica wailing. In the simple form of trio or quartet, he mixed blues-rock with jazz and traditional music elements. Rory brought together the best of the Mississippi bluesmen, Clifton Chenier's Zydeco with Chuck Berry's Rock, Lonnie Donegan's Skiffle and the depths of John Coltrane. A summarised musical encyclopaedia in a unique style, which was exactly what we needed in

necesitábamos en España en aquellos tiempos. Después, al profundizar en la vida del músico, encontramos nuevas y agradables sorpresas: Rory era la antítesis de la rock star, alejado de extravagancias publicitarias, un tipo sencillo sin máscaras, como su música.

Rory fue, sin duda, uno de los intérpretes más importantes en la evolución musical de los españoles de mi generación. Suele ocurrir que, con el paso de los años, nuestros viejos ídolos van cayendo en el olvido, reemplazados por otros gustos. En mi estima por Rory, sólo han cambiado dos cosas: la primera es que hoy pocas veces lo escucho en discos de vinilo, sino en nuevos formatos digitales, aunque de vez en cuando desempolvo antiguos LPs; la segunda es que sus temas, desde 'Sinner Boy' y 'Used to Be' (1971) a 'I Ain't no Saint' (1987) o 'The Loop' (1990), me parecen cada vez mejores. Y, aunque no sea de Cork, después de escuchar a Rory durante tantos años, cuando visito su ciudad, ¿cómo no cantar a voz en grito: 'I'm going to my hometown; sorry, baby, but I can't take you!'?

Spain in those times. Afterwards, when indulging deeper in the life of this musician, we discovered new and nice surprises: Rory was the antithesis of the rock star, far removed from limelight extravagances. He was a simple guy without personas, just like his music.

Rory was, without a doubt, one of the most important musical interpreters in the musical evolution of the Spanish of my generation. As the years pass, our old idols are left by the wayside and forgotten, replaced by other genres. In my admiration for Rory, only two things have changed: firstly, nowadays I hardly ever listen to him on vinyl, but usually on more modern digital forms, although every now and then, I dust down my old LPs; secondly, his songs, from 'Sinner Boy' and 'Used to Be' (1971) to 'I Ain't no Saint' (1987) or 'The Loop' (1990), sound better and better to my ears. I may not be from Cork, but after listening to Rory through the years, when I visit his town, how can I not want to sing out loud 'I'm going to my hometown; sorry, baby, but I can't take you!'?

English translation by Nancy Serrano, jnr.

Vlad Mureşan
(2004)

Romanian text written for this volume.

CORK – UN PRIM CONTACT

CORK. ORAŞ simbol al însoritului sud irlandez. Plouă când ajung acolo întâia oară. Prima vizită, primele impresii. Cer câteva informaţii asupra locaţiei unei clădiri. Mi le dă un bărbat în vârstă ce turuie de zor o limbă uşor cântată ce aduce pe ici, pe colo cu engleza. Nu înţeleg mare lucru dar mulţumesc politicos şi-mi încerc norocul cu un alt trecător. Nu pricep nimic nici de data aceasta dar începe să îmi mai treacă spaima: nu e engleza mea de vină. E doar celebrul accent de Cork. Multe sunete guturale, frazare incredibil de rapidă, cuvinte delimitate printr-o intonaţie cântată şi nu prin pauze, suficiente elemente pentru a cere prezenţa unui translator. (Prieteni din Dublin mă preveniseră de altfel că voi avea nevoie de unul.) Renunţ la a mai avea o ţintă precisă şi hoinăresc la întâmplare pe străzile umede. E ora prânzului şi, în pofida ploii subţiri, pietoni numeroşi se înghesuie pe trotuarele din faţa fast-food-urilor. O clădire înaltă, vopsită în albastru, cu ornamentaţii albe polarizează atenţia furnicarului uman. Pe faţada ei de o arhitectură elegantă şi conservatoare tronează culorile McDonald's, un veritabil Mecca al înfometaţilor pelerini din jurul meu. Un indicator îmi spune în irlandeză şi în engleză că sunt în St. Patrick's Street. Urmez traiectoria ei şerpuindă. Magazine se înşiră de-o parte şi de alta. Predomină cele mici, multe din ele cu exteriorul vopsit în culori vii, ţipătoare, parcă extrase direct din coşurile cu flori suspendate deasupra vitrinelor. Din loc în loc, sedii AIB sau Bank of Ireland îşi semnalează discret prezenţa. Mă deplasez cu destul de multă greutate. Pe şoseaua îngustă lucrurile nu sunt deloc mai roz. Toate maşinile din lume par a-şi fi dat întâlnire pe St. Patrick's Street.

Încă o buclă a drumului. Uşor, peisajul comercial se schimbă. Nu şi cel arhitectural. Deşi mult mai mari, Brown Thomas, Dunnes Stores, Eason's şi Roches Stores sunt găzduite în clădiri ce încearcă să păstreze aparenţa arhitecturală de secol XVIII sau XIX. Încercare destul de reuşită. Nu vezi nicăieri modernitatea construcţiilor din oţel şi beton.

Vlad Muresan
(2004)

(Three literary pieces)

CORK – A FIRST CONTACT

CORK. A symbol city of the sunny Irish south. It is raining as I first get there. The first visit, the first impressions. I ask for some information about the location of a building. I get some help from an elderly man that chatters away in a sing-song lingo that is but vaguely reminiscent of English. Although I do not make much out of it, I thank him politely and I have a bash at it with another passer-by. I do not grasp much this time either, but at least my fear fades away: it's not my English that is amiss. It is just the famous Cork accent. Many guttural sounds, an incredibly fast phrasing, words that are severed not by pauses but by quaint intonation – enough to require the presence of a translator. (My friends from Dublin had warned me that I would need one.) I give up seeking a precise target and I wander aimlessly about the wet streets. It is lunch time and, despite the light shower, many passers-by throng the sidewalks in front of the fast-food joints. A tall building painted in blue and decked with white decorations captures the human swarm's attention. Its façade of elegant and conservative architecture sports the colours of McDonald's, the Mecca of the ravenous pilgrims around me. A street sign tells me in Irish and English that I am on St Patrick's Street. I follow its meandering route. Shops are strung out on both of its sides, most of them small and painted in gaudy colours that seem to have been drawn from the flower baskets hung above the shop windows. Here and there a bank – AIB or Bank of Ireland – makes its presence known discreetly. I elbow my way along the crowd, whose flow is funnelled by the narrow street. All the cars in the world seem to have met on St Patrick's Street.

One more meander of the road. Little by little the mercantile setting changes, while the architectural scenery remains unaltered. Despite being much bigger, Dunnes Stores, Brown Thomas, Easons and Roches Stores are still hosted by buildings that seek – successfully enough – to preserve the architectural outlook of the eighteenth or nineteenth century None of those modern steel-and-concrete buildings are to be seen here.

Blocuri masive, cioplite din piatră cenuşie sunt folosite mai peste tot.

Ajung la capătul străzii. Statuia unui bărbat aşezată pe un piedestal înalt marchează intersecţia pe care St. Patrick's Street o face cu şoseaua ce mărgineşte râul Lee. Ulterior aflu că înfăţişează un prelat pe nume Fra Theobald Matthew şi e atât de cunoscută încât localnicii o numesc pur şi simplu 'statuia'. Toată lumea ştie unde e, aşa încât constituie un punct de reper ideal.

Dincolo de intersecţie e St. Patrick's Bridge. Ploaia s-a oprit când păşesc pe el şi brusc apare soarele. O mulţime de case răsar din aerul limpezit de ploaie. Par mici şi sunt cocoţate peste tot pe dealurile ce pleacă imediat de lângă râu. Turle ascuţite de biserici franjurează linia orizontului. Cork e dintr-o dată un oraş mult mai mare. Îmi place.

REPUBLICA POPULARĂ CORK

Urbea corkoniană se mândreşte cu dubla calitate de oraş si republică. Această calitate nu e menţionată în nici unul din documentele oficiale ale guvernului irlandez (ignoranţa guvernului e de vină, fireşte), însă ea e perfect observată în atitudinea condescendentă a băştinaşilor faţă de 'restul lumii'. Evident că toţi ceilalţi irlandezi (în special cei din Dublin) şi-ar dori cetăţenie corkoniană însă sunt suficient de ghinionişti încât să nu realizeze ce le lipseşte.

Deşi Cork-ul reprezintă doar 1/8 din suprafaţa Dublin-ului, republica este pentru toţi cetăţenii ei cel puţin la fel de întinsă ca Atlantida. Cercetătorul studios care ar încerca să o plaseze undeva între braţele râului Lee, mare şi dealurile ce înconjoară estuarul, ar avea mari dureri de cap. Limitele geografice sunt dificil de stabilit deoarece, la fel ca Atlantida sau Camelot, o bună parte din republică există doar printre neuronii locuitorilor ei.

Limba oficială aduce vag cu engleza în special înainte de rarele momente când vorbitorii îşi încarcă plămânii cu oxigen. Corkonianul tipic cântă, nu vorbeşte, are întotdeauna dreptate, iar când nu are, se încăpăţânează să demonstreze contrariul. Tema favorită de conversaţie este propria-i persoană sau performanţele sportive ale echipei locale de fotbal irlandez.

Politica republicii este una strictă, de conservare şi promovare a valo-

Massive blocks cut of grey stone are used almost everywhere.

I reach the end of the street. The statue of a man set on a high pedestal marks the junction between St Patrick's Street and the road along the Lee river. I was to find later that it portrays a cleric named Fr Theobald Mathew and is so well known that the local people call it just 'the statue'. Everyone knows where it is, so it constitutes an ideal landmark.

Beyond the junction there is St Patrick's Bridge. The rain has stopped as I step on it, and the sun comes out unexpectedly. A host of houses emerge in the air cleansed by the rain. They seem tiny and appear to be perched everywhere on the hills that rise from the river banks. Pointed church steeples jag the horizon. All of a sudden Cork is a much bigger town. I like it.

PEOPLE'S REPUBLIC OF CORK

Cork boasts a double quality: it is a city and also a republic. This quality is not mentioned in any of the official documents of the Irish government (this omission is the fault of the government, of course), but it may be easily noticed in the patronising attitudes of the natives relative to 'the rest of the world'. It is obvious that all the other Irish people (and especially those from Dublin) subconsciously yearn for Corkonian citizenship, yet are unaware that they lack it.

Even though Cork barely amounts to one-eighth of the area of Dublin, to the eyes of its inhabitants the Republic is at least as vast as Atlantis. The learned scholar who might attempt to establish its precise location somewhere among the branches of the Lee, the sea and the hills surrounding the estuary would be in a terrible predicament. Its geographical limits are hard to establish as – just like Atlantis or Camelot – a large part of the Republic exists just within the neurons of its inhabitants.

Its official language is vaguely reminiscent of English, especially just before the rare moments when its speakers fill their lungs with oxygen. The typical Corkonian sings rather than speaks, he is always right and when he is not, he obstinately struggles to prove the contrary. The favourite topic of conversation is his own person or the athletic performance of the local Gaelic football team.

The policy of the Republic is a strict one, of conservation and promotion of its autochthonous values, which are actually the only ones existing in the world. As a result, topics like Sonia O'Sullivan, Roy Keane or Murphy's beer

rilor autohtone, de altfel singurele existente în lume. Ca atare, subiecte precum Sonia O'Sullivan, Roy Keane sau berea Murphy's trebuie abordate cu multă delicatețe și cu respectul cuvenit Sfântului Finbarr, patronul urbei. De asemenea, la capitolul valori naționale, pruncilor corkonieni li se spune încă din fașă ca republica adăpostește singurul port din lume pe care Titanic-ul l-a considrat demn de o scurtă escală înainte de nefericita-i întâlnire cu un iceberg.

Destul de bine dezvoltată economic, republica își datorează în mare parte bunăstarea cohortelor de turiști americani veniți să studieze retorica și oratoria după metoda faimoasei școli de la Blarney. Sărutarea unui bolovan din vârful castelului Blarney este rețeta corkoniană garantată pentru o carieră de succes în relații publice. Folosirea pietrelor pentru remedierea unor defecte de vorbire și de către antichitatea greacă ar putea duce la concluzia că republica lui Platon ar avea ecouri profunde în republica de pe țărmurile fluviului Lee. Nimic mai fals, vor protesta imediat corkonienii, indignați că unicitatea statului lor e pusă sub semnul îndoielii. De altfel, singura republică cu care Republica Populară Cork acceptă că ar fi avut ceva în comun este cea venețiană. Prin eliminarea însă a canalelor din South Mall Street, Grand Parade și St. Patrick's Street corkonienii au îndepărtat și pe acest neplăcut contestatar al singularității lor.

METODA PEȘTIȘORULUI CORKONIAN
Peștișorul corkonian este o specie ce trăiește exclusiv în apele râului Lee. Gurile rele susțin că ar fi fost creat artificial de către Oficiul pentru Promovarea Turismului din Cork. Adevăr sau ficțiune, nu există ghid turistic mai dedicat decât acest mic pește ce te așteaptă mișcând politicos din coadă la intrarea dinspre Ballincollig a orașului, la marginea pajiștei verzi din dreapta râului Lee.

Cu un plici discret, peștișorul își începe turul. Nu se grăbește. Îți dă timp să-ți cufunzi pașii în catifeaua de clorofilă ce îmbracă Lee field. Să scarpini cu unghia coaja copacilor umbroși de pe malul apei. Să topești sub pleoape imaginea malului opus inundat de vegetația luxuriantă tivind clădiri elegante. Un prag ce dă naștere unei microcascade pe Lee sparge soarele în mii de diamante. Peștișorul alunecă cu studiată indiferență

should be approached with the caution and respect owed to St Finbar, the patron of the city. Besides, still under the heading of National Legacy, the Corkonian infants are told from the earliest age that the Republic hosts the only harbour in the world that the *Titanic* deemed to be worthy of its brief stopover before rushing to its unfortunate encounter with an iceberg.

Fairly well developed economically, the Republic greatly owes its welfare to the hordes of American tourists coming to study the rhetoric and oratory according to the famous school of Blarney. The kiss of a rock on top of Blarney Castle is the guaranteed recipe for a successful career in PR. That the ancient Greeks also used pebbles to heal speech defects might imply that Plato's Republic has deep echoes in the Republic on the banks of the Lee. One couldn't be more wrong, would be the protest the Corkonians would utter in unison, outraged by this questioning of the uniqueness of their state. Actually, the only republic that the People's Republic of Cork accepts to have something in common with is the Venetian one. However, by getting rid of the canals in South Mall Street, Grand Parade and St Patrick's Street, the Corkonians have eliminated that last disagreeable contender of their singularity.

THE METHOD OF THE CORKONIAN FISH

The Corkonian fish is a species that lives exclusively in the waters of the Lee. The rumour goes that it was artificially engineered by the Office for the Promotion of Tourism in Cork. Whether this is a fact or fiction, there is no tour guide more dedicated than this tiny fish that awaits you, wagging his tail fin politely as you enter Cork from Ballincollig, by the green meadow on the right riverside of the Lee.

With a discreet splash the fish marks the start of our tour. He is in no hurry. He gives you some time to sink your feet into the chlorophyll velvet that covers the Lee fields: To grate with your fingernail the bark of the shady trees on the river bank; to let you dissolve under your eyelids the image of the opposite bank, flooded by lush vegetation pierced by elegant buildings. A weir across the river creates a small waterfall that shatters the sun into thousands of diamonds. The fish glides with studiedinsouciance past all these. By following him, you reach the wall that skirts the Kingsley Hotel. A short stop for a cup of coffee on the terrace at Poacher's Bar. Good for the tourist. Your guide – quite explicably – avoids these premises. Don't

printre ele. Urmărindu-l, ajungi la zidul care delimitează Kingsley Hotel. Mic popas pentru o cafea pe terasa de la Poacher's Bar. Pentru turist. Ghidul, perfect explicabil, evită localul. Nici o problemă. Îl vei regăsi plutind alene printre pilonii de la Thomas Davis Bridge, puțin în aval de locul unde râul se desparte în două brațe.

Din dreapta podului și paralelă cu brațul nordic, pleacă o alee firavă. Nu are un aspect îngrijit dar o urmezi impulsionat de plescăitul nerăbdător al călăuzei. Șapte, opt pași pe alee și te trezești în mijlocul unui tunel vegetal cu bolta din crengi și frunze ce filtrează pe pământ o lumină difuză. Trunchiuri de copaci înconjurate de ierburi înalte te separă treptat de zgomotele orașului. Din loc în loc, mici ferestre înspre râu oferă ochiului cocori încremeniți într-un picior și cohorte de rațe guralive. Sălcii pletoase și tufișuri dese, crescute parcă direct din apă ascund vederii malul opus. E o altă lume.

Bolta vegetală dispare brusc. Peștișorul corkonian face cercuri largi și apoi începe o serie de salturi acrobatice în aer. Nu vânează musculițe deși acestea abundă, indică doar încă un punct de atracție: plutind deasupra copacilor, un pod suspendat leagă cele două maluri. E Daly's Footbridge. Vibrează ușor sub tălpi, legănat de o părere de vânt. De la înălțimea lui poți îmbrățișa panorama puzderiei de case înfipte în versanții dealurilor. Clădiri imense sau cottage-uri minuscule, construcții vechi sau moderne, majoritatea sunt din piatră și parțial îngropate între copaci, arbuști, garduri vii sau grădini de flori.

Rămânând pe partea dreaptă a râului, urmărirea peștișorului năzdrăvan te duce în Fitzgerald Park. Găsești aici alei asfaltate, un gazon îngrijit, copaci plantați estetic, rondouri cu flori aranjate în pattern-uri geometrice, un muzeu și numeroși vizitatori. Peștișorul corkonian susține că după sălbăticia relaxantă a porțiunii dintre Thomas Davis Bridge și Daly's Bridge, parcul arată ca un copil bucălat duminica, spălat, pieptănat și gata de trimis la biserică. Își marchează afirmația cu o bătaie energică din coadă și dispare într-un vârtej de stropi. Următorul punct de întâlnire – Bachelor's Quay.

E locul pe unde brațul nordic al râului își face intrarea în orașul propriu-zis. Vegetația rămâne undeva în spatele unui pod de fier forjat. Betonul și gresia îi iau locul. Clădiri cu două sau trei etaje se înșiră pe

worry. You will meet him again floating slowly between the pillars of Thomas Davis Bridge, downstream from where the river branches off.

To the right of the bridge, a tiny alley sets out and runs parallel with the river's northern branch. It does not look too well groomed, yet you follow its motion along by the impatient splash of your guide. After a dozen steps on the alley you find yourself in the midst of a vegetal tunnel whose leafy bower allows a subdued light to filter in. Tree trunks hugged by tall weeds gradually insulate you from the noises of the city. Here and there tiny windows to the river let you glance at cranes standing on one leg or flocks of talkative ducks. Weeping willows and thick shrubs that seem to grow from the very water conceal the opposite bank. It is another world.

The bowery gallery comes to an unexpected end. The Corkonian fish swirls in wide circles and then performs a series of acrobatic leaps in the air. He does not chase the flies that swarm over the water, no, he just points to a sight: hovering above the trees, a suspension bridge connects the two banks. It is Daly's Bridge. You feel it vibrating slightly under your feet, swung by a barely perceptible wind. From its height you can embrace the panorama of the multitude of houses stuck onto the hill slopes. Huge buildings and diminutive cottages, some old, some new, most of them made of stone and partly buried amid trees, shrubs, hedges or flower gardens.

Your chase of the magic fish takes you to Fitzgerald Park, still on the right bank. Here you may find asphalted lanes, tidy lawns, nicely planted trees, flower beds arranged in geometric patterns, a museum and numerous visitors. The Corkonian fish claims that, after the soothing wilderness of the stretch between Thomas Davis Bridge and Daly's Bridge, the park looks like a chubby child on a Sunday morning, freshly washed, neatly combed and ready to go to church. The fish stresses his statement by means of a vigorous beat of his tail fin and disappears in a whirl of water drops. The next meeting point – Bachelor's Quay.

This is the point where the northern branch of river enters the inner city. The greenery remains somewhere behind a bridge with wrought iron railings and is replaced by sandstone and concrete. Two-storeyed houses flank the river quays. These are former warehouses converted into apartment blocks, offices or stores. The Lee flows leisurely between the wharfs whose walls have been streaked by the tides with mossy

cheiurile mărginite de şosele. Sunt foste depozite de mărfuri transformate în locuinţe, birouri sau magazine. Lee curge lin între diguri pe pereţii cărora mareele au mânjit lungi dungi verzi. Peştişorul corkonian e agitat. Bancuri de somoni veniţi din mare îi fac concurenţă neloială. Sezonieri, pufneşte el indignat. Nu au habar că într-o clădire de lângă Bachelor's Quay a locuit George Boole. Confundă clopotele de la Shandon Church cu sirenele vapoarelor şi clădirea operei cu staţia de autobuz. (Îţi arată mişcând din aripioare opera – o construcţie din sticlă cu linii futuriste, şi, mult mai departe, staţia de autobuz ce arată ca o benzinărie ceva mai răsărită.)

Numeroase poduri conectează traficul de pe cele două cheiuri. Puţin mai jos de ultimul pod, braţul nordic îl întâlneşte pe cel sudic. Aici Lee este mult mai lat şi vapoare sunt ancorate lângă cheiuri. Plin de aplomb, peştişorul trece pe lângă ele urcând contra curentului pe braţul sudic.

Atmosfera generală se modifică sensibil imediat după docuri. E ca şi cum ai intra de pe un bulevard central pe o străduţă provincială cochetă. Canalul sudic este mai îngust şi, exceptând primăria, mai toate clădirile mici ce-l mărginesc ţin mai degrabă de o zonă rezidenţială sau de agrement decât de una comercială. Peştişorul călăuză e mai relaxat, a adoptat o atitudine uşor boemă şi pendulează între cele două maluri. Se opreşte în dreptul bisericii dedicate memoriei părintelui Matthew (Father Matthew Memorial Church). E un ansamblu neobişnuit de piatră gri ce desenează pe cer un portal uriaş deschis în faţa unei biserici cu un aspect modest. Parcă blocuri de aer au fost folosite pentru construcţia ei.

Nu departe de ea, peştişorul corkonian începe să mişte din coadă dezarticulat şi face tumbe fără noimă. Salută fiecare bolovan şi dă buzna năuc între cârduri de somoni. Motivul acestui comportament se ridică pe malul drept sub forma unor cilindri de inox mirosind a hamei. E Fabrica de Bere Beamish-Crawford şi pentru depăşirea ei e nevoie de multă tenacitate corkoniană. Puţin mai sus pe malul stâng, de după un pod acoperit cu petice de muşchi, cerul se împodobeşte cu turlele catedralei St. Finbarr. Aici e cheia de acces spre sufletul oraşului şi locul unde peştişorul alege să dispară.

green lines. The Corkonian fish is getting nervous. Ocean-bornsalmon shoals shooting upstream make up an unfair competition. Seasonal commuters, he sniffs outraged. They have no idea that in a building by Bachelor's Quay once lived George Boole. They mistake the bells of Shandon Church for the ships' foghorns, and the Opera for the bus station (with a motion of his fins he points to the Opera House – a futuristic glass building – and farther away, the bus station that looks like an overgrown petrol station).

Several bridges connect the traffic of the two quays. Downstream from the last bridge, the northern branch meets the southern one. Here the Lee is much broader and many ships lie at anchor along the wharf. The fish passes them by and swims against the current along the southern branch.

Past the docks the scenery changes visibly. It is as if – after having walked on a downtown avenue – you suddenly entered a quaint provincial lane. The southern canal is narrower and, with the exception of the city hall, most of the small buildings that flank it seem to pertain to a residential or leisure area rather than to a commercial district. More relaxed now, the fish guide has adopted a bohemian mien and zigzags between the two banks. He stops by Fr Mathew Memorial Church, which is a curious compound of grey stone that outlines against the sky a giant portal open in front of a humble-looking church. It is as if blocks of air were used for its construction.

Not far from it, the Corkonian fish begins to wag its tail fin in a rambunctious manner and somersaults pointlessly in the air. He bows before every boulder and he scampers about, dashing into the shoals of salmon. The reason of this demeanour can be seen rising on the right bank: several stainless steel cylinders that reek of hops. This is Beamish & Crawford Brewery and to swim past it requires a great deal of Corkonian tenacity. A little further upstream on the left bank, beyond a bridge covered with patches of moss, the sky adorns itself with the steeples of St Finbar's Cathedral. This is where the access key to the soul of the city lies and where our tiny fish chooses to disappear.

English translation by Adrian Otoiu.

Elena Toniato
(2004)

(Italian text written for this volume)

RICORDI DI CORK … LIKE!

I PRIMI ricordi di Cork? Il cielo grigio ma con tonalità luminose e la pioggia piuttosto incessante sui finestrini del taxi che, il 25 settembre del 1999, dall'aeroporto mi portava a Abbey Wharf, quella che sarebbe stata la mia residenza per i prossimi otto mesi. Finalmente ero nella terra che avevo tanto sognato, ed era proprio come recita la canzone dei Modena City Ramblers: 'È in un giorno di pioggia che ti ho conosciuta'.

La prima cosa che mi colpì fu l'accento, una musica che mi ricordò subito un'altalena. Devo dire che ebbi un po' di difficoltà nel capire quello che il custode della residenza cercava di dirmi. Tra me e me pensai che tutti gli anni passati a studiare inglese non avevano dato molti frutti ma pian piano mi ci abituai a quell'accento tanto che, dopo alcuni mesi, io stessa parlavo con quell'intonazione.

Non ci volle molto per individuare i posti che sarebbero diventati i miei punti di riferimento. Prima di tutti l'Università, U.C.C., con il piccolo ponte all'entrata e i salici piangenti, il verde del *Quad* e gli alberi di *cherry blossom* sotto i quali trascorsi indimenticabili ore a leggere poesie e a scherzare con gli amici dopo le lezioni durante la primavera. Seguii corsi di letteratura molto interessanti e notai presto l'approccio informale dei professori nei confronti degli studenti, aspetto a cui non ero abituata in Italia. E poi la Boole Library, dove passai molte ora a studiare o a curiosare tra i libri di poesia irlandese e dove infine trassi ispirazione per l'argomento della mia tesi, la poesia di John Montague.

Poi le strade del centro, Grand Parade e Patrick Street, il cinema, i pub e l'English Market che frequentavo spesso, essendo io amante dei mercatini di ogni tipo. Davanti a casa mia il Lee che scorrendo offriva colori e giochi di luce..e purtroppo anche carrelli della spesa. Faceva anche paura il Lee quando la pioggia era incessante ed il fiume arrivava quasi a straripare.

Elena Toniato
(2004)

(Views of an Italian student at UCC)

MEMORIES OF CORK ... *LIKE*!

MY FIRST memories of Cork? The grey but brightly toned sky and the incessant rain on the window of the taxi which on the 25th of September 1999 brought me from the airport to Abbey Wharf, my home for the next eight months. I had finally arrived in the country I had dreamed so much about and it was just like the Modena City Ramblers had sung in their song, 'I got to know you on a rainy day'.

The first thing that struck me was the accent, a music which immediately reminded me of a seesaw. I must admit that I found it difficult to understand what the caretaker of the residence was trying to say to me. I thought to myself that all those years spent learning English hadn't been much use but I slowly got used to the accent, so much so that after a couple of months, I was even speaking with that intonation.

It didn't take long to identify the places that would become my reference points in the city. First of all the university, UCC with the small bridge and weeping willows at the entrance, the green of the Quad and the cherry blossom trees under which I spent unforgettable hours reading poetry and messing with friends after lectures in springtime. I followed very interesting literature courses and I was immediately struck by the informal approach of the lecturers to the students, something I was not used to in Italy. And then the Boole Library where I spent many hours studying or leafing through Irish poetry books where I finally found inspiration for the topic for my thesis: John Montague's poetry.

Then there were the streets in the centre, the Grand Parade and St Patrick's Street, the cinema, the pubs, and the English market where I went regularly (I am a lover of all sorts of markets). The Lee flowed in front of my house offering colours and light games ... and unfortunately shopping trollies. The Lee was also frightening: whenever the rain was incessant the river came close to flooding.

Amavo camminare per North Mall fino a Sunday's Well, una piccola oasi nella città. Mi piaceva guardare la città, soprattutto dal dipartimento di musica dell'Università dove andavo a trovare la mia amica Róisin che suonava il pianoforte. Róisin l'avevo conosciuta attraverso uno scambio di conversazione, italiano-inglese e la nostra amicizia dura tutt'ora. E poi dietro al dipartimento di musica la casa di Simon, l'altro mio caro amico. Entrambi venivano da altre parti dell'Irlanda, eh sì, perché, per quanto i *Corkonians* fossero gentili e amichevoli, trovai difficile fare amicizia con loro. Forse non erano ancora 'pronti' a convivere con tanti giovani provenienti da altri paesi.

Ma ritornando ai miei *favorite spots*, da Sunday's Well mi piaceva attraversare lo Shaky Bridge e camminare per Fitzgerald Park dove trascorrevo piacevoli momenti sulle panchine, sotto gli alberi colorati o vicino al monumento alla balena. Di Cork poi mi sono ancora familiari gli odori, in particolare quello della birra che si poteva annusare già da casa mia, proveniva dalla Beamish *brewery*. Proprio lì davanti c'era An Spailpín Fánach, il pub dove andavamo spesso ad ascoltare musica tradizionale e a gustare le pinte, Murphy's in particolare nel mio caso. A pochi metri dal pub c'era Tribes, la caffetteria aperta fino a tardi con il suo stile etnico, i divanetti, le candele, gli infusi e i buonissimi *scones!*

Ho un bel ricordo della piazzetta Rory Gallagher con i caffè, i negozi alternativi e i personaggi della città. Da qualche parte conservo ancora la fotografia di due anziani, moglie e marito, che suonavano per le strade e che non disdegnavano scambiare quattro chiacchiere se ti fermavi con loro, che spirito! Un altro punto di riferimento per me era poi Vibes and Scribes, il negozio di libri al di là del Lee dove mi piaceva fare una capatina anche se non compravo sempre qualcosa. Il lago invece era un po' *eerie*, forse quella parte della città mi sembrava più nascosta, più consona alle ombre e ai crepuscoli dei mesi invernali.

I loved to walk down the North Mall as far as Sunday's Well, a small oasis in the city. I loved observing the city, especially from the Department of Music where I would go to meet my friend Roisin who played the piano. I had met Roisin through an Italian-English conversation exchange and we are still friends today. My other close friend Simon lived in a house behind the music department. Both came from other parts of Ireland because, although Corkonians were kind and friendly, I found it difficult to make friends with them. Maybe they were not yet 'ready' to live with lots of young people from other countries.

But coming back to my favourite spots, from Sunday's Well I liked to cross the Shaky Bridge and walk though Fitzgeralds Park where I spent enjoyable moments on the benches, under the colourful trees or near the monument to the whale. I can still remember the smells of Cork, in particular the smell of beer which floated up to my house from the Beamish Brewery. Right in front of the brewery was the Spailpín Fánach, the pub I went to regularly to listen to traditional music and to try the pints, particularly, in my case, the Murphys. A few feet from the pub was Tribes, a coffee shop open until late with an ethnic style, couches, candles, incense and excellent scones!

I have good memories of Rory Gallagher Square with its coffee shops, alternative shops and characters from the city. Somewhere, I still have a photo of an elderly couple, a husband and wife, who used to busk in the streets and who were not above chatting to you if you stopped by them. What characters! Another point of reference for me was Vibes and Scribes, the bookshop across the Lee where I liked to make a flying visit even if I didn't always make a purchase. The lake on the other hand was a bit eerie, maybe that part of the city seemed more hidden to me, more given to shadows and dusks in the winter months.

English translation by Anne O'Connor.

Martín Veiga
(2004)

(Galician poems written for this volume)

NA RÚA

Así, de súpeto, ela díxolle riseira
ao pasaren de mans dadas College Road abaixo:

'Sempre a mudar. Como o vento'.

E el: 'Talmente como o vento no Lough
un domingo de outono, entre os cisnes'.

E brillaron os seus ollos na mañá morna de maio
xusto en fronte da tenda de Connolly, na esquina.

RÍO LEE

Non é regato cativo: río fachendoso
que baixa follas mortas cara ao mar,
bulsas plásticas e cisco, cabichas, pétalos mirrados.

Aboia abondo refugallo nas augas pardas, lamacentas,
que o levan todo cara ao mar, cara á badía.

Vidros rotos xacen na ribeira mansa
a coruscar como escuras alfaias no bulleiro.

Nas marxes, corvos aleutos peteiran no lixo,
gargallan algareiros sobre muros de pedra,
erguen as negras asas levando o ceo da noite

Martín Veiga
(2004)

(Two poems)

ON THE STREET

As they walked hand in hand down College Road,
out of the blue, she said, smiling:

'Always changing, you are. Like the wind.'

And he said: 'Just like the wind on the Lough
on an autumn Sunday, among the swans.'

And their eyes shone in the warm May morning
there in front of Connolly's shop, on the corner.

THE LEE

It is no small brook. Proud river
that brings dead leaves down towards the sea,
plastic bags and wood, dog-ends, withered petals.

All this rubbish floats on the brown, muddy waters
that carry everything out to sea, through the bay.

Splinters of broken glass lie on the still banks
glinting as dark jewels in the swamp.

There cunning crows peck at the rubbish,
cackling noisily on stone walls,
lifting their black wings, bringing the sky of the night

ás nubes asolladas da cidade, ás ramaxes de espiño.

A garza cincenta espreita nunha ponla
de salgueiro, queda e concentrada,
inmóbil, insensible ao trafegar dos paseantes.

Nenos pescan
muxo voraz, peixe fedorento
que sobe ata a cidade co devalo da maré
e enreda con vermes, garabullos,
o corpo túmido ateigado aínda
de auga salgada, da longa travesía.

Entre as rochas abalan oucas dondas, visitadas
por insectos diminutos.
                              Unha lavandeira afagadora
osma desde a pena esvaradía, cuberta de mofo,
pois que a chuvieira rebeirou a terra
e lentas agroman tórpidas miñocas.

O río é un camiño vello, preguizoso,
que o leva todo cara ao mar,
que a todos leva cara ao mar, cara ao esteiro.

Un antigo rumor de turba no interior
revela a fin do inverno, o estoupido
da luz, de altivos amarelles.

Non hai cobras aquí, áspera ausencia.

to the sunny clouds of the city, to the hawthorn branches.

The ash-grey heron lies in wait on a willow
bough, in locked motionless concentration,
oblivious to the to-ing-and-fro-ing of passers-by.

Children fish
for voracious mullet, foul fish
that come up to the city at low tide
and play with worms, sticks,
their swollen bodies still full
of salt water, from the long trip.

Among the rocks soft weeds swing, hosts
to minute insects.
　　　　　　　　* A wagtail seems constantly to bow
as he hops about on the mossy, slippery rock,
for the downpour has disturbed the earth,
which now sprouts torpid worms.

The river is an old, sluggish highway
that carries everything down to the sea,
that carries everyone down to the sea, through the harbour.

An ancient murmur of peat within
announces the end of winter, the explosion
of light, of haughty daffodils.

There are no snakes here – blessed non-entity.

English translation by David MacKenzie and Martín Veiga.

Martin Alioth

(2005)

German original in: *Neue Zürcher Zeitung am Sonntag*, 2 January 2005, p. 47-48.

Pökelfleisch, Bier, Viagra

'Schon als Kind habe ich Cork immer als europäische Stadt wahrgenommen', bekennt Grace Neville, Französisch-Dozentin an der idyllischen Universität. Sie habe nie verstehen können, wie man von 'Europa' sprechen und damit bloss den Kontinent meinen konnte. Passenderweise ist sie jetzt Mitherausgeberin einer Sammlung von Beobachtungen aus der Feder kontinentaler Besucher von Cork. Vielsprachig durchschreiten die Texte acht Jahrhunderte. Was sehen die fremden Augen? 'Spektakuläre Landschaften, spektakuläre Gastfreundschaft, spektakuläre Armut', fasst Neville nüchtern zusammen. Aber von einem Minderwertigkeitskomplex der zweiten Stadt will sie nichts hören. 'Ich kenne Paris, London und New York besser als Dublin, aber Dublin fühlt sich nicht wie eine Hauptstadt an.' Etwas eng möge die Sicht gelegentlich sein, das gibt sie zu. Schon Thomas McCarthy hatte auf die ummauerte Insel verwiesen, um die Mentalität zu erfassen.

In der Mitte des 19. Jahrhunderts lebten hunderttausend Menschen in Cork – mehr als dreimal so viele wie damals in Basel. Heute ist Basel etwas grösser, aber die Gemeinsamkeiten sind auffallend: das Gepräge einer patrizischen, engen Kaufmannschaft, die Bedeutung der chemischen Industrie, der schräge Blick auf die grössere Rivalin, das Beharren auf Andersartigkeit.

Cork wendet sich allmählich seinen unzähligen Wasserstrassen zu, die das Weichbild bestimmen. Selbst in der Einkaufsstrasse, der Patrick's Street, sind noch Hauseingänge im ersten Stock übrig geblieben; aus der Zeit bevor der Flussarm 1783 überdeckt wurde. Jetzt, im Zuge des Frühjahrsputzes als Kulturstadt, hat eine katalanische Architektin die

Martin Alioth
(2005)

(*Interviews in connection with Cork 2005*)

SALTED MEAT, BEER, VIAGRA

'ALREADY AS a child I perceived Cork as a European city', says Grace Neville, French Lecturer at the idyllic University. She could never understand how people could talk of 'Europe' and only think of the continent. Quite appropriately she is now co-editor of an anthology of images of the city which have flowed from the pens of continental visitors to Cork. In their multilingual form the texts move through eight centuries. What do these foreign eyes see? 'Spectacular landscapes, spectacular hospitality, spectacular poverty', is Neville's sober summary. But she does not accept the concept of an inferiority complex due to being the 'second city': 'I know Paris, London and New York better than Dublin, but Dublin does not feel like a capital.' Views may be a bit narrow at times, she admits. Thomas McCarthy had already evoked the image of a walled city to capture Corkonian mentality.

In the middle of the nineteenth century Cork had 100,000 inhabitants – more than three times as many as Basle. Today Basle is a good bit bigger, but the similarities are striking: the impact of a narrow patrician merchant class, the important role of the chemical industry, the suspicious glance at the bigger rival, the insistence on difference.

Cork gradually turns its face towards the numerous waterways which define the cityscape. Even in the main shopping street, St Patrick's Street, one can spot entrance doors on the first floor; remnants of a time before 1783, the year the arm of the river was filled in. Now, in the course of a facelift which the Capital of Culture year initiated, a Catalan architect has redesigned the street. Slanted gallows carrying the street lighting

Strasse neu gestaltet. Schräge Galgen tragen die Beleuchtung und erinnern an die Hafenanlagen, als Corks Zukunft im Süden lag. Im
Spannungsfeld zwischen provinzieller Genügsamkeit und hochfliegen-
den Ansprüchen wird sich dieses Kulturjahr bewegen. 'Nichts verfängt
daheim so sehr wie die Gerüchte von Erfolg im Ausland', zitiert Thomas
McCarthy zum Abschied und empfiehlt sich, nicht ohne dem Gast ein
Päckchen Türkenhonig geschenkt zu haben.

recall the docks and a time when Cork's future lay southwards. This Year of Culture will be characterised by the tension between provincial contentment and high-flying ambitions. 'Nothing has more impact at home than rumours of success abroad', Thomas McCarthy quotes upon my departure. He says goodbye, not without presenting his guest with a box of Turkish Delight.

English translation by Joachim Fischer.